Frontispiece : *Assyrian Art.* Ibex. *Til Barsip. Eighth Century B.C. Louvre, Paris. Wall Painting, fragment.*

CONTENTS

AM 501
Library of Congress Catalog Card Number : 61-6746
Printed in France

ANDRÉ PARROT

S U M E R

THE DAWN OF ART

TRANSLATED BY STUART GILBERT
AND JAMES EMMONS

GOLDEN PRESS · NEW YORK

Sumer

THE ARTS
OF MANKIND

EDITED BY ANDRÉ MALRAUX
AND GEORGES SALLES

Preface

by

André Malraux

IF Delacroix, a hundred years ago, had been shown the works illustrated in this volume, he would not have *seen* them; they lay outside his range of vision and, had his attention been directed to them, they would have seemed to him devoid of any aesthetic value. As little as fifty years ago Sumer was a *terra incognita* and Mesopotamian art, prior to Assyrian, meant simply the art of Lagash, that so-called 'Chaldean' art which, but for the Bible, would have interested only a few specialists. Even as late as 1930 a good two thirds of the works figuring in this volume were still undiscovered and unknown. Now, however, not only have they been discovered, but the scales have fallen from our eyes and they have become *visible* to us for what they are: authentic works of art in their own right, not just 'museum pieces.'

Nineteenth-century aestheticians had not the slightest conception of what this art would come to mean to us today—and that is understandable. For quite evidently the makers of these works were not concerned with 'beauty'; their concern was with a theme that has inspired many other arts, from Egyptian to Romanesque: *the sacred.* True, art historians knew those other arts, but knowledge did not lead to understanding, and, even after the revelation of Japanese prints, they always took it for granted that the artist based his work on visual experience.

To begin with, art was associated with imitation and idealization; then with spiritualization: idealization on Christian lines. Next, under the auspices of Egyptian and Byzantine art, came the idea of stylization. I have tried elsewhere to show that the purpose of idealization was to arouse admiration and that it related both to life and to the immortality bestowed on individuals by works of art associated with them; whereas the stylizations of early epochs were intended to evoke, not admiration, but veneration, and related to eternity. Hence their pre-occupation

MARI - WORSHIPPER WITH A LAMB (2ND MILL. B.C.). — ALEPPO MUSEUM

XIII

TASSILI, SAHARA - FOUR TUTELARY GODDESSES (XVIIITH DYNASTY). — IN SITU

with death: not so much individual decease as the ineluctable *fatum* of the universe.

That was Egypt's message and how can we fail to be reminded of it when we turn to Sumer? Little is known of the beginnings of Egyptian art; the most that can be said is that it seems unlikely that so advanced an art as that of the Old Kingdom can suddenly have sprung up *ex nihilo* (and the Sahara may still have many surprises in store for us). In Sumer, as in Mexico and Egypt, the sacred was pre-eminently the realm of the fantastic, and it is through art alone that this 'world invisible' takes form. But such art is never conscious of itself as art and its efficacy stems from a quasi-divine power peculiar to the artist: that of figuring forth what necessarily escapes the eyes of earthbound man.

Of this power Mesopotamia gives us an expression, elementary and elemental, in the figurines found in tombs. The Egyptians, Chinese

and Mayans placed in their tombs images that were reminders of their daily life. But, from Sumer to Babylon, the Mesopotamians placed in their tombs images that were utterly unlike anything they and their artists had ever set eyes on.

It is with these images of an unseen world that, for us, their sculpture begins. At the time when, in ceramics, a rigid geometrical design seems to symbolize the victory of the mind over chaos, the fantastic goddesses, half snake, half woman, clasping to their bosoms a child with the head of a startled fox, make their appearance. Contemporary seals show us bird-men whose remote ancestors may perhaps be found in certain prehistoric figures; one of their last expressions is the eagle-headed Assyrian god. Throughout its development, the image of the bird-man becomes more and more elaborate, whereas the snake-goddesses, and even the images of fecundity which followed them, did not point the way to any great Sumerian figure. For over a thousand years an underground art was engaged in creating forms whose evolution is so hard to follow that the art historian, being unable to place them by their style, has to fall back on the conditions of their discovery when he wants to date them.

(A) SUSA - SEAL IMPRESSION (FIRST HALF, 3RD MILLENNIUM B.C.). — LOUVRE
(B) MAGDALENIAN ART - CUEVA DE LOS CASARES, SPAIN

XV

But, though they have no defined place in history, a whole host of these figurines has entered, as of right, into our 'Museum without Walls.'

Some of them are almost amorphous; others have a specious originality due to clumsy execution. This is easily recognizable, since the same awkward gestures have brought similar figures into being in many different cultures. Yet we can also recognize in them the authentic accent of creation. For already the slope of the heads of the snake-goddesses and their composition in the form of a triangle, extending from the jutting shoulders to their feet, show that their makers had in mind a pre-determined schema that is not found, for instance, in the male figures of Eridu. The *Goddess* in the Baghdad Museum, if enlarged to human stature, would pass for an impressive 'barbarian' statue.

We can disregard the inferior reproductions of truly creative works, and even the plaquettes, since they have the same relationship to the major works that Tanagra figurines have to Greek statues. Yet throughout this art there runs a subterranean current of freedom that rises to the surface, dies down and reappears, from the snake-goddesses to the latest figurines, from the images of fecundity to the

(A) GODDESS (3RD MILL.). — BAGHDAD MUSEUM
(B) GODDESS OF FECUNDITY (3RD MILL.). — PRIVATE COLLECTION

(A) IDOL. — ALEPPO MUSEUM   (B) IDOL. — BAGHDAD MUSEUM

A   B

GODDESS OF FECUNDITY, DETAIL (3RD MILL.). — PRIVATE COLLECTION

XVIII

'idols' of Aleppo. Whenever it dies out, we find that seeming deference to human forms which characterizes the large-scale sculpture and tends to make us overlook the freedom of the figurines. Yet this creative freedom orients all Mesopotamian art, like an unseen lodestone.

Let us picture the *Fecundity* illustrated here and the *Idol* of Aleppo remade life-size. They seem even more perplexing than the Baghdad goddess because they quite obviously belong to a more fully evolved art. Their whole conception is at a far remove from that of Egyptian art, if less remote from that of Mexico, with which the great creations of the Mesopotamians have a vague affinity by reason of the fantastic stairways of their ziggurats, their cult of astrologers, and even their taste for gold and garments made of feathers.

For the *primum mobile* of Mesopotamian art is the sacred, rendered in a vein of fantasy. The convolutions of the Aleppo *Idol* remind us of the ornate figures of Mayan steles and the Borgia Codex, or the interlace-man of Irish miniatures. They, too, belong to the world of that which does not exist on earth, and could not exist were there not artists to discover these hieroglyphs of the invisible.

IDOL (3RD MILL.). — ALEPPO MUSEUM

IDOL, DETAIL (3RD MILL.). — ALEPPO MUSEUM

IDOL, DETAIL. — DAMASCUS MUSEUM

None the less, the genius of Sumerian art has the austerity of the desert. Rejecting the possibilities of a copious and colourful mythology, its statuary figures forth a multitude of worshippers and gods. When its creations are intended for the living, not the dead, it is the human form it calls on to reveal that which is not man; but sometimes also asks of it what its artists asked of the figurines made to be placed in tombs.

Here we see the basic ambivalence characteristic of most of the arts resuscitated in our time: an ambivalence due to an attempt to express man by means of that which is not man. In this context we may note that Buddhist and Christian art has familiarized us with a 'sentimental' spiritualization whose means of expression are wholly different from those of sacred spiritualization. Our sacred sculpture died with Romanesque, and an ambiguous relationship exists between *The God Abu* and the Moissac *God of the Second Coming*, whereas there is none at all between the former and a Fra Angelico 'Christ.'

Sumerian gods, like Mexican gods, are still commonly described as idols—but what exactly is an idol? The conquistadors did not regard the Aztec gods as statues but as demons and therefore burned them; and the Aztecs built a jail for the gods of the conquered. The nineteenth century saw idols and fetishes alike as objects to which their worshippers ascribed fictitious powers; there was no basic difference between an African masterpiece and a 'sacred' block of wood. The way the idol was represented raised no problems; if Africans carved their figures as they did, the reason was that they were incapable of imitating or idealizing the human body. (The Spaniards felt less sure about the Aztec figures, since in Mexico they had found an empire, and a luxurious way of life.) Once idols cease being written off as merely ludicrous, the problem set their makers becomes clear: it is that of creating a figure *other than what it represents*. Just as we cannot bring ourselves to admire as a work of art a purely illusionist picture, so no Sumerian could have prayed to a statue in which he saw merely an imitation of a man. The numinous power of a statue was ensured by all that *differentiated* it from any such imitation.

Some of the methods employed by these sculptors are easily accounted for: the projecting elbows and shoulders taken over from the snake-goddesses; the beaked nose inherited perhaps from the prehistoric bird-man; the drastic schematization, as in the beards staged like the stairways of ziggurats; and, above all, the huge staring eyes of gods and goddesses. We know nothing of the atmosphere in which the figures of Tell Asmar and Khafaje had their being, nor can we gauge without an effort the feelings these forms aroused in the men who saw them, not as statues, but as visitants from a world beyond the world. Moreover, there was a remarkable diversity of forms in the first half of the third millennium, from the Warka *Head* to the *Great Singer*.

Thus the heads from the Diyala region have less of a family likeness than those of Tell Asmar, indeed they differ amongst themselves almost as much as do our Christian angels. And in some worshipper figures—the one from Khafaje for instance—there is an attitude of shuddering awe differing *toto caelo* from the hieraticism of the figures of the supreme gods. But common to all alike is their creators' will to liberate them from the world of men and to give them access to another world. Allusion to the human form is permitted only in so far as it can serve as a means of expression—necessary partial, no more than suggestive—of the supramundane.

The works we here are dealing with used once to be regarded as imitations of imaginary models.

TELL ASMAR - MAN HOLDING A CUP (3RD MILL.). — ORIENTAL INSTITUTE, CHICAGO

But *The God Abu* is far from being a clumsy imitation of an imaginary figure; it does not imitate anything. Such statues made the sacred beings present in the spectator's emotion, as their ideograms made them present in his mind. If the Tell Asmar deities act on the imagination, they do not do so in the way Raphael's *School of Athens* may be said to do so, but in the sense in which we say this of music. *The God Abu* does not suggest a person who might look like him; such a person is unthinkable. Nor does the company of figures attending him suggest a *human* assemblage invested with an aura of the sacred; it is sacred in respect of all that differentiates it from any human assemblage. For we now know better than to attribute to inexpertness the flagrant disproportion between the tiny hands of the goddess of Tell Asmar and her enormous eyes. During five centuries these strange eyes, with their corneas of bone and eyelids in bitumen, reappear again and again. In making them, the aim of the Sumerian sculptor was not to express himself as an individual; they are means to creation in the fullest sense, since the sculptor was releasing the human figure from man's estate and allying it with the figures of the gods; illuminating a human visage with a gleam of the divine.

TELL ASMAR - GODDESS (?) (FIRST HALF, 3RD MILL.). — BAGHDAD MUSEUM

Mesopotamian art reminds us of a submerged continent parts of which still emerge as an archipelago that we are now discovering, isle by isle. We cannot hope to understand the creative processes of its great artists as we understand those of Michelangelo and Rembrandt. We are familiar with the conflict of these masters with their immediate predecessors, but we know nothing of the statuary preceding that of the Sumerians. Doubtless in an age when the chief concern of craftsmen was to reproduce certain conventionally approved images, there still were master artists, inventors of new forms, and the history of Sumerian art was, like all others, one of a series of new creations. *Gudea* followed on *Sargon*, worshippers on worshippers, as Gothic Virgins followed on Romanesque Virgins. From Uruk to Babylon great sculptors did away with ancient or hostile figures, in the service of a faith of which we know little except its gods, and of venerable legends none of which said anything about the physical aspects of its heroes. Reading the epic of Gilgamesh, who could possibly conjure up any of the successive forms given him by sculptors? But of this long cortège of reflections of the sacred only a few mutilated sequences have come down to us.

Yet it is by them that we can best divine the *intentions* of the creators, for while it is futile to compare the *Woman holding an Aryballos* with any living Mesopotamian woman, we can compare it to advantage with the *Woman with a Kaunakes*, several centuries previous to it. It would be easier to grasp the significance of *The Smiling Angel* of Rheims—assuming we knew nothing of its immediate predecessors—by comparing it with a Romanesque angel than with a good-looking youngster from that part of France. And we better understand the creative urge behind the *Gudea* in the British Museum if we confront it with the *Grandson of Lugalkisalsi*, than by picturing some lifelike 'Gudea' suited to a waxworks show. For this much anyhow is clear: that the evolution of Sumero-Akkadian art is not to be confused with a progressive mastery of appearances.

The rendering of appearances had been mastered—so far as Mesopotamian artists sought to master it—as early as the Stele of Naram-Sin and the bronze head of Sargon, which is so little 'primitive' that it was once thought to be Assyrian. The early artists, the craftsmen who made the harps of Ur, carved animal forms with a skill and sensitivity unexcelled by their successors. As yet we have only a shadowy idea of Akkad, and presumably new discoveries will follow that of the *Sargon* which, despite the antagonism of Akkad and Sumer, may rank—technically speaking—as a brilliant successor of Queen Shubad's golden bull. But the Stele of Naram-Sin marks a break with the untrammelled freedom of the art of the city states. The amazing alabaster head in the Louvre, certain Gods, the *Captives*, the Bismaya head and some minor figures are affiliated to this Stele by an elaborate finish and a fidelity to appearance equalling those of the art of Lagash. If we picture the decapitated statue of Manishtusu, as compact as the *Gudeas*, as being completed by a head comparable to the bronze *Sargon*, this would surely be one of the key works of Mesopotamian art. And, like the *Sargon*, the wealth of ornaments on the seals seems to foreshadow Assyrian opulence.

If Neo-Sumerian art, with its justly famous Gudea statues, whose lustre has not been dimmed by the recent discovery of their fore-runners, seems still to orient all the art preceding it in the sense that Pheidias seems to orient all Greek art from Delphi to the Acropolis, the reason is primarily that its statues are more complete and numerous than those of Akkad, and also that its hard, polished surfaces as well as its forms suggest an art that has achieved fruition.

TELLOH - WOMAN'S HEAD (SECOND HALF, 3RD MILL.). — LOUVRE

The beardless worshippers of the first dynasties seem, when standing, to point towards the *Gudeas* and, when seated, to the *Architect with a Plan*. . . Because they are better 'likenesses'? But, if so, likenesses of what?

Of their models presumably, certainly of men, the nineteenth century would have replied. Yet the *Seated Figure* in Copenhagen is more like a man than the *Seated Gudea* which it preceded by five centuries. And the *Gudea* keeps closer to the human form than does *The God Abu*, but not closer than the *Woman with a Kaunakes*, the alabaster head in the Louvre, or the bronze *Sargon*. Neo-Sumerian statuary does not owe its accent to skilful imitation but to the sculptor's total mastery of his means, a mastery directed, not to recording a man's appearance, but to translating him into a world beyond the world.

A world that, belonging as it did to the supernatural, must have been, to start with, that of the temple. What doubt can there be about the link between these statues and their vanished architectural settings? This was less a harmony of forms than a spiritual affinity like that between the column-statues and the Romanesque churches to which they belong.

NINEVEH - HEAD OF KING SARGON (?) (SECOND HALF, 3RD MILL.). — BAGHDAD MUSEUM

The temples are in ruins, but reconstructions of them evoke the prodigious stairways and trapezoidal masses of an astrologically-minded civilization. It is doubtless at Teotihuacan when, beyond the geometrical fantasies of the citadel, the moon lights up the emptiness of the Way of the Dead, the Pyramid of the Sun and that of the Moon stepped like a ziggurat, that we best can visualize the star-enchanted nights of Ur and Lagash. The realm of the living is the chaos of their streets and the great rivers, the desert with its wild beasts and the fields with their harvests; but the realm of the statues is the temple freed from chaos as are the geometric patterns of its walls and those of the ceramics. The Toltecs devised for their rain goddess a representation that was simultaneously a monument and an effigy. We may feel uncertain about regarding the standing *Gudeas* as the master pillars of Sumerian spirituality, but there is no possible doubt about the link between the *Architect with a Plan* and the sanctuary. For this majestic statue (as I have remarked elsewhere) is a creation in which a human form has become at once worshipper, god and temple.

(A) WOMAN WITH A KAUNAKES (FIRST HALF, 3RD MILL.). — LOUVRE   (B) CHARTRES CATHEDRAL - WOMAN'S HEAD (1145-1150)

From Ur to Lagash the constant function of this art is one of the loftiest that art can undertake: the imposition on the visible of a sacred order, as it were a cosmic orchestration, that both orients men's veneration and frees it from the chaos of appearances. Its purpose is not to imitate, but to reveal forms enabling men to enter into communion with their gods. And so transcendent is this purpose that the artist is unaware of it, as the saint is unaware of his own sainthood.

Reference to living forms is so habitual, so instinctive, that it is not enough for us to know its limitations in order to rid our minds of it. We can discard this frame of reference only by substituting another. Thus we are led to compare a Sumerian masterpiece with works competing with

(A) MARI - IDI-NARUM, THE 'MILLER' (FIRST HALF,
3RD MILL.). — ALEPPO MUSEUM

(B) SAINT-LOUP-DE-NAUD -
BISHOP SAINT-LOUP (1170-1175)

it on its own ground, and perhaps to liken it (as we liken so many sacred figures) to our twelfth-century statues. And though comparison of the *Woman with a Kaunakes* with one of the Chartres statues, or the *Miller* of Aleppo with the *Saint Loup* at Saint-Loup-de-Naud, may not bring out so clearly the intentions of the Sumerian masters as does a comparison of their works with those of their predecessors, it helps us to grasp the nature of their spirituality and their monumentalism. Far-fetched though they may seem, such comparisons are helpful when they serve to deepen our communion with works of the remote past, especially when, as here, we are dealing with works created by men of whom we do not even know their feelings about such major issues as love and death.

That a family likeness existed between the arts of Mesopotamia and Egypt was recognized at an early date and nineteenth-century authorities often saw in the former a somewhat 'barbarian' equivalent of the latter. This was but natural, since the only Mesopotamian arts with which they were acquainted, that of the Gudea statues and that of Assyria, are the most fully elaborated arts of Mesopotamia. But today we are less impressed by the resemblances due to this kinship than by their differences, for it is these that throw most light on the special characteristics of the arts of Sumer and Akkad.

Yet of what Egyptian statue would we venture to say that it is 'at once worshipper, god and temple'? Perhaps the Sphinx of Gizeh is the nearest Egyptian approximation to the *Architect with a Plan*. But we can hardly picture the Sphinx in a temple, no matter how colossal. Together with the pyramids with which its trapezoidal head-dress harmonizes it—only in front view does it make its full effect—it is the most superb decoy for the constellations the mind of man has ever conjured up, but it holds converse with the night sky, not with the shadows of a temple. As against Neo-Sumerian statues, it seems vaguely inharmonious, and

EGYPTIAN ART - SAQQARA - SEATED SCRIBE
(SECOND HALF, 3RD MILL.). — LOUVRE

when, instead of comparing them
with this unique masterwork, we
compare them with the 'mass-pro-
duced' Sphinxes with which Egypt
teems, we are startled by the relative
puerility of the latter. True, these
are merely incidental figures, for
the genius of Egypt does not lie
in excursions into fantasy, but
in its commerce with eternity; yet
the Egyptian genius for 'doubles,'
which created an incomparable
'double' of the whole earth, knew
nothing of that amazing conjunction
of psychic and artistic powers to
which Akkad and Sumer owed their
noblest creations. A death that
eternizes life becomes as diverse as
life itself, and confronted by the
elemental art of Lagash, that of
Egyptian Thebes and Memphis,
hieratic though it is, comes to seem
an 'open' art, accessible to all the
forms of life; confronted by the
Seated Gudea, even the finest *Scribes*
regress to the ephemeral. In certain statues of seated dignitaries
enveloped in their cloaks, Egypt
created figures somewhat resembl-
ing the *Architect*, but their cubic
mass, modulated by curves, is made
to harmonize discreetly with the
face. In *Gudea* it is the face that
is attuned to the mass; and the
arms linked on the chest seem to
incase the statue, sealing it with the
locked hands.

TELLOH - SMALL SEATED GUDEA
(22ND CENTURY B.C.). — LOUVRE

(A) TELLOH - SMALL SEATED GUDEA, DETAIL. — LOUVRE   (B) LUGALKISALSI'S GRANDSON, DETAIL (3RD MILL.). — LOUVRE

The Egyptian hieroglyph is an image, the cuneiform character an abstraction, and abstraction underlies the art of Sumer as it underlies its writing. The function of most of the worshipper statues was to perpetuate the prayers of those who placed them in the temple. They symbolized the worshipper, but not in the manner of a signature; they are expressive signs and their expression is inseparable from that which associates them with the cultic deity. The Egyptian 'double' ranks as a 'double' in virtue of all that differentiates it from its model; nevertheless it resembles him, as an Egyptian hieroglyph resembles what it signifies. A Sumerian 'worshipper,' from Tell Asmar to the last figures, rarely if ever imitated the man who dedicated it to the god—*it was not meant to imitate him.* This is why, when the finds made by excavators are brought together, they often give an impression of belonging to 'families.' But, while the worshipper figures are not likenesses of the individuals whose names they bear, they often resemble the gods who are being worshipped: gods from whom specialists would often have difficulty in distinguishing them, were it not for certain gestures, the dimensions of the statues and, above all, the inscriptions.

The creation of these sacred figures was much more arbitrary in Sumer than in Egypt since Sumer did not ask of art that ambiguous parallelism with appearance which characterized it in Egypt. Thus the Sumerian artist enjoyed greater freedom. For such a figure to be acceptable, all

(A) SEAL IMPRESSION - MYTHOLOGICAL SCENE   (B) SEAL IMPRESSION - WHEAT BEARER   (C) STELE OF SARGON - NAKED CAPTIVE

that was needed was that priests and worshippers should recognize it as sacred. Moreover two vast fields of art, independent of sculpture, were available to the Sumerian and Akkadian artists: cylinder seals and figurines. Under the early dynasties they made simultaneously abstract compositions, figures with holes drilled in them, and bulls as masterfully executed as those of Babylon. Their glyptic art alone would suffice to prove that the art of the Sumerian bas-reliefs was governed by laws of its own and that there was no question of an effort to overcome 'clumsiness.' Contemporaneously with the *Stele of the Vultures* an artist was engraving on a cylinder seal the Baghdad *Naked Man*, and others had already engraved sheaf-bearers quite as realistic as were to be the figures on Lagash plaquettes. It should be noted that by associating the Assyrian bas-reliefs with those of Sumer and Akkad art historians tend to slur over the special characteristics of the latter. In them we look in vain for the 'landscape' settings of the figures in Assyrian and Egyptian scenes, whose makers, though ignorant of perspective, depicted trees and mountains more or less convincingly. Whereas in the *Stele of Naram-Sin* the tree and the mountain are symbols pure and simple. What lingers in our memory of the sculpture of Sumer and Akkad is—with some rare, masterly exceptions—the statuary.

But alongside the statuary there was a glyptic art that, unlike the bas-reliefs, reveals the co-existence of very different art forms, which, duly noted by the sculptors, contributed to their freedom, a freedom reminding us of the liberties taken by European sculptors in the eleventh century. Its mark is found on figures from the Diyala region, on the Mari *Women with a Polos*, and on a host of worshipper statues from the Tell Asmar *Worshipper* to the *Worshipper with a Young Goat*. Often this art appears to be spontaneous, and yet. . . one wonders? Some Diyala heads (which would intrigue us less if the bodies had not been lost) are akin to those of Khafaje. Those from Mari, which look so peculiar when isolated by photography, seem quite at home in the Damascus Museum, in the company of a divine family like the one from Tell Asmar. Here instinct is more oriented than one might suppose at first sight; sometimes by a poignant emotivity, and almost always by the artist's insistence on a curious, trance-bound stare produced by ridges of bitumen around the eyes and giving them the accent that the Tell Asmar *God Abu* and *Goddess* had owed to their enormous irises. Both tendencies find masterly expression in the Akkadian alabaster *Head*, but a still profounder creative liberty is apparent in the *Great Singer*. True, this strangely haunting face, emerging from the darkness of the past with the instancy of a primitive mask, had had forerunners. But the harmony of the geometric planes of the bust (no photograph can convey this statuette's compelling accent) with the globe formed by the buttocks, reveals a thorough-going independence whose equivalent is far to seek in any historical art. Something of the same spirit can be seen in the contrast between the Lilliputian hands of the Tell Asmar *Goddess* and the huge staring eyes incrusted in the large globular head. Yet these gestures of far-ranging freedom are exceptional, submerged in the over-all current of Mesopotamian art, as those of eleventh-century sculptors are submerged by Romanesque. For, wars and racial mutations notwithstanding, the major works display an indefeasible continuity from the first dynasty to the very last days of the art of Lagash. The *Great Singer* had no progeny, and the most fertile of the Akkadian figures was not the alabaster *Head* but the bronze *Sargon*, precursor of the Gudeas. A *Sumerian* in the Louvre reappears in numbers of small Neo-Sumerian heads and even, a thousand years later, in the *Warrior with a Chin-piece*.

An emotive undertone, a sort of *cante jondo*, permeates most sacred arts, though it is always subordinated in them to the expression of the sacrosanct. But the most favoured mode of expressing this in the profoundly religious art of Sumer was not emotional, but took the form of a schematism whose significance is brought out by the many works assembled for the first time in this volume. Some have seen in this a reduction of forms to their essential characteristics. This explanation—it would apply equally well to Egypt—which was presumably suggested by the standing *Gudeas*, holds good only partially for the *Architect with a Plan* and not at all for the Tell Asmar figures or the *Great Singer*. For obviously this latter is not the 'reduction' of a model; it is the *transformation* of a model. And it is seen to have a latent kinship with the *Architect*, when in imagination we restore the relation of the bust with the masses below it—for the over-all volume of the upper part of the figure has been wrecked by mutilations. Confronted, these two statues represent the two poles of Sumerian schematization. This found expression sometimes in a geometrical treatment of the figure, drastic to begin with (as in *The God Abu*), then less apparent, operating as an unseen architecture; sometimes, especially in the female figures, in a recall of such primordial forms as the sphere and the egg. A recall that at first was brutally direct, then discreet as

MARI - UR-NINA, "THE GREAT SINGER" (FIRST HALF, 3RD MILL.). — DAMASCUS MUSEUM

(A) ASSUR - WOMAN'S HEAD. — BERLIN   (B) TELLOH - MAN'S HEAD (GUDEA?). — METROPOLITAN MUSEUM

in some modern sculpture; the *Woman's Head* in Berlin is no more 'elementary' than Brancusi's works.   There is no question here of the pure oval found in certain idols from the Cyclades; nor of the schematization of a *face*, in the sense in which an Egyptian sculptor stylized a dead man's face to make his 'double.'   For the Egyptian sculptor, the human face had a structure, bones and muscles, and he always took them into account, though doing what he could to soften them; the *Woman's Head* in Berlin would have seemed to him unthinkable because its planes are *not those of a head*.   We must not be misled by the *Gudea with a Turban* figures which owe their prestige to those very qualities which seem to ally them with Egyptian sculpture.   Possibly they are portraits (in which case the *Gudea* in the British Museum cannot be one); possibly, too, those strangely rectangular jaws were not really Gudea's, but means enabling an artist of genius to harmonize the face with the body below and the head-dress it was to wear.   Every great artist aims at unity, and the unity of the

TELLOH - WOMAN'S HEAD (22ND CENTURY B.C.). — BERLIN MUSEUM →

London *Gudea* is markedly inferior to that of the large *Gudea with a Turban* in Paris. However this may be, the style of the turbaned kings certainly did not derive from the Patesi's face, because no style arises from a face, because we can watch this style developing on independent lines, and because the schematization of these heads is of the same order as that of all other heads carved in the same material. That the Sumerians found in stones the suggestive power that Far Eastern artists found in mountains and the Celts in menhirs is amply proved by the boulder on which King Eannatum commemorated the glories of his reign. And this silent, obsessive colloquy between the sculptors and the forms of pebbles or boulders becomes explicit when we compare the *Man's Head* in the Metropolitan Museum with the *Woman's Head* in Berlin, in which the coiffure is so tightly compressed as to acquire the volumes of the shaven cranium of the *Man's Head* from Telloh. It was the same creative process as gave rise, turn by turn, to the Tell Asmar *Goddess*, the *Woman of Telloh* and the *Woman with a Kaunakes*, that pointed the way to the Mari *Warrior with a Chin-piece* and made of the Berlin *Woman's Head* the very symbol of Neo-Sumerian art.

(A) TELL ASMAR - GODDESS (?). — BAGHDAD MUSEUM
(B) TELLOH - WOMAN'S HEAD. — BERLIN MUSEUM
(C) WOMAN WITH A KAUNAKES. — LOUVRE
(D) WARRIOR WITH A CHIN-PIECE. — ALEPPO MUSEUM

← TELLOH - MAN'S HEAD (GUDEA ?). — METROPOLITAN MUSEUM

CONSTANTIN BRANCUSI - MADEMOISELLE POGÁNY - (A) BRONZE (1913) - (B) MARBLE (1931)

This creative process tended at first to adapt human forms to those primordial forms whose effect on us we sense though its causes are obscure, but with which many very early arts, and our own as well, have now familiarized us. When between 1913 and 1931 Brancusi made successive versions of his *Mlle Pogány*, he cut up the ovoid of the first version into more and more summarily indicated but always more distinctive volumes. Like the Sumerian sculptors, he ended up by transforming the eyelids into massive reliefs set in grooves below the superciliary arches. We get an impression that he was seeking to attain (as he attained in *The Bird* and as some of the sculptors of the Cyclades had achieved before him) an elemental purity, a purity regained by imperceptible degrees, but bearing the imprint of a human hand. Yet, though the last version may seem more abstract than the first, the first being nearer the pure oval would have been more so, but for the scarf. And so as to impose on a primordial form a form created wholly by himself, Brancusi spanned his last head with the arch of the eyebrows of Gudea.

Admittedly comparisons between our modern art and the arts of very early periods should not be pressed too far; but such comparisons have the merit of showing, better than the analytic method, how the creative process operates. In 1931 Brancusi obviously set out to carve *a head*, not the face of Mlle Pogány, and those admirable volumes are not a simplification of the volumes of a head but a metamorphosis of it into a work of sculpture—intended for a gallery or museum. But Sumerian heads of worshippers were intended *for a temple*. When the sculptor simplified forms, it was to set man free from the human condition, as artists of other cultures did by dissolving him into hieroglyphs or interlaces, and the makers of Mesopotamian figurines sometimes did by reshaping a face into an arbitrary and inexplicable rosette. Such references to the immemorial, by way of the assimilation of a worshipper's head to a pebble and Gudea to a menhir, are clearly means of transposing the ephemeral into the eternal. But the process is twofold, for Gudea does not become a menhir but a statue.

Brancusi's ideal was not that of carving an egg, nor was this the ideal of the maker of the *Woman's Head*. Cézanne's concern with 'cylinders and cones' did not lead him to paint cylinders but to paint *The Lake of Annecy*, and when applied to *Guernica* the term 'Cubism' is an absurd misnomer.

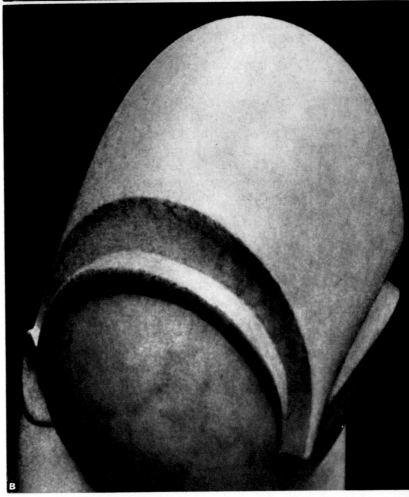

(A) TELLOH - GUDEA, DETAIL (22ND CENTURY B.C.). — BRITISH MUSEUM

(B) CONSTANTIN BRANCUSI - MADEMOISELLE POGÁNY, DETAIL (1931)

The Sumerian sculptor was possessed by a craving for primordial forms and the elementary forms they imposed on him. Hence the pyramid formed by the statue of Manishtusu, the garments shaped like bells or pillars of the standing *Gudeas*, and the aquiline heads of so many Mesopotamian statues, from *The God Abu* to the *Warrior with a Chin-piece*. It was as if the sculptor felt that such forms were *per se* means of communion with the eternal. But for them to impart their power of communion to a statue, the latter had to remain distinct from them, and the primordial form was no more the 'model' of a worshipper figure than was the man who dedicated it, or Man in general. It was in the nature of a schema—a secret mentor urging sculptors to tighten up their line and expand their volumes so that the figures they created could share its numinous power.

Hence that will to schematize and to 'see big,' which characterized, to Baudelaire's thinking, the only sculptures of early epochs that he knew. But also the artist's need to give the human or near-human features which make the head of his statue differ from a round or oval pebble, an accent according them to the subjacent primordial schema he had in mind. When Rodin

AUGUSTE RODIN - BALZAC - NUDE
STUDY. — MUSÉE RODIN, PARIS

XL

decided to make of his *Balzac* that oaktree struck by lightning, unique in his œuvre, he had to abandon the head intended for a naked Balzac and to harmonize everything, down to the planes of the eyebrows, with the ravaged trunk. With their beetling eyebrows and eyelids the Lagash sculptors achieved a similar unity and replaced the inlaid eyelids and antlike or enormous, spellbound eyes of the previous period by a new harmony with the latent primordial form.

Time and again artists were to rediscover the plenitude given the human face by that 'ideal pebble' which is suggested by the cheeks of the Delphi *Charioteer* and by the neckerchiefs of Gothic widows: the superb plenitude we find in the arts of Egypt, India, China, Cambodia and Siam. But in none of these arts does the lower eyelid exactly correspond to the upper, and in all Buddhist art the eye is engraved. For, as in Christian art, it conveys a religious sentiment, whereas in Sumerian art it invariably expresses a transcendent spirituality. No historical civilization has represented worshippers so powerfully *dehumanized;* when compared with those of the great Sumerian effigies, the most famous faces in the arts of Egypt, Greece, India, Mexico and Peru, of the

AUGUSTE RODIN - BALZAC (1891-1897). — MUSÉE RODIN, PARIS

Buddhist lands and even of Byzantium, have a curious vulnerability—it is as though their makers had just discovered the frailty of all living flesh. And never did the human visage regain the accent given it in these 'pebbles' transmuted into kings.

Sumerian abstractionism alone does not explain this difference. The Siamese bronze-workers invented a cloak no less allusive than Gudea's, but they treated it with an almost Persian subtlety and attuned it to that music of the otherworldly which imbues their divine figures, and whose purest modulations are the arabesques formed by the hands of their statues. Nothing is more revealing than the contrast between these hands (indeed those of all great Buddhist sculpture) and the clasped hands towards which all Sumero-Akkadian art seemed constantly aspiring, up to their realization by the sculptors of Lagash. The gestures of the Buddhist figures are symbolic and, long before the flower-like fingers of Siamese sculpture, Asia had discovered that position of the hands in which the Buddha's arms seem to be softly closing on the mystery of the universe. How different they are from that superb gesture, solid as a seal, which we find in the interlocked hands of the Gudea statues—hall-

THAI ART - WALKING BUDDHA (AFTER THE 13TH CENTURY A.D.). — FORMERLY PEYTEL COLLECTION

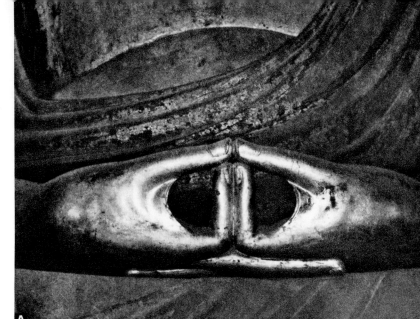

mark as it were of all Neo-Sumerian art! That 'seal' is not a synthesis of real hands; no one can lock his hands in just this way, and those preceding it were more lifelike. It is an ideogram signifying prayer in a culture in which the act of worship was one long prayer, an endless invocation of the sacred: an ideogram by which the sculptor signified the morsel of eternity immanent in man, and in virtue of which the statue stands in the same relation to him as the hands in the *Architect with a Plan* to human hands. We do not know why the age of great creations ended with the Lagash masters—but neither do we know why great Renaissance sculpture ended with Michelangelo. Thereafter, only in the art of modelling clay and in that of bronze (in some ways a dependency of clay modelling) do we find some minor innovations, as when at long last the bronze-workers came to impart to large-scale lions the ferocity that glyptic art had been giving them for centuries. In sculpture the great artists followed in the footsteps of their predecessors. *Ishtupilum* (as the back shows) descends from the *Gudeas;* the *Warrior with a Chin-piece* implements a long tradition; the *Goddess with a Flowing Vase* makes us think of a large terracotta figurine whose maker has

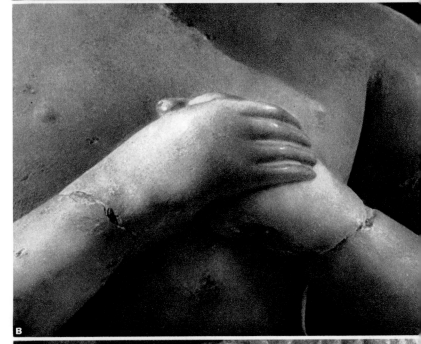

(A) JAPANESE ART - AMIDA, DETAIL (11TH CENTURY A.D.)
(B) MARI - EBIH-IL, DETAIL (FIRST HALF, 3RD MILL.)
(C) SUSA - ELAMITE WORSHIPPER, DETAIL (3RD MILL.)

kept in mind the boldly rectangular faces of Lagash art; the Mari *Worshipper with a Young Goat* might pass for a great-grandson of the Tell Asmar *Worshipper;* the *Elamite* in the Metropolitan for one of the bronze *Sargon.* On the stele inscribed with the Code of Hammurabi the king looks like a suppler Patesi and his eyes, too, imitate Gudea's. Some Kassite figures and the huge scenic effects of Babylon notwithstanding, no true style emerges until we come to the narrative magnificence of Assyrian bas-reliefs and their sinister pageantry.

Some of the works here reproduced claim a high place in our Treasury of world art. Unimpaired, perhaps seconded, by two drastic metamorphoses—that which has stripped the statues of their colour and that which has transferred them from the temple to the museum—Sumerian art has a singular appeal to modern man, by reason of its rejection of illusionism, its schematization and its freedom, so well in keeping with the art trends of today. It came back to life when our own art and the resurrection of great forgotten arts led us to discount those aspects of the masterworks of Sumer and Akkad whereby they seem to resemble what they represent, and to appreciate all that in them does not resemble it. These statues, written off as dumb or stammering when appraised in terms of nature-imitation or idealization, speak to us with no uncertain voice now that they forgather with all the rediscovered works in the 'Museum without Walls' that our new world-culture has brought into being. To the question we have been asking ourselves since 'artist' ceased to signify 'aesthete,' they reply that in the civilization to which we today belong, the art-lover or connoisseur is the man who, looking at the work of art, responds to forms created by the artist, not to the forms of appearance they closely or remotely resemble: the man whose frame of reference is no longer 'nature' but the world of art.

The forms created by artists fall into two classes: those subservient to nature or the idealization of nature, which from Pheidias to Delacroix constituted the art heritage of the nineteenth century; and, secondly, the forms, notably the works of sculpture, which the present century has either invented for itself or resuscitated, and has learned to admire. These are the forms of the Ancient East, but only up to, approximately, the sixth century B.C.; the creations of Buddhist art, but above all Wei sculpture; of Hindu art, but above all Gupta sculpture; of Christian art, but above all Romanesque sculpture. In Egypt and China, as elsewhere, our resuscitations cease at the period when subservience to appearance has become the rule.

For, be it noted, the effect that works of art produce on us is of a specific kind and relates primarily to *forms*. We learned to admire the sculpture of the races of the Ancient East before coming to know (and how imperfectly!) their faith and ways of thinking. The great Resurrection now in progress began in artists' studios, not in learned institutions for the study of compared religions. The entry of Sumer and Babylon into our 'Museum without Walls' was one of a long series of accessions that took place successively: the Primitives, Japanese painting, Gothic, Chinese, Khmer, Greek Archaic, Gandharan, Hindu, Pre-Columbian, Romanesque, Scythian, Etruscan, African and Oceanian sculpture. Does this mean we are travelling back in time and mere remoteness is the criterion of our modern preferences? Not altogether; for we do not admire the paintings at Lascaux or Tassili more than the Ravenna mosaics, or Aurignacian sculpture more than the *Architect with a Plan* or the *Pouting Koré*. What counts for us in the works we are resuscitating is not their remoteness in time but their emancipation from appearance. And these forms which substitute their own order for the order of appearance, in the current usage of the word, are the forms of arts refractory to Appearance in its metaphysical sense.

Not that we are unaware of the part played by metamorphosis in this respect; for actually that vast realm of seeming freedoms is made up of bygone tyrannies. Brancusi was free to carve as he liked, Picasso paints as he likes; it was not so with the Sumerian artists, or those of Ellora, Lung-Mên, Moissac. If these sculptors were untrammelled by appearance, it was because they set out to express what, for them, was truer than Appearance. Their works have not, for us, the Truth they had originally—which is why I once said that very early styles strike us as so many Zarathustras invented by so many Nietzsches; but no present-day Nietzsche can write an *Avesta*, no Picasso carve the Moissac tympanum. A stage mask does not move us in the way an African mask moves us. Sumerian religious faith conjured up forms that could not have existed without it and we respond to them not only in the way that we respond to forms born of the creative impulse, but as we respond to the forms created by other religions. Such forms are not capricious; these sacred arts were 'functional' to the soul, and common to all the arts we have rediscovered is the revelation of a world with which man can enter into communion, but which he cannot know: the sacred world of the gods and of the dead.

The little gods of tribes and towns and the great gods of darkness, of the sun and of desire, the gods of whom men asked eternity—all alike have lapsed into oblivion, the endless night of the dead religions of the East. That the images which we admire today should not have died along with the faiths they sponsored is one of the major mysteries of art. For we have not only realized that their forms were not due to clumsy attempts at imitation, but also that they mean far more to us than 'volumes arranged in a certain order.' Yet that very mystery has made clear what all these arts of the sacred have in common: an aspiration to the inapprehensible. True, they have undergone a metamorphosis; the Gudea figures are no longer those of worshippers in temples and have become statues, and keep company in the world of art with African *Ancestors*, the *Kings* of Chartres, the figures of Rembrandt and Cézanne. But the very loss of that quality of the inapprehensible discloses the new significance they have acquired and share with all the works assembled in our 'Museum without Walls'; even with works that have no religious purpose. Our resuscitation of the arts of the past is gradually bringing to light—as against the elements that make for 'resemblance' in the work of art—that manifest or hidden quality which accounts for their basic dissimilitude from the thing seen, a dissimilitude that orients resemblances even when the artist's aim is nature-imitation. Confronting the intentions we ascribe to Greece and Italy is another 'programme,' that of Sumer and Byzantium; the world of all that can be seen without art's help is confronted by the world of that which art alone enables us to see. A world whose successive reincarnations, making of every great artist a destroyer of that correlation of appearances which constitutes 'reality' and a revealer of a Truth once proclaimed though obsolete today, may well suggest that our deepest response to art is of a metaphysical order. . .

July 1960.

André Malraux

L

Introduction

by

André Parrot

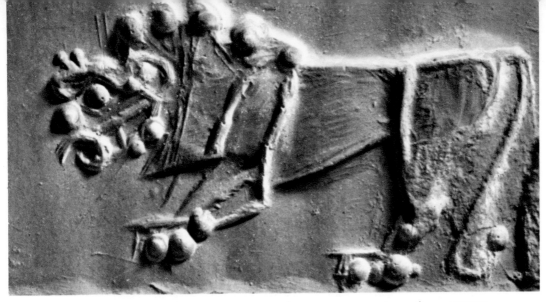

INTRODUCTION

A T the time when Europe was still in the throes of learning the
bare rudiments of social, artistic and political life, the Near East
had long since crossed the threshold of civilization and had also
passed through many of the phases in which man, assured of his ascendancy, makes steady progress on the path of culture. *Ex oriente lux...*
and who can deny that from the East came enlightenment? For Chris-
tians, doubtless, the light of revelation, but for all men that first decisive
flowering of life whose after-effects are still perceptible today.

Mesopotamia and the Nile Valley gave birth to two of the greatest
civilizations the world has ever known. Discussion as to which came
first serves little purpose, but on the whole it now seems probable that
Mesopotamia got under way a little sooner and in the earliest period
gave more than she received. Whether it be so or not, this much is
certain: that on the scroll of history must be inscribed, long before
'the miracle of Greece,' that twofold creative uprush of human genius
which took place some six thousand years ago in two different lands,
and which marked so decisive a step towards man's mastery of his
environment. Thereafter civilization took flame and spread through
subsequent cultures like a forest fire. Not that for a moment we would
wish to deny to other peoples a share in this collective achievement.
Our purpose is solely to point out that every conflagration has a starting-
place and that, in the case of civilization, Mesopotamia was one and

by no means the lesser of the two places whence a flame of enlightenment leapt forth to illuminate surrounding regions. These regions themselves had perhaps already begun to emerge from total darkness but hitherto they had lacked the mighty wind which fans flickering embers into brilliant sheets of fire. It was as if man, after creeping for ages on all fours, at long last stood erect and followed the trail blazed by the torchbearers towards the heights. The gods were now to open wide a door which never again would close, and like a giant with flaming shoulders,

2 · THE GOD SHAMASH (MID-THIRD MILLENNIUM). — BRITISH MUSEUM

the Mesopotamian sun strode forth upon his conquest of the sky.

That sun bathed in its light not only the plain and basin of the two great rivers, Tigris and Euphrates, but also the entire surrounding region. So-called Oriental civilization thus claims as its domain the whole vast area which, bounded on the west by the Mediterranean, extends eastwards to the Afghan frontier. Bounded on the north by the Black Sea, it covers in the south the entire Arabian peninsula. Of its two names, Western Asia and the Near East, each is apt; for both, while specifying a continent, indicate the direction in which it faces. This is important to bear in mind in the following pages.

Yet in the Ancient Near East one region, where the initial flame shone brightest, has unquestionable pride of place. This region comprises not simply Mesopotamia, meaning as the name indicates 'the country between the rivers,' but also its fringes, that is to say its extensions beyond the Euphrates to the west and the Tigris to the east. Its precise geographical content is difficult to define, since it often comprises Iran, so closely allied and interdependent at times were the two cultures.

Its diversity is both ethnical and geographical. We shall encounter, according to the period, several nations in different parts of the country: Sumerians in Lower Mesopotamia; Proto-Elamites, Elamites, Medes, Persians, Achaemenians in Iran; Semites and Akkadians in Middle Mesopotamia; Assyrians in Assyria; Hurrians on the Upper Tigris; Mitannians on the Khabur and to the south of the Taurus range. Looking further north or west, we shall discover Hittites in Anatolia, Aramaean Syrians in the Orontes valley, Phoenicians on the Mediterranean littoral and Canaanites in Palestine. And this is to list only the main branches, leaving out of account their many offshoots.

The names cited above suffice to show that the civilization of Western Asia had not the basic unity we find in Egypt, but varied in terms of localities and races. From which it follows that there was not one art of Western Asia but many arts; not one culture but several. Nevertheless, despite this multiplicity and diversity, there is a ground common to all and always more or less discernible: this is the far-reaching influence of the culture which had its origin in Mesopotamia. Thus it is essential to define and describe as accurately as possible the nature of this culture, to which so many others in the Near East owe so much. As will frequently be seen in the course of this study, Mesopotamia was the birthplace of traditions and themes which, after travelling from region to region and being taken over and remoulded locally, ended up by forming part of the cultural heritage of races that had not originated them. However, this power of assimilation, whose thoroughness may frequently surprise us, was (as is often the case with borrowings of this kind) never strong enough to submerge entirely local idioms and idiosyncrasies.

This holds good in ancient times not only for all Western Asia but also for the very centre of this art, the land of Mesopotamia itself, where there was a continuity lasting for several millennia. Our study begins with protohistory, a term defined at a later page, and ends with the fourth century B.C. when Alexander's victories in his Persian campaign mark a decisive turning-point in the history of the Near East. Once the West secured a foothold in Asia and established its political and military supremacy, a whole world of culture passed away, never to return. Such events had taken place again and again in the area, as the result of wars as ruthless as any today. Sumerian, Assyrian, Babylonian, each had followed the other into the death-pit of oblivion. Now that we know what manner of men these were and what were their achievements, we hardly understand how they can have disappeared so utterly. Paul Valéry coined the very term for such events when he called them shipwrecks. The word serves to remind us that just as modern divers explore hulls of sunken ships and bring to light the treasures they contain, so do archaeologists plumb the very depths of history. The enthusiastic but often haphazard research-work of the pioneers in the field has given place to disciplines that are nothing if not rigorous. In dealing with these buried chronicles of a distant past we have first, as it were, to break the seals and then to uncover, one by one, the successive pages of history, remembering always of course that they disclose themselves to us in the reverse order to that in which they were deposited by the passing generations. As archaeologists, we have to proceed from the known to the unknown, doing our best to compile a methodical inventory of our finds and taking care not to omit anything of consequence. And we have to assign to each object and monument not only its inherent value but also a value relative to the chronology which it has been our first task to establish on a sound basis.

This brief account of the problems involved will give some idea of their complexity. It is obvious that the work has entailed more than any one man, even a man of genius, could carry through. Not only international collaboration has been needed, but the combined, if independent, research-work of whole teams of specialists. At least three generations of experts have participated. When we read books written less than half a century ago, we realize not only the quite amazing quantity of new material accumulated during the last two or three decades, but also the drastic revisions that formerly accepted theories have undergone. It nevertheless seems unlikely that half a century hence our own findings will have to be so drastically overhauled, though doubtless some details of our interpretation may call for modification. By and large, however, that interpretation will probably hold good. For it is difficult to believe that the discoveries made at Ur for instance, or at Mari, a site whose existence was not even suspected thirty years ago, will ever be outclassed. Except for Akkad, all the great capital cities of the Ancient East have now been located. The hundreds of tells as yet unexcavated cover sites of small provincial towns, and it may be doubted whether anything unearthed in them will do more than recall or implement finds already made.

The time seems, therefore, ripe for gathering in the crop, and the harvest is indeed a bounteous one. The following pages present a copious sheaf of richly diverse works of art which have preserved, despite the ravages of time, the wonderful vitality their creators breathed into them millennia ago.

André Parrot

4 - THE TOWER OF BABEL - PIETER BRUEGEL THE ELDER (16TH CENTURY)

I

HISTORY OF THE DISCOVERIES

WHEN in 1882 Georges Perrot and Charles Chipiez published the first volume of their *Histoire de l'Art dans l'Antiquité* they embarked on an enterprise that no two present-day specialists would feel capable of undertaking without collaborators. They set out to cover not only the entire area of the Near East, but Egypt as well, and even Greece. Seven bulky volumes succeeded each other in a period of sixteen years. Infinitely varied as was the material they had to cope with and relating as it did to so many different civilizations, their efforts prove that at the close of the nineteenth century there still existed men who could master a subject of this nature and handle it with authority and competence. In that age of all-inclusive syntheses, often products of a single brain, Perrot and Chipiez's work was followed at the turn of the century by another: Gaston Maspero's *Histoire ancienne des Peuples de l'Orient classique* (1895-99). If Maspero, essentially an Egyptologist, employs a wide canvas and gives a magnificent picture of the birth of two great civilizations and the clashes of early Empires,

5 — KHORSABAD - FIRST DISCOVERIES OF BOTTA - REPRODUCED AFTER HIS DRAWINGS (1844)

from the Nile to the Tigris, Perrot, the Hellenist, feels even less qualms about covering a still wider field. He ranges from the nuraghi of Sardinia to Achaemenian palaces, from the marbles of Paros and pink granite of Aswan to the diorite statues of Gudea. Both, as was then the custom, had draughtsmen for collaborators, men whose industry we cannot but admire when we realize the many painstaking hours they spent sketching what can now be recorded in the fraction of a second, thanks to the camera. Botta, too, in 1848, had no camera, but fortunately for him

6 - (A) STATUE OF GUDEA. — (B) THE BABYLON LION. — (C) THE DYING LIONESS. — (D) STATUE OF ASSURNASIRPAL

he had available the talent of the French artist Eugène Flandin, without which nothing would remain to tell us of the hundreds of yards of reliefs unearthed in the Assyrian palace at Khorsabad. Such encyclopaedic works as Perrot's not only characterize an epoch; they also admirably reveal the state of knowledge at the time. Moreover, we have often to refer back to them for monuments which then existed but have since disappeared or have suffered so greatly from the ravages of time that we can get only a poor idea of them today.

7 - TELLOH - 'TURBANED HEAD' (ENGRAVING AFTER CHIPIEZ)

8 - TELLOH - HEAD OF GUDEA (22ND CENTURY B.C.). — LOUVRE

Against such encyclopaedic works we have Salomon Reinach's *Apollo*, a volume remarkable for its extreme brevity. This is a summary of lectures the author gave in 1902-03 at the Ecole du Louvre, dealing in one hour with 'Egypt, Chaldea and Persia'; there are only twelve pages of text, illustrations included! Half of them are deemed sufficient to cover the subject of the whole of this book and to describe the monuments then considered essential: the Stele of the Vultures, for the Sumerians (described as Chaldeans, a misnomer we are surprised still to find employed occasionally even by serious authors today); the Gudea statuary (the Architect and the Turbaned Head); a selection of Assyrian reliefs (the Gilgamesh, the inevitable Human-headed Bull, the Assurbanipal Hunting, the Wounded Lion, the Dying Lioness); the Frieze of Archers from Susa; and the Hittite Lion of Marash. Architecture in Mesopotamia is represented by a reconstruction by Chipiez, entitled 'Chaldean Temple,' an attempt at representing a ziggurat which, given the state of knowledge at the time, was remarkably successful.

Half a century later a new start had to be made on a very different, much enlarged basis and nowadays the individual researcher is replaced by teams each member of which is asked to deal with his speciality, that is to say

9 - 'CHALDEAN TEMPLE' - RECONSTRUCTION BY CHIPIEZ

the subject he hopes to know least badly. The rapid increase of documentation has led to a degree of specialization that, despite its drawbacks, was inevitable. In the following pages we give an account of the successive stages by which the data fundamental to our work were brought to light, beginning with the pioneers. Needless to say, our survey will be brief and confined to essentials.

At the beginning of the nineteenth century nothing more was known of the Assyrians than the references to them in the Bible. The chief Mesopotamian monument was the 'Michaux Stone' brought to France in 1786 by the botanist of that name, acquired by the government and placed in the Bibliothèque Nationale (Cabinet des Médailles). Ornamented with reliefs and bearing an inscription, it was the object of studies which today have only a retrospective interest. The cuneiform script was then a complete mystery, and even the names of the Sumerians, Akkadians and Hittites were unknown. Only Phoenician had at that time been deciphered: in 1764, by Abbé Barthélemy, thanks to a bilingual text discovered in Malta.

Yet there was then no dearth of travellers in the Ancient East: traders, European officials and a host of adventurers in the full sense of the term. Their 'explorations' were haphazard and superficial. The year 1842 marked the beginning of a new era when, for the first time, excavations were made in some of the artificial mounds, or tells, which contained the ruins of buried cities whose very names were then unknown. This was the period when diplomats turned amateur archaeologists. Thus the French consul at Mosul, P.E. Botta, excavated Kuyunjik (Nineveh) and Khorsabad (Dur Sharrukin) in 1843-44,

12 - SIR AUSTEN HENRY LAYARD (1817-1894)

13 - ERNEST DE SARZEC (1837-1901)

14 - P.E. BOTTA (1802-1870)

15 - WALTER ANDRAE (1875-1956)

16 - ROBERT KOLDEWEY (1855-1925)

17 - HENRI FRANKFORT (1897-1954)

13

and in 1845-47 Austen Henry Layard, an Englishman, investigated Kuyunjik, Nimrud (Kalakh) and Qalaat Shergat (Assur). To these two pioneers we owe the first collections of Assyrian antiquities in Europe: in the Louvre (May 1, 1847) and in the British Museum (October, 1848). These were much increased by subsequent researchers; the Louvre's, by the consul Victor Place at Khorsabad (1852-54); the British Museum's, by Layard and Rassam on the same Assyrian sites (1849-54), under the supervision of H.C. Rawlinson, political agent at Baghdad.

Interest was next to shift to the south. Fresnel, French consul at Baghdad, explored Babylon in 1852; W. K. Loftus, an Englishman, worked at Warka (Uruk) and Susa (1851-53), while the English consul J. E. Taylor investigated Muqayyar (Ur) in 1854

18 - THE FIRST ASSYRIAN ANTIQUITIES COLLECTION AT THE LOUVRE (1847)

and 1855. Thus the Sumerian area had at last been broken into, though no one then guessed this, and, given the poorness of the finds, attention soon reverted to the north where reliefs emerged at

19 - THE 'CHALDEO-ASSYRIAN' ANTIQUITIES AT THE LOUVRE (1890)

14

20 - THE FEAST IN A GARDEN - RELIEF FROM ASSURBANIPAL'S PALACE (7TH CENTURY B.C.) — BRITISH MUSEUM

almost every turn of the spade. Loftus returned to Nineveh where he had the luck of unearthing the famous 'Feast in a Garden' (1855), and in 1872 George Smith discovered a fragment of a tablet completing the cuneiform story of the Deluge, which he had identified some months previously in the storerooms of the British Museum.

It was yet another consul, Ernest de Sarzec, stationed at Basra, who from 1877 on explored the Telloh hills and made known the existence of a civilization and an art attributable to the Sumerians. De Sarzec too discovered, at Telloh, much later, the amazing series of Gudea statues, while at Nippur the Americans John P. Peters and John Henry Haynes, who in 1889 had only recently come on the scene, were garnering a harvest of cuneiform tablets. The quest of museum pieces was, however, to give place to a more judicious view of the way in which scientific excavation should be conducted. Thus began the period of the great clearances which henceforth were supervised by engineers and architects.

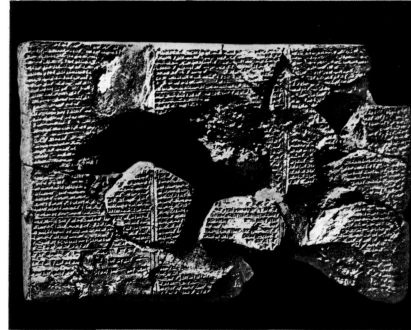

21 - 'DELUGE TABLET' (7TH CENTURY B.C.) — BRITISH MUSEUM

15

22 - THE RUINS OF BABYLON (C. 1850) - BEFORE EXCAVATION

23 - SUSA - THE TELL BEFORE THE LOFTUS AND DIEULAFOY EXCAVATIONS

24 - NIMRUD - THE EXCAVATIONS CONDUCTED BY RASSAM

The site of Susa, to exploring which the Dieulafoys had devoted two seasons (1884-86) and to which the Louvre owes, *inter alia*, some Achaemenian monuments (the Archers Frieze and a capital adorned with kneeling bulls), was entrusted in 1897 to an expedition headed by Jacques de Morgan, a mining engineer, who had a large staff at his disposal. Babylon, meanwhile, was assigned to a German architect, Robert Koldewey, who enlisted some young collaborators, also architects: Andrae, Jordan and Nöldeke. Andrae and Jordan, from 1903 on, were in charge of the Assur expedition and from 1912 on, of that at Uruk. Victor Place had already given an example, at Khorsabad, of the best method of digging horizontally on a large scale, and the German architects followed suit. The latter brought to their work an extreme minuteness, anticipating the procedures of modern 'microscopic' research.

Meanwhile several sites were being reworked and new ones opened up. An American professor of ancient history, E. J. Banks, was sent to Bismaya (Adab) where he worked in 1903-04. Captain Cros, a Saharan officer, took over from Sarzec and worked for four seasons (1903-09) at Telloh. Henri de Genouillac, the Assyriologist, began in 1912 the excavation of al 'Oheimir (Kish), a site which had suffered considerably at the hands of freelance excavators.

25 - NIMRUD - WINGED BULLS OF ASSUR-
NASIRPAL (DRAWING BY LAYARD)

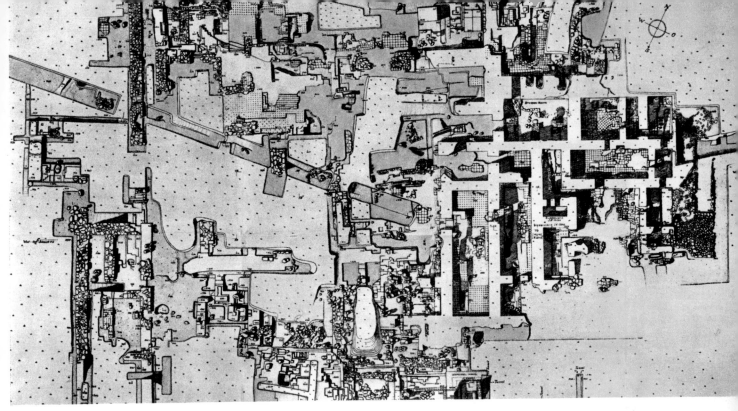

26 - ASSUR - DETAIL OF EXCAVATION PLAN

In 1911 the German Herzfeld had started work at Samarra where he discovered, below Arab remains, a protohistorical level which was to give its name to a phase of Mesopotamian civilization. In the same year Baron von Oppenheim, who was excavating Tell Halaf (at the source of the Khabur) also discovered among the successive strata one that pointed to a cultural and artistic phase hitherto unknown. But the true significance of this phase was not to be fully grasped until after the First World War when, thanks to improved techniques, its chronology could be established.

The outbreak of the 1914-18 war put an abrupt end to many expeditions. Exceptionally, the Germans stayed on at Babylon until 1917, when they were dislodged by the advance of the British Expeditionary Force. After the signing of the Armistice at Mudros (October 30, 1918) had brought peace to the Middle East, the truncation of the Ottoman Empire and the mandates accorded Britain and France for Iraq and Syria completely changed the conditions under which archaeologists carried on their work. Hitherto research had been obstructed by the touchiness of petty officials who were practically all-powerful (owing to their remoteness from the central government) and by the hostility of local tribes. This is illustrated time and again in the reports made by the heads of expeditions; now, however, the researchers were officially aided and encouraged. Thus the period 1919-39 is coming more and more to be regarded as the Golden Age of Oriental archaeology.

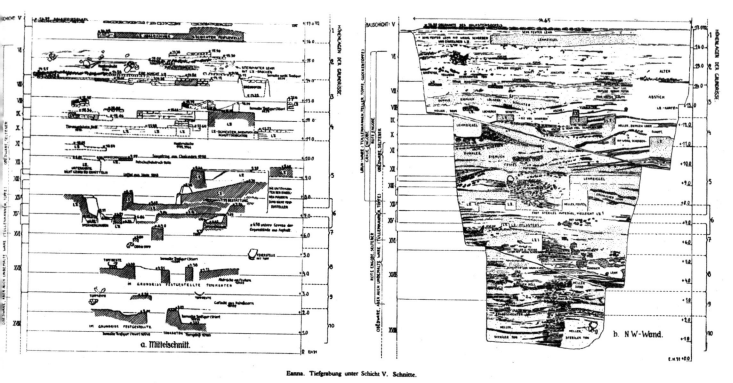

Eanna. Tiefgrabung unter Schicht V. Schnitte.

J. Jordan: Ausgrabungen in Uruk 1930/31. — Taf. 12.

27 - WARKA (URUK) - STRATIGRAPHIC CROSS-SECTION OF THE EXCAVATIONS

Protracted operations, an expert staff and methodized research were now the order of the day and it soon became clear that the buried treasure of these lands was far from being exhausted, as some had supposed; only the surface had been scratched. Meanwhile clandestine excavators, taking advantage of the vast dispersal of the sites and the inability of the various Services of Antiquities to protect them, made here and there some startling discoveries and drew attention either to places long known to be promising (Lagash-Telloh, Larsa-Senkereh) or to others whose importance was not yet recognized (e.g. the Diyala area, east of Baghdad). This led to new expeditions which confirmed the vast resources of this region and revealed an art whose scope and wonderful achievements surpassed all that had been expected in the light of the discoveries made before 1914.

Here again we must confine ourselves to a brief summary of this reconquest of the past. With that tenacity of purpose which is the prime condition of success, four nations joined in the great venture. Techniques were much improved, and besides horizontal excavations,

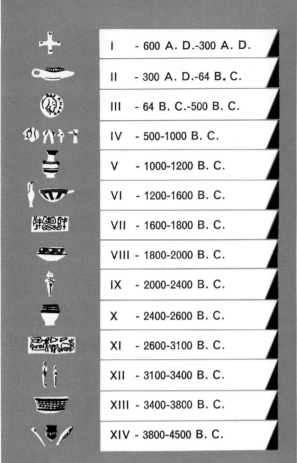

I	-	600 A. D.-300 A. D.
II	-	300 A. D.-64 B. C.
III	-	64 B. C.-500 B. C.
IV	-	500-1000 B. C.
V	-	1000-1200 B. C.
VI	-	1200-1600 B. C.
VII	-	1600-1800 B. C.
VIII	-	1800-2000 B. C.
IX	-	2000-2400 B. C.
X	-	2400-2600 B. C.
XI	-	2600-3100 B. C.
XII	-	3100-3400 B. C.
XIII	-	3400-3800 B. C.
XIV	-	3800-4500 B. C.

28 - JEDEIDEH - STRATIGRAPHIC CROSS-SECTION OF THE EXCAVATIONS - CHARACTERISTIC OBJECTS AT EACH LEVEL

vertical shafts were sunk, beginning with the surface strata (most recent in date) and striking down to virgin soil, that is to say the very earliest vestiges of human habitation. Thus, for the first time in archaeology, a careful study came to be made of the successive levels of a site. Thanks to this it now was possible to trace the cultural and artistic evolution of those who had lived there and to tabulate chronologically successive manifestations of their activities and ways of life. Many indications of these had been found in previous investigations but, in the absence of a stratigraphic technique, could not be interpreted correctly. It was soon discovered that intermediary phases had to be added to those already classified (*Halaf, Samarra*). They were named after the sites where they were discovered or defined for the first time (*al 'Ubaid, Jemdet Nasr, Uruk*). It now seemed that all protohistoric Mesopotamia had been brought to light. Actually, however, the first phase still was lacking; but this could be documented only in the lower part of the country, peopled later than northern Iraq. This was done, at the height of the Second World War, by an Iraqi expedition.

29 - UR - EXCAVATIONS IN THE 'ROYAL' CEMETERY

Since Great Britain had been given the mandate for Iraq, the first on the scene were Englishmen, who for a time had the field to themselves. Campbell Thompson (1918), Hall (1919) and C. L. Woolley (1922) concentrated on the Ur region which, though already explored by Taylor, was soon shown to be worth returning to: hence the excavations at Abu Shahrein (Eridu) and Muqayyar (Ur) and the discovery of al 'Ubaid. Abu Shahrein proved disappointing, but al 'Ubaid, besides yielding a finely decorated shrine, gave its name to an important protohistoric stratum. And the splendours of the 'royal tombs' discovered at Ur (1927-29) eclipsed even those of the tomb of Tutankhamen (1922-24).

An Anglo-American expedition led by the Oxford Assyriologist Langdon, assisted by Mackay and Watelin, put in ten years' work at Kish (1923-33) on the site formerly explored by Abbé Henri de Genouillac. Though it yielded few museum pieces, some important scientific observations were made. A few miles away the Jemdet Nasr Tell (excavated 1925-28) revealed another protohistoric stratum subsequent to the one that German archaeologists were soon to discover (1930-32) at Warka (Uruk), where they resumed work in 1928.

The city of Gilgamesh, Uruk (the Erech of the Bible) was uncovered by the Germans with a meticulous care that let nothing escape.

30 - UR - HYPOGEUM OF SHULGI

Indeed the field work directed by two architects, Jordan, and then Nöldeke, both of them trained in the school of Koldewey, was a model of what such work should be, and it is to them we owe the chronology of this important period of protohistory, whose after-effects are clearly visible in all domains: architecture, sculpture and the written language.

Finally, at Telloh, where free-booters had been operating with a success that was reflected by the number of 'antiquities' that now came on the market (1923-24), Genouillac took over from Cros and Sarzec in 1929. The author assisted him in 1930, and from 1931 to the spring of 1933 took charge of the researches at Sen-kereh (Larsa), where sporadic ex-cavations had led, shortly before, to several spectacular finds.

This succinct enumeration—to which should be added a men-tion of the University of Penn-sylvania expedition, led by Erich Schmidt in 1931, which made Fara (Shuruppak) its base—indicates that all the great cities of Sumer, with the exception of Nippur, the 'Holy City,' were systematically explored by teams which, working on the spot, perfected a technique facilitating not only effective clearances of sites but the discovery of cultures. Thanks to these me-thods, objects have ceased to set conundrums and can be correctly assigned to their period and cul-tural environment.

31 - UR - THE 'ROYAL' TOMBS - SACRIFICIAL PROCESSION

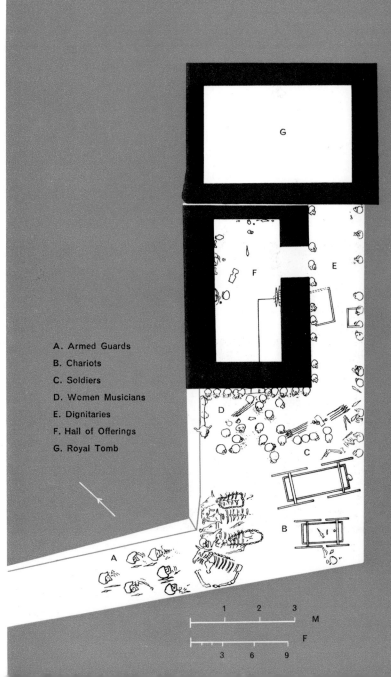

A. Armed Guards
B. Chariots
C. Soldiers
D. Women Musicians
E. Dignitaries
F. Hall of Offerings
G. Royal Tomb

32 - UR - PLAN OF THE TOMB OF SHUBAD —
ARRANGEMENT OF THE SACRIFICIAL VICTIMS

Methodical exploration was now to extend far beyond the Sumer area. About 1924 freebooters extracted from the tells of the Diyala region, east of Baghdad, a quantity of statuettes testifying to a local art well worth scientific study. The Oriental Institute of Chicago, founded in 1919 by John D. Rockefeller Jr, whose moving spirit was the Egyptologist J.H. Breasted, sent an expedition to this area; it was led by Henri Frankfort (1930) who worked there till 1936. Their activities centred on four sites: Tell Asmar (Ashnunnak), Khafaje (?Tutub), Ishchali (?Neribtum) and Tell Agrab, and met with much success. They brought to light not only archaic buildings but a wealth of statuary whose distinctive features sharply differentiate it from that of other Mesopotamian art centres. There could be little doubt, in fact, that this was the work of a quite different race.

The exploration of Assyria, a field that might have seemed exhausted, was also resumed. Members of the University of Pennsylvania, which had already shared, in the far south, in the excavations at Ur, fixed their choice on several sites in northern Iraq: Yorgan Tepe (Nuzi), Tepe Gawra and Tell Billa. They worked from 1925 onward, with the collaboration of the American School of Oriental Research and other organizations, under the supervision of Chiera, Pfeiffer, Starr, Speiser and (in 1938) Bache. Experts from the Oriental Institute took over (1928-35) at Khorsabad the work begun by Place and Botta. Returning to Nineveh, English archaeologists in 1927 began a stratigraphical survey which, combined with the discoveries at Gawra, led to a scientific classification of all the phases of Assyrian protohistory. This we owe to Thompson, Hutchinson, Hamilton and still more to Mallowan, who excavated Arpatchiya (1933) and revealed the so-called Halaf culture.

The exploration of the Upper Tigris valley was accompanied by that of the Middle Euphrates, since it seemed probable that Mesopotamian culture had developed new seminal centres and flowered in that region. Results confirmed this view. After the Dominican Fathers of the French Biblical and Archaeological School at Jerusalem had sunk shafts in the Neirab Tell (1926-27) between Aleppo

33 - TELL ASMAR - STATUETTES FROM THE TEMPLE OF ABU

22

34 - MARI - EXCAVATIONS OF 1934-35. CLEARING OF THE PALACE (EARLY SECOND MILLENNIUM)

35 - DISCOVERY OF THE GODDESS OF THE 'FLOWING VASE'

36 - THE GODDESS AND MEMBERS OF THE EXPEDITION

and the Euphrates, a return was made towards the valley. The Thureau-Dangin expedition investigated Til Barsip (Tell Ahmar) on the bank of the river, from 1929 to 1931, after excavating in 1928 Arslan Tash (Hadatu).

From 1935 on, Mallowan explored the province of Khabur, making borings in several tells: Chagar Bazar, Germayir, Arbit and, above all, Brak (1937-39). In 1933 we made Tell Hariri, near Abu Kemal, our headquarters. In 1934 its identification with Mari, the dynastic capital,

37 - MARI - STATUETTES FROM THE TEMPLE OF ISHTAR (1934)

23

38 - MARI - CLEARING THE THRONE ROOM OF THE PALACE (1935)

was established, and we watched the great city emerging from the desert sands with its buildings (temples and palace), sculptures, wall paintings and archives (twenty-five thousand cuneiform tablets).

While work thus proceeded in the west, activity continued in the east. Susa was still being explored by R. de Mecquenem, but other Iranian sites were soon broached, notably Tepe Giyan near Nihavend (1931-32) and Sialk near Kashan (1933-37). Discoveries made by Contenau and Ghirshman threw light on the cultural exchanges between Iran and Mesopotamia, which, beginning in the very earliest period, never ceased throughout their history.

But once again a World War brought to an abrupt end a golden age of scientific research. Its after-effects, above all the drastic changes in the political structure of the Middle East, were particularly disastrous from the archaeological standpoint and the peace which followed did nothing to favour the return of expeditions. New states, now independent, wished to give priority to their own Services of Antiquities; as a preliminary to sanctioning new researches they began by revising the agreements made with foreign organizations, and the economic problems which all ex-belligerents had now to face, inevitably led to reductions in the grants allotted to post-war research. Several governments now ceased allowing expeditions to remove any of the objects discovered; all had to be delivered to local museums. For these reasons archaeological activity has fallen off, as compared with the period between the wars.

In Iraq, the Department of Antiquities, under Naji-al-Asil, has worked on several sites: Uqair (1940-42), Aqar Quf (Dur Kurigalzu, 1939-45), Tell Harmal

39 - EXCAVATIONS AT NIPPUR (1890)
THE SCRIBAL QUARTER

2

(1945-47), Eridu (1945-49) and Hassuna (1943-44). The most striking discovery was made at the last-named site, where the oldest proto-historic phase—anterior to Samarra and Halaf—was identified and positively dated. And the expedition sponsored by the Oriental Institute of Chicago and led by Braidwood had the luck to discover at Jarmo (1948) and Muallafat (1955) the earliest links with prehistory properly so called. Nothing is missing in the sequence of cultures from the early fifth millennium on, and we can now keep track of all its manifestations up to the fourth century B. C.

40 - NIMRUD - MALLOWAN'S EXCAVATIONS (1949)

Two other sites, which might have been thought to be abandoned for ever, came to life again: Nimrud (Kalakh), where from 1949 on Mallowan proved that the excavations of the last century had been far from exhausting the possibilities of sites of this size; and Nippur, where the joint (American) expedition of the Oriental Institute and the University Museum, after its return in 1949, had the same experience. Finally, at Warka (Uruk), German archaeologists have resumed the exploration cut short by the Second World War and are carrying on their researches with the scrupulous exactitude which characterized their pre-war work.

Still in the Mesopotamian plain, though in Syrian territory, the only excavation in the Euphrates valley that has been re-opened and relates to the period we are concerned with, is that at Mari, where digging recommenced in 1951. Mention must also be made of the Moortgat expedition to Fecherijeh, a site in the Upper Jezireh (1955). Mari, Nimrud, Nippur and Warka are the four Mesopotamian towns in course of being explored today and so large are they that many years will be needed before we can say that they have yielded all their secrets.

41 - WARKA - EXCAVATIONS OF 1930-32 :
INTERIOR OF THE 'WHITE TEMPLE'

42 - CHOGA ZAMBIL - THE ZIGGURAT (12TH CENTURY B.C.)

The same is true of Susa, scene of so many wonderful finds. This site is now being explored by Roman Ghirshman who has also started an excavation at Tepe Choga Zambil.

Now that we can view the Mesopotamian basin in its collective splendour, it is becoming clear that this flame which blazed up so suddenly in the Middle East and shed so wide a light, was kindled at several points, each with its own nuance and distinctive lustre. Susa, Lagash, Ur, Uruk, Ashnunnak, Assur, Nineveh, Mari—all alike were centres where civilization advanced from strength to strength, until at last, thanks to the genius of a few and the boldness of many, there was wrought forth, as in an alchemist's crucible, a prodigious, manysided art.

43 - CHOGA ZAMBIL - THE ZIGGURAT STAIRWAY (12TH CENTURY B.C.)

The tempo of the discoveries —sometimes rapid, not to say precipitate, sometimes slow, then accelerating—led specialists in the history and art of the Ancient Orient to periodical reappraisals of their stock of knowledge. This was only to be expected, and we find reflections of their changing viewpoints in their terminology.

Thus the monumental work (five large folio volumes) in which Botta published his discoveries at Khorsabad was named *Monument de Ninive*, and as a result there was much talk of 'Ninevitic art.' Then, when Sarzec uncovered vestiges of Lagash in the Telloh hill country, the Gudea statues were described as 'Chaldean' and this epithet was also applied to the buildings in the plain.

At the same time a heated controversy was raging between two schools of linguists, as to whether alongside Assyrian, a Semitic language, there existed another non-Semitic language, that of the 'Sumerians,' its presumed inventors, and whether they were not also creators of the earliest civilization brought to light in 'Chaldea.'

Thereafter experts were divided into two camps. Some held that Mesopotamia as a whole was the cradle of the Sumerian civilization. To others it seemed preferable—since it was impossible to deny the co-existence of ethnically different populations—to adopt a less exclusive attitude and, so as

44 - TELL HALAF - STATUE OF THE GODDESS WITH HANGING BRAIDS (10TH CENTURY B.C.)

to make allowance for both contributing elements (Sumerian and Semitic), to speak of an Akkadian-Sumerian civilization as regards the early periods and of an Assyro-Babylonian civilization as regards the later, when the Sumerians had disappeared from the scene.

But here too the terminology is misleading, since it overlooks the new discoveries which have greatly complicated the problem. For alongside the Sumerians and Semites a place must be allotted to a still older race, the Subarians, and a different, though later, factor cannot now be left out of account: the Hurrians. The peculiar sculptures that Oppenheim discovered in 1911 at Tell Halaf revealed a new world intermediate between Assyrians and Hittites, whose work was being unearthed (from 1906 on) on the Anatolian uplands.

Meanwhile new finds were constantly being made. In the period between the wars the Oriental Institute of Chicago, following clandestine excavators, discovered the art of the Diyala region, i.e. the central zone of the Mesopotamian plain. Unquestionably the culture to which this relates had a character peculiar to itself (though not homogeneous), and radically different from that of the Sumerians.

A similar problem arose when a whole world of statuettes emerged from the soil of Mari. The culture to which they belonged was modelled

on that of the southern Sumerian area, and objects found in Ur and Mari are to all intents and purposes interchangeable. But, strictly speaking, we cannot describe the art and civilization of Mari as Sumerian, since the habitat is specifically Semitic.

As a way out of these difficulties we propose to treat the civilization of 'the land between the rivers' not from the ethnical but from the geographical angle. The term 'Mesopotamian civilization,' and its corollary 'Mesopotamian art,' cover both a period of time—from the origins to Hellenism—and a specific area, from the Assyrian cliffs or the Khabur plain to the marshes near the Persian Gulf. But clearly this overall appellation must be defined from the outset in terms of the races and historical events on which modern research-work has thrown so much light and of which it can now provide a just view and an appropriate classification.

Thus all our data must be set out in strictly chronological order and appraised in terms of periods and places of origin. To leave these two factors out of account would be a methodological defect, and to treat them perfunctorily would lead to false conclusions. For it is quite impossible to come to a reliable decision about a work if we isolate it from its triple context and overlook what preceded it, the contemporary setting, and what came after.

49 - THE GUDEA ROOM AT THE LOUVRE - 1947 ARRANGEMENT

This principle is, moreover, illustrated by the museographical arrangement now in favour. Nowadays all objects are shown in their chronological order and in their geographical context. That total lack of discrimination which prevailed in all museums at the beginning of this century, when no qualms were felt about housing, for instance, in the same room, Sumerian Gudea statues, the Babylonian Code of Hammurabi, and Assyrian reliefs from Nineveh or Khorsabad, has happily become unthinkable.

Thus the visitor to the Louvre can now obtain a precise and, we believe, correct impression of each of the separate, successive forms of art discovered in the Ancient East. And as he walks from room to room, he will become acquainted with the chief phases of a long cultural evolution. Within a few minutes he is able to traverse several millennia; but whenever he wishes, he can linger or retrace his steps.

For an ancient object does not always convey its message at first sight. Patience is sometimes needed but, given patience, a proper understanding soon develops between it and the spectator. We quickly weary of a too frankly seductive work, and often form a more lasting attachment to one which is discreet enough to veil under a somewhat forbidding aspect the very real charm of an inner presence.

In the preceding pages we have given a perforce brief account of the explorations in Mesopotamia. The number of finds we owe to them is so great that only a fraction can be illustrated in the present work. The vastness of our documentation is due not only to organized excavations (those officially conducted by recognized authorities and erudite organizations) but also to the activities of the clandestine excavators, which were, needless to say, quite haphazard and governed solely by the desire to unearth as much as possible with the utmost speed. Most of the results of these explorations are now preserved in various museums but many are in private collections. There has been a tendency in certain circles to deprecate the removal of these objects to museums, especially objects discovered at the end of the last century or the beginning of the twentieth. We would do better, however, to be grateful for the protection museums afford, since during this period the preservation of ancient monuments was often, and indeed commonly, regarded as quite unimportant. At Khorsabad quantities of the reliefs were ground up in plaster kilns and, elsewhere, ornamented slabs were used as door-sills or for the lips of wells. The modern town of Hilleh is known to have been built with baked bricks taken from the monuments of Babylon and Borsippa. The 'Tower of Babel' was exploited like a quarry, since it contained a mass of ancient building material ready to hand and in good condition. Thus museums act as repositories, and it is thanks to them that so much has been salvaged.

That the ancient world now attracts so much attention is due not only to the field work of so many explorers but to the attempts at explanation made by profound and accurate thinkers who are also great savants. In reading the monumental studies of historians like Toynbee or Teilhard de Chardin (who unhappily did not live to bring his work to completion), we cannot fail to be struck by the points they have in common in their attitudes to history. And history necessarily comprises art, as well as life and civilization. One of the most spectacular achievements of twentieth-century science is its reconquest of Space and Time. This has constrained us to readjust our knowledge to its true scale, the scale the Psalmist had in mind when he wrote: 'A thousand years in Thy sight are but as yesterday when it is past.' A dazzling intuition, yet still inadequate. For, as Jacques Madaule has rightly remarked, 'the field of history, covering at most seven thousand years, is incredibly narrow when we compare it with the life span of the human race, which goes back at least five hundred thousand years, and, if Eddington is to be trusted, is due to last another two million years. If we assimilate the existence of mankind to the lifetime of a man, all that we call history represents barely a single day of it.'

50 - KHORSABAD - RELIEFS FROM THE PALACE OF SARGON OF ASSYRIA, DRAWN BY FLANDIN

Even if Toynbee is (as we think) wrong in his estimate of the number of 'societies' or civilizations (twenty-one according to him), and perhaps on other points, he is assuredly right in stressing the multiplicity as well as the contemporaneity of civilizations. Thus we are justified in comparing similar events which took place in very different epochs and environments: for when all is said and done, what can a mere seven thousand years signify as against several millions of years? Roger Caillois had this in mind when he observed that 'every civilization reveals itself as a fragment of a whole,' suggesting that 'there is a common destiny for all mankind.' This Teilhard de Chardin named 'the great spiral of life, rising irreversibly stage by stage, in compliance with the guiding line of its evolution. Susa, Memphis and Athens could pass away, but an ever better organized conception of the Universe was to be handed down, its splendours growing with the ages.' Thus we need to reconsider all three as a whole: History, Civilization, Art. There was a time when the question of choosing between Rome and the East gave rise to acrimonious controversies. How far away it seems! The alternative is no longer stated in such narrow terms; we are becoming more and more convinced that identical arts and techniques could prevail in different periods and regions without any borrowings or interaction. Let us take care that specialization, inevitable today, does not blind our eyes to the 'tremendous whole' in its two dimensions, Space and Time. When we bear in mind the fact that 'the youth of the "first men" had behind it many thousands of years,' we are somewhat less surprised by their manifold achievements, brought off almost spontaneously, it would seem, and in a spirit of play.

MAP OF THE
DISCOVERIES AND EXCAVATIONS

In Roman letters : ancient names of sites.
In *Italics :* modern names of sites.
Dates for each site indicate when excavations
began and when they came to an end. Excavations still in progress are indicated by a dash.
The country sponsoring the archaeological
expedition is indicated as follows :

Am. = United States - D. = Denmark
F. = France - G. = Germany
GB. = Great Britain - Ir. = Iraq - It. = Italy - J. = Japan.

CHRONOLOGY
OF THE EXCAVATIONS

1842 - Nineveh *(Kuyunjik)*	1929 - Til Barsip
1843 - Dur Sharrukin	*(Tell Ahmar)*
(Khorsabad)	1930 - *Tell Billa*
1845 - Kalakh *(Nimrud)*	Ashnunnak
1847 - Assur	*(Tell Asmar)*
(Qalaat Shergat)	*Khafaje*
1849 - Uruk *(Warka)*	1931 - *Tepe Giyan*
1851 - Larsa *(Senkereh)*	Shuruppak *(Fara)*
Susa	*Re-excavated*
1852 - Babylon	1933 - *Arpatchiya*
1854 - Ur *(Muqayyar)*	*Kakzu*
Eridu	Larsa *(Senkereh)*
(Abu 'Shahrein)	*Re-excavated*
1877 - Lagash *(Telloh)*	Mari *(Tell Hariri)*
1884 - Susa	1934 - *Ishchali*
Re-excavated	1935 - *Chagar Bazar*
1888 - Nippur	*Tell Agrab*
1897 - Susa	1936 - *Choga Zambil*
Re-excavated	1937 - *Tell Brak*
1899 - Babylon	*al 'Ubaid*
Re-excavated	*Re-excavated*
1902 - Shuruppak *(Fara)*	1940 - *Tell 'Uqair*
1903 - Adab *(Bismaya)*	*Fecherijeh*
Assur	1942 - Dur Kurigalzu
(Qalaat Shergat)	*(Aqar Quf)*
Re-excavated	1943 - *Tell Hassuna*
1911 - *Tell Halaf*	1945 - *Tell Harmal*
Samarra	1946 - Eridu
1912 - Kish *(al 'Oheimir)*	*(Abu Shahrein)*
Uruk *(Warka)*	*Re-excavated*
Re-excavated	1948 - *Jarmo*
1918 - Ur *(Muqayyar)*	Kalakh *(Nimrud)*
Re-excavated	*Re-excavated*
1919 - *al 'Ubaid*	Nippur
1923 - Kish *(al 'Oheimir)*	*Re-excavated*
Re-excavated	1951 - *Shanidar*
1925 - Nuzi *(Yorgan Tepe)*	1955 - *Muallafat*
Jemdet Nasr	*Fecherijeh*
1926 - Neirab	*Re-excavated*
1927 - *Tepe Gawra*	1956 - *Telul eth Thalathat*
1928 - Hadatu	1957 - *Shemshara*
(Arslan Tash)	1958 - *Shemshara*
Dur Sharrukin	*Re-excavated*
(Khorsabad)	
Re-excavated	

34

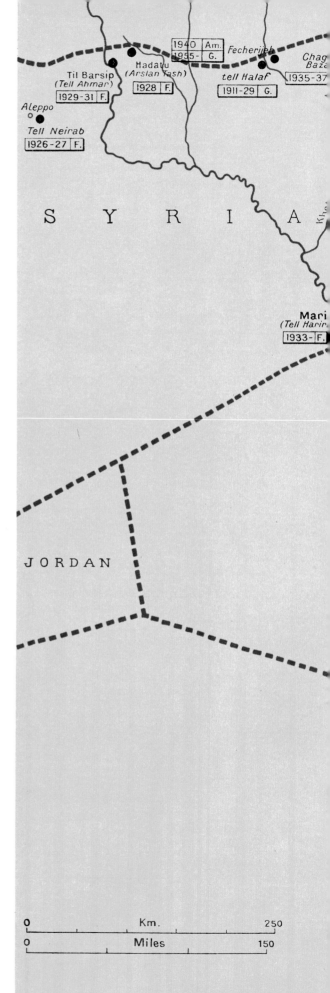

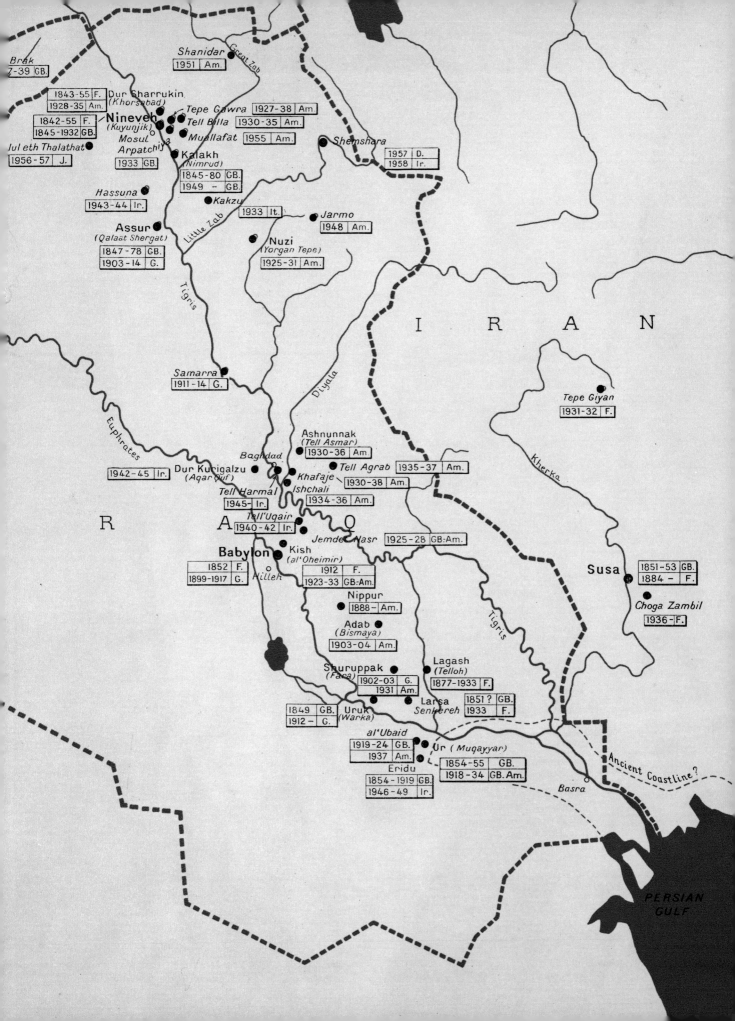

Brak
7-39 GB.

Shanidar
1951 | Am.

Great Zab

1843-55 | F. | Dur Sharrukin
1928-35 | Am. | (Khorsabad)

Tepe Gawra | 1927-38 | Am.

Tell Billa | 1930-35 | Am.

1842-55 | F. | Nineveh
1845-1932 GB. | (Kuyunjik)

Muallafat | 1955 | Am.

Mosul
Arpachiya

Jul eth Thalathat | Kalakh
1956-57 | J. | (Nimrud)

Shemshara

1957 | D.
1958 | Ir.

1933 GB.

1845-80 | GB.
1949 – | GB.

Hassuna
1943-44 | Ir.

Kakzu

1933 | It.

Jarmo
1948 | Am.

Assur
(Qalaat Shergat)

Nuzi
(Yorgan Tepe)

1847-78 | GB.
1903-14 | G.

1925-31 | Am.

I R A N

Tigris

Little Zab

Samarra
1911-14 | G.

Diyala

Tepe Giyan
1931-32 | F.

Ashnunnak
(Tell Asmar)
1930-36 | Am.

Euphrates

Baghdad

Kherka

1942-45 | Ir. | Dur Kurigalzu
(Aqar Quf)

Tell Agrab | 1935-37 | Am.

Khafaje
Ishchali

1930-38 | Am.

Tell Harmal
1945- | Ir.

1934-36 | Am.

R

Tell Uqair
1940-42 | Ir.

A

Jemdet Nasr | 1925-28 | GB:Am.

Q

Babylon

Kish
(al'Oheimir)

Susa

1851-53 | GB.
1884 – | F.

1852 | F.
1899-1917 | G.

Hilleh

1912 | F.
1923-33 | GB-Am.

Choga Zambil
1936- | F.

Nippur
1888 – | Am.

Adab
(Bismaya)
1903-04 | Am.

Tigris

Lagash
(Telloh)
1877-1933 | F.

Shuruppak
(Fara)
1902-03 | G.
1931 | Am.

Larsa | 1851 ? | GB.
Senkereh | 1933 | F.

1849 | GB. | Uruk
1912 – | G. | (Warka)

al'Ubaid
1919-24 | GB.
1937 | Am.

Ur (Muqayyar)

1854-55 | GB.
1918-34 | GB. Am.

Ancient Coastline ?

Eridu
1854-1919 GB.
1946-49 | Ir.

Basra

PERSIAN
GULF

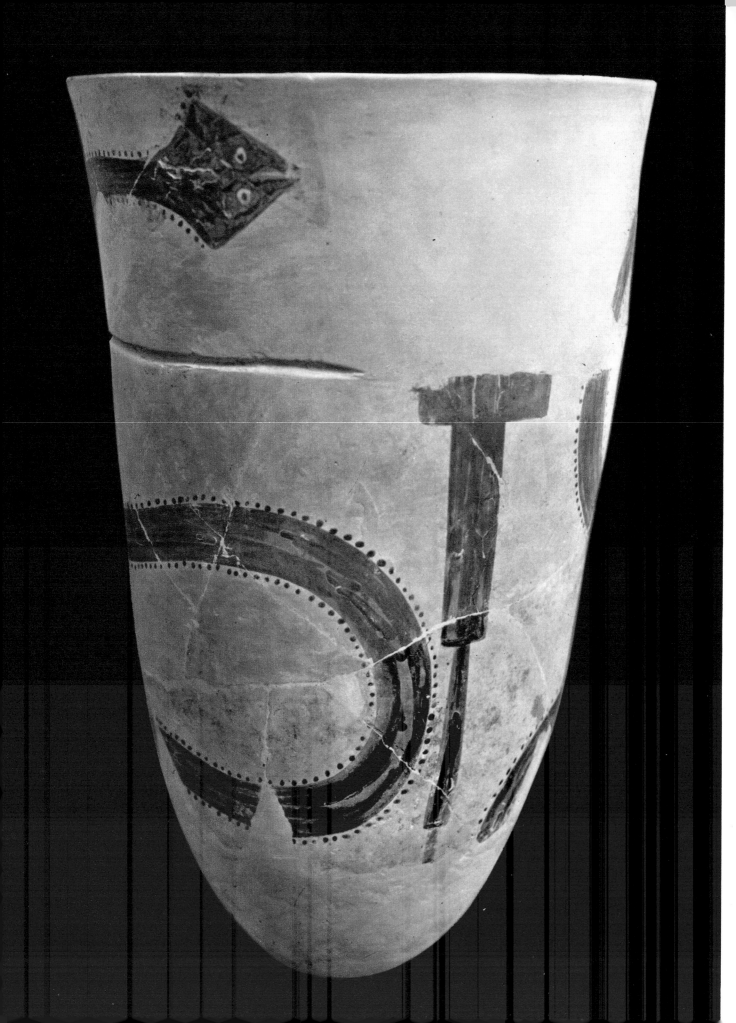

53 - IMPRESSION FROM THE SO-CALLED TEMPTATION SEAL (MID-THIRD MILLENNIUM). — BRITISH MUSEUM

II

THE 'GARDEN OF EDEN'
FROM THE ORIGINS TO HISTORICAL TIMES
(5000-2800 B.C.)

And the Lord God planted a garden eastward in Eden; and there he put the man whom he had formed. And out of the ground made the Lord God to grow every tree that is pleasant to the sight, and good for food... And a river went out of Eden to water the garden; and from thence it was parted, and became into four heads. The name of the first is Pison... And the name of the second river is Gihon... And the name of the third river is Hiddekel: that is it which goeth toward the east of Assyria. And the fourth river is Euphrates. (Genesis ii, 8-14.)

IN all Oriental literature there is, we believe, no passage that evokes so lucidly man's first awakening to his infinite possibilities of well-being in the highly favoured land of Mesopotamia. Biblical tradition saw it as a vast garden, an oasis of shade and coolness watered by four rivers, two of them the Tigris (Hiddekel) and the Euphrates. But though reminiscences of these four waterways lingered on for centuries, as we shall see, in the iconography of the region, there is little hope of ever finding a depiction of the First Man, the Woman and the Serpent beside the Forbidden Tree. The famous cylinder seal in the British Museum, which in the first flush of enthusiasm was promptly named 'the seal of the Temptation,' certainly does not relate to the scene in Genesis. Nevertheless it conveys well enough the atmosphere of the Biblical Paradise (Genesis, iii), since the elements of its design are a god, a tree, a woman and a serpent side by side.

52 - SUSA - VASE OF THE 'SUSA I' STYLE
(FOURTH MILLENNIUM). — LOUVRE

54 - MESOPOTAMIAN LANDSCAPE

The common modern view is that this is a mere coincidence, but what is important for our purpose is that this representation, from the third millennium B.C., is perfectly applicable to the Mesopotamian conception of the primaeval world, a world in which the first men forgathered with the gods under shade trees, sharing their happy lot with birds and animals, none of them unfriendly or alarming. This land so richly endowed by nature had had to be conquered before it could be planted, and we now know much about the early stages of its conquest.

Though etymologically Mesopotamia signifies 'the land between the rivers,' culturally, as we have already indicated, it covers a much wider area. It overlaps both sides of the two great waterways, especially to the south-east, where it encroaches deeply on present-day Iran. Thus it comprises a vast plain some six hundred miles in length, extending from the mountains of Armenia on the north to the Persian Gulf on the south, and ending, westwards, in the Syro-Arabian desert. To the east it is bounded by the Iranian highlands. The rich, exceptionally fertile alluvial soil enjoys an abundance of sunlight and water. So it need not surprise us that this ideal region of the world came to be occupied at a very early date, the northern part to begin with, then, as the marshlands gradually receded, progressively further south.

Two English geologists, G.M. Lees and N.R. Falcon, in 1952, put forward a revolutionary theory. Contradicting the usual opinion that in the earliest periods the head of the Persian Gulf began several hundred miles north of its present position, they maintained instead that it had varied relatively little in five thousand years. Their theory is a challenging one and will need to be carefully verified.

Yet there is always the possibility that some day traces of human habitation will be discovered to the south of Abu Shahrein (Eridu) and Tell el-Lahm, hitherto regarded as the most southerly inhabited sites.

This study need not take account of the first manifestations of human activity that have been found in present-day Iraq. The Shanidar grotto which supplies the earliest archaeological data (34,000 to 30,000 B.C.) belongs to prehistory and there is no question of speaking of civilization, still less of art, in its connection. So far, no wall engravings, no sculpture and no modelled objects have been reported that could be assigned to the Palaeolithic or the Neolithic period.

A line of demarcation must be drawn between the two phases of human evolution: the one in which man still lives in caves and *collects* his food, the other in which he *produces* it. At the latter stage he has moved out of natural shelters and set up house in the open. This is the beginning of the village, and Muallafat in the province of Erbil, in north-eastern Iraq, was identified by R.J. Braidwood in 1955 as the oldest village in Mesopotamia. In point of fact it is not in the plain but in a mountainous region, and if we refer to it, this is due to its priority; it is assigned to an earlier date than Jarmo, another inhabited site in open country. Jarmo was discovered in 1948 and Carbon 14 tests have shown its date to be around 5000 B.C. (4857 ± 320 years). Though using only stone implements, the men who lived there made clay figurines: among them animals, and what is evidently a prototype of the Mother Goddess invoked everywhere, and depicted under a variety of forms, by mankind in its infancy. Here we have what well may rank as the earliest manifestation of creative art. It is an art that draws its inspiration from religious faith. Art and religion went hand in hand from the start and continued to be indissolubly united throughout the long, eventful annals of Mesopotamia.

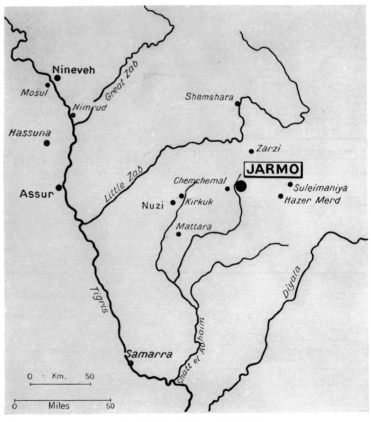

55 - NORTHERN MESOPOTAMIA - FROM THE 'ASSYRIAN TRIANGLE' TO THE DIYALA

Thus we can now determine with some precision the time and place of origin of Mesopotamian art. It is also possible to trace its initial phases, those belonging to what is now known as 'protohistory': a period which, beginning at the margin of prehistory, spans almost two thousand years. More and more, man made proof of his reasoning faculty and creative power. He domesticated many animals and mastered the soil, while developing and multiplying the amenities of life. After the village came the city; that is to say the individual, having acquired a social sense, saw that there was more to be gained than lost by living in close touch with a community. Needless to say, such changes had far-reaching effects on human behaviour, which was from now on to leave ever clearer traces of its manifestations.

Civilization had come into being and nothing could be more remarkable than the speed with which it gave rise to achievements that still compel our admiration. In some fields, notably that of art, works were produced, with natural ease, which we have merely reiterated, sometimes much less well, several millennia later. Only one thing was missing: a script, in other words a coherent, organized system of signs serving to stabilize language and, *a fortiori*, thought. Without writing there can, strictly speaking, be no history, since history comprises names of persons and places, and chronicles of facts and events. Writing did not begin in Mesopotamia until a little before 3000 B.C. Thus, for two thousand years, from the time of the settlements at Muallafat and Jarmo (late sixth—early fifth millennium) to the invention of writing (late fourth millennium), we can speak only of protohistory.

Documentation for this long period is extremely diversified and copious. When we add that practically none of it was available thirty years ago, the reader can gauge the rapid advance of knowledge in the field. Not only has archaeology retrieved from oblivion two thousand unchronicled years, but it has retrieved them in their

56 - SITES OF ANCIENT MESOPOTAMIA - FROM TELL HALAF TO ERIDU

57 - SENKEREH (LARSA) - THE SITE BEFORE EXCAVATION - THE ZIGGURAT MOUND (1933)

exact chronological order. This reconquest of the past is largely due to the new technique of excavation 'in depth.' Beginning at the surface, excavators dig down through successive strata until they come to virgin soil, that is to say the level where all trace of human activity ceases. Layer by layer, all is methodically cleared and scrutinized down to the very least detail before being shovelled away. Thus we retrace the course of history, travelling back through centuries, sometimes millennia, of past time.

Following the prehistorians, specialists adopted the practice of naming each successive phase after the site where its manifestations were discovered for the first time. Until the Second World War this nomenclature prevailed; thus we read of the *al 'Ubaid* Period (1919), the *Uruk* Period (1931) and the *Jemdet Nasr* Period (1926). Each of these sites is in the plain of Lower Mesopotamia. But two northern sites cannot be ignored, Samarra and Tell Halaf (both explored in 1911), where finds of an 'archaic' type were made, which owing to the imperfect state of knowledge before the First World War were not correctly dated. Only after the more recent exploration of Hassuna (1943-44) was it possible to determine the chronology of these strata and the successive stages in the progress of Mesopotamian civilization. At the same time, thanks mainly to the exploration of the Iranian area, at Tepe Giyan (1931-32) and at Sialk (1933-37), the remarkable material discovered at Susa (from 1897 onwards) could be 'placed' correctly and no longer isolated from the culture of Mesopotamia proper. Still more recent discoveries made at Eridu (1946-49) confirmed these findings, while enlarging the foundations of

41

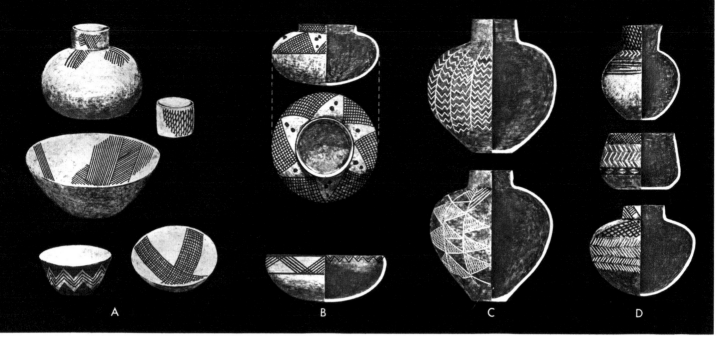

58 - HASSUNA POTTERY. — (A) PAINTED ARCHAIC. — (B) TYPICAL PAINTED. — (C) TYPICAL ENGRAVED. — (D) ENGRAVED AND PAINTED

the already existing knowledge of the subject. The objects revealed by these excavations show that, from the very start, even in his tools and household goods, Mesopotamian man often sought to create things of beauty, or at least things which he evidently regarded as beautiful.

In studying Mesopotamian art, however, we need to bear in mind two major difficulties that it had to contend with. Since there was no stone or mineral ore in the country, at any rate in the south, the inhabitants had to make do with earth and import their stone and minerals. The latter were therefore reserved for articles of prime necessity. The Sumerians never had an opportunity of carving in Paros marble or the pink granite of Aswan. As a rule they had to content themselves with basalt or a calcareous conglomerate. That they could cope so successfully, on occasion, with diorite, a particularly hard rock, demonstrates their amazing technical skill, especially when we allow for the tools they had to work with. These handicaps inevitably left their mark on Sumerian art which, generally speaking, is forceful rather than graceful. It has a rugged, sometimes ponderous power. Its charm is usually elusive, though here and there we find some lighter touches: liberties promptly repressed, however, but resumed, as we now know, whenever a majority of the population was Semitic and a freer, less stereotyped and rigid view of life prevailed. Figures became humanized, life was breathed into inert masses, yet none the less and to the very end the smile remained frozen on the lips. It was left to the Greeks and the cultures of the West to discover the lighter side of life.

If Muallafat and Jarmo were merely starting-points and their value is chiefly that of symbols, the tiny site of Hassuna is one where man speedily grew conscious of his powers. Cave-man and nomad here gave place to the man of settled life who, as cultivator and breeder of livestock, appears to have preferred a permanent abode, the house, to that moving home, the tent. Architecture came into being, and the 'functional' qualities of this new-found skill are truly remarkable: planning becomes harmonious and lay-outs ingenious. Everything has obviously been thought out beforehand.

Most striking of all is the fact that in the making of household ware utility was not the only aim; their makers sought to add a touch of fancy, of ornamentation, to articles intended for daily use. This ornamentation is in no way superfluous, for the images have potency and meaning, and something quite definite to say. From the start two techniques are employed: painting and engraving, used either separately or combined. To begin with, the themes are exclusively non-figurative; in some of the more complex compositions we even find total asymmetry, an absolute disdain of order and proportion, not due to inexpertness, but significant and purposive. Thus, and the point is worth stressing, we have here a beginning of what today is known as abstract art.

59 - (A) EXCAVATIONS OF THE HASSUNA TELL
(B) PLAN OF DWELLINGS (FIFTH MILLENNIUM)
(C) RECONSTRUCTION OF A HOUSE

If Hassuna is only a beginning, the art of Samarra marks an obvious advance, and there is a noteworthy improvement in technique and craftsmanship. Utility is increasingly allied with elegance. More attention is given to form, and clay pots are so richly decorated that they are by way of becoming *articles de luxe*. No sooner has the potter shaped his ware than it is handed over to the decorator. Once again, to start with, all is pure abstraction: combinations of horizontal, vertical or slanting lines, zigzags, herring-bone and simple Greek-key patterns and the like. Next come geometrical designs: squares, rectangles, lozenges. Finally we have elaborate combinations of primary elements and highly complex composition. Had the decorators kept to this repertory, they would probably not have gone beyond the stage of honest workmanship, that of the painstaking artisan who makes linear patterns and assembles them. But they did far better, since they turned to nature, to the animal and vegetable kingdoms, for inspiration.

Animals, particularly, are delineated with an amazing sureness and simplicity. Everything is rendered with a racy schematism expressing only the essentials: life and movement. Here, we see four deer-like creatures gyrating wildly round a tree whose branches point in opposite directions; there, four long-plumed water-birds, each gripping in its beak a fish which it has just pulled from a pond, one of a group that are scuttling away as fast as their fins can take them. On another cup four women, surrounded by a ring of scorpions, outline the four limbs of a cross, their long, loose hair streaming in the wind. For all its drastic simplifications, this style is eminently figurative, indeed naturalistic.

It is interesting to observe how easily transitions from the figurative to complete abstraction took place in the art of Samarra. A familiar example is that enigmatic symbol, the Maltese cross, which originally represented four he-goats running round a drinking-pool. By a process of intensive schematization the bodies have ended up by forming triangles and, with horns, tails and feet suppressed, what remain are the four structural elements of the cross. Here we have a reversion from figurative to frankly non-figurative art; but with the very important additional factor that this abstract style has a precise significance and conveys a specific message.

For implicit in these decorative patterns is a whole *Weltanschauung*. All these symbols are meaningful; they express the hopes and fears of a race, a race that has already developed a strong religious faith. The circling goats, the swastika formed by the four women's hair are clearly intended to suggest the life-force immanent in all created beings, propelling men and animals alike in never-ending cycles.

SAMARRA POTTERY (FIFTH MILLENNIUM) -
60 - FIGURATIVE, NATURALISTIC STYLE
61 - TRANSITION TO THE ABSTRACT

A

B

A

C

B

D

C

So, even in this early, so-called Samarra, period we have, it would seem, intimations of idealism, that is to say a spiritualization of reality. Religion has already moulded so effectively the human personality that art finds in religion its chief, almost its only source of inspiration. Henceforth we shall very rarely find in Mesopotamia a work of art that is not, more or less, a cultic object.

Another favourite theme is the garland so often found around the necks of vases. It consists of a frieze of circular or lozenge-shaped elements with fringe-like pendants hanging from it. Here again a purely abstract motif conceals another, clearly figurative: a line of human beings linking hands in a ritual dance. For there is no question that this represents a rite, its purpose being to call down rain. In a later era the priests of Baal did likewise on a famous Biblical occasion when, in the presence of Elijah, they 'leaped up and down,' at the altar set up on Mount Carmel (I Kings, xviii).

The human figures on some potsherds are also found on a vase from Hassuna whose neck is decorated with a boldly stylized face, almost certainly a god's. Just how 'primitive,' one wonders, were the artists who showed such scrupulous regularity and rigour in their designs? Notice the highly schematic rendering of the hair, the nose, the eyebrows and eyelashes on this vase.

62 - SAMARRA POTTERY - GARLAND AND DANCERS DESIGNS

63 - NECK OF A HASSUNA VASE WITH A HUMAN FACE (5TH MILLENNIUM)

64 - TELL HALAF - SEATED FIGURINE OF
MOTHER GODDESS (5TH-4TH MILL.)

65 - TELL BRAK - HEADLESS FIGURINE OF
MOTHER GODDESS (5TH-4TH MILL.)

In the course of his excavations at Samarra, Herzfeld found some objects executed in a different technique. They testified not to a break with the earlier art but to a continuation and extension of it. This new cultural development is named after Tell Halaf, the site on the Upper Khabur where it was first identified (in 1911), but we believe that it originated in the Upper Tigris region, north of Samarra; more precisely, at Arpatchiya, a few miles from Nineveh, a site which Mallowan explored in 1933.

This later phase is characterized, particularly, by the discovery of methods of working metal; copper tools come into general use, leading to drastic changes in technique and to ever bolder creations. But though stone, always in short supply, now is carved more frequently, clay remains the staple medium of this culture. We have already mentioned the modelled figurines found in the village of Jarmo. More and more such figures are produced and they have some peculiar characteristics. All are women, usually squatting, their bodies modelled in large masses with sagging breasts. The head is sketchily indicated, a mere bulb of clay. No one dares, it seems, to carry to the end these representations of the Mother Goddesses, whose bodies, patterned with transversal stripes, symbolize fertility, but which, being left incomplete, remain impersonal. The artist stops half way, as if he dares not make his gods in his own image.

66 - TELLOH - HEADLESS FEMALE FIGURINE - -
(AL 'UBAID STYLE, 4TH MILL.). — LOUVRE

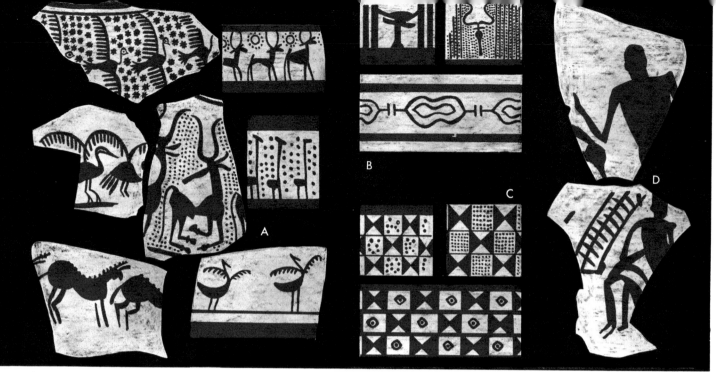

67 - TELL HALAF AND ARPATCHIYA - PAINTED POTTERY - (A) ANIMALS. — (B) BULL SKULLS. — (C) DOUBLE-HEADED AXE. — (D) FIGURE

Yet wherever the religious taboos do not operate, the artist gives proof of an observant eye and charming fantasy. The animal kingdom has no secrets for him, and his renderings of antelopes crouching on all fours and pricking up their ears, of startled birds observed at the moment they are preparing to take wing, of galloping animals, or of flying creatures with their wings outspread against a starry sky, are all recorded in a few telling lines, with the liveliness of snapshots. But even now schematism and stylization add a note of fantasy, and naturalism is by way of becoming decorative.

Thus gradually the figurative veers towards abstraction; a very wide range of geometric forms is brought into play, accompanied by a freedom unknown in the previous phase, though these compositions have invariably an underlying significance.

We have already noted that the Maltese cross, with its four triangles pointing inwards, corresponds to a pattern of four goats running round a pool in their attempt to escape the hunter's net. A dish from Arpatchiya, adorned with rosettes and crosses, evokes the sky, both with the sun of daytime and the stars spangling it on cloudless nights.

On other vessels, two motifs persistently recur: the double-headed axe and the bull's skull (more or less distorted). They are religious symbols associated with the ideas of fecundity and fertility. The bull is, *par excellence*, the animal that propagates the species, while the axe is plied by the god to cleave the clouds and release the rain storms so needful for the crops and pastures of an arid land.

While the art of Tell Halaf evidences a keen interest in, and feeling for, plants and animals, human figures are rarer. We have already mentioned the qualms these artists felt about modelling the human form. On the few vases which have painted figures on them, these figures are never particularized; the head, like the body, is only a dark patch, nor are any attributes delineated. Thus the figures cannot be identified; there is no knowing whether they are gods or ordinary mortals.

On the fringes of Mesopotamia and on Iranian soil we find an art so closely akin to this that some of its decorative or symbolic motifs are line for line identical with, and indistinguishable from, those discovered on the banks of the Tigris and the Khabur. The design of a handsome vase from Sialk displays an harmonious combination of geometric, vegetable and animal motifs. The graceful convolutions of the plants and, more eloquently still, the lithe ferocity of the circling panthers tell us of a great art which, long before Seurat, uses a pointillist technique. And on the potsherd from Ray we see dancing girls about to fling themselves into the mazy circle of the dance. Their nakedness has not the least immodesty; their attitudes are ritual, instinct with the spirit of religion. For, in its origin, the dance was a sacred rite and the dancers formed part of the temple staff.

68 - IRANIAN ART - SIALK - PAINTED VASE -
PANTHERS IN A WOODLAND SETTING
69 - RAY - PAINTED FRAGMENT - DANCERS

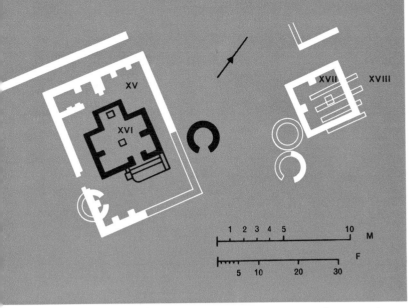

70 - ERIDU - PLAN OF TEMPLES - LEVELS XV TO XVIII (5TH MILL.)

Thus far, all the data cited with regard to the earliest manifestations of Mesopotamian art have related to the northern area. This does not mean that civilization had not developed in the south. Mention has been made of recent theories as to the original location of the shores of the Persian Gulf, but they cannot be accepted without careful investigation. So far nothing has been discovered in the far south (that is to say south of Eridu or Tell el-Lahm), corresponding to the earliest village culture named after Hassuna. On the other hand, recent excavations at Eridu (1946-49), the town of Enki (Sumerian god of the waters), have brought to light the remarkable fact—probably unique in the annals of archaeology—that no less than eighteen temples were built here one above the other on a single site.

At Level Sixteen a temple was found whose lay-out, if extremely simple, is impressive. It is the oldest built temple ever to be discovered and contains elements which have persisted up to our time, through many millennia and cultures. It consists of a rectangular shrine which seems to have been divided in two zones by partition walls. At one end is a niche, made to contain a mud-brick pedestal. Here we have, as it were, the lay-out of the typical Christian church: narthex, nave, and chancel containing an altar. The temple of Solomon had exactly the same tripartite arrangement: portico, Holy Place, and Holy of Holies. Thus two of the world's great monotheistic religions reproduced the structure of the Mesopotamian temple.

The 'furnishing' of the temple, too, has its significance. Men felt that, when the god deigned to dwell on earth, they should not appear before him empty-handed; offerings were indispensable. Two structures in baked brick were set up inside the sanctuary. One of these, in the apse, served as the pedestal for the god; the other, in the antecella, as the offering table. In the Christian sanctuary, however, the offering table was eliminated and the god's pedestal became the altar, at once place of sacrifice and habitation of the divine. That such a lay-out was employed at Eridu suggests that, even at this early stage, primitive superstitions had given place to an organized religion whose canons were universally accepted.

There is no knowing what divinity was worshipped in this age-old temple. If Enki was later the chief god at Eridu, he was not the only one. This well-established early cult, however, can hardly be accounted for except with reference to the local patron god. True, we know Enki's iconography from the third millennium on, when he was shown as a man with waves flowing from his shoulders; but nothing is known of the way he was originally represented—assuming that he was represented at all in this early phase.

The men of Eridu had given a lead; those of al 'Ubaid were now to follow it up and impose their religious tenets and hegemony throughout the whole of Mesopotamia. This is evidenced by the fact that the evolution of the north, at the very time of the full flowering of the Halaf culture, was suddenly cut short and the whole region forced to comply with the austerity of which Eridu had set the example. On this subject, too, the ceramics have much to tell us. For we find that now the naturalism hitherto so much in favour in the Upper Tigris area was almost entirely abandoned. Artists had to make shift with a non-figurative geometric repertory of lozenges, triangles, ladders and chevrons: in other words straight lines arranged in various ways. There were some rare exceptions to this embargo; thus timid attempts at figuration have been discovered at Gawra, in the suburbs of Nineveh, and at 'Uqair and Telloh we find goats and birds which seem strangely out of place in decorations otherwise of the most strictly abstract order.

How is this obvious regression to be accounted for? Certainly the culture of the time is far from giving an impression of losing any of the ground it had gained so triumphantly. And—a sure proof of cultural progress—never before had architecture made such rapid strides. In this respect, particularly, the excavations of the last twenty years have been rewarding. Hitherto it had been thought that, for the most part, the inhabitants of al 'Ubaid, presumed in 1919 to have been the earliest dwellers in Mesopotamia, had lived in huts of mud and woven reeds; now, however, it is clear that they were indefatigable builders.

71 - TELLOH - PAINTED FRAGMENTS ('UBAID PERIOD, 4TH MILL.). — LOUVRE

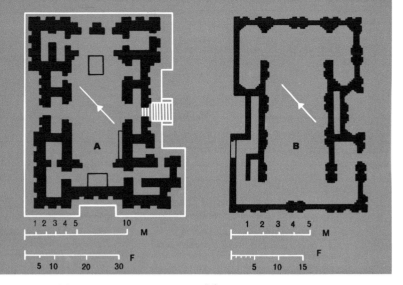

72 - (A) ERIDU - TEMPLE VII. — (B) GAWRA - TEMPLE - LEVEL XIII

In that town so rich in revelations, Eridu, three new temples (VI to VIII) were discovered, built one above the other, and they testify to a sense of composition based on symmetry and orderly arrangement. The sanctuary of the god, no longer a room of the simplest shape, is now a complex structure whose central cella, containing an altar pedestal and an offering table, is flanked by small rooms, while numerous doorways provide for the comings and goings of the worshippers. The god and his retinue are not only welcomed with all the reverence due to them, but have more space at their disposal. However, the zone reserved for worship retains its original lay-out in three parts. Undoubtedly, from now on, a trained personnel was needed to celebrate the rites, which had become too esoteric and intricate to be performed by any but adepts of the cult. Not that the public were excluded; the number of doorways in the shrine proves the contrary.

We get the same impression, even more strongly, from the ground-plan of one of the Gawra temples, that known as the North Temple. (In the absence of inscriptions or written records, its attribution is still uncertain.) This is of a novel type and no other temple seems ever to have been built on these lines. There is a central nave abutting at each end on a short transept. The lay-out is skilfully disposed so as to provide an easy division of the central space between two occupants, in other words to accommodate two deities without giving umbrage to either. Clusters of pilasters, supporting the interior and exterior walls, comprise the architectural ornamentation. How can we fail to be reminded of cathedrals, with flying buttresses outside and engaged pillars within, while the pilasters mark off recesses which might on occasion serve as chapels?

The intense religious feeling of an age which gave so much care to its sanctuaries in unquestionable. Does its figurative art in any way define, or illustrate, this preoccupation with the numinous?

Though stone carving had not yet come into existence, much can be learnt from the clay figurines in the round. The male figures are a curious assortment, and so too are the 'female,' very different from the earlier Great Mother types. Slim, always standing, sometimes holding a child, sometimes with their hands resting on their hips, these naked 'women,' whose bodies are picked out with touches of paint or inlaid with tiny pellets of clay on the shoulders, have heads no longer amorphous but given a snake-like aspect and crowned with wigs in bitumen. The purport of the hybrid snake-woman is still a mystery. Since the snake had always been associated with fertility, this conformation might seem easily accounted for. However, recent excavations at Eridu have brought to light a figurine of the same type: this time a man's—which further complicates the problem. Gods, demons, beneficent or malefic beings? It is hard to reach a conclusion. These weird figures, embodying man's superstitious fears, seem to illustrate a phase of culture which, after banning figures from vase decorations, sanctions them modelled and in the round, but with the important reservation that what is represented must not belong to the visible, tangible world. Yet, though these awe-inspiring beings were imaginary, imperceptible to the senses, they were none the less regarded as 'real,' and we can be sure that their existence was vouched for by the religious beliefs of the age. Here, once again, while the existence of these daemonic powers was taken for granted, qualms were felt about giving them a purely human appearance; specific differences were called for, indicating their supramundane attributes and functions.

73 - UR - HEADLESS FIGURINE - WOMAN WITH A CHILD (AL 'UBAID PERIOD, 4TH MILL.). — BRITISH MUSEUM

77 - UR • WOMAN HOLDING A CHILD (AL 'UBAID PERIOD, 4TH MILL.) — BAGHDAD, MUSEUM

9

78 - SUSA - GOBLETS - SUSA I STYLE (4TH MILL.). — LOUVRE

Austerity may have been the rule in southern Mesopotamia but this was not the case in the outlying areas. On the south-eastern border and in the Susa plain, there flourished an art that was nothing if not colourful. Iran, as already noted, was not satisfied with unadorned objects, and had enriched its wares with painted decorations. At the height of the al 'Ubaid period Susa had become the Sèvres of antiquity. The Louvre possesses magnificent collections which prove that no similar industry in the Ancient East could vie with the pottery of Susa.

Large goblets, cups and bowls were the prototypal forms. Working in carefully refined clay coated with a greenish yellow slip, the decorator could give free rein to his inspiration, and sometimes he expressed it with an ease and elegance that bear the stamp of genius. Not that all the works in question have this high quality. Some were made by expert craftsmen who merely copied their masters' creations, while others must be written off as failures.

The general effect of the best works is one of effortlessness, as though these handsome objects were produced instinctively, without taking thought. Actually, however, preparatory designs and calculations were certainly needed to assemble such well-balanced compositions, often very far from simple. True, it was relatively easy to score the bellies of certain drinking-vessels with a double, broken line, to adorn the angles with lozenges or hatchings, and to cast some palmettes on the field. But the artist's task was much less easy when it was a

60

matter of covering the entire object and when he desired to avoid the effect of over-all monotony that repetitions of the same motif would produce. On one of the big goblets in the Louvre the leading theme is boldly stated in its exact centre, where a stylized goat figures within a trapezoidal cage of thick, straight lines. Its horns, preternaturally elongated and swung back in a sweeping curve, enclose a circle filled out with cross-hatchings and a row of chevrons. Above it is a narrow strip of running gazelle-hounds, flattened out so as to fit the narrow space. The top of the goblet is decorated with a frieze made of the necks of a row of birds, craning their beaks towards the lip of the vessel, as though trying to drink from it.

Typical of Susian decoration and its twofold motivation, this work is at once figurative and abstract. Its naturalism is often greatly schematized. Here, for example, although the hunting dogs are relatively lifelike, the goat is rendered with an eye to decorative effect, and the birds with their fantastically elongated necks are barely recognizable. In other drinking-vessels there is still more difficulty in identifying certain semi-abstract details; thus in one case some authorities see storks arising from a nest where others see arrows in a quiver. The same uncertainty prevails in the case of the so-called 'bird-comb' motif, which may equally well be a

79 - SUSA - GOBLET - SUSA I STYLE (4TH MILL.). — LOUVRE

stylized rendering of two black goats with shaggy pelts, standing side by side. They have come to drink at one of the irrigation canals known as *seguia* in the East, which on this bowl are represented as flowing into a central reservoir.

Despite the vast number of works turned out, human beings very seldom figure on pottery of the Susa school, and the rare instances of their appearance are, therefore, of particular interest. On one of these bowls we see a tall, wisplike man standing between two objects which look like lances ; on another, an archer with a plumed headdress. In neither is there anything giving a clear idea of the man's face. We are reminded of figures in a shadow-theatre, mere silhouettes profiled on a light-hued ground.

It would certainly be a mistake to see in these *de luxe* objects no more than household utensils of a somewhat superior quality. (The large goblets have been found in Susa only, and they may have served as models, setting a standard for the mass-production of such articles.) For we cannot doubt that their designs had a symbolic meaning—as is proved by the frequent use of swastikas, Greek and Maltese crosses. They relate probably to a solar cult and to notions of fertility, since all ancient religions were obsessed with such themes.

80 - BOWLS - SUSA I STYLE
(4TH MILL.). — LOUVRE

We have been dealing with the al 'Ubaid period, which must have begun in the early fourth millennium and whose subsequent developments can be traced through several centuries. Discoveries at several sites have proved that it lasted longer than used to be thought. At Eridu we have discovered three temples, one above the other, and six levels of human habitation; and at 'Uqair, seven levels all belonging to this same period. Civilization progressed slowly in these early phases, but they were decisive. However, one thing, the most essential, was still to come: writing had not yet been invented. Was it that the al 'Ubaid peoples lacked time to make this invention, or were they incapable of making it? There is no knowing. Rather it seems that they were fated to be overrun and submerged by invaders whose native energy, allied with high intellectual powers, was now to inaugurate throughout the land an age of rapid progress. Mesopotamian culture, like a rocket, was to soar suddenly aloft and very soon to shoot forth in brilliant flowers of fire.

* *

The great epoch which now began and lasted till the coming of the first dynasties used to be named after the two sites which had first revealed its existence. It was divided into two phases: the earlier Uruk period and the later Jemdet Nasr period. Only the first of these two towns merited this distinction, since it was a royal city and is referred to in the Book of Genesis under the name of Erech. (It is also known as Warka.) The second has kept its Arab name, since its identification with Kidnum has not been confirmed. In any case, even if it was never more than a large village, it was one which won considerable renown in 1926 owing to the discovery on the site of pottery of a new type, associated with tablets bearing inscriptions and pointing to a cultural phase of which there had hitherto been no inkling.

Present-day specialists prefer to study these two periods as a whole, since it is extremely hard to draw a clear demarcating line between them. We shall follow their example, instead of embarking on interminable, and largely unprofitable, discussions of conflicting theories. For a whole new world of culture now emerged. No province of art was unaffected by the ferment of ideas due to the coming of a race which, after conquering the country, promptly set to building up a new civilization on wider, stronger foundations. These newcomers, the Sumerians, brought with them a culture far in advance of that of the original inhabitants. Not that the earlier achievements were valueless; to write them off as such would be to do them gross injustice. If the Sumerians so quickly scaled the heights this was because they

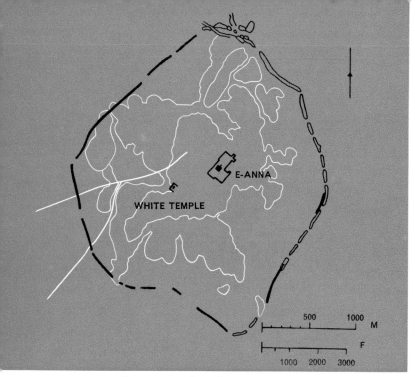

81 - WARKA (URUK) - PLAN OF THE SITE

profited by the discoveries and inventions of their predecessors, the progressive achievements of several millennia.

Whence did these people come? What was their racial background? It is not easy to give a positive answer, and specialists have not yet reached agreement on the subject. This much can certainly be said: that the Sumerians were not Semites; that their language is unlike any other known language; and that their country of origin lay somewhere beyond, perhaps very far beyond, the Caspian. Also that their coming brought a drastic and decisive change and left its imprint on all Mesopotamian civilization.

The first indication of a change of government is the abrupt disappearance of painted ceramics in all southern Mesopotamia. Anton Moortgat, the eminent orientalist, has spoken of the 'laicization' of the household ware, until now our chief source of information. Evidently its decorations were regarded as subversive by the new rulers of the land, who, not content with imposing their laws and customs, sought to impose their religion also. Yet, while in this respect the al 'Ubaid pottery with its severely geometric patterns and infrequent animal motifs should have seemed innocent enough, that of Susa was clearly much more imaginative and suggestive. It, too, now was doomed to be replaced by an industry whose productions seem all the more commonplace, coming as they do after those we have described above. Yet, fairly soon after this imperious call to order, we find a return to the old style. Ornamentation is resumed, but shorn of its previous brilliancy. Indeed the falling-off can be seen at a glance. Artists, now discountenanced, make way for artisans.

To say this may seem to suggest a general decline of civilization, but, on the contrary, the genius of these grave, realist-minded Sumerians may be measured from the fact that architecture now advanced from strength to strength, while sculpture, hitherto non-existent, not only made a start but gave rise to a series of masterpieces. Above all, writing was at long last invented.

64

82 - WARKA (URUK) - THE ZIGGURAT AND E-ANNA SECTOR

Several towns have yielded a quantity of valuable finds, but none has the renown and prosperity of Uruk, home of the hero Gilgamesh, within whose legendary walls the largest complex of sacred architecture so far discovered has been brought to light. Stratigraphical research has uncovered no less than eighteen successive levels, and these for the protohistorical period alone. Naturally the edifices are to be dated and appraised in terms of these levels. Truly coherent and imposing architecture does not make its appearance until we come to Level Five, where limestone blocks, and this in a stoneless country, were employed for its foundations. Several temples are grouped in a part of the city which is described in later inscriptions as E-Anna (House of Anu). Here Innin, the goddess of fertility and fecundity, was worshipped and doubtless also, Dumuzi, the god adored in all parts of the East under various names (e.g. Tammuz, Adonis). In this land where the fierce heat of summer parches vegetation and brings cultivation to a standstill, the return of a kindlier season was associated with gods who died and came back to life with reassuring regularity. Nowhere else had a pair of gods like these been so indispensable, each seconding and complementing the functions of the other, the first doomed to inutility unless the second lent his aid.

65

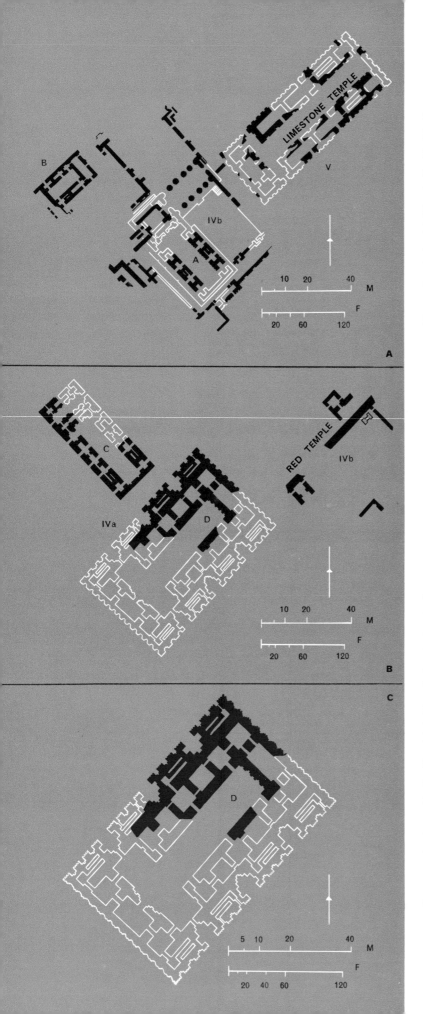

No dwelling could be too vast, too sumptuous for housing these beneficent powers. If, as regards their temples, the Sumerians did no more than take over the creations of their predecessors, they gave them a spaciousness and majesty that were wholly new. Architects of genius made plans that skilled workers carried into effect with unremitting care. Since, in the absence of written records, the attributions of these temples cannot be determined with certainty, they have kept the names their discoverers gave them in the first instance: the Limestone Temple, the Red Temple, etc., or their designation by letters, A, B, C, D. Temple D, the fourth, is by far the largest : 262 by 98 feet (outside measurements). The central nave, 203 by 37 feet (much bigger than the temple of Level Thirteen at Gawra, 40 by 28 feet), could contain a very large congregation. Prayers were made to one or more divinities placed at the far end of the edifice, where we have what is either a central chapel flanked by two sacristies or three adjoining chapels housing a trinity of gods. The striking thing is that the ground-plan, as at Eridu, anticipates, three millennia in advance, the lay-out of the Early Christian sanctuary: narthex, nave, transept and a central apse flanked by two rooms, a diaconicon and a prothesis. Moreover the outside walls were not left bare, but adorned with semi-engaged columns and

83 - URUK (SECOND HALF OF 4TH MILL.)
(A, B) TEMPLES AT LEVELS V, IV B AND IV A
(C) DETAIL PLAN OF TEMPLE D

niches. The only material available for architecture being grey mud-brick, the builders made breaks in the monotonous expanse of wall which, creating effects of light and shade and a play of contrasts, embellished the otherwise unattractive exterior. Often, too, they covered the outer sheath of mud (indispensable as weather-proofing) with whitewash, frequently renewed, thus giving a dazzling brilliance to the edifice. Sometimes, too, not content with this, they added 'cone mosaics,'

84 - URUK - (A) CONE MOSAICS. — (B) MOSAIC PANELS IN AN ARCHAIC TEMPLE

beyond all doubt a specifically Sumerian invention. To diversify interior walls and ponderous columns, they drove into the mud plaster thousands of small pointed cones, black, red and white, in such a way that only their heads were visible and formed zigzags, diagonals, chevrons, lozenges and triangles patterning the surface with a variety of colours. The general effect resembled a tapestry that, instead of being woven with coloured wools, was composed of innumerable tiny pellets of earth.

So yet again the soil of Mesopotamia supplied all that was required by her architects and craftsmen.

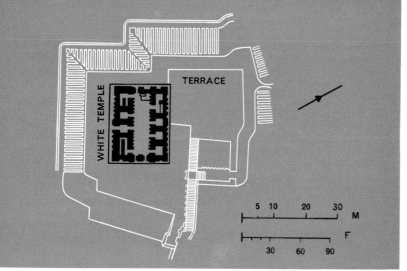

85 - URUK - PLAN OF THE WHITE TEMPLE OF THE ANU ZIGGURAT

The temples grouped in the E-Anna sector were not the only ones at Uruk. The town could boast of another sacred edifice, of a very different type and inaugurating a long architectural tradition: that of the staged towers, named ziggurats, prototypes of the Tower of Babel described in the Book of Genesis.

In a part of the town consecrated to Anu, god of the sky, a small edifice, known to archaeologists as the White Temple, had been built on an artificial mountain, irregular in shape and some forty feet high. It took its name from the large whitewashed inner shrine (61 by 16 feet). Here the Sumerians obviously followed the precedent set by Eridu, and the lay-out is remarkably similar: a large hall, a series of small rooms, with the same ritual accessories (offering table, altar) and several entrances for the convenience of the public. But here we find a marked contrast with Temple D, briefly described above. For one thing, the reduced scale indicates that the builders were already catering for the god himself rather than for a large concourse of worshippers. And, for another, this temple, mounted on a gigantic platform, answers doubtless to an essentially theological preconception. We have attempted to describe this elsewhere, on the strength not only of observations made at Uruk but also of similar edifices of the same period discovered at other sites: at Eridu, at 'Uqair in northern Sumer and also, most surprisingly, at Tell Brak in the far north, between the Euphrates and the Tigris. This heaven-aspiring architecture testifies to an ardent religious faith, as do, still more evidently, the later ziggurats of five and seven stages. From the end of the fourth millennium on, men constantly desired to build a ladder between earth and heaven so as to facilitate the descent of their gods, no matter what the cost. Hence these artificial, ever higher 'mountains.' At the summit a special type of sanctuary was made ready for visitations of the god. A large one was not needed, as the populace was not invited; only the priests awaited the celestial visitant who, after sailing through the empyrean, made his landfall here. Offerings were provided, and, after this homage of the faithful to their overlord, the god came down from the heights to the residence prepared for him long in advance in the town below. Henceforth he would dwell among men and make his presence known and welcome by ensuring them the staples of

86 - URUK - THE WHITE TEMPLE (SECOND HALF OF 4TH MILL.) →

existence. Indeed all Sumerian ritual centred on this give-and-take between earth and heaven.

For a long time next to nothing was known of Mesopotamian religion; the message of the ground-plans had still to be deciphered and elucidated. Then, quite suddenly, thanks to certain figural representations, their significance was understood; everything fell into place. For in several stone carvings we see religious rites in process of being solemnized.

The finest example is the great alabaster vase found at Uruk ornamented with reliefs in several registers, typically Sumerian in their clarity and precision. The reliefs can be read from top to bottom or vice versa, without in any way affecting their general significance. (It is known invariably as the Warka vase.) The theme is the cult of the goddess Innin, here represented by her emblems: two bundles of reeds, which, placed side by side, symbolize no doubt the entrance of a temple. A long line of offering-bearers is approaching it: naked men carrying baskets of fruit and vegetables, and vases. One of them leads the way and immediately behind him is a dignitary whose face has unfortunately been broken off. Presumably he was the king of the city or its high priest. His long-tasselled belt is held up like a train by an attendant, and he is greeted by a woman just come out of the temple, perhaps the goddess herself, but

87 - URUK - VASE WITH RELIGIOUS SCENES (4TH-3RD MILL.) — BAGHDAD MUSEUM

more probably, in our opinion, the High Priestess. Behind her, within the sacred precinct, is a great pile of offerings: baskets and dishes of fruit, animal-shaped vases and other objects. More problematical are the two rams bearing small figures. Finally, in the lowest band, we see a procession of animals moving along a strip of fertile land which, given the luxuriance of the barley and other vegetation, is evidently on the riverside.

This, the oldest ritual vase in carved stone that has so far been discovered in Mesopotamia, can be dated to round about 3000 B.C. It initiates us into the atmosphere of the age and with it we get for the first time a notion of the way in which man entered the presence of his gods. Never would he have dared to come empty-handed, and the huge mass of offerings witnesses to his gratitude towards one of the supreme goddesses of the city. Field produce and the pick of the herd enter into the composition of the sacrifice. Thus in Genesis (iv, 3, 4) we read that Cain and Abel offered to Jehovah 'the fruit of the ground' and 'the firstlings of the flock.'

This, the simplest interpretation of the scenes depicted on the vase, is carried a stage further by some specialists who see in them a celebration of the rites of hierogamy, the 'mystic marriage' in which two human beings played the leading roles, the high priestess impersonat-

88 - DETAIL OF THE WARKA VASE

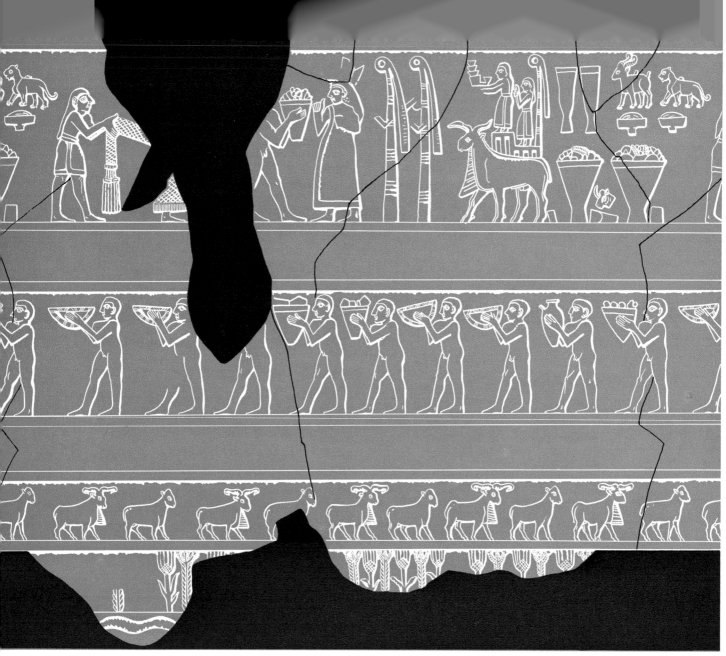

89 - URUK - THE THREE REGISTERS OF THE WARKA VASE (4TH-3RD MILL.). — BAGHDAD MUSEUM

ing Innin and the high priest (or king) acting as the god's representative. During the season of sterility, when the Mesopotamien soil was parched and the crops were languishing, the god who personified the generative forces of nature was thought to have left the land, and the goddess, his consort, to have suffered a bereavement. Only the god's return and reunion with his spouse could remedy the situation. Thus regular solemnization of this auspicious reunion, in which Innin wedded Dumuzi, was indispensable, and most particularly at that critical moment, the turn of the year. Reliefs in stone were later to record these New Year celebrations, which also included a ceremonial banquet.

90 - DETAIL OF THE TOP REGISTER

91 - SEALS - (A) URUK - SACRED BOAT. — BERLIN MUSEUM. — (B) TELL BILLA - RITUAL SCENE. — BAGHDAD MUSEUM

This alabaster vase is not the only illustration of a Sumerian religious rite. The engravings on the small objects known as cylinder seals represent scenes that are highly interesting on several counts. While some of them reproduce, in part, the design of the Warka vase, others show different rites and also have much to tell us about the daily life of the dwellers in this vast plain criss-crossed with canals. Eridu had already supplied us with the model of a boat in terracotta; others were found at Uruk and Tell Billa, but carved in stone. Above, we have a skiff, manned by two sailors, on which is a bull carrying on its back a staged altar with two tightly bound sheaves rising from it. Below, we have a scene of worshippers going to a temple which, being shown in vertical projection, gives much valuable information, since none of the tops of buildings have survived. Someone is coming by water and, being unable to find room for him in the boat, the engraver has placed him above it, hung in air. Three other men are going on foot to the temple, two of them holding a garland and a belt, doubtless intended to deck the cult image. It is impossible to say what deity this represented. Once again we have only symbols to go on.

74

Thus on each side of the temple is a pole composed of various elements and topped by six projecting loops. Doubtless initiates could read these symbols at a glance.

Here we have an art at once accomplished, descriptive and evocative; there is nothing tentative about it. Seemingly these artists knew nothing whatsoever of perspective, nor is there any regard for proportions. In the Tell Billa cylinder the worshippers bringing the collar and belt are given the same height as the dwelling of their god. In the Uruk cylinder, the poop and prow of the boat conveying the bull to the altar are so unnaturally high that a line drawn between their tips would pass over the head of the central passenger. He is accompanied by the bull and a rectangular panel whose purport remains a mystery. If it represents a much simplified fragment of a building, perhaps the façade of a temple, the man beside it, the leading figure in the little scene, could enter the temple only by crawling into it on all fours.

92 - URUK - THE LION-HUNT STELE (EARLY 3RD MILL.). — BAGHDAD MUSEUM

But it would be a mistake to assume that this art is still in its infancy, as the Lion-Hunt Stele, also from Uruk, might, for similar reasons, lead us to believe. This stele consists of a rough-hewn block of basalt smoothed on one side to take the figures. Here there are no registers, only two superimposed scenes. In the upper one we see a bearded man thrusting a spear into a lion's throat; below, he is shooting arrows at two lions, wounded but still dangerous. Originally there was yet another lion behind him. Frankfort believes that 'with this monument the commemorative stele makes its first appearance in the history of art.' This may be so and once we expressed the same view. It is certainly the first of that great series of combats with wild beasts which Assurbanipal was later to commemorate to such spectacular effect. Assurbanipal however hunted on horseback, whereas his predecessor at Uruk is depicted on foot.

75

In both periods, the hunting of wild beasts was as much a defensive measure as a royal sport; the cattle needed constant protection. The theme is illustrated on several vessels adorned with animal figures in high relief. They are rendered with power and monumentality, on a more or less hard ground of white sandstone or greenish blue steatite.

A vase from Uruk shows lions attacking bulls. On a bowl from Ur we see a row of bulls advancing with ponderous tread, and in the field behind each animal, is represented an enormous ear of wheat. The part does duty for the whole; the ear for the entire field ripe for harvesting.

93 - TELL AGRAB - RITUAL VASE (EARLY 3RD MILL.). — CHICAGO

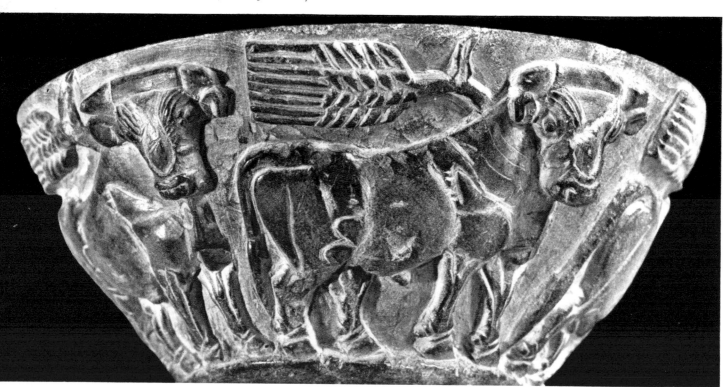

94 - UR - DECORATED RITUAL BOWL: BULLS AND WHEAT (EARLY 3RD MILL.). — BAGHDAD MUSEUM

96 - URUK (?) - DECORATED RITUAL VASE: GILGAMESH, BULLS, BIRDS (EARLY 3RD MILL.). — BRITISH MUSEUM

But not only men take part in the defence of crops and cattle-pens. They are often assisted by a curious being with whom we may identify the legendary hero Gilgamesh. He is depicted naked, for the girdle he wears can hardly count as a garment, and his face already has the traits given him in a later age. Shaggy-haired, bearded, his curly locks streaming behind his head, this kindly giant is performing his appointed task, the protection of the herd. Sometimes he is shown with his arms resting on the bulls; sometimes he is holding back lions who would otherwise wreak havoc on the livestock.

It is only a brief remove from scenes like these to a world of fantasy and archetypal myths. The monster in crystalline limestone in the Brooklyn Museum is a dramatic embodiment of the primaeval fears haunting the mind of early man.

78

97 - HUMAN-BODIED, LION-HEADED MONSTER (EARLY 3RD MILL.). — BROOKLYN MUSEUM

This grim creature has the body of a sexless human being and a lioness's head. Nothing of this sort could be seen in nature, any more than could these four confronted quadrupeds, whose elongated necks, twining around each other two by two, end in serpents' heads. These animals have a curious likeness to those on Egyptian cosmetic palettes.

We here come against the problem of the relations between Egypt and Mesopotamia: the exchanges or influences already implied by the carved handle of the Jebel el-Arak knife, which represents not only boats with just the same high extremities as those plying on the Tigris and Euphrates but also a man with hair and a costume of the Mesopotamian type, thrusting back two lions. Moreover, the fighting animals represented on that knife have striking correspondences with the iconography of many Mesopotamian cylinder seals.

There can be no doubt of a definite connection between these figurations, and all specialists agree that the themes originated in Mesopotamia, and that Egypt took them over. It is interesting to note that some of the 'heraldic' designs of the seals were reproduced in armorial bearings of the feudal era, and also that we sometimes find Romanesque twelfth-century sculptors employing definitely Mesopotamian motifs on the capitals of pillars.

98 - (A) CYLINDER SEAL. — LOUVRE
(B) NARMER PALETTE. — CAIRO MUSEUM
99 - THE JEBEL EL-ARAK KNIFE. — LOUVRE

100 - VOTIVE BULL. — BRITISH MUSEUM

IOI - RITUAL VASE DECORATED WITH LIONS IN HIGH RELIEF (EARLY 3RD MILL.). — LOUVRE

There can be no question here of dealing in its entirety with the huge mass of artifacts discovered on the sites of Uruk, Ur, Lagash, Tell Agrab and Khafaje. After the decorated stone vases and cylinder seals, we will now turn to the representations of animals which display to such effect these artists' technical ability. The figures of bulls and rams in the round have a fine sobriety and density. With an unfaltering hand the sculptor carves domesticated animals at rest, sometimes pierced with cavities for coloured incrustations. For the Sumerians set much store on this decorative technique based on colour contrasts. Polychrome ornamentation in geometric motifs (chequers, lozenges, rosettes) is found on some of the long-beaked ritual vases, excellent specimens of which have been unearthed at Uruk.

Closely akin and no less effective, but with an imprint peculiar to itself, is Susian sculpture in the round. We have already described the painted ware, and in the field of sculpture, too, there are many works that show gifts of observation combined with remarkable sobriety of expression. First we have the animal figures, which are modelled in clay, and then baked. All is rendered in large masses without any lingering over superfluous details; in short, more is suggested than is represented.

The ram shown above is poised in an attitude of feral vigilance. Prominence is given to the horns, their sharp tips pointing forward, formidable weapons ready for any emergency. The body is ponderous, but some light pressures on the clay have brought it aggressively to life.

A

B

C

Modelling in clay was easier and could serve as a preparation for carving in stone: more or less close-grained breccia or translucent alabaster. We have a great number of small objects that give the impression of having been models for works to be executed, later, on a larger scale.

The art of Susa was extremely varied and, besides small recipients reproducing forms with which the pottery has familiarized us, we often find vessels shaped like animals: birds, frogs and ducks with holes in their backs intended to contain perfumes, unguents or cosmetics. Sometimes, too, we come across a highly stylized human figure: for example a man squatting on his buttocks with his head flung back, his hair plastered and hanging down his back in the form of a triangle. With both hands he holds forth a vase cut in the same block of stone; it, too, was intended to contain some ritual offering or precious substance. All is conceived in terms of a very simple canon, giving the statuette an extreme compactness, and a simplification that modern artists would not disdain.

The same impression is produced by the dog-headed man in limestone, sitting on his haunches, rapt in silent contemplation, and by the kneeling woman, lost in ecstasy or in pious meditation on the god she is adoring, with her hands folded on her breast and her long hair bound in a scarf.

103 - SUSA - (A, B) PERFUME JARS.
(C) STATUETTE. — LOUVRE

Power, self-confidence and elegance characterize this art which reached full fruition at the end of the fourth and the beginning of the third millennium B.C. During the last twenty years we have also become aware of its amazing sensitivity. We owe this revelation to the woman's head found at Uruk in the excavations of 1938-39 and known as the Warka Head.

This nearly life-size head in white stone is far more than the plastic representation of a face; it is at once a presentment of the eternal feminine and emblematic of the mystery of the human situation. Originally the head had eyes and eyebrows inlaid with coloured substances, lapis lazuli and shell. And today, despite the black cavities and the damage to the nose, the expression of the face is unimpaired. We seem to catch a gleam of living eyes within the empty sockets and behind the forehead, patterned with smooth curves of hair, we sense an alert, lucid mind. The lips have no need to part for us to hear what she has to say; their undulation, complemented by the ripple of the cheeks, speaks for itself. Here we have a woman unsure perhaps of herself, yet dimly conscious nevertheless of an enigmatic power.

An ordinary mortal, a high priestess, a king's wife, or even a goddess? The face might answer to any of these roles, for it is in fact a synthesis of all. It is when we compare it with other figures of the period, the Praying Woman of Khafaje, or the Man's Head from Tell Brak, that bold anticipation of Cubism pure and simple, that we best appreciate its superiority. In the 'Museum without Walls' the Warka Head is one of those masterworks of sculpture which, defying explanation, stand supreme on their own merits. And it is no exaggeration to say that we have here one of the peak points of man's creative genius.

Such were the heights scaled by the art of the banks of the Euphrates at the close of the protohistoric period. An impressive beginning, but of its very nature hard to follow up. How were the men of the historical period to treat this legacy of the past? What were they now to make of it?

86

106

107

108

109

110

111

112

113

114

115

116

117

119

118

MESOPOTAMIAN SEAL IMPRESSIONS
OF THE URUK AND JEMDET NASR PERIODS

CHAPTER II

THE 'GARDEN OF EDEN': FROM THE ORIGINS TO HISTORICAL TIMES
(5000-2800 B.C.)

PERIODS	SITES	ARCHITECTURE
End of Prehistory	SHANIDAR MUALLAFAT	
C. 5000 B. C.	JARMO	
Hassuna Period	HASSUNA ERIDU	Temple (Level XVIII)
Samarra Period	SAMARRA BAGHUZ	
Halaf Period	HALAF	
	ARPATCHIYA	' Tholoı '
	CHAGAR BAZAR	
	GAWRA	' Tholos ' (XX)
	ERIDU DJOWI SIALK	Temples (XVI-IX
al 'Ubaid Period	AL 'UBAID	
	UR	
	LAGASH	
	URUK	
	ERIDU	Temples (VIII-VI
	UQAIR GAWRA	Temples (XIII)
	SUSA	
Uruk and Jemdet Nasr Periods (3500-2800)	URUK	E-Anna Temples Anu Ziggurat 'Riemchen' bricks 'Patzen' bricks
	LAGASH UR ERIDU	Temples V-I
	UQAIR	Temple on high platform
	AGRAB	
	KHAFAJE	Temple of Sin (I-V)
	BILLA GAWRA	Temples (VIII)
	BRAK	Temple with decorated podium
	MARI SUSA	

The account of Paradise in the Book of Genesis: its perfect applicability to Mesopotamia, a garden land that men were called on to conquer and to cultivate.

Muallafat and Jarmo: two of the earliest Mesopotamian villages.

The so-called Hassuna culture: its buildings and decorated pottery; the beginnings of abstract art.

The Samarra period: from figurative to abstract art; first expression of religious faith.

The Halaf period: the animal kingdom; the Mother Goddesses; the first temple of Eridu.

The al 'Ubaid culture: architecture; male and female demons. Susa: the Sèvres of Antiquity.

The great age of Uruk and Jemdet Nasr. The coming of the Sumerians: rapid progress in architecture and sculpture, both arts centring on ritual and religion. The Warka Head.

SCULPTURE	TERRACOTTA	METAL	SHELL AND IVORY	PAINTING	EGYPT	AEGEAN
	'Mother-Goddess' Figurines					
	Engraved and Painted Pottery					
	Painted Pottery Painted Pottery					
	'Mother-Goddess' Figurines					
Amulets	'Mother-Goddess' Figurines	Copper Implements				
	Painted Pottery Bull-Skulls, Ibexes, etc.					
	'Mother-Goddess' Figurines					
	'Mother-Goddess' Figurines					
	Painted Pottery					
	Painted Pottery					
	Painted Pottery					
	Painted Pottery Figurines					
	Painted Pottery Figurines					
	Painted Pottery Figurines					
	Painted Pottery Figurines					
	Painted Pottery Figurines					
	Painted Pottery					
	Painted Pottery Figurines			Level XVI Wall Paintings		
	Painted Pottery Figurines					
Alabaster Vase Lion-Hunt Stele Woman's Head Cylinder Seals				Wall Paintings (houses)	Pre-Thinite Period (3300-3000)	
Cylinder Seals						
Cylinder Seals						
				Wall Paintings Podium and walls of the temple		
fragment of a vase with reliefs male Worshipper						
Cylinder Seals						
Man's Head Idols Vases male Worshippers Animals	Engraved Pottery				Thinite Period (3000-2778)	Early Minoan I (3000-2800)

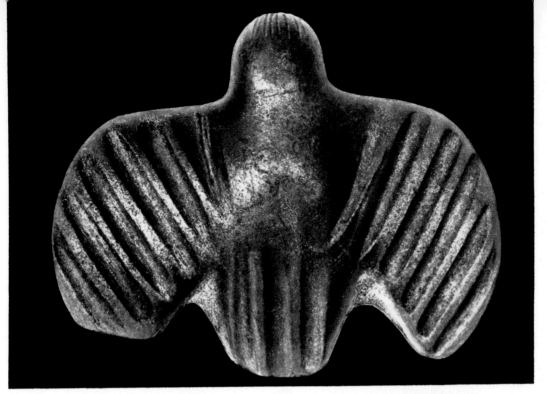

III

THE CITY STATES AND SUMER'S GOLDEN AGE

(UR, LAGASH, MARI, 2800-2470 B.C.)

With the invention of writing by the Sumerians, round about 3000 B.C., civilization took a decisive forward step. But much time must have been needed before the complex system of signs which Sumerian writing involved could be fully worked out and standardized. At Uruk, to begin with, upwards of nine hundred signs, not counting numbers, were employed, while at Jemdet Nasr there were roughly four hundred and twenty. The usage of these hundreds of sometimes intricate signs must have been confined to a very small body of specialists, men who came to be known as 'scribes.'

Writing in its early phase was essentially pictographic; that is to say, its forms derived from things that met the eye in daily life: man and his dwelling, domesticated livestock, game animals, canal and river fish, cultivated plants and vegetables, weapons, household utensils and agricultural implements. The pictorial genius of the Sumerians is evidenced in their schematic renderings of these motifs; they had a gift for singling out what was essential in each object and delineating it in a few unerring strokes.

120 - URUK - BIRD IN FLIGHT (EARLY
3RD MILL.). — BRITISH MUSEUM

hut		rope
niche in wall		wheat stalk
tent		sheaf
city wall		date palm
plough		vine leaf
vehicle		plants in water
sled		bull
boat		cow
canal		calf
spade		goat
axe with handle		dog
arrow		pig
spearhead		chamois
bow		deer
curved weapon		fox
stake		lion
bundle		donkey
brazier		swan
forge		stork
pot		fish
beaked pot		human head
pot with handle		hand
pot with handle		arm
double container		foot
cup		legs
full goblet		female sex
covered basket		male sex
tablet		man
lyre		star
pestle and mortar		comet

In the earliest script a sign could stand both for a word and for a sound. That is to say, some signs served a twofold purpose, having at once a phonetic value and that of an ideogram. This ambivalence was obviously a complicating factor and it led in time to the use of 'correctives' designed to simplify reading and to obviate the risk of misinterpretation. Pictographic to begin with, writing became progressively linear before ending in complete abstraction. The signs were incised with a stylus which, on the soft clay tablets, made rectilinear marks tapering to a point. Hence the name Cuneiform (from the Latin *cuneus*, a wedge).

With the invention of writing begins the recorded history of mankind. In the opinion of the best qualified specialists, the earliest written records so far discovered relate to what are essentially economic matters: workmen's accounts, lists of livestock and possessions, etc. Of religion at first there seems seldom any mention, but in time the texts grow more explicit and their interest widens accordingly. Names appear, which relate to cities, kings and gods. Chronology, no longer relative and amounting indeed to little more than guesswork, becomes absolute, that is to say accurate to within a few dozen years. Such accuracy is all the more remarkable when we remember that the events thus pin-pointed occurred nearly five thousand years ago.

Art in this new phase is inseparable from History. One cannot be correctly understood without the other. The work of art is often said to convey a timeless message, but it can only be explained by a fairly exact knowledge of the circumstances giving rise to it. It is a link in an endless chain; a link as closely connected with what preceded it as with what was to follow.

The art of the early third millennium falls logically into place in the cultural evolution of Sumer and Mesopotamia as a whole. There is no trace in it of any break of continuity; rather, a constant evolution, as is natural enough in the case of a living organism still in process of growth. And this holds good also for the political and cultural developments of the age.

The political developments can now be followed, thanks to our collation of recently excavated monuments with early historical inscriptions, and in particular with the 'dynastic lists' drawn up by scribes of the early second millennium. Though compiled long after the period they cover, these lists are not so fanciful as historians and archaeologists formerly supposed; personages once regarded as legendary and invented, it was assumed, merely for mythological purposes, have been found to figure in inscriptions contemporary with the events commemorated. The most striking example is that of Mesannipadda, a king of the First Dynasty of Ur, mention of whom was found by excavators on a foundation tablet brought to light in 1919 in the temple of al 'Ubaid.

So far, the reader will note, we have been speaking only of Sumerians, the people who firmly established themselves in Lower Mesopotamia towards the middle of the fourth millennium B.C. It fell to them, we believe, as already said, not only to bring the al 'Ubaid type of civilization to a close but also to initiate the magnificent flowering that followed. There is no doubt that this transformed the southernmost part of the country into a thriving cultural centre whose impact and influence extended well beyond the region and penetrated areas peopled by other races and nations. Nor is there any doubt that by the end of the fourth millennium, if not earlier, the Upper and Middle Euphrates areas had been occupied by a Semitic race which had also settled in the plain of the Upper Tigris. Midway between Semites in the north and Sumerians in the south lay a third zone with a mixed population. This was in the region watered by the Diyala, south-west of present-day Baghdad.

These different population strains left their mark on art. For this reason, as observed above, it is perhaps better to describe so homogeneous an art and civilization as Mesopotamian rather than Sumerian or Semitic, considering that its habitat extends from the Khabur basin in the north to the shores of the Persian Gulf in the far south.

This civilization which had developed within what is after all a fairly narrow compass was limited to a few outstanding centres: Nippur, Uruk, Ur, Eridu, Lagash. The political fortunes of these five cities were not the same. The consensus of opinion now is that each constituted an independent city state ruled by a king. This local autonomy, however, was to some extent restricted by the action of a central authority. While tradition has it that 'after the Flood kingship descended from heaven,' it appears from the 'lists' that local dynasties succeeded at times in extending their hegemony over the surrounding regions. Both Uruk and Ur several times gained control of the entire country. Yet despite their highly developed civilization, the kings of Lagash were never able to impose their law on Mesopotamia; only on their immediate neighbours. Nippur and Eridu remained essentially religious centres to the end, without political ambitions, or anyhow ones that were openly pursued. At times the south had to come to terms, it seems, with cities of the north: Kish, in particular, made good its ascendancy several times, but so also did Akshak (on the Tigris) and, more surprisingly, Mari, on the Middle Euphrates. What is certain, nevertheless, is that no one dynastic city was successful in maintaining for long its hold over the country from north to south, and that this region was frequently partitioned between contending powers.

This semi-anarchic state of affairs had lasted nearly four centuries when a great warrior appeared on the scene, Sargon of Akkad. His emergence is one of our reasons for describing the period before him as Pre-Sargonid, in preference to 'Early Dynastic,' the term current among British and American specialists. They have also proposed to divide the period into three phases. Against this we have nothing to say; it was only to be expected that progressive changes of style should take place in the course of several centuries. It will be found, however, that these changes are most noticeable when we move from one centre to another. A Mari statue is far from being a replica of a Lagash statue. Here we have Sumerians, there Semites. Racial differences led to these stylistic modifications, which however by no means disrupted the unity and homogeneity of the civilization as a whole, whose creative vigour is illustrated by a wealth of monuments.

We may begin by considering the case of architecture. There is no question that the Pre-Sargonids—as we shall call them, leaving aside for the present the problem of their racial background—did a great deal of building. Unfortunately most of the monuments assignable to them have been found in very poor condition and convey no more than an imperfect idea of their pristine splendour. Often standing on solid foundations of stone slabs, as at Mari, they employ, in the south, a new

123 - TELL 'UQAIR - THE TEMPLE ON A HIGH PLATFORM (EARLY THIRD MILLENNIUM)

building material: a type of brick whose top surface is not flat but bulges out, and which is therefore known as 'plano-convex.' These brittle prefabricated elements were fired to give them added strength. The result was a brick as hard as stone, and of a much improved appearance. Whereas sun-dried bricks were jointed with clay mortar, baked bricks were laid more carefully, each course being bonded to the next with bitumen. The Book of Genesis (XI, 3) refers to this technique when it describes the materials used by the men of the plain of Shinar for building the Tower of Babel: 'And they had brick for stone, and slime (i.e. bitumen) had they for mortar.'

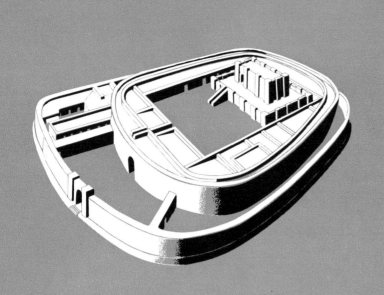

We have said before that the early Mesopotamians sometimes built their sanctuaries on a high terrace-like platform, intended to represent a mountain in miniature. The Pre-Sargonids continued to build them in the same manner. Such are the temples of al 'Ubaid and Khafaje, each surrounded by one or two egg-shaped enclosures, relating to a symbolism which eludes us but must have had something to do with fecundity. Upon this raised platform the architects proceeded to erect successive storeys.

It is a pity that no ziggurats of this period have been found; they undoubtedly existed, for we see them pictured on the designs of early cylinder seals, and once too on a vase from Susa. Rising higher and higher above the plain, these towers, crowned with a temple, were surely intended to facilitate the descent of the gods to earth.

Many Pre-Sargonid sanctuaries have been brought to light in the course of excavations. The best known today are those in the Diyala region and at Mari and Assur. They cannot be described as 'cathedrals,' as at Uruk, but are shrines or temples built on a more modest scale and intended rather for the god, it would seem, than for the faithful. What the builders obviously had in mind was a residence to accommodate the god during his earthly sojourn. The sign representing it, moreover, which is read as 'E,' actually signifies 'house.' The room set aside for the divinity

124 - KHAFAJE - TEMPLE (RECONSTRUCTION)
125 - KISH - ZIGGURAT ON A CYLINDER SEAL
126 - SUSA - ZIGGURATS ON A VASE

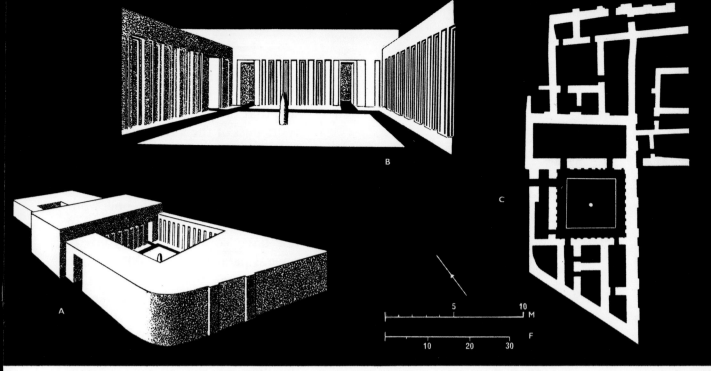

127 - MARI - (A) TEMPLE OF NINNI-ZAZA. — (B) INNER COURT. — (C) PLAN OF THE TEMPLES OF ISHTARAT AND NINNI-ZAZA

is the *cella*, which characteristically takes the form of an oblong room, with a side entrance and the podium at the very back, as far from the entrance as possible, just where the domestic hearth would have been.

Known to us now at Mari are the temples of Ishtar, Ninhursag, Shamash, Ishtarat, and Ninni-Zaza. Their plan is perfectly clear: these are houses in which particular care has been taken with the divine apartment, the cella, and with the court. The latter varies from temple to temple. In that of Ishtar it has a columned portico along two sides. No better prototype could be found of the monastery cloister, where the monks walk and meditate before and after services. In the temple of Ninni-Zaza the court has plainly been designed with an eye to processional rites. In the centre stands the sacred stone, the 'baetylus' peculiar to Semitic forms of worship. In paying homage to it, the assembled priests walked in procession on a path laid in bitumen that did duty for a carpet. The other rooms in the temple complex served to house the staff of guardians and priests, or anyhow some members of it. Built entirely of unbaked bricks, these flat-roofed edifices were outwardly indistinguishable from the dwelling-houses of well-to-do citizens, but certain architectural refinements within indicated that the occupant was a sacred personage. The courtyard of the temple of Ninni-Zaza was entirely adorned with pilasters and recessed niches having a very fine decorative effect. Touched up with bitumen and whitewash, forming contrasts of black and white, they created a rhythmic, balanced play of light and shade.

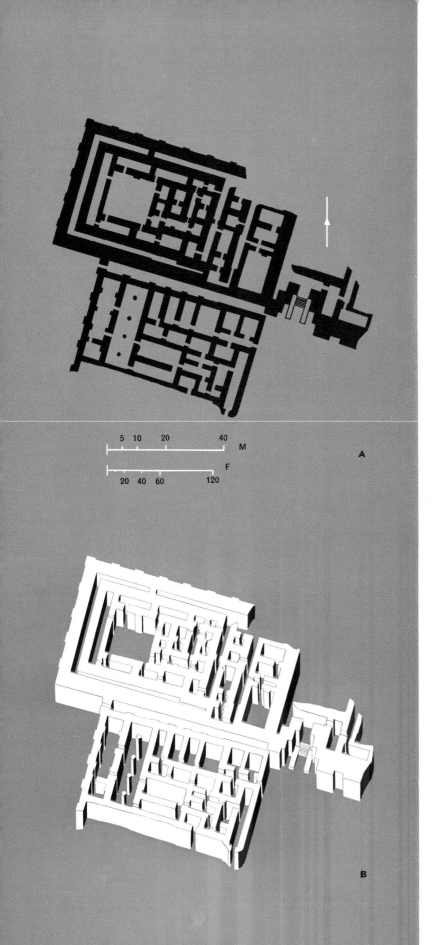

5 10   20   40
                      M
20 40 60   120
                      F

A

B

As the temple was designed as the abode of the god, so the palace was that of the king. Of the royal residences of the Pre-Sargonid period we still know very little. So far not a single one has been discovered at Mari. The palace of Kish is the most imposing; indeed, one wonders whether, in actual fact, it may not have consisted of a group of several palaces side by side. While the ziggurat was the triumph of vertical architecture, the palace of Kish illustrates a lay-out in horizontals. The home of the ruler reproduces on a larger scale the dwelling of the average citizen, with the addition, however, of improvements and amenities which the latter could not afford.

These divine and royal residences were built in the face of many material difficulties, notably the extreme scarcity of both timber and stone. When we uncover the surviving ruins and proceed to examine them, we can only wonder how they could have housed so many masterpieces. These great constructions of mud-bricks, so drab and weather-beaten now, seem unworthy of all the alabaster, the lapis lazuli, the ivory and gold with which this civilization filled them in such bewildering profusion. And when today we contemplate the unprepossessing tombs of the 'royal' cemetery at Ur, we cannot help being struck by the contrast between the simplicity of these 'eternal abodes' and the splendour of the grave furniture.

128 - KISH - PLAN AND RECONSTRUCTION OF THE PALACE (FIRST HALF, 3RD MILL.)

129 - TELL ASMAR - STATUES FROM THE FAVISSA OF THE TEMPLE OF ABU (FIRST HALF, 3RD MILL.). — BAGHDAD MUSEUM AND CHICAGO

The material brought to light of this period is so copious that a selection has to be made. But what criterion is to guide our choice? A history of art should include all schools, even if some of them offend our taste or transgress our present-day canons of beauty. It is quite obvious, moreover, that our tastes and canons may in many particulars be very far removed from those of antiquity; and all attempts to interpret and explain ancient art are necessarily hypothetical. Still, the works themselves are there and challenge us to decipher their message.

By and large, it may be said this message consists primarily in the revelation of a theocratic social system; individuals are portrayed with their hands clasped in prayer, their gaze directed heavenwards. Any doubts we may have in the matter are removed at once when we see the group of twelve statues discovered together by Henri Frankfort in the temple of Abu at Tell Asmar. Mesopotamian art of the third millennium found in religion almost its only source of inspiration.

130 - WORSHIPPERS (FIRST HALF, 3RD MILL.) - (A, B) STATUETTES FROM KHAFAJE. — (C, D) STATUETTES FROM TELL ASMAR

Unquestionably, in the period of three or four centuries under consideration, this art evolved. Frankfort has defined its evolution on the basis of his own discoveries and observations. He considers that, cubist and geometric to begin with, the style became realistic, that is to say it endeavoured more and more to render visual reality, with lifelike details, individual and personal characteristics. In other words, it advanced from the abstract to the figurative. This is certainly true of the Diyala region where, on the sites of Tell Asmar, Khafaje and Tell Agrab, we can watch the changes taking place. However, it may be that this stylistic evolution was confined to that region alone. Neither in the extreme north, at Mari and Assur, where the stratigraphical order has been respected, nor in the lower, specifically Sumerian part of the country, has any mutation of the kind been traced. Ur and Uruk are admittedly poor in sculpture of this period, but Lagash has yielded much, and all of it is in the purest naturalistic vein.

It is true that we have to sort out what was merely due to clumsiness and inexperience (certain sculptures of worshippers, for example, in the temple of Nintu at Khafaje) from other works in the same style, like the group of twelve statues found together in the *favissa* at Tell Asmar. The latter, with their geometrical lines, protruding shoulders, angular

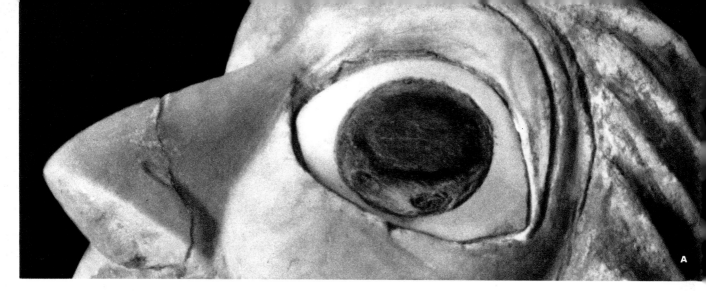

134 - TELL ASMAR - (A) THE GOD ABU (?), DETAIL OF THE HEAD. — (B) THE EYES OF THE GODDESS (?)

elbows, their trapezoidal trunk and skirt in the shape of a truncated cone, were obviously designed with a view to their power of suggestion. The huge eyes, staring out from a head sunken between the shoulders, seem focussed upon a distant scene, plunged in an hypnotic trance. Frankfort has suggested, chiefly on the strength of their preternaturally large eyes, that the two biggest statues of the group may represent two gods. We should be more inclined to see in them the king and queen of Ashnunnak, and in the other statues the highest dignitaries of the city, praying to the gods, in particular to those who grant fertility and fecundity to the region. Their lips are shut, but the tenseness of the bodies and the keen stare of their eyes are more eloquent than words. From this petrified group there emanates something of that awe and apprehension which historians of religion have described in analysing the sensations primitive man experiences in the presence of the numinous.

135 - TELL ASMAR - GODDESS AND THE GOD ABU (?) (FIRST HALF, 3RD MILL.). — BAGHDAD MUSEUM

There was a decisive change in the next phase, when sculpture reverted from flat-edge carving to modelling. Despite their dynamism, the geometric effigies jar on our sense of harmony. After all, are not the human face and body among the marvels of creation? So it was but natural that a new generation of sculptors should attempt to reproduce the finest specimens of them available, and idealize the others.

138 - FEMALE HEADS FROM THE DIYALA REGION (FIRST HALF, 3RD MILL.). — (A) TELL AGRAB. — (B) TELL ASMAR

This basic change of attitude is particularly striking when we find it taking place in one and the same locality, among one and the same people, as was the case in the cities along the Diyala, where there arose a school whose vigour and boldness can be explained only as the outcome of a creative urge untrammelled by the disciplines of the earlier age.

These statues are invariably of worshippers, both men and women, but the faces have now a smiling composure, an amiability and good humour, which prove that the age of abject apprehension of the gods was definitely ended. Humble folk and well-to-do mingle without distinction. Calm and confident, they approach the altar, at the foot

139 - FEMALE HEADS FROM THE DIYALA REGION (FIRST HALF, 3RD MILL.). — (A) KHAFAJE. — (B) TELL AGRAB

141 - TELLOH - HEAD OF A WOMAN (FIRST HALF, 3RD MILL.). — LOUVRE

of which they place their offerings: statuettes of gypsum, alabaster or pink conglomerate which perpetuate the suppliant's presence and prolong his prayer. To this belief we owe the abundance of statuary which has come down to us, and it gives us, in the form of effigies, a vivid impression of the appearance of the Mesopotamians of the first half

142 - WOMAN WITH A KAUNAKES (FIRST HALF, 3RD MILL.). — LOUVRE

143 - MALE HEADS FROM THE DIYALA REGION (FIRST HALF, 3RD MILL.) - (A) UM EL-AGHAREB. — (B) KHAFAJE

of the third millennium. All of them wear the garments known as *kaunakes*, kilts made of strips of cloth which, strange as this may seem, are almost certainly a conventional representation of sheep's fleece.

Not all this statuary, of course, was the work of master sculptors. There was mass production even then, and we can easily picture what these workshops were like: very similar no doubt to the craftsmen's booths we see today in the bazaars adjoining many Eastern sanctuaries. There, day in, day out, in a stone supplied in abundance from quarries close to the city, and therefore at a very low cost, the workers carved these 'interchangeable' statuettes: men standing bare-chested and bare-footed, with a kilt drawn tight at the waist; women usually standing but sometimes seated, wearing a long robe leaving the right shoulder more or less bare, or a cloak covering the entire body, from neck to ankles. Worshippers of both sexes stand or sit in the same characteristic attitude: their hands clasped in fervent prayer, their gaze fixed in rapt contemplation.

Made for travellers, pilgrims and the local townsfolk, these figurines, almost all anonymous, represented the permanent supplications of the men and women who placed them in the cella of the sanctuary, at the feet of the deity or on the offering table.

Alongside this standardized production, it seems certain that expert artists were sometimes called in by kings and high-ranking officials, and it is quite possible that in some instances we have actual portraits. This

144 - AL 'UBAID - STATUE OF KURLIL (FIRST HALF, 3RD MILL.). — BRITISH MUSEUM

145 - MARI - STATUE OF KING LAMGI-MARI (FIRST HALF, 3RD MILL.). — ALEPPO MUSEUM

seems especially likely in such a city as Mari, which has yielded dozens of small statues and statuettes. The Semitic type is portrayed with unmistakable fidelity, yet it is well differentiated from one individual to another: Lamgi-Mari in no way resembles Iku-Shamagan. Both were kings. Nani is distinguishable from Idi-Narum, known as the

146 - MARI - HEAD OF KING IKU-SHAMAGAN (FIRST HALF, 3RD MILL.). — DAMASCUS MUSEUM —

147 - MARI (FIRST HALF, 3RD MILL.) - (A) STATUE OF NANI. — (B) THE STEWARD EBIH-IL. — LOUVRE

'miller,' a name certainly not to be taken in the literal sense. Both were officials of high rank and cannot be confused with Ebih-il, the steward. This rule was not always to hold good: in Neo-Assyrian times, from the ninth to the seventh century B.C., it is impossible to tell Sargon from Sennacherib or Assurnasirpal from Assurbanipal. Their grand

148 - MARI - IDI-NARUM, THE 'MILLER' (FIRST HALF, 3RD MILL.). — ALEPPO MUSEUM ·

149 - MARI - HEAD OF A WORSHIPPER ('THE BEDOUIN') (FIRST HALF, 3RD MILL.). — DAMASCUS MUSEUM

viziers all look alike, a stock effigy serving for all and being reproduced without the change of a single feature. There is nothing of this in third-millennium statuary, in which, despite family likenesses, individuals stand out sharply, each with his personality clearly indicated. An instance is that nameless face from Mari, whose huge, deep-set eyes seem to burn with a flame ceaselessly fanned by the desert wind.

150 - MARI - HEAD OF A WORSHIPPER (FIRST HALF, 3RD MILL.). — DAMASCUS MUSEUM

151 - UR - FEMALE WORSHIPPER (FIRST HALF, 3RD MILL.). — BRITISH MUSEUM

The women, too, have much of the grace and delicate appeal we have already met with in the Diyala region. The figure of a female worshipper from Ur, now in the British Museum, is full of smiling charm despite the empty eye-sockets. Her robe, leaving the right shoulder bare, exemplifies the asymmetrical style of dress so frequently found in statues of young women. At Mari, where young women were often represented in this way, the queens stand at the head of the procession of suppliants. Wearing a high crown of the *polos* type, they have always a faint smile that at once fascinates and intrigues us.

152 - MARI - FEMALE WORSHIPPER (QUEEN ?) WITH
A BRANCH (FIRST HALF, 3RD MILL.). — LOUVRE

155 - MARI - (A AND B) UR-NINA, 'THE GREAT SINGER' (FIRST HALF, 3RD MILL.). — DAMASCUS MUSEUM

None, however, has the gracious aristocratic charm of Ur-Nina, 'the great singer.' If she is wearing pantaloons, the reason is that she was also a dancer and performed her figures to the accompaniment of her songs. Though placed in a temple, and in some respects a religious work, this statue has also much to suggest about the court life of the period.

156 - MARI - 'THE GREAT SINGER'

157 - MARI - 'THE EMBRACING COUPLE' (FIRST HALF, 3RD MILL.). — ALEPPO MUSEUM

The 'Embracing Couple' from Mari, a work unique in Sumerian art, brings us a little closer to this remote world of flesh-and-blood beings moved by passions like our own.

But these wonderful achievements of sculpture in the round must not lead us to overlook the carvings in low relief.

158 - (A, B) TELLOH - MAN WITH A PLUMED HEADDRESS. — (C, D) NIPPUR - VOTIVE RELIEFS DEDICATED TO ENLIL

Far less numerous, they are of very unequal merit and answer to two different requirements. Some are plaques with a hole bored in the centre; others are slabs or blocks of stone on which figure mythological, religious or historical scenes. The techniques also differ. The simplest consists of linear engraving, for example the bas-relief of a man with

159 - TELLOH - (A, B) BAS-RELIEF OF UR-NINA (FIRST HALF, 3RD MILL.). — LOUVRE. — 160 (A) - MACE-HEAD OF MESILIM

a plumed headdress, from Lagash (Telloh), and the Nippur plaques illustrating the cult of Enlil, the earth god. In the other type of bas-relief, figures stand out more or less sharply on a uniform background. They treat a variety of subjects: sometimes scenes of real life are illustrated, sometimes the figuration is wholly or partially inspired by local myths.

160 (B) - TELLOH - MACE-HEAD OF MESILIM, DETAIL (FIRST HALF, 3RD MILL.). — LOUVRE

Obviously mythological, though hard to interpret, are the figures on a mace-head inscribed with the name of Mesilim. On top is a lion-headed spread eagle; on the circumference is a frieze of six sketchily indicated lions. Rough, inexpert sculpture, not without power, however, in its schematic patterning.

Better executed, already, is the plaque known as the 'genealogical bas-relief of Ur-Nina.' The king of Lagash, Ur-Nina (now more often read 'Ur-Nanshe'), appears on it twice, with his children and his cup-bearer. We see him standing to the left with a basket on his head; underneath, he is seated, holding a cup. The linear inscriptions in some of the spaces between figures and on their skirts give no clue to the meaning of the scene, which, however, obviously represents the laying of the first brick of a new temple and the feast that followed.

Real persons figure also in a votive plaque from Khafaje, where we find once more the superimposed registers already employed on the vase from Warka, a typically Sumerian lay-out. The upper band contains a banquet scene, with a man and a woman as guests of honour; the middle register shows the preparations for the banquet; below is a chariot. According to some authorities scenes of this kind represent the New Year's celebrations, when 'sacred marriage' rites were solemnized so as to ensure the fertility of the soil in the coming year.

We have also reliefs partly mythological, such as the Telloh plaque showing a naked celebrant offering a libation to the goddess of the mountain; and others wholly so, like the plaque from al 'Ubaid with a human-headed bull attacked by a lion-headed eagle. Many explanations of this symbolism have been suggested. We will content ourselves with pointing out that these imaginary scenes always contain four type figures, grouped in pairs, which were destined to play major roles in this art: man and bull, eagle and lion.

161 - PLAQUES AND RELIEF (1ST HALF, 3RD MILL.)
  (A) KHAFAJE - VOTIVE PLAQUE
  (B) TELLOH - LIBATION BEFORE NINHURSAG
  (C) AL 'UBAID - EAGLE ATTACKING BULL

133

A

B

C

164 - TELLOH - STELE OF THE VULTURES, DETAIL: KING EANNATUM AT THE HEAD OF HIS TROOPS. — LOUVRE

That famous work, the Stele of the Vultures, combines history and religion in its commemoration of a notable feat of arms: the victory won by King Eannatum of Lagash over the neighbouring town of Umma. It comprises a summary of the course of the battle, running from top to bottom. At the same time, the two sides of the stele give complementary versions of what happened: on one, the exploits of the warriors; on the other, the decisive intervention of the gods.

The men of Lagash advance in close formation, carrying leather shields, ready to attack with their spears. The king stands at the head of his troops, a thick protective hide draped slantwise over his body. Actually, however, the battle is already won: Eannatum's troops are marching over the prostrate bodies of the enemy, which birds of prey are already beginning to devour. Immediately below, on the second register, light infantry march by, bare-chested, their spears on their

165 - TELLOH - STELE OF THE VULTURES, DETAIL: THE GOD NINGIRSU WITH HIS MACE. — LOUVRE

shoulders. Here, again, the king takes the lead, but riding now in his war-chariot. Dressed as before, he brandishes his weapons, a spear in his left hand, a falchion in the right, as though the battle were still in progress. His leather helmet is reinforced behind with a false chignon, giving additional protection to the nape of his neck. The king had taken care to let his hair down before giving battle—a rite which, we learn from the Bible, was still observed in Israel in the time of the Judges and Samson. Once sighting ends is theirs and the men of Lagash have won the day, they proceed 'in the third register' to count their dead on the field of battle and, most important of all, to provide decent burial for them. The bodies are collected in a heap and covered with earth; the customary funeral sacrifices are offered. Next came, presumably, the epilogue of all successful wars: a scene of the prisoners being led away into captivity. This, no doubt, was represented on the lowest register. But all that has survived is the clean-shaven head of some recalcitrant captive, seen just as a spear strikes his forehead.

This memorial of a successful campaign had, as we have said, a religious aspect. To this the other side of the stele is devoted. If Eanna-tum was victorious, it was only because the gods themselves came down and took a hand in the proceedings. Indeed, the fragments of the shattered stele that have been pieced together make it clear that a whole pantheon of gods threw themselves into the fray. Two crowns, still intact, point to the presence of two goddesses, presumably Inanna and Bau. But the mighty figure of Ningirsu, tutelary god of Lagash,

136

166 - TELLOH - STELE OF THE VULTURES, DETAIL: THE PRISONERS IN THE NET. — LOUVRE

dominates the scene. In his right hand he lifts the stone mace with which he is about to bludgeon the luckless warriors trapped in the wide-meshed net held in his left hand, which also grips the symbolic emblem (a lion-headed eagle and two lions), while his huge eye is fixed on an unseen enemy who, we may be sure, is soon to undergo the fate in store for all who resist the will of Ningirsu.

So far we have been dealing with a narrative style in which every element is stated and depicted with such clarity that no serious problem of interpretation can arise. Very different, indeed purposively esoteric, is the style of the bituminous plaque of Dudu, high priest of Lagash: one of the series of so-called 'perforated plaques.' The procedure followed here is quite different; heterogeneous elements are grouped in combinations whose purport is far from evident at first sight. In this plaque we have successively the lion-headed eagle between two lions, which are biting its wings; the priest Dudu, bare-chested, wearing the *kaunakes* skirt; a heifer lying down, but looking as if it were about to rise to its feet; and a thick tress with four convolutions. Of course explanations can be found, and there has been no lack of them. The fact remains that we are faced here with a symbolic figurative language, a kind of rebus or picture puzzle, which the Sumerians themselves, however, must have had no particular difficulty in deciphering.

One cannot help wondering, on the other hand, what their reactions were to the ornamentation of certain votive vases, deposited in shrines, whose belly is covered with strange scenes belonging to a world that is utterly foreign to our own. What we have in mind are not the vases decorated with divine figures, like the fragment in Berlin, from Lagash, on

167 - LAGASH (FIRST HALF, 3RD MILL.) (A) PLAQUE OF DUDU. — LOUVRE. (B) THE GODDESS NINHURSAG. — BERLIN MUSEUM

168 - VASES (3RD MILL.) - (A) SUSA. — LOUVRE. — (B, C) MARI. — ALEPPO MUSEUM. — (D) KHAFAJE. — BRITISH MUSEUM

which we see the goddess Ninhursag, 'Lady of the Mountain,' with a leafy crown on her head, her shoulders covered with sprouting branches, her hair flowing out behind her, and holding the branch of fertility in her hand. Nor are we thinking of those vessels in greenish steatite, decorated with composite geometric patterns (plaitwork, chevrons, imbrications, incurved lintels), architectural elements or animal motifs (coiled snakes speckled with inlays). What we have in mind, rather, are the vases covered with a weird assortment of animal forms. Here all is blind ferocity, elemental chaos. From Khafaje come several examples of this turbulent style. The same site has yielded another vase, now in the British Museum, on which we can detect signs of a return to order. Beside a group of wild beasts and birds of prey stripping the carcass of a bull, stands a woman, a remote prototype one would say of the *Potnia Therôn* of the Greeks, who seems to have succeeded in taming some selected members of this otherwise unruly menagerie.

This scene is relatively easy to interpret. It is otherwise with the vase from Mari illustrated here, whose decoration is all the more puzzling for being sadly incomplete. Who will ever know why, at the foot of a palm tree, a man is kneeling while a snake devours his genitals? It is only fair to add that one is no less intrigued by the motifs of several cylinders and the decorative inlays of some of the panels discovered at Ur. In these the real world is closely interwoven with a world of purest fantasy, or anyhow the two coexist at every turn. But for the Mesopotamians of the third millennium there was nothing anomalous in scenes where the invisible powers were embodied in seemingly preposterous forms. The previous generation was already familiar with these hybrid creatures, half human, half animal. We meet them again and again in glyptic art. The bull-man of the Khafaje vase reappears, carved in the same manner, on the stone rollers whose impressions on the soft clay of tablets, stoppers and labels depict similar combats with wild beasts. This hybrid figure is Enkidu, comrade of Gilgamesh, the hero with curly hair and a long beard who single-handed was more than a match for two lions and, thanks to his Herculean strength, could handle them like children's toys. How strange, too, is the atmosphere of the scene of beasts of prey attacking peaceful

169 - MYTHOLOGICAL SCENES (3RD MILL.)
(A) VASE FROM MARI. — DAMASCUS MUSEUM
(B) SEAL IMPRESSION. — THE HAGUE
(C) SEAL IMPRESSION. — CHICAGO

170 - ARM-RESTS (FIRST HALF, 3RD MILL.) (A) LOUVRE. — (B) KHAFAJE - PHILADELPHIA

cattle, while Gilgamesh and Enkidu vie in feats of strength—a scene at once symbolic and boldly schematized. After outlining a human face and trunk, both dextrously foreshortened, the engraver, greatly daring, has joined to them two lions, heads downwards. It seems certain that this was originally intended to remind the viewer how once a hero, unaided, had subdued two lions. The three elements combined have given rise to an absurd, yet strangely compulsive, figuration of a human trunk grafted on to the lion's bodies: a singular hybridization which, surprisingly enough, was to reappear millennia later in Romanesque art.

Such conjunctions of the real and the fantastic are also to be found in animal sculpture in the round. We have already observed how in the previous period, named after Jemdet Nasr, sculptors had delighted in representing animals. Pre-Sargonid animal art is in no way inferior, and its achievements testify to the same creative power. During the Second World War the Louvre acquired the muzzle of a bull which had evidently served as the arm-rest of a throne. This bull's muzzle is a prolongation of the block of stone of which it forms a part, and the massive head with its short horns, is rendered with fine sobriety. This carving may well have been done from life in some Sumerian cattle-pen. From Khafaje comes an identical arm-rest with a bull, but this time the bull has a man's face. Strange though it is, this hybrid creature seems placid enough; evidently it was not meant to inspire fear or awe. Indeed it has all the aspect of a 'good genius.'

141

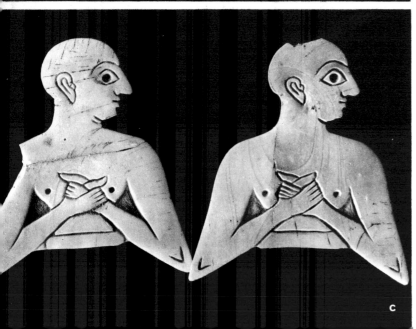

The same observation holds good for another class of objects in which Pre-Sargonid artists excelled, and which they carried to a pitch of perfection never to be attained by any of their successors. We have in mind the works in ivory and shell inlays, elaborate compositions in which the Mesopotamians displayed to fine effect their imagination and their technical proficiency. The materials employed, the mother of pearl especially, being extremely brittle and not permitting any retouching, each line had to be cut with absolute exactitude and pentimenti were ruled out. One often wonders how the engravers of cylinder seals could have produced the work they did without a magnifying glass, so fine, so meticulously precise is their chiselling. But in the ivory-carvers they had rivals who often equalled and sometimes excelled them. When we inspect some of the small plaques that have been discovered at Mari, we cannot see how they could possibly have been bettered, even with modern tools. It would indeed be impossible to improve on such marvellous creations as these profiled dignitaries in full ceremonial dress, a smile curling their lips as they await the naked captives who are being led forward by the victorious soldiery. We get the same impression of perfection from a ritual scene of two men slaying rams, for sacrifice. These are but shattered relics of

171 - STANDARD FROM MARI (FIRST HALF, 3RD MILL.) (A) DIGNITARIES. — LOUVRE (B) RITUAL SACRIFICE. — ALEPPO MUSEUM (C) WORSHIPPERS. — DAMASCUS MUSEUM

172 - MARI - SEATED FIGURE WITH A GOBLET (FIRST HALF, 3RD MILL.). — DAMASCUS MUSEUM

some large-scale composition; yet, fragmentary though they are, they conjure up, across the ages, the dignitaries, priests and worshippers, both men and women, whom we have already seen portrayed in stone, but whose forms incised in ivory or shell are yet another revelation of these early artists' amazing skill.

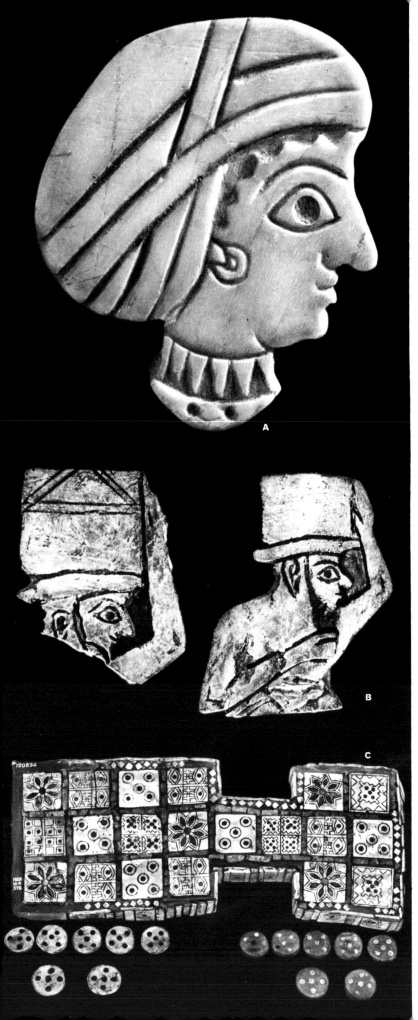

Mention has been made at an earlier page of the technique of inlay and the juxtaposition of simple elements in the case of cone mosaics. The ornamented panels from the royal tombs of Ur derive from this traditional technique, but show it at a stage of singular perfection. Several gaming boards and soundboxes of lyres are decorated with plaques composed of geometric designs (rosettes, chessboard patterns, dotted circles, the 'magic eye'), incrusted in a wooden ground. The use of different materials (shell, mother of pearl, lapis lazuli, schist, bitumen, pink stone) admits of polychrome effects which add a shimmering lustre to the surface. These fine inlays became even more effective when precious metals, gold and silver, were added to them.

Yet this purely geometric decoration might in the end have become monotonous, had it not been varied with figurative motifs. The scattered remnants of this art from Mari, Kish and Lagash reveal their true significance only when studied in the light of the complete ensembles found in the excavations at Ur. One of the most famous, and justly famous, examples is known, incorrectly, as the 'Standard.'

Shaped like a lectern, this object consists of four panels (front, back and two sides) decorated with inlays. The two main panels, longer than the others, are the most characteristic. They illustrate

I

175 - UR - THE 'STANDARD,' DETAIL: WAR CHARIOT (FIRST HALF, 3RD MILL.). — BRITISH MUSEUM

two complementary aspects of existence, the dark and the bright side of life: on the one, war; on the other, peace. Only when the former had come to a successful end could the blessings of peace be enjoyed to the full. The theme of war is treated more elaborately than on the Stele of the Vultures, and here the gods are dispensed with altogether. Credit for the successful issue of the conflict goes to the fighting men themselves. The episodes leading up to it should be read from bottom to top. They include the earliest known representation of a chariot fight, a type of warfare that must have introduced some sweeping changes into the old infantry tactics. We have already met with these war chariots on the Stele of the Vultures. But here for the first time we see them in action; or rather we see *one* in action (the part for the whole) but represented four times, at different moments, with its team of onagers advancing first at a walk, then speeding up, then at a mad gallop. Here we have the first armoured cars in the history of warfare and also the world's first animated newsreel, for this attempt

176 - UR - THE 'STANDARD': PANEL REPRESENTING WAR
177 - UR - THE 'STANDARD': PANEL REPRESENTING PEACE
(FIRST HALF, 3RD MILL.). — BRITISH MUSEUM

178 - UR - THE 'STANDARD.' PEACE, DETAIL: LIBATION SCENE (FIRST HALF, 3RD MILL.). — BRITISH MUSEUM

to render movement anticipates the motion pictures of today. The chariots clear the way and the supporting infantry bring up the rear. Helmeted soldiers advance relentlessly, protected by heavy leather cloaks; all that remains for them to do is to round up the miserable herd of captives and drive them to the king, who has alighted from his chariot and is awaiting them, for the fight is over.

After the storm and stress of battle comes the feast to celebrate the victory. No caption is needed to explain what is going on. Bearers and menials are seen conveying to the palace the spoils of war, together with the animals and supplies required for the banquet. The king has doffed his battle dress and appears in his peacetime kilt. Seated, with a cup in his hand, he takes refreshment with his guests (all men), who sit facing their sovereign. While they regale themselves, a woman sings to the accompaniment of a harpist. Both stand well outside the group, but their music helps to take the minds of the warriors off the recent horrors of the battlefield.

149

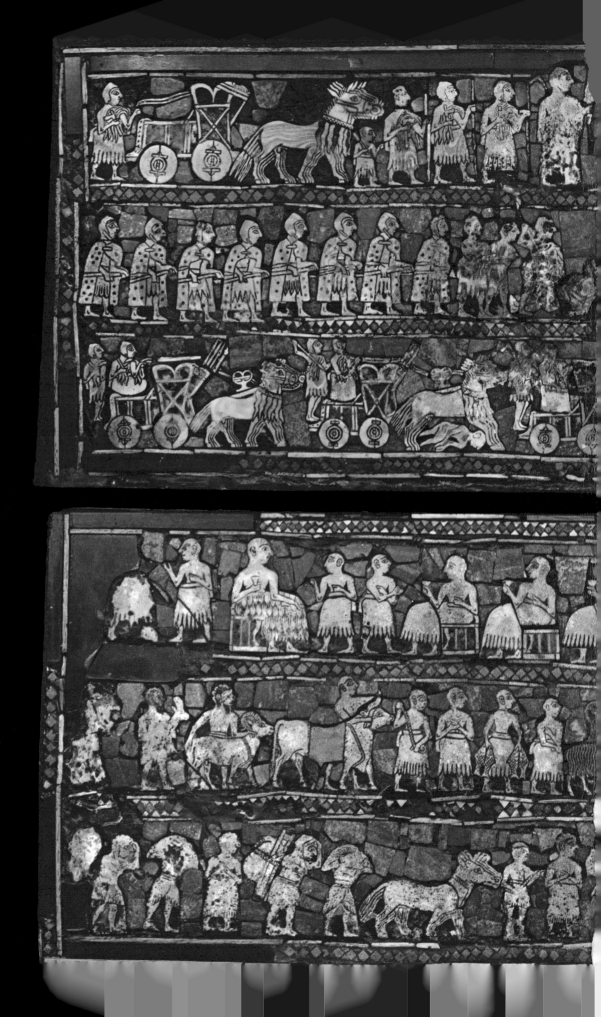

The 'Standard' of Ur is a page from the book of history. Some of the inlays on the soundboxes of harps bring us back to the world of myth and legend, for none of the incidents they represent relates to real life. After a naked Gilgamesh grappling with two human-headed bulls, comes a series of animals impersonating men: a dog, with a dagger stuck in its belt, carrying a laden table, followed by a lion with a cup and a large jar. Obviously preparations for a banquet, at which an ass will play the lyre, a jackal the sistrum and tambourine, and a bear will perform a dance. Next comes a scorpion-man with a scroll in his hand, followed by a gazelle holding two goblets, which it has just filled from the large vessel behind it.

It is hard to say exactly what this elaborately composed scene is intended to convey, and to sum up and criticize all the interpretations so far proposed would take us too far afield. Probably it is an evocation of the myth of Gilgamesh. That such a theme should have been used to decorate a lyre need not surprise us. By this time the epic of Gilgamesh had certainly assumed its literary (though still oral) form and was chanted by bards to a musical accompaniment. What could be more natural than to decorate the soundbox of the accompanying lyre with characteristic episodes from the epic? Here again we have a Sumerian theme, the music-making ass, destined to recur through the ages; it reappears in the satirical papyrus of Turin, in the ostraca from Deir el-Medina, in the fables of Aesop and Phaedrus, and finally in Romanesque capitals.

Metal came into general use early in the third millennium. The result was nothing short of a revolution in the technique of tool-making, for tools had hitherto been almost exclusively made of stone or clay. The effects of this innovation made themselves felt in art, which was the first to benefit by it. Such metals as copper, bronze, silver, electrum and gold, in all grades from the commonest to the finest, were now available for many purposes.

Here again a selection has to be made in order to show the most representative prototypes of these workshop products, which doubtless were beginning to compete with those of the stone-carvers. We find, however, that on the whole the bronze-founders and goldsmiths seem to have made efforts to work on a different line, and thus to avoid duplication; they produced, for example, very few figures of worshippers, while any number of them still were carved in stone. The small statuette of a man, in the Louvre, wearing a kilt of long vertical bands, has his hands clasped like those naked, bearded men from Khafaje, erect on a four-legged stand, on whose heads rested a small vessel. These figures were cast in almost pure copper, like the foundation figurines from Lagash, which also reproduce the features of a beardless, long-haired man, with clasped hands, whose lower body tapers into a nail; for this was a cult object intended to keep under control, in the depths of the edifice, evil spirits or hostile powers.

180 - KHAFAJE - WORSHIPPER (FIRST HALF, 3RD MILL.). — CHICAGO

181 - TELL AGRAB - VOTIVE CHARIOT DRAWN BY FOUR ANIMALS (FIRST HALF, 3RD MILL.). — BAGHDAD MUSEUM

A copper chariot, discovered in a temple at Tell Agrab during the winter excavations of 1936-37 conducted by the Oriental Institute of Chicago, calls for special mention. Though barely three inches high, this object nevertheless constitutes a unique piece of evidence for the history of transportation. A two-wheeled chariot is drawn by four animals, which are certainly not horses, but are in all probability to be identified as asses or onagers. The animals are harnessed side by side, the two in the middle being joined by a yoke solidly locked to their collars. The reins are passed through a ring fastened to the upper lip of each of the four animals.

The driver, a bearded man with long hair, holds the two central reins in his left hand; the slack is coiled round a centrepiece made fast to the axle of the chariot. His right hand is left free and must have plied a whip or a goad (this accessory has disappeared). Since he is unprotected, this can hardly be the model of a war chariot, like those represented in the Stele of the Vultures and the 'Standard' of Ur.

182 - TELL AGRAB - VOTIVE CHARIOT DRAWN BY FOUR ANIMALS (FIRST HALF, 3RD MILL.). — BAGHDAD MUSEUM

We are inclined rather to regard this quadriga as serving only for quick journeys over the steppes, the driver being both a courier and a bearer of news. Only a very sturdy vehicle could stand up to the rough cross-country tracks of those days. This one was exactly what was needed. In the original of which this is a model, the wheels were solid and spokeless, each of them being composed of three strips of wood fitted together and clinched by four double pins. For added resistance, the wheels were reinforced with an intermittent rim of metal plates, which served both to protect the wood from wear and tear and to ensure a better grip on the road.

To give an expression of intenser life both to the animals and the driver, the bronze-founder set a particle of mother of pearl into their eye-sockets, and made it fast with bitumen. This combination of metal and shell is often found in other copper figurines of the same period, also from the Diyala region; but as we shall see at a later page it was a technique still in favour in all parts of Mesopotamia.

A

B

C

A

B

184 - (A) LAGASH - BULL'S HEAD. — LOUVRE — (B) SHURUPPAK - GOAT'S HEAD. — UNIVERSITY MUSEUM, PHILADELPHIA

From the same site at Tell Agrab comes a remarkable and, in some respects, intriguing group. Two men are engaged in a wrestling match of a peculiar kind, each participant having to keep balanced on his head a vase whose enormous size is out of all proportion with his body.

Apart from the team and chariot described above, we have so far dealt only with human figures. Let us now turn to a few examples of that animal art in which, precisely because of their close contact with nature, the Mesopotamians excelled. This bull's head discovered at Lagash—but strikingly reminiscent of similar pieces from Ur— seems almost alive, with its formidable horns, its pricked-up ears, and its flashing polychrome eyes of shell inlaid with lapis lazuli. The same impression is produced by a goat's head from Shuruppak, home

183 - BRONZE FIGURINES (3RD MILL.) - (A, B) WORSHIPPERS. — (C) WRESTLERS

185 - AL 'UBAID - BULL FROM THE TEMPLE FRIEZE (FIRST HALF, 3RD MILL.). — BRITISH MUSEUM

of the Babylonian Noah, with its long spiral horns and tapering nostrils. Equally fine is the mighty procession of bulls from al 'Ubaid, which so dramatically vivified one of the friezes on the façade of the temple. Yet nothing can match the head of a bearded bull in copper, acquired in 1952 by the City Art Museum of St. Louis. This head is rendered in a compact, sober style, with close-set muzzle and massive horns. Against the green patina the eyes of lapis lazuli strike a bright note,

186 - BULL (FIRST HALF, 3RD MILL.).
CITY ART MUSEUM, ST. LOUIS

187 - AL 'UBAID - LION-HEADED EAGLE BETWEEN TWO STAGS (FIRST HALF, 3RD MILL.). — BRITISH MUSEUM

recalling the gaze of an animal that is steadily observing the scene before singling out the victim to attack, charge and gore. On the other hand, the lions which guarded the temple gate at al 'Ubaid, their bodies consisting of copper sheets hammered over a bitumen core, seem petrified, inert, and convey no sense of power, despite the inlays of their eyes and hanging tongues. On the whole, the execution of these animal figures is ponderous and coarse.

This is not the case with the great panel of hammered copper which stood over the doorway of the temple: a lion-headed eagle

188 - (A) UR - REIN RING (FIRST HALF, 3RD MILL.). — BRITISH MUSEUM

with its wings outspread between two stags, who are moving placidly away. The pity is that this relief should have been in such bad condition when discovered, for the restoration has certainly done injustice to the original. It is beyond the power of even the most expert restorer to reconstruct in its entirety an incomplete piece of ancient art. Compare, for example, the lion-headed eagle from the temple of al 'Ubaid with the one that spreads its wings so majestically on the silver vase of Entemena: the differences are plain to see.

Here we have another fine example of the metal-workers' skill. This handsome vase in the Louvre owes its outstanding importance to the engraved friezes decorating it. Round the belly of the vase the theme of the bird of prey

188 - (B) TELLOH - SILVER VASE OF ENTEMENA (FIRST HALF, 3RD MILL.). — LOUVRE

gripping two animals recurs four times. Lions alternate with stags and goats, and snap at them ferociously. Above this symbolic scene, on the shoulder of the vase, is a frieze of heifers. There are seven, the sacred number; truly impressive is the contrast between the calm of their green pastures and the combats of animals, over which Im-Dugud presides.

Very different from the hieratic treatment of the silver vase of Entemena is the rendering of an onager in electrum mounted on a rein ring, found at Ur. It is instinct with the quivering life of an untamed animal; indeed it would be impossible to convey more tellingly the fierce resentment of a proud, mettlesome creature that will not let itself be harnessed without a struggle. It is prancing, raising its head defiantly, as if to sniff the heady air of freedom.

This piece from the 'royal tombs' of Ur is but one example among many of those superb works which justify us in ranking the Sumerians as the greatest of all early artists. No other civilization in the world, in that first half of the third millennium, can boast of such an abundance of works executed with such consummate craftsmanship. It is not

just the glitter of gold—which would be merely a token of material wealth. What holds us spellbound is the brilliance of the creative achievement behind it.

But here we come up against a still unsolved problem. The 'royal' tombs of Ur we have called them, keeping to the established terminology; but this is precisely the point at issue. Akalamdug and Meskalamdug, each described as 'king' on various objects, do not figure on any dynastic list. Nor does 'Queen' Shubad. Dozens of human sacrifices, both men and women, have been found near most of these 'royal' burial vaults; yet no tradition tells us that the obsequies of Sumerian monarchs were attended by such hecatombs. Archaeologists, Assyriologists and historians of religion have tried to solve the mystery. Rites connected with the myth of Tammuz, thinks Moortgat; others relate them to a fertility cult and the renewal of the seasons; some hold them to be foundation sacrifices on an unusually large scale. Each hypothesis is tenable, but none has been confirmed as yet.

The fine goblet and bowl of 'Queen' Shubad could hardly be eclipsed by any royal table service. A few chevrons and zigzags, a rosette, creasings of the metal sheet and linear patterns of the utmost simplicity—these testify to the exquisite taste of the Sumerian goldsmiths. Not that

189 - UR (FIRST HALF, THIRD MILLENNIUM)
(A) GOLD PLATE OF SHUBAD. — (B) BULL'S HEAD. — UNIVERSITY MUSEUM, PHILADELPHIA (C) HELMET OF MESKALAMDUG. — BAGHDAD MUSEUM

190 - UR - RAM AGAINST A FLOWERING SHRUB (FIRST HALF, 3RD MILL.). — BRITISH MUSEUM

I

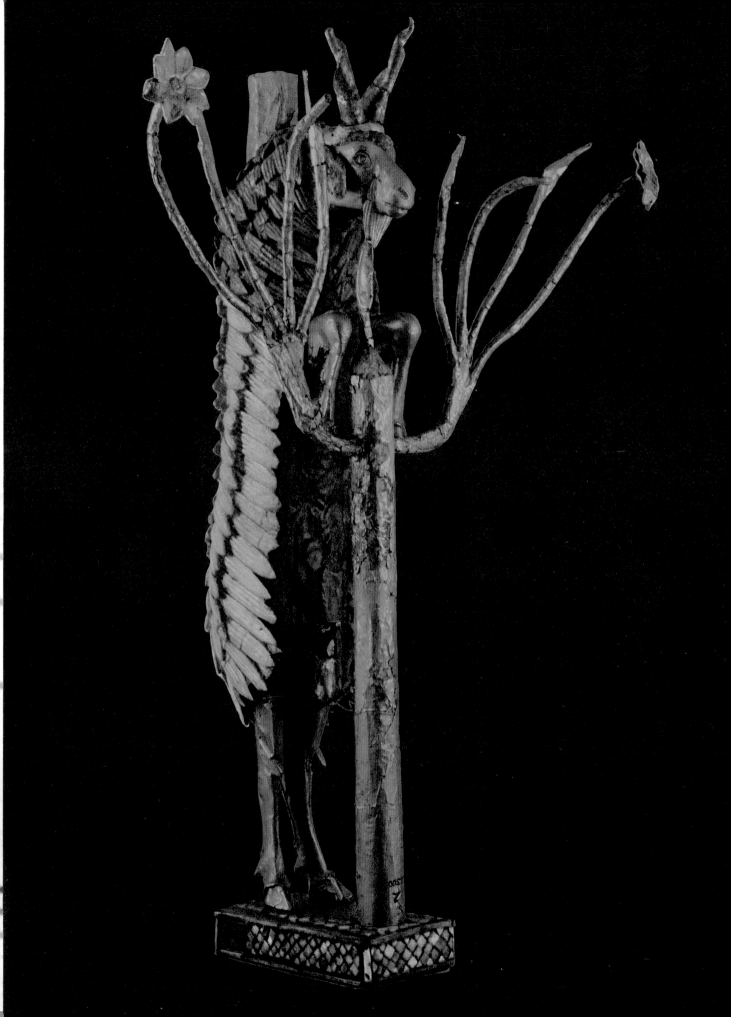

they shirked more complicated techniques. They were no less adroit when it came to cloisonné work; witness the dagger from Ur and the ring from Lagash. Equally perfect of its kind is the helmet of Meskalamdug, whose wavy hair, braids, chignon and curls are so flawlessly carved in the body of a single metal plaque.

No less striking are the bulls' heads serving as 'figure-heads' to certain lyres, either all in gold or in gold and lapis lazuli. Here again we find a consummate form of animal art in the full vigour of its expression, an art untrammelled by limitations and sometimes greatly enhanced by imaginative touches, as in the case of the ram standing on its hind legs and resting its forefeet on a flowering shrub. Here the artist has employed a variety of materials: besides gold and lapis there is silver, shell and red stone. The polychromy thus obtained adds to the charm of the work, but does not make it any easier to interpret. We cannot help feeling that Woolley was over-bold when he saw in this a prescient allusion to Abraham's sacrifice, and in particular to the 'ram caught in a thicket by his horns' which the patriarch offered up to God instead of his son Isaac (Genesis, xxii, 13). The motif of two animals propped against the sacred tree and confronting each other is a recognized Mesopotamian theme, but its significance is still an open question. We can have little doubt, however, that it was related in some way to the fertility rites which never ceased to be the main concern of a race whose daily life was one long struggle against the devastating heat of the Mesopotamian sun. To protect their livestock against predatory animals and to ensure the fertility of their fields by propitiating and invoking the gods were prime conditions of their survival.

They led at best a precarious existence, challenged and imperilled again and again, for no political regime succeeded in establishing itself on a secure and permanent footing. Though kingship had 'descended from heaven' and was indeed regarded as a supernatural institution, the king himself was never safe from the machinations of ambitious rivals. Yet, though dynasty followed dynasty, the Sumerians succeeded for a long time in imposing everywhere their civilization, their art, their religion and their writing, even on parts of the country where different ethnic and racial groups might have been expected to resist assimilation. There is no question that in the Diyala region, on the Upper Tigris and the Middle Euphrates, the Semites had, so far, received and taken over much from the Sumerians. But now they embarked on a venture calculated to make them masters of the country. They succeeded thanks to the leadership of a great warrior, Sargon, a man of obscure origin who suddenly emerged as the founder of a dynasty and an empire-builder.

191 - UR - BULL'S HEAD, FROM THE SOUNDBOX OF A HARP
(FIRST HALF, 3RD MILL.). — BAGHDAD MUSEUM

192

195

193

194

196

197

200

198

201

199

202

MESOPOTAMIAN SEAL IMPRESSIONS
OF THE PRE-SARGONID PERIOD

CHAPTER III

THE CITY STATES AND SUMER'S GOLDEN AGE
(UR, LAGASH, MARI, 2800-2470 B.C.)

The invention of writing, a new and decisive stage in the progress of civilization. The sign alphabets of Uruk and Jemdet Nasr. From picture writing to cuneiform script.

Architecture of the Pre-Sargonid period: shrines on lofty platforms, temples, palaces (al 'Ubaid, Khafaje, Mari, Kish).

Statuary and the cult rituals. Geometric patterning and realism in the sculpture of the Diyala region. Standardized statuary and the collection of portraits at the court of Mari. Queens, the 'great singer,' female worshippers.

Low relief. Its technique and inspiration: mythology, religion, history. Works from Lagash, Nippur, Khafaje, al 'Ubaid.

Ritual vases and their ornamentation.

Animal art and its realistic and mythological inspiration.

Inlays of ivory and shell. The great panel mosaics. The 'Standard' of Ur.

Artifacts in metal: statuettes, figurines, animals.

The 'royal' tombs of Ur. Their significance and their treasures.

PERIODS	SITES	ARCHITECTU
First Dynasty of Ur	UR	'Royal' Cemet
	AL 'UBAID	Temple of Ninhurs
	LAGASH	Plano-conve bricks
	URUK	Plano-conve bricks
	NIPPUR	Temple of E
	ADAB	
	SHURUPPAK	
	KISH	Palace
	ASHNUNNAK	Temple of A
	KHAFAJE	Temple Ov Temple of N Temple of S
	AGRAB	Temple of S
	ASSUR	Temple of Is
	MARI	Temple of Is
		Temple of Ninhurs
		Temple of Shamas
		Temple of Ish
		Temple of Ninni-Za
		Ziggurat

SCULPTURE	TERRACOTTA	METAL	SHELL AND IVORY	PAINTING	EGYPT	AEGEAN
...nale ...rshippers { Perforated plaques / Libation to Nannar; ...tue of ...temena		Heads of bulls gold, silver, bronze; Goblet and bowl of Shubad; Helmet of Meskalamdug; Weapons; Ram (gold, electrum, shell, lapis); Lion-headed eagle; Bulls; Lions (with bitumen core)	Standard (B.M.); Soundbox of harps and lyres; Gaming boards; Casket of Shubad; Cone mosaics; Decorative frieze		Old Kingdom (2780-2280)	Early Minoan II (2800-2400)
...ce-head ...Mesilim / Steles of Ur-Nanshe Vultures Dudu Ninhursag; ...Vor-...hipper ...atues ...udu	Figurines; Inlaid and engraved pottery					
{ Cult reliefs	Figurines				Zoser Saqqara Pyramid	
		Goat's head				
Worshipper statues	Inlaid and engraved pottery		Various elements		Kheops Khephren Mykerinos	
...or-...pper { Relief-plaques; ...or-...pper { Relief-plaques / Vases with reliefs	Pottery	Foundation figurines			Gizeh Pyramids	
...Vor-...pper { Vases with reliefs		Chariot Wrestlers				
Worshippers	Pottery Altars					
Ebih-il Lamgi-Mari Idi-Narum Statuary	Figurines		Standard Decorated dagger			
...tuary { Vase with reliefs			Various elements	Decoration of a chapel		
...tuary { Vase with reliefs			Various elements			
Iku-Shamagan Ur-Nanshe			Various elements			
			Various elements			
			Various elements			

204 - GODS IN COMBAT (SECOND HALF, 3RD MILL.) — MRS WILLIAM M. MOORE COLLECTION

IV

SARGON AND THE AKKADIAN EMPIRE

(2470-2285 B. C.)

THE rise to power of the Akkadians was probably due to a concerted reaction against the brutal aggressions of the Sumerian Lugalzaggisi, king of Uruk, who, by about 2500 B.C., had extended his iron rule over the whole of Mesopotamia. With fire and sword, for a quarter of a century, if the dynastic lists are to be trusted, the Sumerians controlled the whole area extending from the 'lower sea' to the 'upper sea,' i.e. from the Persian Gulf to the Mediterranean. Their despotic rule was brought to an end by an Akkadian soldier.

His father was of humble origin, a water carrier (*naq-me*). He himself was an officer, who, with the body of troops at his command, rebelled against the 'master of the lands.' We know nothing of the details or circumstances of his campaign; only that it succeeded. The rebel officer had Lugalzaggisi shut in a cage and exhibited his prisoner at the gate of the temple of Enlil at Nippur: a convincing demonstration of his victory and proof that the old order had been overthrown. The conqueror assumed a new name: Sharrukenu (lawful king). He has come down to history under the name of Sargon, and more specifically Sargon of Akkad or Agade, so as to connect him with the country and race from which he sprang. To

◄ 203 - SUSA (SECOND HALF, 3RD MILL.)
THE GODDESS INNINA. — LOUVRE

205 - 'THE FOUR QUARTERS OF THE WORLD.'

put the seal on his success, the new king decided to establish himself in a new city and make it his capital: this was Akkad, which archaeologists have not yet identified with certainty. The Sumerian kingdom of Lugalzaggisi soon fell entirely into the hands of Sargon, whose full title proudly proclaimed him to be lord and master of the 'four quarters of the world,' namely Amurru to the west, Subartu to the north, Sumer and Akkad to the south and Elam to the east.

While taking over the reins of political power, the Akkadians at first were sensible enough to carry on rather than undo the work of their predecessors in other spheres. There is no apparent break in the advance of civilization, no gap in artistic developments. Yet the Semitic temperament makes itself unmistakably felt, impressing the peculiar tinge of its sensibility and fantasy on works of art, and for a time counteracts the rigour and perhaps excessive hieraticism of the Sumerians. The ancient dykes were broken down, and the stream of life could flow more freely. But this freedom was far from countenancing disorder or anarchy. An autocrat like Sargon would certainly never have tolerated any lawlessness in his dominions.

The bronze head discovered at Nineveh—which can very plausibly be identified with the founder of the dynasty himself—leaves no room for doubt: here again we have an actual portrait. So striking is this face that it holds us spellbound, even though the flashing eyes have been gouged out. Their sockets stand empty, and one has been wantonly hacked and enlarged by a vandal hand. Yet the bronze mask has lost none of its nobility of character. A faint smile, at once ironic and disdainful, hovers on the fleshy, sensual lips. With his hair bound closely round his forehead and bunched at the nape of his neck in a chignon held by three gold rings, and with his elaborately curled, carefully groomed beard, Sargon takes his place in the line of the great dynasts whose headdress he has adopted. The helmet of Meskalamdug of Ur is no more delicately chiselled; and in itself

206 - NINEVEH - KING SARGON (?) (SECOND HALF, 3RD MILL.). — BAGHDAD MUSEUM

170

this fine bronze head proves that the ruler of Akkad was determined to safeguard his artistic heritage.

He showed the same fidelity to tradition in commemorating his victories. A diorite stele has battle scenes carved in the Sumerian manner. The scenes are set forth in rows, as in the time of Eannatum, and vultures and a great net figure in them. Their arrangement could scarcely be more orthodox. But in the reign of Rimush, Sargon's son, who ascended the throne at his father's death, artists began to break, if to a limited extent, with the old conventions. In the Louvre are some large fragments of a stele which also commemorated a battle. It keeps to the usual lay-out in superimposed registers, but a noticeable change has taken place in the representation of figures. Instead of being grouped in the compact phalanx of the Sumerians, the Akkadian fighting men move in looser

formations. Their arms and accoutrements are also different. They are more lightly clad and less hampered in their movements; moreover, armed as they are with bow and arrow, they must have been effective at long range. Fragmentary though it is, this Telloh stele already points the way to the stele of Naram-Sin.

Sargon's grandson, Naram-Sin was one of the greatest of Oriental rulers. Renowned both as a soldier and as a builder (he had a palace at Tell Brak, in the Khabur region), he led his armies in many victorious campaigns, which he sometimes commemorated on the spot, as for example at Pir-Hussein, deep in Kurdistan, to the northeast of Diarbekir. But the monument that immortalizes Naram-Sin is the great stele in the Louvre, erected originally at Sippar, city of the god Shamash, but discovered at Susa, to which it was carried off among the spoils of war some thousand years later. Here we find Akkadian art at its splendid best, expressing itself with its own peculiar genius and liberated entirely from disciplines of the past.

On this stele of pink sandstone, a monolithic boulder whose natural shape has been only slightly altered by the sculptor's chisel, fifteen figures are represented. The general effect produced is that of two contending armies, with eight soldiers on one side, seven on the other. The king in front of his roops stands head and shoulders

209 - SUSA - STELE OF SARGON. — LOUVRE
210 - TELLOH - STELE OF RIMUSH. — LOUVRE

211 - PIR-HUSSEIN - STELE OF NARAM-SIN
(SECOND HALF, 3RD MILL.). — ISTANBUL MUSEUM

212 - SUSA - STELE OF NARAM-SIN, DETAIL: THE KING TRAMPLING ENEMY SOLDIERS (SECOND HALF, 3RD MILL.). — LOUVRE

above them all. The setting is a wooded, mountainous region, that of the Lulubi. The Akkadian warriors are seen moving up the mountain side in a double column of light infantry, with flying colours, while the opposing army is in flight before them, crying for quarter. Naram-Sin tramples two entangled bodies, while another falls headlong from a rocky ledge. With his bow and battle-axe in one hand and his javelin in the other, helmeted like a god (he is wearing the horned crown), the king has reached the foot of a boldly schematized mountain. In the sky shine two stars, alluding to the auspicious deities who have presided over a victory no longer in the balance, the enemy forces having been reduced to a motley horde of dead, wounded and fugitives. It is interesting to compare this work with the Stele of the Vultures; both figure in the same room at the Louvre. Their spirit and manner are strikingly different: one is all massive strength and power; the other, all aerial

213 - SUSA - STELE OF NARAM-SIN. — LOUVRE

214-215 - SUSA - ROBE OF MANISHTUSU AND OBELISK OF MANISHTUSU (SECOND HALF, 3RD MILL.). — LOUVRE

lightness, but none the less impressive. In the first, chronological order is observed with rigorous accuracy, answering to a desire for clarity and precision. Noteworthy in the second are the sculptor's freedom of handling and his soaring imagination. The Sumerians keep to the analytical method; the Akkadians aim at and achieve an immediate, brilliantly successful synthesis of the essential, determinant elements of the scene. These fifteen figures carved in pink sandstone bring to mind Velazquez's famous painting, *The Surrender of Breda,* in which twenty-eight lances conjure up a whole army. Genius alone can bring off effects like these. And the anonymous maker of this Akkadian stele was certainly a genius, indeed one of the greatest sculptors of all time.

216 - SUSA - FEET OF A STATUE OF NARAM-SIN
(SECOND HALF, 3RD MILL.). — LOUVRE

Sculpture in the round of the Akkadian epoch is less well represented than that of the Pre-Sargonid period. The royal statues have been systematically mutilated, and broken fragments are all we have to go on. But, even so, they prove that the sculptors had thoroughly mastered their medium and did not shrink from pitting themselves against one of the hardest of all stones: diorite. In this close-grained stone, polished to perfection by tools of which we still know very little, several statues were carved for Manishtusu, son of Sargon. In one of these, of which only the robe survives, fringed diagonally with a row of knotted tassels, we still can sense the very pulse of life, subtly conveyed by the slanting undulations of the robe. Of another only two bare feet remain, resting on a pedestal whose inscription justifies us in assigning it to the reign of Naram-Sin. The whole Neo-Sumerian revival (to be dealt with presently) is not merely foreshadowed here, but has become a *fait accompli*. Already we find, fully realized in the monumental inscriptions of the period, that aesthetic quality which entitles them to rank as works of art in their own right. Thus the obelisk of Manishtusu, a block of diorite entirely covered with inscriptions is both an invaluable historical document and an artistic achievement heralding, half a millennium ahead, the Code of Hammurabi.

217 - BISMAYA (ADAB) - MAN'S HEAD (SECOND HALF, 3RD MILL.). — CHICAGO

A few nameless heads in a softer stone have come down to us. One of these, found at Bismaya (the ancient Adab), portrays a bearded man wearing a turban. Another comes from Assur and represents a woman. The features in both cases have been softened; every trace of harshness has been eliminated. These heads, which doubtless belonged originally to full-length worshipper statues, are sculptured in the great tradition, and the only clue to their dating lies in certain stylistic peculiarities, the turban for example. Even so, they can seldom be dated positively, for identical types were reproduced century after century, and in the absence of other criteria it seems to us impos-

218 - ASSUR - WOMAN'S HEAD (SECOND HALF, 3RD MILL.). — BERLIN MUSEUM

219 - HEAD OF A BEARDED MAN (SECOND HALF, 3RD MILL.). — LOUVRE

sible to distinguish Akkadian sculpture from later work, contemporary with the Third Dynasty of Ur or even with the Isin and Larsa dynasties. Such is the case with the head of a bearded man, in the Louvre, pursing his lips, with deep-set eyes carved in relief; this work could be assigned with equal plausibility to any of these periods.

The same difficulty occurs in dating other objects. Were it not for the stone tablet and its inscription copying the text engraved on the metal plaque which a roaring lion seems to be defending against some approaching enemy, we should never have ventured to assign this figurine, acquired by the Louvre in 1948, to the Akkadian period. Cast in bronze, the animal is represented lunging forward with its paws resting on a tablet of the same metal. The shaggy head, with its slightly projecting ears and stylized mane, is fiercely alert, charged through and through with nervous energy.

This work anticipates the realism characteristic of animal sculpture in the Larsa period. But the inscription leaves no room for doubt: the piece comes from the Subartu region, in other words from northern Mesopotamia, and dates in all probability to the beginning of the Akkadian period. Though on a smaller scale, this lion dedicated by Tisari, king of Urkish, is in no way inferior to the bulls of Ur (later it was to have a perfect counterpart in the dog of Sumu-ilu, found at Telloh). Here we have yet another example of the extraordinary dynamism of Akkadian art, whose chief concern was, everywhere and always, to render movement and life with vivid actuality.

220 - URKISH - LION AND FOUNDATION TABLET (MID-3 MILL.). — LOUVRE ▸

223 - IMPRESSION - SEAL OF SHARKALISHARRI (SECOND HALF, 3RD MILL.). — DE CLERCQ COLLECTION

The same observations hold good in the field of glyptics, a minor art no doubt, but one in which the Akkadians gave abundant proof both of their conservatism and of their originality. If a typical illustration had to be singled out, there could be no hesitating: our choice would unequivocally fall on the cylinder seal of Sharkalisharri. A single theme is treated, but treated twice, reversed. Kneeling, with the lower half of his body seen from the side, and his trunk and head full-face, Gilgamesh, the Sumerian hero, is holding a vase with both hands; a buffalo with annelated horns, tilted at a curious angle so as to bring out their breadth and sweep to full effect, drinks the water gushing from the vase. Both man and animal are treated with a vigour and forcefulness that emphasize their volume. Carved on a large slab of stone, the work

224 - MARI - SEAL IMPRESSION, DETAIL:
GILGAMESH GRAPPLING WITH A
BUFFALO. — DAMASCUS MUSEUM

would have been in high relief. As it is, this delicate piece of sunk carving has been executed on a Lilliputian scale; a fact that can but enhance our admiration of its expert craftsmanship. The scene is set in mountainous country, beside a stream suggested by a wave pattern running between two imbricated bands. This is obviously a mythological subject, but its meaning eludes us, as will almost invariably be the case from now on.

To this initial manner, whose realism contains a certain hieratic element, the Akkadians added other, livelier modes of expression. The earlier theme of the two friends, Enkidu and Gilgamesh, fighting wild animals, is one of their favourites and they treat it with exuberance and even gaiety, for the triumph of the two heroes is always a foregone conclusion. They are more than mere slayers of wild beasts; they make sport with them and put them through paces of the most diverse kinds. Lions and buffaloes are no match for these Herculean athletes, who have no trouble in swinging them aloft or cracking their joints like matchsticks. Here, kneeling and throttling a huge lion, Gilgamesh is about to send the beast flying through the air; elsewhere we see him resting his feet on a buffalo's neck and gripping a horn and hind leg, as a preliminary to rending it limb from limb with his bare hands.

225 - SEAL IMPRESSION, DETAIL: GILGAMESH GRAPPLING WITH A LION. — BRITISH MUSEUM

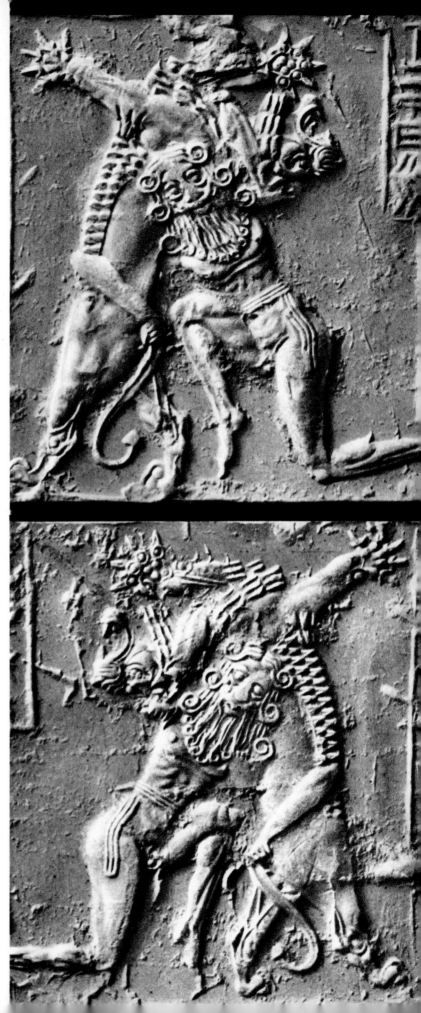

226 - SEAL IMPRESSION - MYTH OF ETANA (SECOND HALF, 3RD MILL.). — BERLIN MUSEUM

Akkadian glyptic art did not confine itself to glorifying the exploits of Gilgamesh and his companion. It was also a medium of expression for theological and dogmatic conceptions, which had never been so fully dealt with before. Hitherto the gods had made only very discreet appearances. Now we find them engaged in multifarious activities, many of which seem of a quite new type. Religion, more than culture, was feeling the after-effects of the change of government. The Sumerian gods had been assimilated by the Akkadians and, under other names, had taken their places in the Semitic pantheon. Utu-Babbar, the sun god, became Shamash; Ishtar, goddess of love and war, superseded Inanna; Ea, the water god, was an extension of Enki; Sin, the moon god, eclipsed Nannar. They are all shown performing specific tasks and represented with a remarkable wealth of detail, but for the most part in a language which for us remains enigmatic.

True, we have no difficulty in recognizing the myth of Etana, the shepherd carried into the empyrean by a mighty eagle, and there is something almost touching in the childlike candour with which the tale is told. The sheep dogs are gazing helplessly skywards, puzzled by their master's sudden disappearance. As against this, however, how many other scenes defy interpretation! A god standing in a chariot drawn by a winged lion with a naked woman on its back, brandishing lightning flashes, advances towards a worshipper who offers him a libation. The scene is easily described, but we should be hard put to it to say what it means. The same is true of another cylinder

227 - SEAL IMPRESSION - PROCESSION OF GODS (SECOND HALF, 3RD MILL.). — PIERPONT MORGAN COLLECTION

228 - MARI - SEAL IMPRESSION - THE GOD ANU AND OTHER DEITIES (SECOND HALF, 3RD MILL.). — DAMASCUS MUSEUM

189

229 - VASE WITH A CAPTIVE, FRAGMENT. — LOUVRE

seal, found recently at Mari, showing the god Anu seated on a mountain top, and beneath him two ducks (?) vomiting streams of water over which tree goddesses and a bearded divinity with a long spear are advancing. These are only a few examples; we could go on citing similar pieces *ad infinitum*. One and all reveal the will to expression, the impulse to communication, which underlies all Akkadian art. But at the same time they testify to the remarkable polyvalence and complexity of Akkadian religious thought, whose tenets and formulas were being constantly enlarged and enriched in an attempt to solve the endless problems set by the human condition. Heaven and earth were intermingling.

The surprising thing is that these new trends of thought should have found expression in a minor art, but for which we might have remained ignorant of their very existence. Akkadian sculpture in the round seldom represented worshippers, and never any god. But innumerable cylinder seals go to show that the divine iconography had been fully worked out and that gods in human form were conceived as taking an active part in mundane affairs. Yet they were powerless to spare the Akkadian kingdom the ordeal of invasion and its aftermath of sweeping political changes. The old dynastic lists remind us of the instability of the times when, after a series of the names of the rulers who followed each other in quick succession on the throne, we find this disillusioned query: 'Who was king? Who was not king?' Its foundations undermined by anarchy, the State fell an easy prey to the foreign invader.

230 - VASE WITH A CAPTIVE, DETAIL (SECOND HALF, 3RD MILL.). — LOUVRE

231

232

234

233

235

236

237

238

239

240

241

242

SEAL IMPRESSIONS
OF THE AKKADIAN PERIOD

CHAPTER IV

SARGON
AND
THE AKKADIAN EMPIRE
(2470-2285 B.C.)

Sargon of Akkad, a Semitic officer, puts an end to the supremacy of Lugalzaggisi, Sumerian king of Uruk. He founds a dynasty which for nearly two centuries rules all Mesopotamia. This political upheaval makes no break in the evolution of art, but the Semitic temperament, with its sensibility and fantasy, softens and tones down the previous rigour and hieraticism of Sumerian art.

This is clearly brought out in the bronze head from Nineveh and above all in the Stele of Naram-Sin, in the Louvre, in which we find the problem of narrating a military exploit solved in a very different way from that of the earlier Stele of the Vultures.

The Akkadians leave so indelible an imprint on sculpture in the round that their tradition maintains itself throughout the Neo-Sumerian phase that follows, and even down to later periods contemporary with the Isin and Larsa dynasties.

In this great artistic flowering, glyptics occupy a prominent place, for they introduce us to a numerous and singularly active company of gods, portrayed with a wealth of detail. But the difficulty of interpreting these enigmatic scenes remains virtually insuperable. Except for Gilgamesh and Etana, literary tradition seldom or never throws any light on the iconography that finds expression in them.

KINGS	SITES	ARCHITECTU
Sargon	AKKAD (OR AGADE)	
Rimush	LAGASH	
Manishtusu	SUSA	
Naram-Sin	UR SUSA MARI BRAK PIR HUSSEIN	Palace
Sharkalisharri and the last kings		
	ADAB ASSUR UR MARI	
2285 Invasion of the Guti End of the Akkadian Dynasty		

SCULPTURE	TERRACOTTA	METAL	SHELL AND MOTHER OF PEARL	PAINTING	EGYPT	AEGEAN
{ Cylinder Seals Gilgamesh and Enkidu, Adda	Figurines	Bronze Head (Nineveh)			End of the Old Kingdom (2423-2280)	Early Minoan III (2300-2100)
{ Stele Cylinder Seals						First palace at Mallia
Obelisk Robe Bust		Foundation Figurines (Urkish)				
Stele		Bronze Vases				
Stele						
{ Cylinder Seal (de Clercq)						
Man's Head Woman's Head Cylinder Seals Cylinder Seals						

244 - TELLOH - CYLINDER SEAL - EAGLE AND CAPRIDAE (22ND CENTURY B.C.). — BAGHDAD MUSEUM

V

THE GUTI AND THE
NEO-SUMERIAN REACTION

(2285-2016 B.C.)

FROM time immemorial the Mesopotamian basin had been a tempting prize for less prosperous neighbours, who looked enviously upon this fertile land, watered all the year round by two great rivers, where the sun ensured thriving crops and abundant harvests. Races that settled there, even the hardiest, tended to grow soft and time and again the region fell, like a ripe fruit, into the hands of enterprising hordes, sweeping down from the mountains. Such were the Guti: wild nomads who descended to the plains in full force from the northeast and irrevocably sealed the fate of the Akkadians. Of what actually took place in the course of this invasion and the overthrow of the established regime, we know little. It is certain, however, that the enslaved Sumerians were not displeased at being rid of their Akkadian overlords, even though their place was taken by barbarians. The Guti seem to have had no great political ambitions. They were content to

245 - FRENCH EXCAVATIONS AT TELLOH (LAGASH)

settle down in a fertile country and live on the fat of the land. According
to the dynastic lists, the Guti occupation spanned nearly a century,
but the number of kings listed in the period (twenty-one) shows that
the average reign lasted only a few years—which implies that the
central power was unstable and continually being challenged.

This instability suggests why it was that the largest Sumerian cities
—Uruk, Ur and Lagash—were so easily able to establish themselves
on a quasi-independent footing in their dealings with these transitory
overlords. And in course of time the independence tacitly granted
them enabled the bolder Sumerian leaders to break free altogether,
until the day came when the occupants, shorn of their power, were
either assimilated with the original inhabitants or driven out.

This complete reversal of the situation was the work of the so-called
Neo-Sumerians. To them we owe the re-establishment of political
and cultural conditions approximating to those which had prevailed
before the advent of the Akkadians. Still, it was impossible to eradicate
the effects of three centuries of history. While the Guti had contributed
little or nothing of their own, this was not so with the Akkadians. Under
them, culture had progressed, and their artists had left an imprint that
could be neither disregarded nor effaced. So that the Neo-Sumerians,

in reverting to the past, inevitably had to reckon with the Akkadian interlude, whose beneficent effect had been to temper, mitigate and soften the rigours of earlier Sumerian art.

Two cities stand out with exceptional brilliance in this new cultural phase, both of them in southern Mesopotamia: Lagash and Ur. There has been much discussion lately of the political relations between them and the extent to which one was dependent on the other. Lagash was never the seat of a dynasty, even though its famous ruler, Gudea, seems to have been more than a match for his immediate neighbours. Ur, however, had political ambitions and pursued them at the expense of Uruk. Ur-Nammu made it a royal city and founded the Third Dynasty, whose five kings ruled for more than a century (2124-2016) over the whole of Mesopotamia. To use our own chronological terms, this brings us to the twenty-second and twenty-first centuries B.C.; the third millennium was drawing to a close. In all parts of the world, the period is known as the Bronze Age, but for Sumer it was also undoubtedly a new Golden Age.

Any doubts one may have of this are dispelled at the sight of the great architectural ruins scattered over the Mesopotamian plain, works of a boldness and magnitude such as only strong, long-lasting governments can have undertaken and carried through. Sargon had reigned for over half a century. Dungi (or Shulgi), king of Ur, occupied the throne for upwards of fifty years, while his predecessor, Ur-Nammu, had held it for eighteen years. Countless monuments bear the imprint of these two rulers. The baked bricks which were now produced in very large quantities and used instead of stone were marked, before being fired, with the royal seal in the form of a brief text or legend either stamped on them or inscribed by hand. Thus the names and pedigrees of these great builders were recorded on the monuments themselves, not only in the foundations as hitherto. Gudea's city, Lagash, unfortunately, being in a more ruinous state than the others, has no place in a discussion of the staged towers, or ziggurats, in building which the Neo-Sumerians excelled.

246 - MATRIX INSCRIBED UR-NINGIRSU. — BAGHDAD MUSEUM

247 - UR - THE THIRD-DYNASTY ZIGGURAT (22ND-21ST CENTURIES B.C.)

Mention has already been made of the elevation given certain shrines in the Mesopotamian plain. Built to begin with on a simple platform or terrace, they were raised higher and higher as time went on. Such edifices are known to have existed as early as the first half of the third millennium, for we occasionally find them represented on contemporary cylinder seals; but none has come down to us from that remote period. The Akkadians do not seem to have improved on this type of architecture. But the Third Dynasty of Ur took it over and developed it with ever-increasing boldness. All the Sumerian cities (except Lagash) are still dominated by these great mounds, now more or less eroded. Ur, Uruk, Nippur, Larsa, Eridu—each has its ziggurat. From three to seven storeys in elevation, built entirely of brick (unbaked within, baked on the outer surface), these monuments remind one at first sight of the Egyptian pyramids, and in particular of the so-called 'stepped' pyramid of Saqqara. But we must not be misled by a superficial resemblance; actually, they served a very different purpose. The pyramids were always designed as tombs; the ziggurats belonged exclusively to a domain of religious architecture, of whose nature and function there

200

248 - UR - RECONSTRUCTION OF THE THIRD-DYNASTY ZIGGURAT (22ND-21ST CENTURIES B.C.)

can no longer be any doubt. The ziggurat forms a gigantic pedestal designed to facilitate the descent of the gods to the earth. No pains were spared to provide a place of reception worthy of the celestial visitant. A temple of welcome stood at the top of the tower, and a second shrine at ground level to accommodate the god during his sojourn. The two were connected by stairways along which processions mounted and descended, and which formed, as it were, a permanent line of communication between heaven and earth. The ziggurat served as a ladder, like the one 'with angels of God ascending and descending on it' which Jacob saw in his dream at Bethel (Genesis, XXVIII, 12).

When we remember that in these gigantic structures only materials of small dimensions were employed (no brick used in them exceeded a cubit in length, i.e. about fifteen inches), we can better appreciate the magnitude of the builders' task. Millions of elements went to their making and masons, engineers and architects had to cope with numberless problems. How well they succeeded we can see for ourselves: for four thousand years the ziggurat of Ur has withstood the destructive violence of man and the ravages of time. And neither dealt with it gently.

A

B

C

D

E

F

250 - TELLOH (LAGASH) - HYPOGEUM OF THE PATESIS UR-NINGIRSU AND UGME (22ND CENTURY B.C.)

In view of such achievements as this, all the others seem less surprising: temples, palaces, groups of dwelling-houses, abodes of the dead. Ur itself offers a complete series of these. Nothing could be more impressive than the hypogea of the kings Dungi (Shulgi) and Bur-Sin, with their stairways leading down to tombs of baked brick, with ogival doors; unfortunately their tombs had already been rifled when archaeologists found them. No less impressive are the underground funerary chambers at Lagash of two *patesis*, Ur-Ningirsu and Ugme. Much damage had been done, but hundreds of offerings were found in them (figurines and cylinders in particular), brought in ancient times by citizens who made pilgrimages to Lagash and left tokens of their piety.

249 - UR - (A) 'QUIET STREET.' — (B) CHAPEL OF PA-SAG.
(C) 'PATERNOSTER STREET.' — (D, E) STAIRS.
(F) HYPOGEUM OF SHULGI (22ND-21ST CENTURIES B.C.)

203

The Neo-Sumerian period is outstanding not only for its architecture but also for its sculpture. In this field Lagash dominated the whole region, and even the whole century, with a production as remarkable for its quantity as for its quality. We owe it almost entirely to a single man, that enigmatic personage Gudea. He ruled for at least fifteen years, perhaps longer, but either declined the title of king or was for some reason debarred from assuming it; instead he contented himself with the position of *patesi*, a high-ranking official exercising both religious and political functions, but standing below the highest echelon in the hierarchy of the State. He made of Lagash an unrivalled cultural centre. Palaces, temples and works of public utility were filled with objects of art, and in particular with statues of Gudea himself. Over thirty of these statues are now known to exist, most them in museums, a few in private collections; they form the most impressive body of sculpture created at the behest of a single man, in a single place, that is to be found in the whole history of art.

254 - GUDEA WITH 'NARROW SHOULDERS'   255 - GUDEA WITH 'BROAD SHOULDERS' (22ND CENTURY B.C.). — LOUVRE

The Louvre is justly proud of its fine series of Gudea figures. These beautifully executed works in diorite and dolerite—stone so hard as to present a serious challenge to the skill of even the ablest sculptor —at once convey an impression of majestic serenity and breathe a religious fervour seldom, if ever, expressed with so much power and simplicity.

256 - TELLOH - GUDEA 'A' (22ND CENTURY B.C.). — LOUVRE

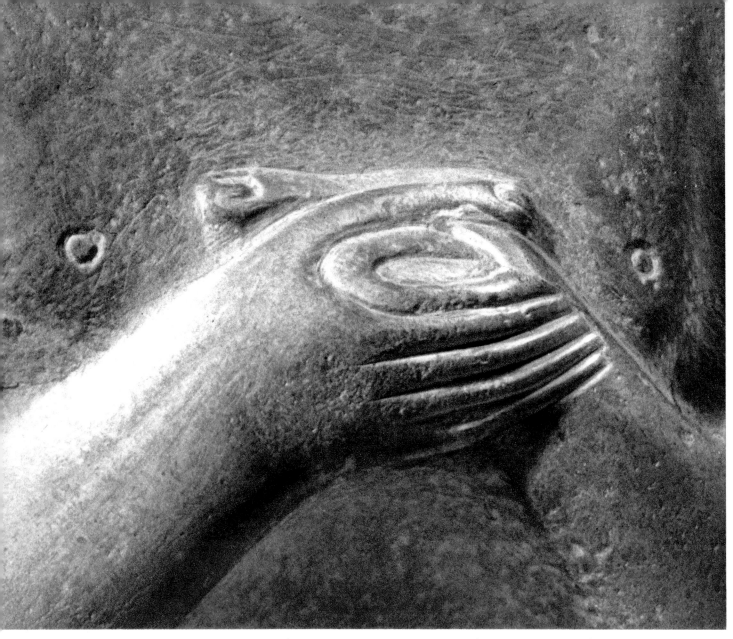

259 - STATUE OF LUGALKISALSI'S GRANDSON, DETAIL: CLASPED HANDS (MID-THIRD MILLENNIUM). — LOUVRE

Gudea always had himself portrayed with clasped hands entering the presence of the god. For all the damage they did to these sculptures, their ancient desecrators failed to rob them of their numinous power, a power their creators had both the intention and the capacity to express. The black or greenish blue stone in which they are carved has preserved an extraordinary 'density' adding to their monumental effect. Gudea is dressed with monkish simplicity: a straight-falling robe, leaving the right shoulder and arm bare; a few folds under the armpit, others on the left forearm; a narrow border to the robe; no more. Plain material, unadorned, unembroidered. The feet are massive, but the hands wonderfully delicate, with tapering fingers and finely chiselled nails.

260 - TELLOH - STATUE OF GUDEA, DETAIL: CLASPED HANDS (22ND CENTURY B.C.). — LOUVRE

Many of these statues have been decapitated, but the heads of
several have been retrieved. The one at first called the 'Turbaned
Head' (it was not then known whom it represented) is unquestionably
a portrait of Gudea. Paradoxically enough, it is a likeness all the more
convincing for the mutilation it has suffered. With its staring eyes,
high cheek-bones, undershot jaw and sharply defined mouth, this is
the face of a self-willed ruler, in the prime of life, who insists that his
orders are obeyed. What the orders were is revealed by the inscriptions which often overflow the tablets, and sometimes spread across the
front of his robe or run round it. These are especially prominent in
the two seated Gudeas, one with the plan of a building engraved on a

263 - TELLOH - (A, B) GUDEA WORSHIPPING. — COPENHAGEN MUSEUM   264 - TELLOH - GUDEA WITH FLOWING VASE. — PRIVATE COLL.

tablet in his lap, the other about to set to work with stylus and ruler, instruments of the architect.   Only once, instead of clasping his hands, is Gudea shown holding to his breast the vase from which the waters of fertility flow: a reminder of the benefits he has conferred on his country, through the intermediary of course of the deities he invokes, in particular Ningirsu, the city god, Ningizzida, his tutelary god, and Bau and Gatumdug, two female divinities.

Gudea, we may be fairly certain, had himself portrayed exactly as he was, without idealization; he is short and sturdy, his head deep-sunk between his shoulders, with a short, thick neck.   A careful comparison of the heads reveals that each successive sculptor took account of his model's age and, as a result, we have a series of portraits showing us what Gudea looked like from about twenty-five to forty.   A wise administrator, devoted to the cause of peace, Gudea kept his ambitions within bounds.   It was above all as a patron of arts and letters that he sought to be remembered.   Thanks to him, and to a propensity he seems to have had for portraiture, we are very well acquainted with Neo-Sumerian sculpture in the round.

265 - TELLOH - GUDEA WORSHIPPING. UNINSCRIBED STATUE (22ND CENTURY B.C.). — LOUVRE

Gudea's son, Ur-Ningirsu, did not share his passion for the arts. Yet we owe to him one statue which is a masterpiece in its own right. If it is difficult, in view of its mutilated condition, to do justice to the bust in Berlin, the headless statue in the Louvre is remarkable and in keeping with the finest traditions of Sumerian art. Carved in gypseous alabaster, a stone much softer than diorite, it reproduces many features of the Gudea statue 'A' illustrated on page 207: it has the same simplicity, the same aristocratic elegance. Now in the Metropolitan Museum, New York, the head with its turban recalls the portraits of Gudea in his youth. The great novelty of this statue is the decoration of the base, with its double procession of kneeling tributaries carrying baskets containing vases. The figures are generally believed to represent foreigners, presumably Semites. Their attitude has a submissiveness and deference which one wonders how Ur-Ningirsu succeeded in exacting. But the scene once more illustrates the familiar gesture of the conqueror lording it over his enemy captives, who in the present instance can probably count themselves lucky to be getting away with their lives.

Kings were not the only ones to commission work from the sculptors. Apart from royal statues, the Louvre has several small heads also in diorite, which are likewise marvels of realism.

TELLOH - (21ST CENTURY B.C.).
267 - UR-NINGIRSU. — BERLIN MUSEUM.
268 - UR-NINGIRSU. — LOUVRE

269 - TELLOH - UR-NINGIRSU, DETAIL: BASE WITH TRIBUTARIES (21ST CENTURY B.C.). — LOUVRE

270 - TELLOH - HEAD OF A YOUNG MAN (21ST CENTURY B.C.)   271 - HEAD OF A MAN (22ND-21ST CENTURIES B.C.). — LOUVRE

Instances are these heads of beardless young men, one thin-faced, the other plump, obviously done straight from the life.   Female figures are rarer.   The most famous (it has survived in several copies) is a statue of a female worshipper—with clasped hands—which, with some plausibility but no real certitude, has been identified as Gudea's wife. Clad in a two-piece costume decorated with braids and buckles, this lady of Lagash wears a necklet of superimposed rings; her hair is caught up in a kerchief with a narrow head-band.

272 - TELLOH - WOMAN WITH A KERCHIEF (GUDEA'S WIFE?) (22ND CENTURY B.C.). — LOUVRE

This survey of sculpture in the round may conclude with a series of small human-headed bulls. Falling over each ear is a twisted coil of hair, framing the mild face. All have a small hollow scooped in their backs, and invariably found empty. What it contained is uncertain: incense or unguents perhaps; unless the animals were the attributes of a divinity, whose statues were plugged into the holes. Anyhow it seems certain that they represented beneficent powers. The four extant examples all appear to come from Lagash; why they should be confined to one particular city is unknown.

When they reappear several centuries later as guardians of Assyrian palaces, the bulls are depicted walking and equipped with wings. So that, after surviving in the form of statuettes in the Neo-Sumerian period, the human-headed bull of ancient glyptic art has, by the first millennium, become once again a colossus.

Except for the Baghdad Museum, the Louvre alone possesses a collection of them. Thanks to an inscription on a recently acquired example, they can now be dated with certainty to the time of Gudea. Wearing a crown adorned with a superimposed series of horns, tapering off as they pile up, the bull is always shown in side view, facing right or left, with its head slewed round towards the spectator, its carefully waved beard curled up at the tips.

TELLOH (22ND CENTURY B.C.)
276 - (A, B) BULLS. — LOUVRE
277 - BULL. — BAGHDAD MUSEUM

279 - UR - STELE OF UR-NAMMU, DETAIL: THE GOD NANNAR (22ND CENTURY B.C.). — UNIVERSITY MUSEUM, PHILADELPHIA

The Sumerian renaissance also bore fruit in another branch of art: the bas-relief. Excavations at Lagash and Ur have yielded several examples, but all are badly damaged and incomplete. Gudea himself boasts in one of his inscriptions of having erected seven steles in one shrine. The stele executed for Ur-Nammu at Ur is very large, measuring almost ten feet in height; it testifies to his veneration for the gods Nannar and Ningal and commemorates his share in the building of the ziggurat. Here one is immediately struck by the return to the traditional lay-out in terms of superimposed registers and it reminds

280 - UR - STELE OF UR-NAMMU (22ND CENTURY B.C.)

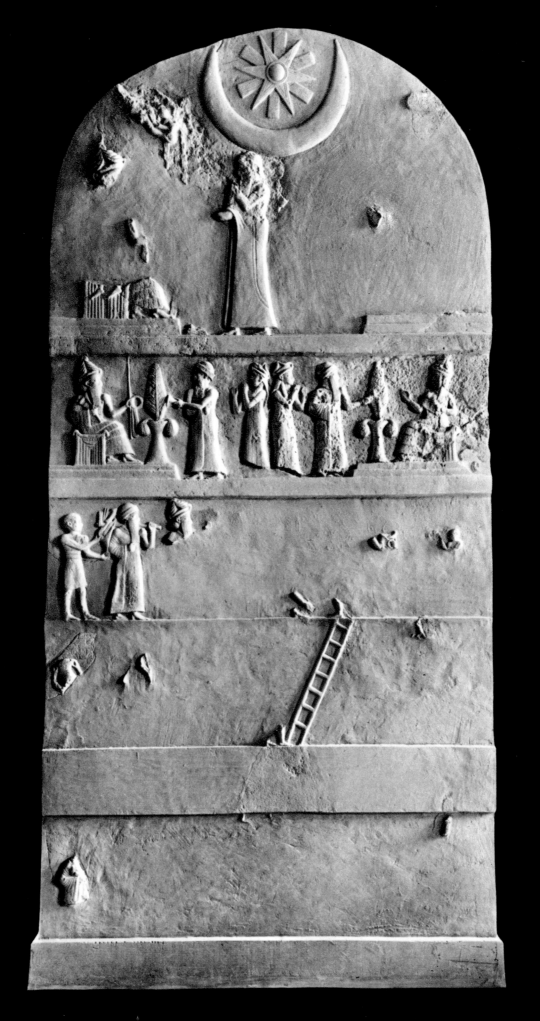

us yet again of the concern for clarity and precision that remained throughout the ages an essential trait of the Sumerian character.

On this stele, the king is seen twice making the same gesture of libation at the foot of a plant rising out of a funnel-shaped stand. On the left he pours out a libation to Ningal, on the right to Nannar. In both cases a goddess is standing by, her hands raised in the ritual gesture of intercession. The repetition of the king's figure, facing first one way, then the other, may well be no more than a conventional stylistic device for representing a rite actually performed not twice, but only once in the presence of the divine couple, seated side by side.

Also to be noted here is the implication that the gods are more involved than ever in the affairs of men, and ready to assist them in all sorts of circumstances. First in religious ceremonies; afterwards, in a scene where we see the king with a mason's tools on his shoulder walking to the workyard of the ziggurat. There is an amusing touch here,

228

282 - UR - STELE OF UR-NAMMU, DETAIL: THE KING WORSHIPPING NANNAR (ABOVE) AND CARRYING A MASON'S TOOLS (BELOW)

showing how observant was the artist of the life around him: the tools carried by the king are so heavy that a servant steps forward to steady them on his master's shoulder, while the king himself remains intent on following the god who leads the way.

The Sumerians were obsessed at this time with gods who acted as intercessors or mediators. It was felt that no one, not even a king, could gain a hearing from the celestial powers of higher rank, unless accompanied and 'presented' by a personal or tutelary divinity. Such presentation scenes are repeated over and over again on cylinder seals, from which however the complicated themes of Akkadian theology have now been altogether eliminated.

On a stele in Berlin, we see Gudea, bare-headed and deferent, following behind Ningizzida, recognizable by the dragon heads rising from his shoulders. The god holds the wrist of his protégé with a grip so firm that he seems about to drag him by force towards a higher deity, whose body, unfortunately, is so badly disfigured as to make identification very much a matter of guess-work. Streams of water pouring down in front of him certainly suggest Enki, the water god, but Ningirsu, the 'nourisher of the fields,' could also have been thus represented. What remains of the iconography of the other participants shows them all to be bearded. Dressed in long flounced robes leaving the shoulder bare, they wear the horned crown indicative of high rank: impassive celebrants steeped in self-importance, yet at the same time full of deference for the decisions to be made by the supreme court of

the gods. The divine hierarchy called for strict discipline, and this obtained at every level. Yet how characteristic it is of human nature that the Neo-Sumerians should have besought the favour of their omnipotent gods through the intercession of female divinities! For it is a goddess, in the great majority of cases, who pleads for the suppliant. And sometimes, when a particular request has to be made in the course of a presentation, it is a goddess who acts as intermediary, raising her hands in a gesture which appears to us one of supplication rather than of benediction.

For the Neo-Sumerians were much concerned with establishing frequent and direct relations between gods and men. Not that the priest had been by-passed, far from it; but there seemed now to be a whole region of man's life that lay beyond the ambit of the priesthood. And what was true of the average citizen must have been doubly true of the king, who moreover had always been regarded as a sacred personage, empowered on earth to carry out the behests of heaven. The Akkadians had deified Naram-Sin by crowning him with the horned tiara reserved for gods. The Neo-Sumerians were equally bold. Dungi (Shulgi), king of Ur, was known as 'the divine' in his lifetime. After his death the people of Lagash gave the same title to Gudea.

287 - SMALL PLAQUE - WOMAN AND DEDICATION TO
NINSUN (22ND-21ST CENTURIES B.C.). — LOUVRE

23

288 - TELLOH - STELE OF GUDEA, FRAGMENT: THE
GODDESS BAU (22ND CENTURY B.C.). — LOUVRE

In Pre-Sargonid times, the worshipper had been content to lay a statuette (with which he identified himself) at the foot of the god's throne. Now he expected to be presented in person to his god and to make his prayer directly. True, he was escorted by intercessors, but piety had certainly grown bolder.

The representation of the gods in human form, though now the rule, did not altogether exclude the use of symbolic figures. To this conservative spirit we owe several fine pieces of work, such as the human-headed bulls mentioned above, sculptured in the round, and some equally fine lion-muzzles, executed in more or less high relief, which once adorned a basin. Other muzzles embellished Gudea's mace. These works mark a significant advance on the same animal forms, sketchily outlined, pursuing and snapping at each other, that had figured on the mace of Mesilim, king of Kish. Yet what we find here, still alive, are the old traditions of relief carving on stone vessels, and this is confirmed by the libation vase illustrated here, bearing Gudea's name. Its decoration is wholly symbolic: two snakes, twined round a pole, rise up to the lip of the vase, as if to drink the liquid poured from it, while two winged dragons stand guard behind them, holding in their front paws a staff with a loop at the top.

These monsters must have inspired the most salutary awe, for they

289 - TELLOH - GUDEA'S LIBATION GOBLET (22ND CENTURY B.C.). — LOUVRE

290 - TELLOH (22ND B.C.) - CENTURY COVER OF A LAMP. — LOUVRE   291 - GUDEA'S MACE-HEAD. — LOUVRE

combine several dangerous animals in one; the eagle contributes its wings and talons, the snake its head, the panther its body, and the scorpion its poison-charged tail. This composite beast has divine prerogatives: witness its horned crown. There can be no room for doubt: this is the animal attribute of the god Ningizzida, and as such protects Gudea, while ensuring the fertility of his dominions through the twining snake accompanying it. Here we have the origin of the caduceus, which through the ages has retained its virtue as a beneficent emblem.

This libation vase has much in common with the cover of a lamp on which we again find two snakes so closely interlocked that we can hardly tell them apart. In trying to follow their meanders, we realize that a third snake (whose head is missing) is included. The pattern of their bodies, beautifully conceived and executed, forms a network of loose meshes strong enough to stand any strain. No stone could better lend itself to these effects than this greenish blue steatite.

The Neo-Sumerians were equally skilful as metal-workers. Leaving aside tools and weapons, we shall deal here only with the foundation

237

figurines, cast in bronze, which have been unearthed in great numbers at Lagash, Ur, Uruk, Nippur and Susa (Susa, now in Iran, then being politically dependent on Sumer). There are three stock subjects which are never departed from: a kneeling god driving a peg into the ground; a basket carrier; and a recumbent bull. All these figurines have one feature in common: they taper off to a point. Nor is this just a coincidence. This point was regarded as having the special power of pinning down evil spirits beneath the building and so preventing them from doing any injury to the occupants or owner.

Of even greater interest, however, than their specific function is the renewed conjunction of god and man in foundation figures, involving a revival of the use of a numinous symbol, for example in the figuration of the bull. Here again, whatever explanation of these figures is proposed, we realize how solidly rooted were the traditions underlying Neo-Sumerian art. The construction of an edifice was evidently a momentous step, an operation that, unless due precautions were taken, might well unleash a horde of malignant powers. It was to foil these powers that the Mesopotamians made a point of burying statuettes or figurines at the corners of new buildings and under the thresholds of doors. This was certainly preferable to the practice of immolating a new-born babe or a young child, as was done at Jericho by Hiel the Beth-elite (I Kings, XVI, 34). 'Foundation sacrifices' are still customary today, though limited to burying a few dated coins in the ground along with a parchment inscribed with the appropriate names. The idea of propitiating infernal powers is now quite forgotten, yet this is the origin of the world-wide practice of laying the 'foundation stone.'

292 - FOUNDATION FIGURINES - (A, B) TELLOH. — (C) SUSA. — (D) NIPPUR

A   B   C   D

In addition to this large output of works in metal, mention must be made of the terracotta figurines which the Neo-Sumerians produced in such abundance. Even though some of these objects may no doubt be regarded merely as family keepsakes, many others, in fact the majority of them, are *ex votos* and idols.

Although the gods honoured with stone statues were few, a fair number of the members of the Mesopotamian Pantheon have come down to us in terracotta (e.g. Enki, Bau and Gula), as well as several legendary figures (Gilgamesh, Enkidu, Humbaba) and effigies of ordinary citizens praying with clasped hands or leading sacrificial animals to the altar.

We also find scenes of family life—a mother suckling her child; a husband casting a fond glance at his wife as he places his hand on her shoulder—while aspects of public life are suggested by likenesses of military leaders and dignitaries.

There is no doubt, furthermore, that some of these figurines can be identified with the 'teraphim' of the Bible, first mentioned in the account of the secret departure of Jacob and Rachel from Laban (Genesis, XXXI). Rachel carried off her father's teraphim, or household images, with which she could not bring herself to part. They must have been just such small statuettes as these, since she was able to conceal them in the camel's trappings.

TELLOH - SMALL FIGURE-PLAQUES
294 - MAN CARRYING A GOAT. — LOUVRE
295 - WOMAN SUCKLING A CHILD. — LOUVRE

296 - TELLOH - SMALL FIGURE-PLAQUE - HUSBAND AND WIFE (22ND-21ST CENTURIES B.C.). — LOUVRE

The Neo-Sumerian figurines, also, were of small dimensions (from six to eight inches high, on the average), though occasionally we find one as big as a child. Two such were discovered at Ur, twenty-four and twenty-eight inches high respectively: one representing Enkidu, the other a goddess with a flowing vase.

There is another episode of Biblical history of which the two figures from Ur give us a clearer understanding—David's escape from Saul's wrath thanks to the ingenuity of his wife Michal, who deceived the officers sent to slay him. 'And Michal took an image, and laid it in the bed, and put a pillow of goats' hair for his bolster, and covered it with a cloth. And when Saul sent messengers to take David, she said, He is sick.' Meanwhile David made good his escape (I Samuel, xix, 12-16). The passage suggests that the teraphim in this case must have been larger than usual for it to have given the illusion of a human body when hidden in the bedclothes.

297 - TELLOH - FIGURINE - OFFERING BEARER (22ND-21ST CENTURIES B.C.). — LOUVRE

Blood sacrifice is known to have been an important religious rite throughout the Ancient East. Abel, the Book of Genesis tells us, offered up to the Lord the firstlings of his flock. Innumerable figurines represent a worshipper approaching the altar with an animal sacrifice: a goat, a ewe, or a lamb. But we also have the evocation of a demoniacal world in this hybrid being, with the trunk of a man and a lion's head, clutching in its two paws a bird it has just captured.

298 - TELLOH - FIGURINE - LION-HEADED DEMON (22ND-21ST CENTURIES B.C.). — LOUVRE

It will be apparent from this survey that the Neo-Sumerians not only rapidly made good the havoc wrought by the invasion of the Guti, but bestowed on their country a new Golden Age. Growing and developing, civilization pursued its evolution and multiplied its conquests. A century whose achievements include the construction of the ziggurats and the thirty statues of Gudea need fear no comparison.

We have seen, too, that this reaction against Akkadian domination by no means involved the destruction of everything that the Semites had undertaken and achieved in the field of art. The Sumerians were too shrewd not to turn the lesson to account. The old inflexibility was relaxed and diversified; hieraticism lost its grimness.

A thorough-going evolution towards a more refined way of life was under way, and it was speeded up as a result of fresh political upheavals, due this time not to barbarians but to those Semites of the West who had been momentarily held in check but were now to take their revenge.

303

304 306

305

307

308

309

310

311

312

313

314

SEAL IMPRESSIONS
NEO-SUMERIAN PERIOD

THE GUTI
AND THE NEO-SUMERIAN
REACTION
(2285-2016 B.C.)

The invasion of a horde of nomads, the Guti, puts an end to the Akkadian empire and gives the Sumerians an opportunity to regain their independence and to initiate the Neo-Sumerian period of civilization and art: a veritable Golden Age, known as the Third Dynasty of Ur. Among its kings are Ur-Nammu and Dungi (Shulgi).

This period of renewal has left the ruins of an imposing architecture, characterized by ziggurats, temples, palaces and impressive hypogea. Ur in this respect is unrivalled.

In addition to monuments of baked or unbaked brick, there is statuary of unprecedented power. Lagash provides a superb group of some thirty statues of the *patesi* Gudea, to which may be added those of his son Ur-Ningirsu and many anonymous works. Statuary in the round and bas-reliefs compete for the sculptors' talent, while the works in metal are in no way inferior. No less interesting are the cylinder seals and clay effigies: glyptics and figurines which together tell us much about a period when, perhaps more than in any other, man yearned for communion with his gods.

KINGS, PATESIS AND DYNASTIES	SITES	ARCHITECTU
Guti Dynasty (2285-2132)		
Patesis of Lagash	LAGASH	
Gudea		
Ur-Ningirsu		Hypogeum of Ningirsu-Ugm
Fifth Dynasty of Uruk (2131-2125)		
Third Dynasty of Ur (2124-2016)		
Ur-Nammu (2124-2107)	UR ERIDU NIPPUR URUK	Ziggurat Ziggurat Ziggurat Ziggurat
Shulgi (Dungi) (2106-2059)	UR SUSA	Ziggurat Hypogeum Temples
Bur-Sin (Amar-Sin) (2058-2050)	UR	Hypogeum
Gimil-Sin (or Shu-Sin) (2049-2041)		
Ibi-Sin (2040-2016)		

SCULPTURE	TERRACOTTA	METAL	SHELL AND IVORY	PAINTING	EGYPT	AEGEAN
					First Intermediary Period (2280-2050)	Early Minoan III (2300-2100)
atues Gudea | Steles	Small figure-plaques Modelled figurines	Foundation figurines: kneeling gods, basket carriers, bulls				
Statue of Ur-Ningirsu						
onymous statuary Human-headed bulls						
Cylinder Seals	Small figure-plaques				Middle Kingdom (2050-1778)	Middle Minoan I (2100-1900)
Stele						
Headless statue						
		Foundation figurines				

316 - SEAL IMPRESSION SCENE OF WORSHIP (EARLY 2ND MILL.). — PIERPONT MORGAN COLLECTION

VI

THE RETURN OF THE AMORITES
AND THE BABYLONIAN HEGEMONY

(2016-1595 B.C.)

ONCE again we must begin with a brief account of the historical background, some knowledge of which is indispensable for a proper understanding of the art of this great period, spanning over four centuries. At its outset (about 2025 B.C.) we find two rival dynasties, those of Isin and Larsa, establishing themselves at the very gates of Ur. At its end (about 1595 B.C.) the sack of Babylon by the Hittites marks the downfall of the Amorite dynasty, whose most brilliant representative was the famous law-giver Hammurabi (1792-1750 B.C.).

Sumerian political power, centred at Ur, collapsed about 2015 B.C. under the combined attacks of Semites of the West and Elamites. As so often happens with coalitions, one of the partners ended up by dominating the other. The Semites proved the stronger and appropriated to themselves the fruits of victory but internecine feuds soon developed among the conquerors. The vast territory governed by Ur in the days of its glory was shared out and passed into the hands of local rulers residing at Assur on the Upper Tigris, at Mari on the Middle Euphrates, at Ashnunnak in the heart of Mesopotamia, and at Larsa, in the far south. A dynasty was also founded at Babylon, which formed the design of subjugating all these competing powers, one after the other. Hammurabi—thanks to a reign of over forty years and a genius for both diplomacy and generalship, of which the royal archives of Mari have much to tell us—was the soul of the enterprise and it was a complete success, one of the consequences of this change being the definitive and total disappearance of the Sumerians from the political scene.

It is usual for historians of ancient art, when they reach this period, to study its cultural manifestations by associating them as far as possible with the various dynasties mentioned above. Such and such a work of art, for example, is said to belong to the Isin-Larsa period, or to bear the stamp of the First Dynasty of Babylon. More recently the American Orientalist A. Goetze has even spoken of 'the age of Mari.'

None the less several eminent authorities, among them Henri Frankfort, have confessed their inability to distinguish the art of Hammurabi's time or that of his successors from the art of the Isin-Larsa period which preceded it, except when monuments bear inscriptions enabling us to date them with precision. The present writer shares these views. This very uncertainty, however, goes far to demonstrate the remarkable unity of this art, a unity due to the fact that the whole area was peopled by the same races. Differences certainly exist, but they can be detected only after careful scrutiny and are usually found to lie in details of works basically akin. When they do so, they are usually attributable to local idiosyncrasies and to 'provincialism'; they never conflict with the general creative trend, essentially Semitic in nature, even though Sumerian reminiscences enter into it here and there. Nor did the Amorites ignore the whole body of Neo-Sumerian work; on the contrary, they not only took it over, but profited by its example and carried it a stage further.

Indeed, there is no visible cleavage in the culture of the age; rather, a steady evolution and constant progress in many fields. The palace of Mari, covering an area of over eight and a half acres, was considered in its time one of the wonders of the world. The ruler of Ugarit requested King Hammurabi to present his son to Zimri-Lim, ruler of Mari, so that the young man might obtain permission to visit the palace and broaden his mind. The work of several generations, the palace had been enlarged again and again so as to meet new requirements. Its arrangement was that of a typical Sumerian house, with an inner court open to the sky, from which different rooms led off. But here it was treated on a very large scale and repeated again and again. In course of time these great interlocking building units came to form a city in itself, within the city of Mari. Here was the heart of the kingdom, with an administrative headquarters where the king held audience and functionaries had their offices; with a sacred zone, including a 'palace

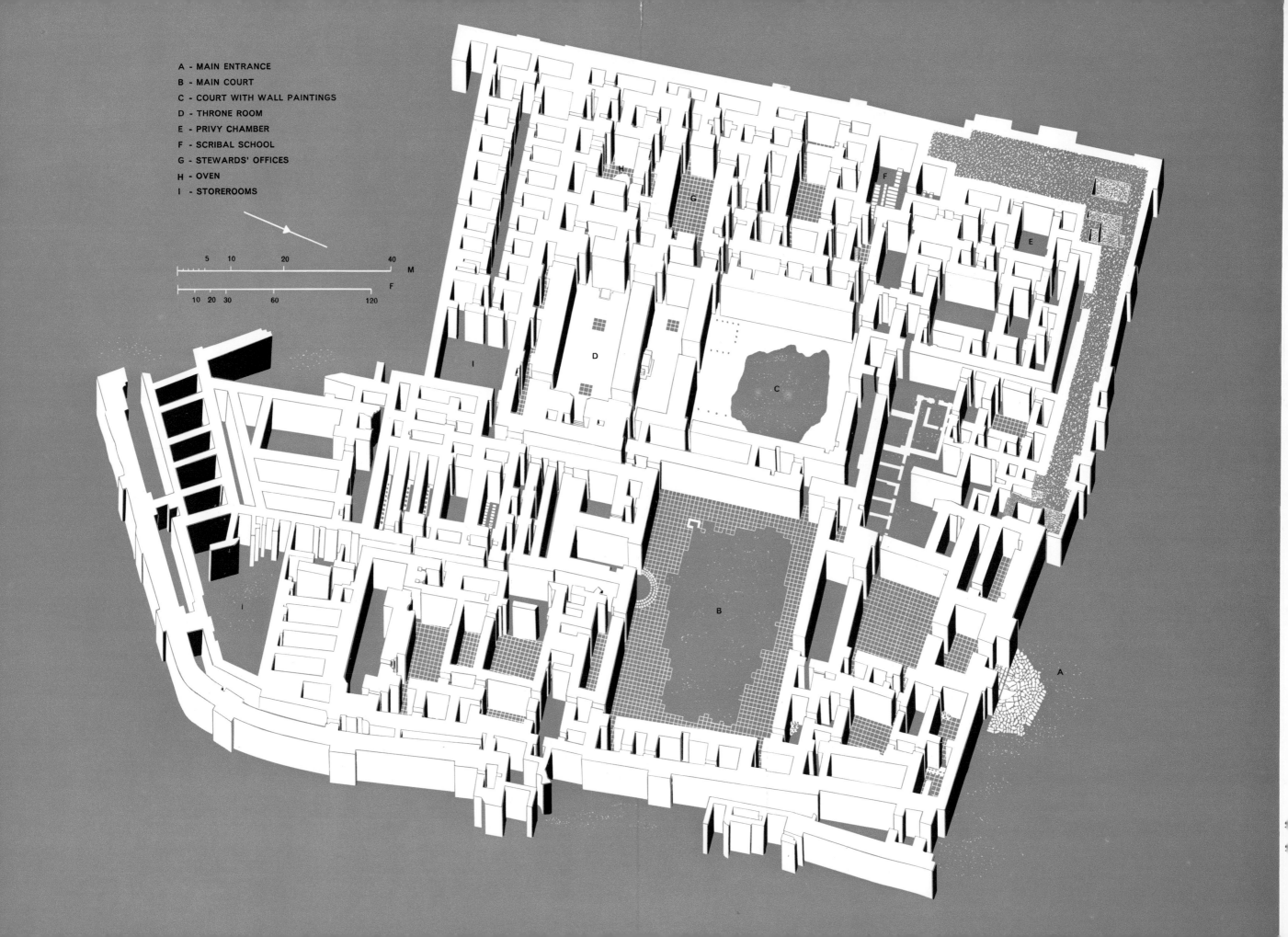

A - MAIN ENTRANCE
B - MAIN COURT
C - COURT WITH WALL PAINTINGS
D - THRONE ROOM
E - PRIVY CHAMBER
F - SCRIBAL SCHOOL
G - STEWARDS' OFFICES
H - OVEN
I - STOREROOMS

5 10   20   40   M
10 20 30   60   120   F

317 - MARI - PALACE OF ZIMRI-LIM (18TH CENTURY B.C.)

chapel'; with private apartments of the court; with outbuildings housing kitchens, workshops and storerooms. With its great walls of sun-dried brick and its single gateway, the palace was designed like a fortress and, in case of need, could withstand a siege. The terraced roofs provided large open spaces where, in times of peace, especially during the summer, the occupants could enjoy the cool of the evenings and nights; in wartime they served as vantage points from which the defenders could dominate any attacking force and hold it at bay.

318 - MARI - THE MOUNDS OF TELL HARIRI BEFORE EXCAVATION

319 - AERIAL VIEW OF THE SITE: TEMPLE OF ISHTAR AND PALACE

320 - MARI - CLEARING THE PALACE (EARLY 2ND MILL.)

DISCOVERY AND EXPLORATION OF MARI

In the summer of 1933, while digging a grave at Tell Hariri, about seven miles from Abu Kemal, in Syrian territory on the right bank of the Euphrates, some Arabs unearthed a mutilated statue distinctively 'Sumerian' in character.

On the initiative of René Dussaud, with the approval of Henri Seyrig, director of the Department of Antiquities in Syria, an expedition was sent out from Paris to explore Tell Hariri.

In January 1934 the discovery of statuettes bearing inscriptions made it possible to identify the site with the ancient city of Mari.

Excavations were made during six successive seasons, from 1933 to 1939. Interrupted by the Second World War, work was finally resumed with the permission of the Syrian government in 1951 and was carried on for four seasons, up to 1955.

From the tell, or mound, that had kept its secret inviolate for countless generations a great capital emerged, and with it a civilization marked by two decisive periods: one in the early third millennium (Pre-Sargonid period) and another in the early second millennium (Amorite period). After many vicissitudes, Mari finally lost its independence, vanquished by Hammurabi, king of Babylon. The city was taken and destroyed about 1760 B.C. Later the Assyrians established a military outpost there. Subsequently it sank to the level of an unimportant country town.

Temples, palaces, dwelling-houses and cemeteries have been successively brought to light. Innumerable monuments have been found in the ruins, works of sculpture in particular, which show that Mari was for a long while an outstanding art centre. Precious

321 - AXONOMETRIC PROJECTION - RECONSTRUCTION OF THE PALACE OF MARI →

wall paintings, dating back to the early second millennium, have revealed hitherto undreamt-of aspects of the Mesopotamian genius. Twenty-five thousand tablets of cuneiform script, constituting the diplomatic and economic archives of the State, tell the story not only of a city but of all Mesopotamia in the age when Hammurabi made good his hegemony, after long years of diplomatic manœuvres and military campaigns.

* *
*

Clearing a lion of the temple of Dagan. The temple of Dagan, at Mari, was guarded by a pack of lions made of bronze plaques hammered over a wooden core. Of those found on the esplanade little trace was left; only their eyes in white stone inlaid with schist testified to their presence. Inside the shrine, however, two lions had survived intact. They were cleared under the direction of Mr F. Pearson of the Dura Europos mission. One is in the Aleppo Museum, the other in the Louvre.

Discovery of the statue of Ishtup-ilum. This figure of the *shakkanak* (governor) of Mari was discovered in the throne room, at the foot of a great staircase leading up to a gallery. Lying on its back, the statue had suffered relatively slight damage, though its nose had been battered out of shape. Brought to light by André Bianquis, it is now in the Aleppo Museum.

Alabaster head. On one of the steps of a stairway leading from a courtyard to a shrine in the palace of Mari, an alabaster head was uncovered, almost miraculously intact, lying only a few inches below ground level. It certainly belonged to a large statue, whose body, however, could not be found. It too is in the Aleppo Museum.

322 - MARI - CLEARING A BRONZE LION OF THE TEMPLE OF DAGAN

323 - CLEARING THE STATUE OF THE 'GOVERNOR' ISHTUP'-ILUM

324 - MARI - CLEARING A HEAD ON THE STEP OF A STAIRWAY

← 325 - MARI - AERIAL VIEW OF THE PALACE

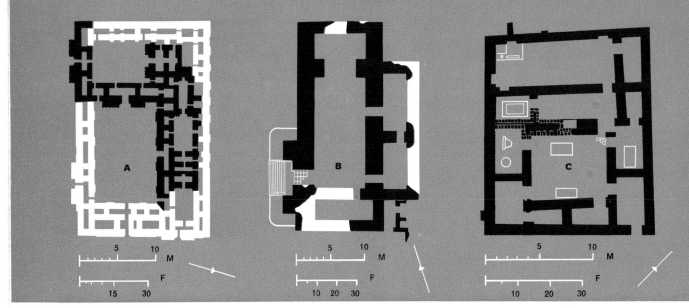

326 - (A) ISHCHALI - TEMPLE OF ISHTAR-KITITUM. — (B) ASSUR - ONE OF THE TEMPLES OF ISHTAR. — (C) TELLOH. — A HOUSE

To this development of the royal residences corresponds that of the sanctuaries. One of the most characteristic of these, located at Ishchali, was dedicated to the goddess Ishtar-Kititum. Being regarded as abodes of the gods, temples were designed on the lines of palaces; they formed a complex, that is to say, consisting of a court surrounded by rooms. But the plan of the sector serving as the private residence of the god conformed to a strictly regulated lay-out. In it we always find a shallow cella, at the back of which a niche marked the place where the idol stood. This was often preceded by an antecella, which also took the form of a room laid out breadthwise and opening on a courtyard at right angles to it. In the typically 'Babylonian' plan all the doorways, including the street entrance, lay along the same axis. So that the worshipper, after crossing the threshold, had only to walk straight ahead until he reached the Holy of Holies. (It was otherwise in the North.)

The dwelling-houses of the townsfolk, though, needless to say, more modest and less roomy, were by no means carelessly designed or built. Each had a door on the street, an antechamber and the usual courtyard, surrounded by rooms. Possibly, in certain cases, there was an upper storey above the ground floor. As in the great residences, the building material consisted of sun-dried brick, though baked brick was frequently used for the foundations. The courtyard and some of the rooms were paved with fine terracotta tiles. The location of the kitchen can be recognized by the presence of a hearth or oven. Sanitary arrangements were quite adequate; floors and cess-pools were made watertight with bitumen. As an added refinement, palaces were equipped with tiled baths and bathrooms. In this respect the palace of Mari left nothing to be desired. All the amenities of life were provided; indeed no other royal residence of antiquity was so well appointed.

327 - ISHCHALI - THE TEMPLE OF ISHTAR-KITITUM (EARLY 2ND MILL.) - RECONSTRUCTION

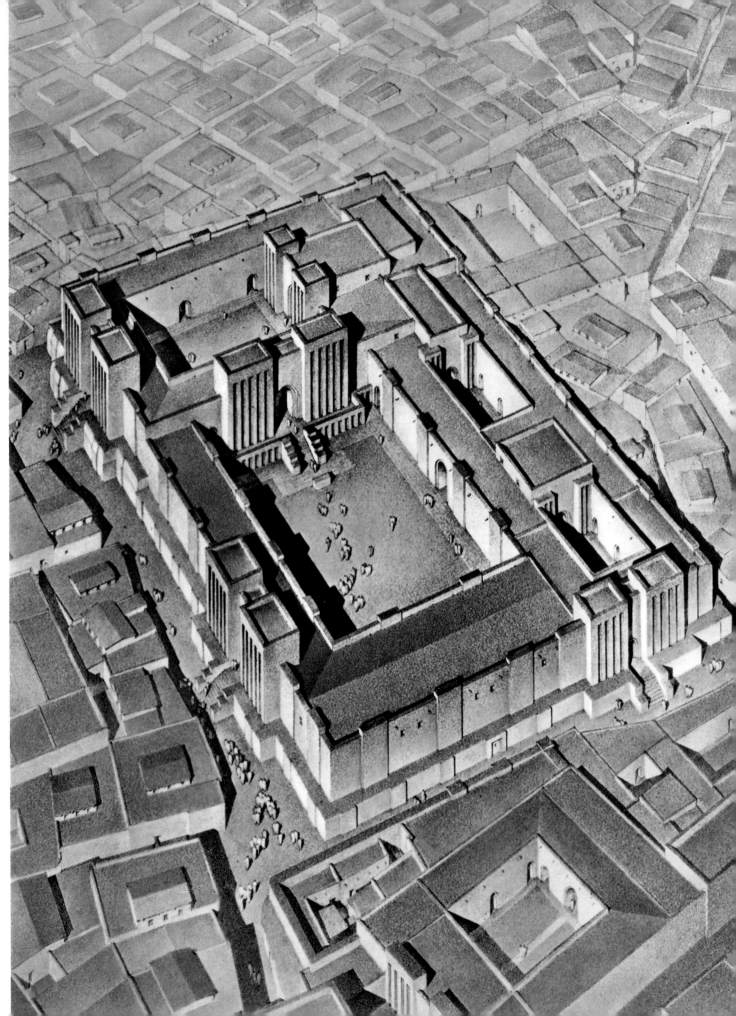

Nor was any other so lavishly decorated; no other, in any case, has yielded such an abundance of *objets d'art*, statues and paintings. Representing the achievement of several dynasties, the palace of Mari is contemporaneous both with the Isin-Larsa period and with the Babylonian period; hence its exceptional importance. When we take stock of the discoveries made before the exploration of the capital of the Middle Euphrates, we realize the extent to which our knowledge has been widened by it. Most representative of the earliest batch of finds had been the statuette of the goddess Bau found at Ur, the sculptures originating from Ashnunnak which Morgan unearthed at Susa, and those which had been taken from Mari to Babylon as war booty and were discovered in the latter city by Koldewey.

Among the later discoveries were the statue of Ishtup-ilum and the headless statue of Idi-ilum, both of them governors of Mari; the white head of the warrior with a chin-piece; and above all the goddess with a flowing vase, one of the most precious of all Mesopotamian sculptures. There are also several small heads of men carrying young goats, found in temples in the centre of the city. This new batch was uncovered only some twenty years ago. In the light of these two successive groups of finds some general conclusions can today be arrived at.

328 - UR - THE GODDESS BAU. — BAGHDAD MUSEUM
329 - SUSA - A WORSHIPPER. — LOUVRE

330 - MARI - STATUE OF IDI-ILUM (EARLY 2ND MILL.). — LOUVRE
331 - ISHTUP-ILUM. — ALEPPO MUSEUM

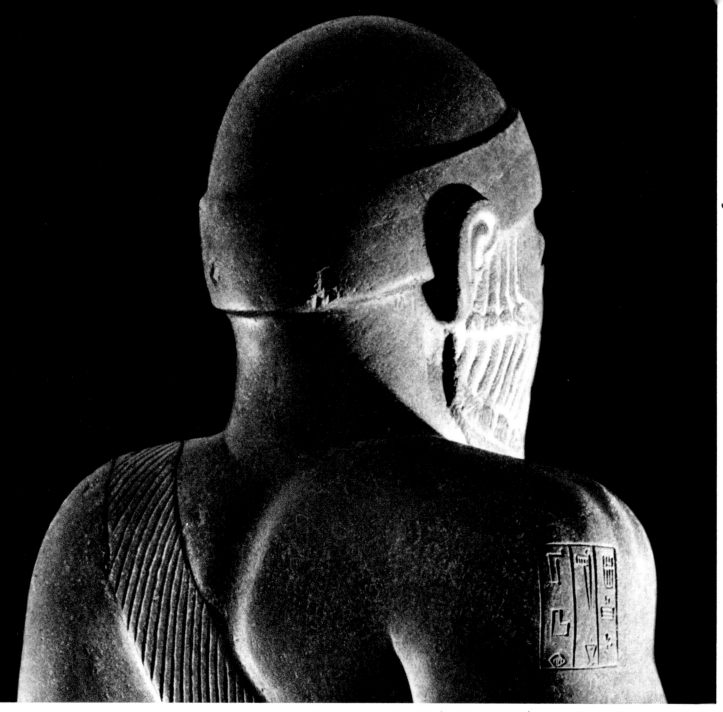

332 - MARI - STATUE OF ISHTUP-ILUM, BACK VIEW (EARLY 2ND MILL.). — ALEPPO MUSEUM

It becomes evident, first of all, that the Sumerian tradition lingered on, with its hieraticism and unbending rigour. The goddess Bau, with her long, flounced robe, is demurely seated with clasped hands. Barefoot, also with his hands clasped, the *shakkanak* Ishtup-ilum keeps to the attitude of Gudea, but the face has an expression of grim severity that is not attenuated by a beard and moustache masking the greater part of it. His garment is remarkably simplified, consisting as it does

333 - MARI - STATUE OF ISHTUP-ILUM, DETAIL. — ALEPPO MUSEUM

334 - MARI - STATUE OF PUZUR-ISHTAR (EARLY 2ND MILL.)

of no more than a strip of cloth, trimmed on both the long and the short sides with a fringed braid, carefully flattened against the body and draped slantwise down the back. This figure diverges sharply from the statues identified with other governors of Mari which, however, seem to be only slightly earlier in date.

In the course of Koldewey's excavations at Babylon two basalt statues were discovered in the 'museum' of Nebuchadnezzar's *Hauptburg*. Both were found headless, but the head of one of them had been looted from the site and acquired by the Berlin Museum. The original head in Berlin, placed on a plaster cast of the corresponding statue preserved in the Istanbul Museum, has enabled one of the two figures to be reconstructed in its entirety.

Reconstructed, the statue raises a number of problems, of which the most difficult to solve is: whom does it portray? A god or a prince? For the statue bears two inscriptions. The first reads: 'Puzur-Ishtar, *shakkanak* of Mari, Milga, priest, his brother,' while the second begins: 'Tura-Dagan, *shakkanak* of Mari, Puzur-Ishtar *shakkanak*, his son, to the god... Lord... God... have devoted for their life.' Then follows a string of imprecations against anyone who violates the statue. Wearing a crown with a single pair of horns, the figure should, normally, represent a deity. Yet serious doubts arise, owing to the fact that this 'god,' whose name has been mutilated, is described by epithets which seem to imply that he should be identified with Dagan, one of the chief gods of the Mari pantheon; but it is scarcely credible that so important a god would have contented himself with a single pair of horns on his crown. We are therefore inclined to see in this statue a governor of Mari, accorded divine attributes.

335 - MARI - HEAD OF PUZUR-ISHTAR (EARLY 2ND MILL.). — BERLIN MUSEUM

336 - MARI - WARRIOR WITH A CHIN-PIECE (18TH CENT. B.C.). — ALEPPO MUSEUM

Closely related to it is that of Idi-ilum, which was found in the palace of Mari and which, though headless, represents a tall, slender prince, with a graceful, aristocratic bearing. The robe closely enveloping his body is the acme of elegant harmony.

This warrior's features have the same distinction. Jutting out over a short chin, the smooth lips curl in a faint smile. If this head had not been found in the course of a scientifically conducted excavation and in an archaeological context dated beyond any possibility of error, who would ever have ventured to assign it to the early second millennium? Had it turned up at an antique dealer's, many a specialist might well have dated it to the final phase of Hellenistic art. Compare this head from Mari with the reliefs on the so-called Sarcophagus of Alexander, discovered at Sidon, in particular the turbaned figures in the hunting scene. The resemblances are striking—yet the two works are separated by nearly fifteen hundred years!

337 - SIDON - SO-CALLED SARCOPHAGUS OF ALEXANDER (HELLENISTIC PERIOD). — ISTANBUL MUSEUM

338 - MARI - WARRIOR WITH A CHIN-PIECE. — ALEPPO MUSEUM

Despite the mutilation it has suffered, this goddess with the flowing vase has something of the same charm. The inlays have been gouged out of the eyes, and the nose has been badly damaged by some vandal. Yet her smile remains, as do the dimple in her chin and the delicate modelling of the cheeks. Somewhat over-shadowed by the massive helmet, the graceful oval of her face is framed in the plaited hair clustered on her shoulders like a fur collar. With both hands the goddess tilts the *aryballos* which, on certain occasions, thanks to a pipe con-necting the vase with a tank, overflowed with the 'water of fer-tility.' Streaming down her robe, the water clothed the lower part of the statue with a rippling, translucent veil.

This theme of the flowing vase was extremely popular throughout Mesopotamia. The Sumerians had already given it a very prominent place in art, and we now see it taken over by the Semites of the West, who passed it on to others.

The same is true of the theme of the sacrificial animal offered to the gods. The scene of the worshipper holding in his arms the animal he is bringing to the altar figured very frequently, as we have seen, on Pre-Sargonid plaques, on Akkadian cylinder seals and in Neo-Sumerian figurines. At Mari this ritual gesture was recorded in sculpture in the round. Several small statues represent

339 - MARI - GODDESS WITH FLOWING VASE
(18TH CENT. B.C.). — ALEPPO MUSEUM
340 - HEAD OF THE GODDESS

worshippers clasping a young goat tightly to their breast with both hands. Here we have an eloquent illustration of man's reluctance to approach his god empty-handed, and an astonishing prefiguration, too (though the significance is entirely different), of the Good Shepherd of Early Christian art.

The palace of Mari was not only a museum of sculpture. Several rooms and courts were decorated with large wall paintings. They were executed in distemper and their brilliant colours must have been a delight for the eyes. It is a miracle that any trace of them survives, subjected as they have been to the destructive violence of men and the inevitable ravages of time. While the private apartments of the royal family were decorated with paintings mostly composed of geometric patterns, the administrative sector was entrusted to practised figure painters. Scenes of warfare and religious worship were equally in favour, but we also get glimpses of daily life in its humblest aspects. A soldier, with his jaws wrapped in a chin-piece like the one we found earlier on a stone head, is seen riddled with arrows, but (not so submissive as St Sebastian) he has torn one from his body. A bearded, dark-haired fisherman walks home with his catch at the end of a stick resting on his shoulder. Both figures are treated somewhat in the manner of a modern charcoal sketch.

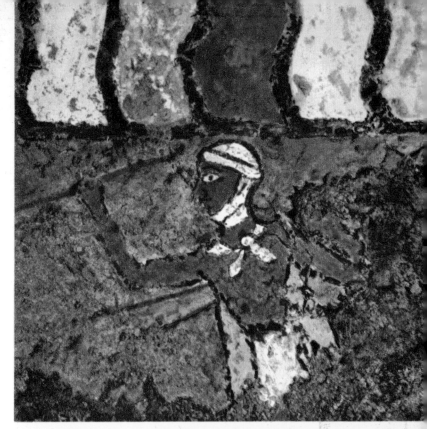

MARI - WALL PAINTINGS
(18TH CENTURY B.C.)
342 - WARRIOR 343 - FISHERMAN

341 - MARI - OFFERING BEARER (EARLY 2ND MILL.). — ALEPPO MUSEUM

344 - MARI - WALL PAINTING - SCENE OF SACRIFICE (18TH CENTURY B.C.). — LOUVRE

In the large fragment of a painting depicting a scene of sacrifice, the composition is more elaborate. It is divided into registers, and we have fragmentary glimpses of a great procession headed by a man of gigantic stature who can be none other than the king. The painting has been badly damaged and nothing remains but the lower part of the king's robe, its edges festooned with rows of flounces, a triple sash wound round his waist, and an arm whose imperious gesture sets the rhythm of the long line of marching figures.

Among the participants another leading figure stands out, his aquiline profile drawn with a vigorous, schematic line. He holds a small white rod or scroll tightly gripped in his left hand. Behind him comes a bearded man, wearing the same white *polos* on his head and leading a sacrificial bull. The tips of its horns are plated with gold or silver, and a crescent of the same metal is tied to its forehead.

345 - MARI - WALL PAINTING - SCENE OF SACRIFICE
(18TH CENTURY B.C.). — ALEPPO MUSEUM

Even more complex, both in inspiration and execution, is the painting which we named 'The Investiture of the King of Mari,' and which decorated the same court (No. 106). This is an extraordinary document, not only for the history of art but also for Mesopotamian religion. Dated with unusual precision (it figured in a palace destroyed about 1760 B.C.), it offers an admirable synthesis of the two mentalities, Semitic and Sumerian: conventional hieraticism on the one hand, graceful fantasy on the other. Hieratic is the upper scene of the central panel, showing the king, no doubt Zimri-Lim, touching the emblems presented to him by Ishtar, the goddess of war, in a ceremony of investiture on which the presence of several deities confers an added solemnity. Hieratic again are the symbolic animals which seem to form a protective barrier, and the two great goddesses supplicating or blessing. On the other hand, fantasy and total unconstraint characterize the figures of date-pickers climbing a palm tree, among whose green fronds perches a magnificent blue bird, with outspread wings, ready to take flight. We had always regarded the bird as a creation of the painter's imagination; but while walking in the palace one day in April 1950 we noticed a great bird of prey almost exactly like it, which, at our approach, flew off in panic from the ruins where it had its nest.

This is not the place to enter into a lengthy interpretation of this painting, each detail of which has its explanation in Mesopotamian religion. Of all the divine beings figuring in it, only one can be identified with certainty: Ishtar, with her weapons and a lion, her animal attribute. But there are two goddesses with a flowing vase, pictorial equivalents of the stone statue described above. It is interesting to note that the four streams gushing from the *aryballos* bring to mind the four rivers of Paradise; and that similarly the fantastic animals guarding the stylized tree recall the cherubim forbidding access to Eden and the tree of life. A mere coincidence, or an anticipation of the Bible story? However this may be, we have once again an illustration of the typically Mesopotamian setting of the opening pages of Genesis.

Other stylistic traits raise other problems: those concerning the relations between the Orient and the Aegean. The painting at Mari has a border of running spirals. This motif was also employed in the decoration of the upper front of the 'podium' in Room 64 of the palace, which we are now inclined to regard as a reception room. It would be hard to find a more typically Aegean motif. The wall paintings of Knossos and the sarcophagus of Haghia Triada, with their spiral bands, have truly remarkable similarities to the decorative pattern used at Mari. Where did it originate, whence did the inspiration come? Some inscribed tablets found in the palace of Zimri-Lim mention the existence of econo-

346 - MARI - WALL PAINTING - INVESTITURE OF THE
KING OF MARI (18TH CENT. B.C.). — LOUVRE

348 (A) - MARI - WALL PAINTING - REGISTERS III, IV AND V (18TH CENT. B.C.). — LOUVRE

The audience chamber (Room 132) in the palace of Mari was decorated with a large mural painting; unfortunately, when discovered, it was in very poor condition, having flaked away from the wall. Only the three lower registers are illustrated, but it seems to have had five in all:

I. A frieze of porters, moving to the right.

II. A soldier wearing a turban and chin-piece, riddled by arrows.

III. The goddess Ishtar receiving an offering made by another goddess; a procession of divine and human beings.

IV. The king making sacrifice (libation and burnt offering) to a god seated on a mountain, above whose head-dress is a crescent moon. The king is accompanied by divine beings. On each side of the scene, a bull passant and a figure seen against a starry night sky.

V. A frieze of fishermen, moving to the right.

The interpretation of this composition is particularly difficult, for two reasons: first, we have no means of identifying the figures; secondly, the scenes apparently inspired by everyday life may well have some religious significance attaching to them.

It seems probable, if not certain, that this painting was meant to commemorate, *inter alia*, a ceremony in one of the city's many temples in the course of which the king of Mari officiated, in a religious capacity.

348 (B) - MARI - WALL PAINTING, DETAIL,
OFFERING OF FIRE AND WATER

347 - MARI - WALL PAINTING - INVESTITURE OF THE KING, DETAIL (18TH CENT. B.C.). — LOUVRE

mic and commercial relations with Crete. It would have been surprising indeed, had art remained unaffected by these contacts. If merchants could travel freely, we may well assume that architects and decorators, too, indulged in foreign travel.

But whatever the reciprocal borrowings and influences that may have taken place between Mesopotamia and the Aegean, Mari remains, with its architecture, sculpture and painting, an art centre such as the East has rarely known. The city had still other treasures, prominent among them being the works executed in bronze. Several pieces found on different sites, and all belonging to this same period, call for mention.

First of all, there are two bronzes from Larsa, where they were unearthed by clandestine excavators about 1930; both convey the typically Semitic effect of movement and life. One consists of three ibexes back to back. The base is decorated with two bearded figures upholding a small basin. The men's faces were covered with silver foil, the animals' heads with gold. From the same workshop, undoubtedly, came the other statue, of a worshipper. A man in a turban, with his right knee on the ground, kneels in an attitude of prayer. His right hand is raised in a gesture familiar to anyone who has lived in the East, where it occurs whenever one man tries to convince another in the course of an argument. The rectangular base is adorned with a low relief (on one side a ram, on the other a worshipper kneeling before a god) and prolonged in front by a small basin. This statuette can be dated from the inscription on it, which tells us that it was dedicated on behalf of the life of Hammurabi by one Awil-Nannar, the man whom it portrays. The hands and face are covered with gold foil, and in this technique of plating certain parts of the figurine with a precious metal, there is something more than a desire to give the object a higher commercial, or artistic, value. This practice, which we shall meet with again well beyond Mesopotamia, has a religious significance, for gold and silver were thought to have purifying properties and were therefore applied to the 'noblest' parts of the body, i.e. the face and hands.

Two bronzes of a new type have been found at Ishchali, in central Mesopotamia. Both are images of gods. In one the god is standing, with one foot on a ram, a curved weapon dangling at his side, and wearing a long flounced robe; the other shows a goddess holding the flowing vase in both hands. The surprising thing about these figures is that each has four faces. A two-faced god recurs frequently in Akkadian seal designs, but this is the first time we find ones with four, and here the artist had to solve a special problem: the four faces had to be neatly joined together to make them in any way plausible. The junctures are more successful in the case of the god, with his beard and beret, than in that of the goddess, with her crown shaped like an altar. These strange works recall Ezekiel's vision of 'four living creatures' each with four faces (Ezekiel, 1, 5-6).

LARSA (19TH-18TH CENTURIES B.C.) — LOUVRE
349 - THREE IBEXES   350 - KNEELING WORSHIPPER -
ISHCHALI (19TH CENTURY B.C.) — CHICAGO
351 - FOUR-FACED GOD   352 - FOUR-FACED GODDESS -

With the bronze lions from Mari, guarding both the entrance and the esplanade of the temple of Dagan, we come back to realism. There was a whole group of lions originally, but only two have escaped destruction. The one in our illustration is an embodiment of savage vigilance. Its sinews are tensed for action, its jaws gaping, and there can be no doubt of its intention to pounce on any rash intruder within the sacred precinct. To add to its terrifying effect the bronze-founder gave it two enormous eyes, made of white stones with a pellet of bluish schist inlaid in the centre. And he also fitted the jaws with a row of fangs, carved in bone. This minute attention to detail in no way detracts from the power of the whole. The artists of the early second millennium were past masters in the rendering of animals.

354 - TELL HARMAL - LION GUARDING THE TEMPLE
(EARLY 2ND MILL.). — BAGHDAD MUSEUM

355 - HEAD OF A ROARING LION (EARLY 2ND MILL.). — LOUVRE

Elsewhere we find other proofs of their ability in this field. The lions of Mari recall those of Tell Harmal, near Baghdad, though there is not the least question of imitation. Modelled in clay and then fired, the Tell Harmal lions were arranged in pairs, keeping guard over two of the entrances to the temple of Nisaba and Khani. Head and body are executed in such a way as to stress every feature capable of inspiring fear. The pelt, rendered with a certain stylization, brings to mind both the *kaunakes* style and the flounced drapery of human figures. Two lion-

288

356 - TELL HARMAL - HEAD OF A ROARING LION (EARLY 2ND MILL.). — BAGHDAD MUSEUM

muzzles, acquired by the Louvre in 1947, belong to this same family of guardian animals, but their characteristics are even more accentuated. Realism is still the artist's main concern, but in one the head is schematically rendered in broad planes heightening the effect of ferocity. Thus the composition combines and harmonizes two very different manners, one naturalistic, the other hieratic. In so doing, the sculptor-modeller obviously aimed at reconciling accurate observation of reality with an architectonic concept.

Exactly the same impression is conveyed by a magnificent ram's head, carved in steatite, discovered at Ur by Sir Leonard Woolley. The animal is certainly taken from life, and belonged to one of the many flocks of sheep roaming the steppe. But it has been given an hieratic aspect that at once idealizes it and at the same time adapts it to some ceremonial purpose. For this head must have figured originally on a sceptre or on some high functionary's staff of office.

Naturalism, however, is the predominant characteristic of the dog of Sumu-ilu in the Louvre. Found at Lagash, its type brings it into line with the series of small-sized animals, such as the human-headed bulls of the Gudea period. The customary hole in its back is here provided with a drinking cup; but as the latter is carved in a different kind of stone, it may well have been a later addition. Particularly noteworthy is the convincing realism of this mastiff; with its slightly parted jaws it seems about to bark and leap up from the slab on which it rests.

Naturalistic, too, are the wild goats from Susa, carved in a bituminous substance, and employed for decorating bowls of which they sometimes form the stem. These animals—for a change—seem docile and timid; they are shown lying down, with their ears pricked up and their eyes on the alert for danger.

357 - (A) UR - RAM'S HEAD. — BRITISH MUSEUM
(B) LAGASH - VOTIVE DOG. — (C, D) SUSA -
BOWLS. LOUVRE (EARLY 2ND MILL.)

358 - SMALL FIGURE-PLAQUES (EARLY 2ND MILL.). — (A) KHAFAJE. — CHICAGO (B) LARSA. — LOUVRE. — (C) LOUVRE

As well as this close contact with nature we now have intimate glimpses of everyday life, which, hitherto altogether absent from Sumerian iconography, makes its appearance in the Isin-Larsa period and in the time of Hammurabi. On the small figurine-plaques, long confined to reproductions of type figures, we now find a repertory of forms which make it clear that definite efforts were being made to strike out in new directions. Thus on a terracotta plaque from Khafaje we see a god driving his sword into the belly of a Cyclops; on a plaque from Larsa, a celestial visitant straddling the walls of a fortress. Many members of the Mesopotamian pantheon are represented under aspects with which we were totally unfamiliar, but which we shall meet with again in the glyptic art of the same period. Also a figure of a wholly new type now makes its first appearance: this is a naked, gracefully proportioned woman, with her hands clasped. She has nothing in common with the buxom, heavily built matron, the 'Lady with a Timbrel' of Gudea's time, but is a kind of Venus who seems quite unconscious of any touch of shamelessness in thus exposing herself to the public gaze.

359 - SMALL FIGURE-PLAQUES (EARLY 2ND MILL.). — (A, C, D, E) LOUVRE. — (B) CHICAGO

But the art of this period is not limited to depictions of gods or to religious scenes and figures. Scenes of everyday life also inspired the modeller: a peasant riding an ox; a musician seated on a folding stool, plucking the strings of his harp; another performing a serenade; an itinerant showman exhibiting monkeys; boxers engaged in a hard-fought match; a carpenter leaning over the wood he is shaping with tools that

361 - MARI - MOULD - STAG-HUNT (18TH CENTURY B.C.). — ALEPPO MUSEUM

have changed little in four thousand years. Many such works have been discovered, and so lively and convincing are these small terracotta plaques that one is plunged into the very atmosphere of the age.

Not only city life, but also life on the steppe is illustrated on some of the terracotta moulds, discovered in the palace of Mari, which were evidently used for stamping cakes and pastries served at the royal table. One of the scenes represents a stag-hunt. A bearded man, with a cap falling on the nape of his neck, is shown leading a stag which he holds by an antler; in front a slender, graceful animal, probably one of the thoroughbred hounds known as slughis, is standing up on its hind legs.

362 - MARI - MOULD - LION ATTACKING OXEN (18TH CENTURY B.C.). — LOUVRE

In the offing is a smaller stag accompanying the captive animal at a safe distance.

The design on another mould evokes the dark side of the husbandman's life, the constant depredations of his livestock by wild animals. We see a lion leaping upon an ox, which moves off to the left, seemingly indifferent to the attack being made on it. Meanwhile, in the background, two peaceful animals, perhaps young calves, are escaping from the danger area.

These doubtless familiar incidents of country life are treated with a simplicity and sobriety enhancing their appeal. A great many figurines

are extant which, with a well-nigh startling realism, depict the 'king of the desert.' And when we look at these lions, their jaws gaping, their formidable claws bared, and their huge bodies tensed for action, we get an idea of the dangers to which the men who went out (or were sent out) to hunt them were exposed. Zimri-Lim, king of Mari, was a great hunter of lions and some of the documents preserved in the palace archives recount his exploits.

Very different is the subject of a small plaque illustrated above, showing a bitch suckling her puppies. Whether the scene is symbolic (the dog was the animal attribute of the goddess Gula) or simply the fruit of observation, it admirably suggests the irresistible life-instinct urging the new-born puppies to their mother's dugs.

364 - MARI - SMALL FIGURE-PLAQUE - LION
PASSANT (19TH CENT. B.C.). — LOUVRE

296

367 - WINGED GODDESSES (EARLY 2ND MILL.). — (A) THE 'BURNEY PLAQUE.' — (B, C) LOUVRE

Though life now was wholly laicized, the sense of mystery and even certain atavistic fears had lost nothing of their hold. The latter are epitomized in the repulsive face of the demon Humbaba, (plate 370, page 303), composed, it seems, of a mass of twisted, writhing entrails. Though less startling than Humbaba, the nude winged goddess of the Burney plaque, with her feet like the talons of a bird of prey, and the lions and owls attending her, hardly gives the impression of a friendly presence. However, another winged goddess, figuring on a vase we discovered at Larsa, seems more kindly disposed. With her open, lifted hands, she appears to be blessing all who appeal to her for aid. She is attended by animals, all of a placid disposition—birds, fish, a tortoise— except for a fierce-looking bull, perhaps the creature sent by Anu to chastise Gilgamesh.

368 - SMALL FIGURE-PLAQUE - THE GODDESS NINTU (EARLY 2ND MILL.). — BAGHDAD MUSEUM

369 - SMALL PLAQUE - HUMBABA (EARLY 2ND MILL.). — BRITISH MUSEUM

The epic of Gilgamesh is one of the most famous creations not only of Mesopotamian but of world literature. This sublimely inspired poem, or anyhow the essential part of it, has been preserved in Assyrian and Babylonian scripts, but a Sumerian prototype and Hittite and Hurrian versions are now known to have existed. The text covers twelve tablets, of which the eleventh is devoted to an account of the Flood. By and large, the epic deals with the fundamental issues of human existence: life and death, friendship and human conflicts, and, dominating all, the problem of immortality.

Gilgamesh, king of Uruk, is unpopular with his subjects. The latter entreat the goddess Aruru to give him a companion. Her choice falls on Enkidu, a wild man who delights in the society of animals, which he protects so effectively as to give offence to the local hunters. Enkidu is to be initiated into the civilization of the cities but the first contact between Gilgamesh and Enkidu leads to trouble, and the two men fight it out on the spot. Then comes a complete reversal of the situation: after the fight they swear eternal friendship. From now on the two men are inseparable companions.

They set out together for the cedar forest, whose approach is guarded by the giant Humbaba (or Huwawa). The two heroes succeed in killing the monster and cut off his head. They return in triumph to Uruk, where rejoicings are held in celebration of their exploits, but Gilgamesh at this point rejects the advances of Ishtar. Piqued at his behaviour, the goddess asks her father Anu to send the celestial bull to punish him. Enkidu rends the animal limb from limb, but himself dies shortly afterwards. Gilgamesh, horrified by the thought that the same fate lies in store for him as well, sets out in quest of immortality. Enkidu is permitted to briefly revisit the world of the living and he describes to his friend the sad lot of the dead in the Nether World, of those in particular who have been forgotten by the living. On this melancholy note the poem ends.

370 - GRIMACING MASK OF THE GIANT HUMBABA (EARLY 2ND MILL.). — BRITISH MUSEUM

371 - MARI - GODDESS SMELLING A FLOWER (18TH CENT. B.C.). — LOUVRE

The gods were not always ill-disposed towards man. We also find them serving as friendly patrons and intercessors, and glyptic art often shows them under this beneficent aspect.

Leaning on his staff, and duly followed by the divinity interceding for him, Idi-ilum, governor of Mari, confidently approaches the goddess, who bids him welcome. Yet, sometimes, the welcome changes to a mood of fierce hostility; it must be remembered that this is the period which saw the first written account of the assembled gods decreeing the destruction of the human race by means of a flood. But there was no need for a natural cataclysm to bring men to disaster; this they could do for themselves. Never had the goddess Ishtar had so many adepts. She is utterly unlike the amiable goddess of Mari, decked in necklaces and bracelets, who delighted in the fragrance of sweet-smelling flowers. Not content with presiding over the embraces of loving couples, Ishtar devoted herself above all else to the profession of arms.

One of her most faithful earthly devotees was Hammurabi who had, it seems, a passion for hegemony at any price. One cannot help wishing that he had remained to the end the sage, enlightened promulgator of the Code. Although we know now that he was not the first to have had the idea of systematically defining the law and recording its precepts in a

372 - MARI - SCENE OF PRESENTATION (EARLY 2ND MILL.). — ALEPPO MUSEUM

written compilation, his Code
nevertheless remains an impressive
achievement. Hammurabi went
further than his predecessors, Ur-
Nammu, Bilalama and Lipit-Ishtar,
who, at Ur, Ashnunnak and Isin
respectively, had endeavoured to
codify the legal procedures of their
dominions.

The law-giver king had himself
represented at the top of the
black basalt stele on which the
two hundred and eighty-two clauses
of his Code are engraved with exquisite precision. Standing in the
attitude of respect, with his right
arm raised, he appears before the
god of justice, Shamash, whose
shoulders are aflame and who
holds in his right hand the attributes of power, the rod and circle,
while he dictates the Law to the
king. Impassive and majestic,
Shamash gazes intently at the man
who acts as his representative on
earth, and who, though exacting
obedience from his fellow men,
must, himself, obey his god. The
setting of the scene is not in the
plain but on a mountain, indicated
by the triple line of imbrications
on which the god's feet rest. Here
the sculptor has brilliantly succeeded in rendering the atmosphere of
the colloquy, serene and dignified
but governed also by a 'categorical
imperative' with which the king
had no choice but to comply.
And looking at this scene, we are
inevitably reminded of Moses, on
Mount Sinai, receiving the tables
of the law.

373 - SUSA - THE LAW CODE OF KING HAMMURABI
(18TH CENTURY B.C.). — LOUVRE

374 - HAMMURABI (18TH CENTURY B.C.). — BRITISH MUSEUM

Preserved in the British Museum is a relief on which we find the figure of the great monarch, treated in a similar fashion but with somewhat less vigour; for this no doubt the relatively poor quality of the stone is mainly responsible. The similarities that there are show us, nevertheless, that the sculptors made a point of keeping closely to the prototype which served as their point of departure and was re-copied, rather clumsily, by other 'image-makers,' as is evident in several steles in the Louvre.

Hammurabi had succeeded in gathering some fine artists around him, and to one of them we owe this head, sculptured in the round, which may very plausibly be regarded as an effigy of the king who had made himself 'master of the world.' In greenish blue steatite, the sculptor has carved the worn, emaciated features, on which perhaps illness has left its mark, of a Hammurabi well advanced in years. The lips are puckered in a faintly sardonic smile, the cheeks are gaunt, the eyes less wide-open than usual; the face is shown exactly as it was at a certain moment in the history of Babylon and in the life of Babylon's greatest king. This is unquestionably a portrait, and one of the most moving in all Oriental art, a chapter of which it brought to a close. With the death of Hammurabi began the decline of the dynasty which, nevertheless, contrived to linger on for another century and a half. But throughout this period Babylon produced nothing calling for mention, nothing worthy to rank as a work of art. So prolonged a period of sterility may perhaps be accounted for by the state of insecurity in which the country lived, constantly harried on the north by the Kassites, on the south by the people of the Sea-lands. Once again barbarian hordes were to triumph over a people to whom civilization had owed an age of unprecedented brilliance. Was the edifice so patiently and tirelessly erected to be dashed to the ground by the foreign invader? Our final chapter will describe what actually took place.

375 - SUSA - HEAD OF HAMMURABI (?), KING OF BABYLON (18TH CENTURY B.C.). — LOUVRE

376

377

378

379

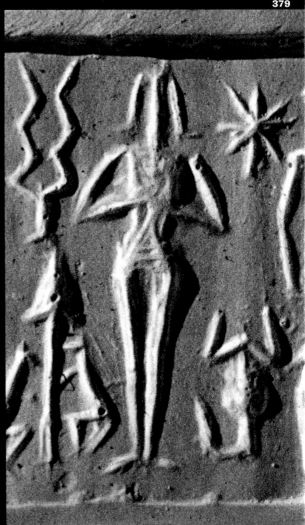

380

381

382

383

384

386 385

SEAL IMPRESSIONS OF THE LARSA PERIOD
AND THE FIRST DYNASTY OF BABYLON

CHAPTER VI

THE RETURN
OF THE AMORITES
AND THE BABYLONIAN
HEGEMONY
(2016-1595 B.C.)

The fall of the Third Dynasty of Ur marks the end of the Neo-Sumerian period. Mesopotamia once again comes under Semite rulers: the dynasties of Isin, of Larsa, and above all of Hammurabi (1792-1750 B.C.) sking of Babylon. Again a great new phase of civilization dawns, and prosperous conditions lead to a magnificent flowering of art.

Great works are produced in all fields of human activity and artistic creation. Mari is an inexhaustible mine, with its palace over eight and a half acres in extent; so too are Ashnunnak and Ishchali, with their grandiose temples and private residences. Large-scale statuary unearthed at Mari shows that sculpture remains within the Sumerian tradition (Ishtup-ilum), but that sculptors are not indifferent to such Semitic qualities as the grace and elegance of garments (Idi-ilum). The wall paintings of Mari confirm this trend; the high originality of these artists' inspiration is unquestionable. Metalwork is equally well represented, and bronze statuettes have the same quivering life that characterizes the works in terracotta (statues and small figure-plaques).

Everyday life, scenes of religious worship, mythological episodes—every facet of civilization is seen in art, which makes these second-millennium men, gods and animals seem very close to us. The whole age is dominated by Hammurabi, king of Babylon, immortalized by his law code. But his rule, as we now know, was far from humanitarian; he wielded the sword with merciless severity.

KINGS, PATESIS AND DYNASTIES	SITES	ARCHITECTURE
Isin Dynasty (2022-1797)		
Larsa Dynasty (2023-1761)	LARSA	Palace of Nur-Adad
	LAGASH	
	UR	
Babylon Dynasty (1894-1595)		
Hammurabi (1792-1750)	SUSA	
	HARMAL	Temple of Nisab and Khani
Patesis of Ashnunnak	ASHNUNNAK	Palace
	ISHCHALI	Temple of Ishtar-Kititur
Kings of Assur Shamshi-Adad		
Princes and Kings of Mari	MARI	
Puzur-Ishtar	BABYLON	
Idi-ilum	MARI	
Ishtup-ilum	MARI	Temple of Daga
Niwar-Mer	MARI	
Iahdun-Lim	MARI	Temple of Shamash Palace
Iasmah-Adad	MARI	
Zimri-Lim	MARI	Palace

SCULPTURE	TERRACOTTA	METAL	SHELL AND IVORY	PAINTING	EGYPT	AEGEAN
					Middle Kingdom (2050-1778)	Middle Minoan I (2100-1900)
Cylinder Seals	Burney Plaque Vase with winged goddess Grey pottery Small figure-plaques Grey pottery Small figure-plaques	Bronze figurines: Worshipper Ibexes				
og of Sumu-ilu						Early palaces at Knossos and Phaistos
Ram's Head						
Head of Hammurabi Code of Hammurabi	Guardian Lions					Arrival of the Achaeans (2000-1750) Middle Minoan II (1900-1700) Frescoes in the early palaces
		Four-faced bronze figurine				
Statues						
Statue Cylinder Seals						
Statue						
		Foundation plaques				
Statue						
tue h ving e	Goddess smelling a flower Head of a warrior	Lions of the temple of Dagan		Palace: Investiture Sacrificial scene Fisherman, Warrior, etc.		

VII

KASSITES AND ELAMITES IN BABYLONIA
(1730-1155 B. C.)

THE Kassites in many ways recall the Guti who had preceded them in Mesopotamia by half a millennium. Like them, the Kassites swept down from the Zagros mountains into the plains watered by the Tigris and Euphrates; but there they met with much more resistance than the Guti had encountered, for Hammurabi's successors were not men to surrender without a struggle. The Babylonians managed to stave off disaster for a while; yet their doom was sealed, and by about 1600 B.C. the Kassites had firmly established themselves in Babylon.

The Kassites displayed a remarkable power of adaptation. A rough, uncultured people, they came into an inheritance fraught with problems for newcomers. Yet what they found they were shrewd enough to keep intact rather than to destroy. For nearly six centuries they maintained precarious sway over a territory coveted not only by their sea-land neighbours to the south, in the marshes along the Persian Gulf, but also and above all by the Elamites, who frequently made swift and profitable incursions into the country. It is in fact in Elam, whither Shutruk-Nakhunte had carried them off as war trophies, that some of the most famous Mesopotamian reliefs have been discovered—the Stele of

387 - BOUNDARY STONE OF NEBUCHADNEZZAR I
(12TH CENTURY B.C.). — BRITISH MUSEUM

389 - AQAR QUF (DUR KURIGALZU) - WALL PAINTING - PROCESSION (14TH CENTURY B.C.)

Naram-Sin and the Code of Hammurabi, for instance, to mention only two. Excavations in Elam have also brought to light Kassite monuments carried off in similar circumstances.

To realize that the Kassites were essentially continuators, not creators, it is only necessary to examine the lay-out of their capital, which stood some twenty miles west of what is now Baghdad, at a place known today as Aqar Quf, but in antiquity called Dur Kurigalzu. Founded in the fifteenth century B.C., the city was dominated by a magnificent ziggurat, the top of which was approached by a triple stairway, and which still overlooks the ruins of the ancient city from a height of nearly two hundred feet. Today one of the most impressive staged towers surviving in Mesopotamia, it was surrounded by several sanctuaries—divine residences dedicated to Enlil, Ninlil and Ninurta. A great palace built in accordance with ancient techniques was decorated with wall paintings comprising geometric themes, floral patterns and processions of men in white tarbooshes, their dark hair and red-tinged faces and arms standing out boldly against the grey walls. Assyrian art later had recourse to these long processions (but executed in stone), which celebrated the grandeur and achievements of kings who no doubt felt a need for propaganda of this kind, both for their own satisfaction and in order to impress their visitors.

390 - AQAR QUF - ZIGGURAT (14TH-13TH CENTURIES B.C.)

314

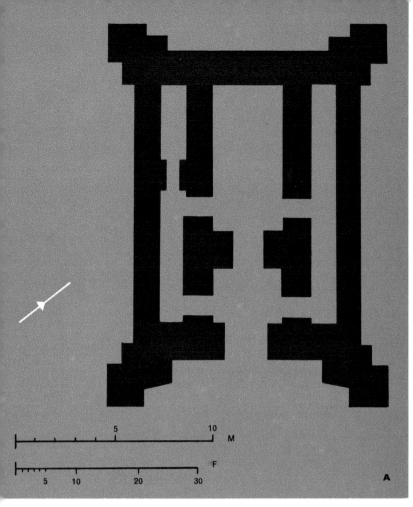

391 - (A) URUK - TEMPLE OF KARAINDASH (B) TEPE GAWRA VIII

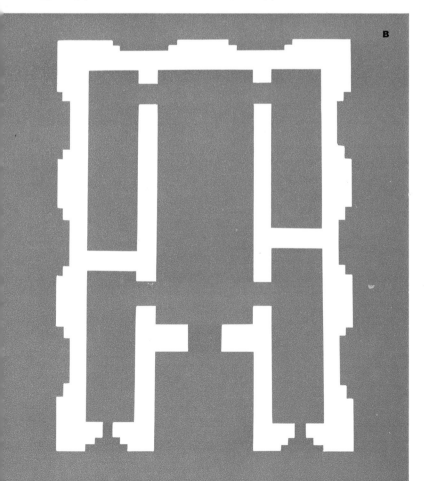

The Kassite leaders not only built for themselves a capital vying with the greatest of the day, but demonstrated their fidelity to Mesopotamian tradition by restoring the ruined monuments of older cities. Traces of these restorations can be seen at Nippur, Uruk and Ur and testify to this people's veneration of Enlil, Inanna and Nannar, whose shrines they not only consolidated but considerably embellished.

Able architects and remarkable builders though they were, the Kassites could never quite overcome a certain native uncouthness and inexpertness, which even in their most painstaking imitations of their predecessors they were unable to disguise. Take, for example, the small temple, dedicated to Inanna, which King Karaindash erected at Uruk. Neither the plan nor the decorative themes belong to the period in which it was built. On the contrary, both lay-out and themes are obvious reminiscences of the archaic temple of Gawra, which pre-dated this sanctuary by fifteen hundred years. The façade of baked brick was decorated with a typically Mesopotamian motif, the flowing vase, but the treatment of it contained several new elements, notably the juxtaposition of gods and goddesses, alternating in narrow recesses. Each figure holds a vase in both hands out of which simulated streams of water flow down in wavy lines, from

3

392 - URUK - MURAL DECORATION OF THE TEMPLE OF KARAINDASH (15TH CENT. B.C.). — BERLIN MUSEUM

niche to niche and over the pilasters between them. Wholly novel, however, was the Kassite use of moulded bricks which, when assembled in sufficient quantities, made up for the absence of stone and could be fitted together in such a way as to form continuous terracotta bas-reliefs.

Temples and palaces must have been full of statues. But no piece of sculpture in the round has come down to us intact. Fragments are all we have, such as those of a colossal statue found at Dur Kurigalzu and inscribed with a text in Sumerian telling of a pious king who restored the sacred precincts after their destruction by some natural calamity or the vandalism of an invading force.

The Kassites also excelled in animal sculpture. A small head of a lioness in terracotta, discovered at Aqar Quf, is in the same vein as the lioness modelled in unfired clay from Warka, though assignable to a later date. In both cases the animal is magnificently rendered, especially in the second, where it is shown advancing lithely with noiseless tread, stalking with grim tenacity some hapless victim it has just caught sight of, and whose fate is sealed.

Very different in inspiration are the boundary stones known as *kudurrus*. Deposited in sanctuaries, covered with inscriptions and decorated with relief carvings, they give us an insight

393 - AQAR QUF - LIONESS (14TH CENTURY B.C.). — BAGHDAD MUSEUM

into the mentality of the Kassites and their conceptions of the Other World. There is some diversity in the composition of these reliefs, though certain elements constantly recur. On a *kudurru* in the Louvre, King Melishipak (twelfth century B.C.) 'presents' his daughter to the goddess Nana, thus renewing a theme frequently employed in the glyptic art of Gudea's time and in that of the Third Dynasty of Ur. The king has taken the place of the intercessionary god, in the same way as Marduk-apal-iddin was later to enact the role of a divine being. The shift of emphasis, if slight, is unmistakable; but this does not mean that religion was losing ground. On the contrary, on certain boundary stones, wholly covered with symbols, the religious motif is predominant.

One of the best examples is a boundary stone also bearing the name of King Melishipak. The sculptor has reverted to the Sumerian

394   WARKA - LIONESS - KASSITE PERIOD (?) - UNBAKED CLAY

395 - BOUNDARY STONES: (A, B) OF MELISHIPAK. — LOUVRE. — (C) OF MARDUK-NADIN-AKHE. — (D) OF NEBUCHADNEZZAR. — BRITISH MUSEUM

practice of dividing the surface into superimposed registers, but the imagery adorning them consists of a sequence of cryptograms not always easy to decipher. On the top row we see the supreme triad, Anu, Enlil and Ea, preceding Ninhursag and dominating the celestial triad: the crescent of Sin (the moon god), the star of Ishtar and the rayed disk of Shamash. On the second register are the gods of hell and war: Nergal, Zababa and Ninurta. On the next row down we recognize the emblems of Marduk, Nabu and Gula. Lower still we can identify Adad, wielder of the thunderbolt, Nusku with the lamp, and Ningirsu with the plough. A bird perching near by perhaps represents Shuqamuna, the only specifically Kassite divinity. On the lowest register, the horned snake and scorpion are the attributes of Ningizzida and Ishara; but the symbol on the extreme left defies interpretation. Thus the *kudurru* contains a representation, at once realistic, fantastic and symbolic, of the pantheon of the Ancient East.

The Kassites founded a school and the kings of the Second Dynasty of Isin, who superseded them in Babylonia, took over their figurative language. King Marduk-nadin-akhe (twelfth century B.C.) had himself portrayed on a *kudurru* of just the same form, with a symbolic frieze and altars of the supreme gods above the royal effigy. To the initiative of Nebuchadnezzar I (twelfth century B.C.) we owe a veritable corpus, on six registers, of all the known themes, together with some that appear for the first time, a pseudo-centaur with bow and arrow, for example.

396 - (A, B) CONFRONTED ANIMALS (13TH-12TH C. B.C.). — BERLIN MUSEUM

Underlying all Kassite glyptic art, no less than in the *kudurrus*, is a more or less esoteric theology. In the designs on cylinder seals two very different styles can be distinguished. The first is derived from ancient Babylonian traditions and, above all else, it affirms the direct relationship, without any intermediary, between the worshipper and his gods. Its emblems are few but characteristic: the cross, lozenge and crescent, to which in time are added the rosette, and afterwards various animal forms (fly, bee, seated dog, locust, gazelle's head).

The second style introduces life and movement, with more or less imaginary animals, trees and plants, which look somewhat unreal; there are also figures (the god with a flowing vase and the fishman) taken over from the old iconography. But here, in marked divergence from the static character of the first style, all is pervaded with an intense dynamism—leaping animals, birds in flight—and even the vegetation seems to be caught up in the general exuberance. Notable is the discrepancy between the iconography of the *kudurrus* and that of glyptic art. On the boundary stones there is a profusion of symbols never found on cylinder seals, and, conversely, certain signs and themes employed in the latter—the cross, for example, which figures so frequently in them—are not found on any *kudurru*. Do the differing 'functional' purposes of cylinder seals and boundary stones account for these divergences? The question is well worth investigating.

While the Kassite dynasty was reigning at Babylon, an Elamite dynasty had established itself at Susa. There are several features in common between the arts of these two dynasties, most notably a certain provincial uncouthness. This provincialism is already evident in several steles in the Louvre, carved in Elam in the time of the First Dynasty of Babylon and reproducing one of its favourite themes: the king standing before his god.

397 - SUSA - STELE OF A KING STANDING BEFORE A GOD. — LOUVRE

The Elamites, however, who had already given proof of remarkable energy, ended up by elevating themselves to the level of their neighbours. King Untash-Huban, in particular, built a five-storied ziggurat at Choga Zambil. The splendid temple at the summit, dedicated to Inshushinak, dominated the plain from a height of over one hundred and sixty feet. The size of the tower and the care with which it was built testify to an age of great prosperity.

The mastery displayed by the bronze-founders during the same period thus comes as no surprise. The statue (cast in two parts) of Queen Napir-Asu, wife of Untash-Huban, mutilated though it is, ranks as a document of capital importance, not only for what it tells us of the technical evolution that had taken place, but also for the light it sheds on Oriental iconography as a whole. Though this statue represents a mass of nearly two tons, its bulk in no way impairs the elegance of this truly royal figure—that of a great lady who seems to be gliding along in her period dress, over the carpets of a reception room, from guest to guest, from courtier to courtier. In point of fact, however, the clasped hands show that Napir-Asu is at prayer. Alas that by an irony of Fate the offerings to the gods and the maledictions inscribed on the embroidery of the robe failed to protect this statue from the impious hands of vandals!

398 - SUSA - STATUE OF QUEEN NAPIR-ASU (C. 1250 B.C.). — LOUVRE

399 - STATUE OF QUEEN NAPIR-ASU, DETAIL —

400 - SUSA - PROCESSION OF WARRIORS (LATE 2ND MILLENNIUM). — LOUVRE

Vandalism has also played havoc with several monuments, such as this bronze bas-relief, which commemorated an Elamite victory and is known to have contained at least three registers. Seven warriors are on the march, each brandishing the same curved, long-handled weapon. In this manner of representing a procession of marching men, whose over-all effect depends entirely on the serial repetition of a single type-figure, we find again a procedure favoured by the Hittites, and taken over by the Assyrians, then by the Achaemenians.

A stele erected by King Untash-Huban has also been severely mutilated. A partial restoration goes to show that once again the Elamites drew inspiration from the Mesopotamians (superimposed registers, scenes of the king before his god, the genius with a flowing vase, the bull-man). Some of its elements, however, are original.

401 - SUSA - STELE OF UNTASH-HUBAN, DETAIL (C. 1250 B.C.). — LOUVRE

PLATE 1 OF UNTASH-HUBAN DETAIL (c. 1250 B.C.)

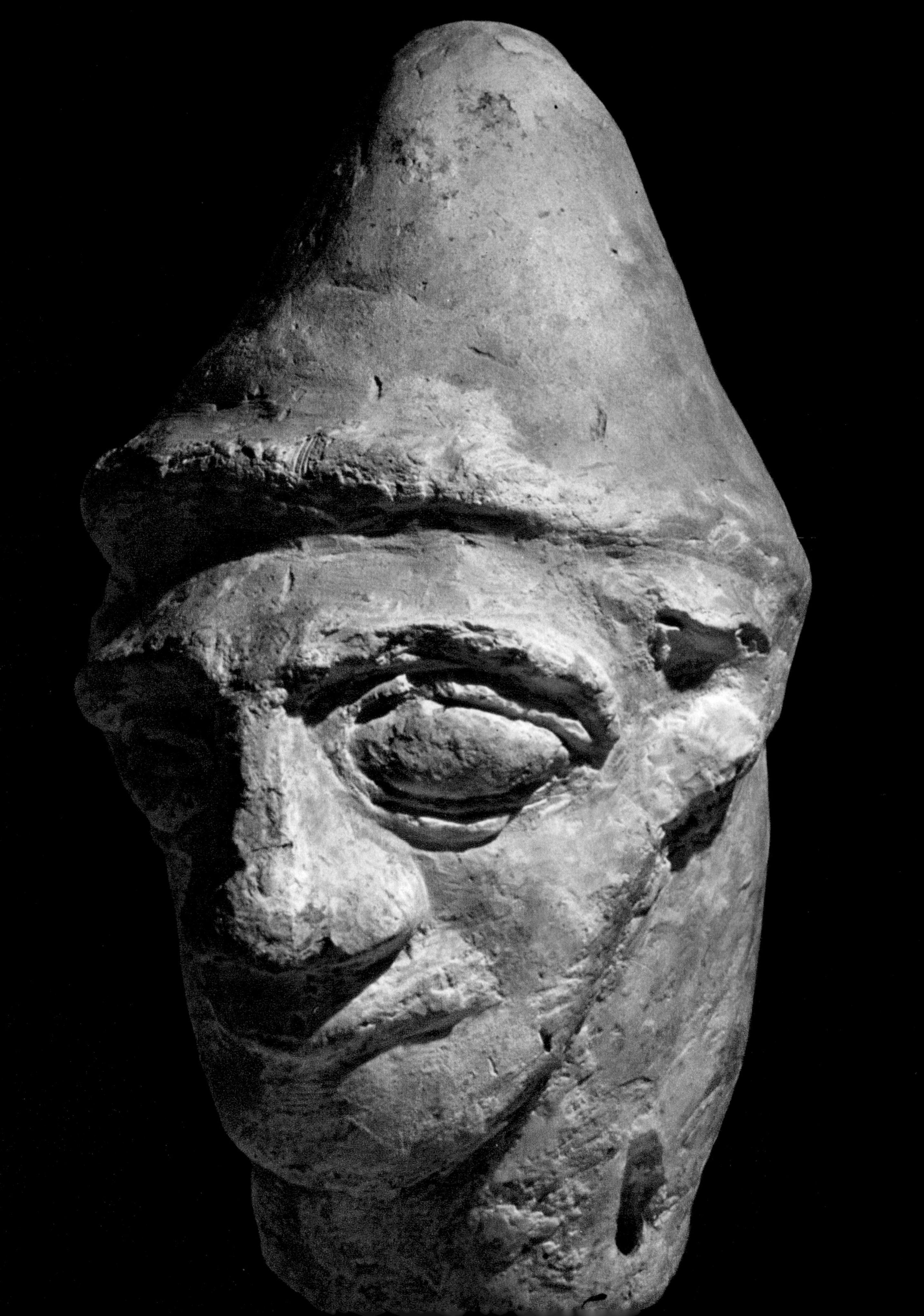

403 - SUSA - HEAD OF A MAN - TERRACOTTA (MID-2ND MILL.). — LOUVRE

404 - SUSA - (A, B) OFFERING BEARERS (MID-2ND MILL.). — (C) WORSHIPPER (2ND HALF, 2ND MILL.). — LOUVRE

But the most striking example of originality is in our opinion the panel of moulded bricks which was discovered at Susa, and whose date is fixed from its inscriptions relating to Kutir-Nakhunte and Shilhak-in-Shushinak, the two sons of the great Elamite raider, Shutruk-Nakhunte (twelfth century B.C.). The panel represents a curious scene: a god, the lower part of whose body is that of a bull, is taking a stylized palm tree under his protection. Beside him is a woman, treated in the manner of a column, raising her hands to her chin.

The bull-god, and reminiscences of Enkidu and the goddess Ninhursag, here combine in the representation of what is certainly a beneficent act. There can be no doubt that in prescribing this decorative technique the Elamite kings were inspired by the Kassite panels in the temple of Karaindash at Uruk.

Ruggedness and schematization are the basic characteristics of this period and province. However, there are some exceptions, for example two statuettes, one in electrum, the other in silver, of a worshipper bringing the sacrificial offering, an ibex or young goat, in which we have a typically Mesopotamian rite reproduced at Susa.

405 - SUSA - BULL-GOD AND THE GODDESS NINHURSAG (2ND HALF, 2ND MILL.). — LOUVRE

407 - SUSA - HEAD OF A BEARDED MAN (EARLY 1ST MILL.?). — LOUVRE

Another exception is the magnificent bronze head of an Elamite dignitary, now in the Metropolitan Museum, New York. The face has an expression of punctilious gravity; the hair is combed flat beneath a turban, tightly encircling the brow. The carefully groomed and curled beard extends well up the cheek-bones. The lips, beneath a neatly trimmed moustache, are thin and tight-shut, expressive of an aloofness that was no doubt to be read in the eyes as well, once inlaid but now empty; yet even so their blank gaze tells of the silent meditations of this monarch or priest.

Later in date perhaps by several centuries, but stylistically belonging

406 - HAMADAN - HEAD OF AN ELAMITE DIGNITARY (2ND HALF, 2ND MILLENNIUM). — METROPOLITAN MUSEUM, NEW YORK

to the same type of art, is the terracotta head from Susa, now in the Louvre. The face is a stern one, and the lips convey disillusionment as well as reprobation. This work is of paramount importance, since it proves that the modellers in clay were far more than mere craftsmen; they were capable of making admirably lifelike portraits.

We conclude this survey of Elamite art with a monument of the late twelfth century B.C.: the bronze tablet known by the name of 'Sit Shamshi,' which represents what is presumably a ceremony solemnized at sunrise. Crouching down, two naked men are performing the rite of ablution in a high place, surrounded by the essential cultic paraphernalia: two ziggurats, an offering table, two columns, some basins, a large jar for the water, and the sacred grove. An inscription in the corner citing the name of King Shilhak-in-Shushinak enables us to fix its date. No document could be more explicit; a glance at the scene conveys at once its meaning. It illustrates not only the Elamite religion but also represents as it were a summary of all the ritual practices of the Ancient East. The ziggurats recall the Mesopotamian plain; the sacred grove exemplifies the veneration of the Semites for any 'green tree.' The large jar brings to mind not only the *apsu* but the 'brazen sea' (I Kings, vii, 23); the two columns subsequently figured prominently in the sanctuaries of Tyre as well as in Jerusalem. To these religious 'constants' there corresponded others relating primarily to the domain of art. The stability of ritual is far from being the only explanation of such recurrences. There are deeper, underlying laws governing the patterns of all human behaviour. Man, the individual, passes away, yet something permanent lives on, whose subsequent reappearances cannot be accounted for, nor can the channels by which they were transmitted be discerned, for all trace of them has been obliterated.

409 - SUSA - SO-CALLED TABLET OF SIT-SHAMSHI, DETAIL: TWO WORSHIPPERS. — LOUVRE

With the Kassites and Elamites, Mesopotamia reached the final stage of an age-old evolution, characterized by mighty achievements in all fields of human endeavour and stamped with the hall-mark of genuinely creative genius. But Mesopotamian culture did not follow a steadily rising curve of progress. The graph rises steeply for a time, then falls back, as is the case with life itself, which cannot continue in a state of constant exaltation. The phase which we have described marks not only a halt but an evident recession. This setback, however, is not permanent; Mesopotamia will resume its forward march and progress for nearly another millennium. Naturally enough, the new developments will not be a simple, logical continuation of the past; they will have a different basis and pursue methods equally efficacious, but very different in inspiration. Fully aware of their past, the Assyrians will be seen to have made a point of remaining faithful to it, though determined to outdo it and to operate on a far grander scale. In this, as we shall see, they are brilliantly successful, but in due course their world too collapses like its predecessors.

← 408 - SUSA - SO-CALLED 'TABLET OF SIT-
   SHAMSHI' (12TH CENTURY B.C.). — LOUVRE

410

413

411

412

385

414

416

415

SEAL IMPRESSIONS
OF THE KASSITE AND ELAMITE PERIODS

CHAPTER VII

KASSITES AND ELAMITES
IN BABYLONIA
(1730-1155 B.C.)

The Guti had put an end to the Akkadian kingdom. The Kassites do likewise with the dynasty of Babylon. Their political success, however, is not attended by destructive violence; on the contrary, they carry on the traditions of the past. They make every effort to keep the cities in repair, to restore the great monuments and to build new ones (an example: the ziggurat of Aqar Quf). They are excellent animal sculptors. Their most characteristic works are the boundary stones, known as *kudurrus*, decorated with reliefs that are often enigmatic, and with a whole family of gods represented in terms of symbolic imagery. Their glyptic art also testifies to a more or less esoteric theology.

In many ways the Elamites recall the Kassites. Excavations at Susa and Choga Zambil have brought to light an abundance of works which enable us to distinguish the special characteristics of their art: monumental architecture (ziggurat of Choga Zambil); bas-reliefs in stone, bronze and brick; bronze figures (e. g. 'Napir-Asu'); small- and large-scale statuary. All go to prove that Elamite art had far more to it than a congenital ruggedness and deliberate schematization.

Mesopotamian civilization has reached the end of a long evolutionary phase; now comes a period of stagnation. A fresh start will be made by the Assyrians, a race determined to excel their predecessors and to operate on a larger scale.

KINGS AND DYNASTIES	SITES	ARCHITECTURE
Kassites (1730-1155)		
Gandash		
Kurigalzu	DUR KURIGALZU (AQAR QUF)	Ziggurat
Karaindash (1445-1427)	URUK	Temple of Inann
Nazimaruttash II (1319-1294)	SUSA	
Melishipak II (1202-1188)	SUSA	
Elamites (1350-1150)		
Untash-Huban	CHOGA ZAMBIL	Ziggurat
Shutruk-Nakhunte	SUSA	
Kutir-Nakhunte (1171)	SUSA	Temple of Shushinak
Shilhak-in-Shushinak	SUSA	Temple of Shushinak
Second Dynasty of Isin (1170-1039)		
Nebuchadnezzar I (1146-1123)	NIPPUR	
Marduk-nadin-akhe (1116-1101)		

SCULPTURE	TERRACOTTA	METAL	SHELL AND IVORY	PAINTING	EGYPT	AEGEAN
Cylinder Seals					Hyksos Dynasties (1675-1580)	Middle Minoan III (1700-1580)
Colossal Statue	Head of a Lioness			Palace: Processions		
	Moulded brick reliefs				New Kingdom (1580-1090)	Later Cretan palaces Late Minoan I (1550-1450) Tombs of Mycenae
Kudurrus					Sethos I (1312-1298)	
Kudurrus					Ramesses II (1298-1233)	
Head of a Dignitary (Metropolitan)					Ramesses III (1198-1166)	Late Minoan II (1450-1400)
Stele		Statue of Napir-Asu Relief with warriors				Late Minoan III (1400-1180) Later palaces of Mycenae and Tiryns
					Ramesses III (1198-1166)	
Stele	Moulded brick reliefs Enamelled and glazed pottery	Sit Shamshi				
					Ramesses III (1198-1166)	
Kudurru						
Kudurru		Bronze Dagger				

337

GLOSSARIAL INDEX

AND

BIBLIOGRAPHY

GLOSSARIAL INDEX

Each work reproduced is listed under the place where it was discovered. Items marked with an asterisk are commented on in separate entries under the corresponding letter of the alphabet.

ABEL — Son of Adam, a shepherd, sacrificed the firstlings of his flock (Genesis, IV, 4). . . *p.* 71, 242

ABRAHAM — Hebrew patriarch, born at Ur, father of Isaac and Ishmael, ancestor of the Jewish people. . . . . *p.* 162

ABU — God of vegetation. Statue from Tell Asmar (discovered 1933-34), dating from the first half of the third millennium B.C. Baghdad Museum . . . . *fig.* 134*a*, 135, 137
— Statuettes from the temple of Abu. . *fig.* 33, 129

ABU HABBA (SIPPAR) — Akkadian city, with temple of Shamash. Excavated by Rassam (1879-82), P. Scheil (1894), and Jordan and Andrae (1927). Famous monument: tablet of Nabu-apal-iddin (British Museum). The stele with the Code of Hammurabi may have been erected here . . . . . *p.* 174
Sculpture: Boundary stone of Nebuchadnezzar I*
fig. 387, 395*d*

ABU KEMAL — Syrian town founded by the Turks in 1887. Near the Iraqi frontier, not far from Mari . . . . *p.* 23, 256

ABU SHAHREIN (ERIDU) — City in southern Mesopotamia, centre of the cult of Enki-Ea, god of subterranean waters. Excavations have revealed here a phase of Mesopotamian protohistory preceding the al 'Ubaid period.
p. 20, 24, 39, 41, 52-55, 63, 66, 68, 74, 90, 96, 200
Architecture:
— Temple VII (plan). . . . . *fig.* 72*a*
— Temples on levels XV-XVIII (plan). . . *fig.* 70
Sculpture:
— Figurine . . . . *fig.* 75
Map . . . . *fig.* 56

ACHAEMENIANS — Persian dynasty, of which Cyrus (546 B.C.) was the first king to reign over the whole country. Ends in 330 B.C. with the death of Darius III Codomannus . . . . *p.* 3, 324

ADAB, see BISMAYA.

ADAD — Akkadian storm god, known as Hadad in Syria-Phoenicia-Canaan . . . . *p.* 19

ADDA — Scribe's name engraved on an Akkadian cylinder seal (British Museum). . . . . . *fig.* 237

ADONIS — Phoenician god of fertility, alternately dying and being reborn, whose Mesopotamian prototype is Tammuz-Dumuzi . . . . . . *p.* 65

AEGEAN SEA — Part of the Eastern Mediterranean between Greece and Asia Minor. Has given its name to an early Hellenic civilization . . . . . *p.* 278

AESOP — Greek writer of fables (7th-6th c. B.C.) *p.* 150

AGADE, see AKKAD.

AKALAMDUG — A 'king' of Ur whose name was found on a cylinder seal in Tomb 1050 of the 'royal' cemetery . . . . *p.* 160

AKKAD — An ancient city (perhaps Deir) and state whose first king was Sargon (25th century B.C.), whose dynasty ended in the 23rd century B.C. The name Agade is sometimes used to designate the city, state or dynasty.
p. 4, 96, 170, 172, 182, 194, 250, 336
Cylinder seals of the Akkadian period:
— Shamash*. . . . . *fig.* 2
— Various· . . *fig.* 223, 225-227, 231, 233-235, 237

AKKADIANS — Name applied to the kings of the Semite dynasty founded by Sargon or to the subjects of their State. . . *p.* 3, 12, 169, 170, 178, 186, 187, 194, 197, 198, 200, 234

AKSHAK — Dynastic city (the 12th after the Flood) whose site is still unidentified. Probably located in the region of Seleucia (Ctesiphon) on the Tigris. *p.* 96

ALABASTER — White calcareous or gypseous stone, sometimes translucent, taking a high polish, in which the Mesopotamians carved their most precious statuettes . . . . *e. g. fig.* 147*b*

ALEPPO — City in northern Syria (population 400,000), already mentioned in tablets found at Mari (18th century B.C.) . . . . *p.* 22, 259

ALEXANDER THE GREAT (356-323 B.C.) — King of Macedon and conqueror of Western Asia. Died at Babylon . . . . *p.* 3

ALEXANDER, so-called Sarcophagus of — Found in the necropolis of Sidon in 1887 by T. Reinach and Hamdy Bey. Istanbul Museum. . . . . . *p.* 270
fig. 337

AL-'OHEIMIR (KISH) — Sumerian city, seat of several dynasties (I-IV), NNE. of Babylon. Excavated from 1912 on (Genouillac), then from 1923 to 1933 (Joint Expedition). . . *p.* 16, 20, 96, 100, 166, 236
Architecture:
— Palace: plan . . . . *fig.* 128*a*
         reconstruction . . . . *fig.* 128*b*
Sculpture:
— Lion attacking a Stag . . . . *fig.* 162
Seal:
— Picture of a ziggurat. . . . . *fig.* 125

AL 'UBAID — Small site near Ur, excavated in 1919, which gave its name to a phase of Mesopotamian protohistory between the Halaf and Uruk periods (4th millennium). . . *p.* 19, 20, 41, 53, 60, 63, 64, 90, 95, 98, 133, 156, 158, 166
Sculpture:
— Bull. . . . . *fig.* 185
— Human-headed bull. . . . . *fig.* 161*c*
— Kurlil* . . . . *fig.* 144
— Lion-headed eagle from the tympanum of the temple door (British Museum). A relief from the same site represents a lion-headed eagle attacking a human-headed bull (British Museum) *fig.* 161*c*, 187
Figurines and plaques:
— Figurines of the al 'Ubaid period. . . . *fig.* 73-77
— Figurine in the al 'Ubaid style . . . . . *fig.* 66
Sherds (of the al 'Ubaid period) . . . . . . *fig.* 71

AMERICAN SCHOOL OF ORIENTAL RESEARCH
— Has conducted many important explorations throughout the Near East (Khafaje, Nuzi, Tepe Gawra, Tell Billa, etc.) . . . . *p.* 22

AMORITES — Semitic inhabitants of the Amurru region . . . . *p.* 254

AMURRU — Region of western Mesopotamia (Middle Euphrates and Syrian desert) . . . . *p.* 170

ANATOLIA — Central part of Asia Minor. *p.* 3, 29

ANDRAE (Walter) (1875-1956) — Famous German architect and archaeologist, disciple of Koldewey and excavator of Assur (1903-14). . . *p.* 16, *fig.* 15

ANTECELLA — Room in many Mesopotamian temples connecting the court and the cella where the divinity resided . . . . *p.* 262

ANTELOPES — Frequently and conspicuously represented in hunting scenes with Gilgamesh and Enkidu . . . . *e. g. fig.* 67a

ANU — Supreme god of the Mesopotamian pantheon. Temple at Uruk*.. *p.* 65, 68, 190, 302, 319, *fig.* 228

APSU — Underground body of fresh water, domain of Enki-Ea . . . . *p.* 332

AQAR QUF (DUR KURIGALZU) — Site of the ancient Kassite capital, west of Baghdad. Excavated by the Iraqi Department of Antiquities (1942-45) . . . . *p.* 24, 314, 317, 318, 336
Architecture:
— Ziggurat: one of the most famous, best preserved staged towers in all Babylonia. Kassite period (14th century B.C.) . . . . *fig.* 390
Sculpture:
— Head of a lioness: fine specimen of Kassite animal art . . . . *fig.* 393
Painting:
— Procession. . . . . *fig.* 389

ARAMAEANS — A Semitic people settled for the most part in central Syria, their three main cities being Damascus, Hamah and Aleppo . . . . *p.* 3

ARBELA, see ERBIL.

ARBIT — Tell in the Upper Khabur region, about 9 miles east of Chagar Bazar. Excavated by Mallowan in 1936 . . . . *p.* 23

ARCH — Architectural form known to the Mesopotamians, e.g. hypogeum of Dungi and Bur-Sin at Ur (late 3rd millennium) . . . . *fig.* 30

ARMENIA — Mountainous region to the north of Mesopotamia, known to the ancients as Urartu *p.* 38

ARPATCHIYA — Small site near Nineveh excavated by Mallowan in 1933. Revealed evidence of several protohistorical cultures (Samarra, Halaf, 'Ubaid). Ancient name unidentified. . . . . *p.* 22, 48, 50
Pottery . . . . *fig.* 62a, 67b, 67c

ARSLAN TASH (HADATU) — Site in Upper Syria excavated by the Thureau-Dangin expedition in 1928. Reliefs, statues and a magnificent collection of ivories discovered there (Louvre and Aleppo Museum) . . . . *p.* 23

ARURU — Female divinity who, with the god Marduk, created humanity . . . . *p.* 302

ARYBALLOS — Round, narrow-necked vase held by deities or genii, from which water sometimes flows (Mari goddesses, Uruk gods and goddesses, Khorsabad gods) . . . . . . *p.* 272, 278, 316, *fig.* 273

ASHNUNNAK, see TELL ASMAR.

ASS, Music-making — Mesopotamian theme found in the decorative inlay of a harp from Ur. Reappears in Romanesque art . . . . *p.* 150, *fig.* 179

ASSUR, see QALAAT SHERGAT.

ASSURBANIPAL — King of Assyria (668-631 B.C.), famous for his palace and library discovered at Nineveh by Layard, Rassam and Loftus. Immortalized by the Lion Hunt and Garden Scene reliefs in the British Museum. . . . . *p.* 10, 15, 75, 118
— Relief from his palace ('Feast in the Garden') *fig.* 20

ASSURNASIRPAL II — King of Assyria (883-859 B.C.) who embellished Kalakh (Nimrud). Palace containing reliefs (British Museum, Louvre, Baghdad Museum) and precious objects (ivories, British Museum and Baghdad Museum). Stone statue (British Museum). . . . . *p.* 118, *fig.* 6d
— Winged bulls of Assurnasirpal II . . . . *fig.* 25

ASSYRIA — Region of the Upper Tigris, several cities of which were great cultural centres: Assur (Qalaat Shergat), Kalakh (Nimrud), Nineveh (Kuyunjik), Dur Sharrukin (Khorsabad). *p.* 3, 22, 37

ASSYRIANS — Inhabitants or natives of Assyria . . . . *p.* 3, 12, 29, 256, 324, 333, 336

ASWAN — City in Upper Egypt on the Nile, famous for its quarries of pink granite . . . . . *p.* 8, 42

ATHENS — Capital of Greece, at the foot of the Acropolis and Mount Lycabettus . . . . . *p.* 33

AWIL NANNAR — Dedicator of the bronze statue known as the Larsa Worshipper. . . *p.* 284, *fig.* 350

AXE, Double-headed — Decorative motif frequent in protohistorical pottery (Arpatchiya, Halaf period), symbol of the storm god . . . . *e. g. fig.* 67c

BAAL — Collective name of the Canaanite gods in the Old Testament . . . . *p.* 46

BABBAR — Sumerian sun god, with particular reference to the rising sun (*cf.* UTU) . . . . . *p.* 188

BABYLON — Great capital city in the heart of Mesopotamia, on the Euphrates, some 50 miles south of Baghdad. Mentioned as early as the 24th century B.C. Particularly prosperous under Hammurabi (1792-1750) and later under the Neo-Babylonians (626-539). Its last king, Nabonidus, was defeated by Cyrus. According to a moderate chronology (S. Smith and Ungnad), which we have adopted here, the 'dynasty of Babylon' lasted from 1894 to 1595 B.C. *p.* 14, 16, 17, 32, 253, 254, 256, 264, 268, 306, 310, 313, 320, 336
Architecture:
— Ruins of Babylon . . . . *fig.* 22
Sculpture:
— Lion from Babylon . . . . *fig.* 6b

BABYLONIA — Region including Babylon. *p.* 313, 319, 336

BABYLONIANS — Inhabitants of the Babylon region. Sometimes used, by extension, to designate the inhabitants of a much wider area, embracing central and southern Mesopotamia. Some archaeologists therefore speak, for example, of an 'Assyro-Babylonian' civilization . . . . *p.* 3

BACHE (Charles) — American archaeologist who explored Tepe Gawra . . . . *p.* 22

BAETYLUS — Aniconic sacred stone, often erected in places of Semitic worship. An example found at Mari, in the temple of Ninni-Zaza, is now in Damascus Museum . . . . *e. g. fig.* 127*b*

BAGHDAD — Capital of Iraq, founded in 760 A.D. by the Abbasid Caliph Mansur. Originally built on the right bank of the Tigris, the city now stands largely on the left bank. Just outside Baghdad is the site of Tell Harmal*. *p.* 14, 18, 22, 95, 224, 288, 314

BANKS (Edgar James) (1866-?) — American excavator of Bismaya* (Adab). . . . . *p.* 16

BARTHELEMY (Jean-Jacques) (1716-1795) — French scholar who first deciphered the Phœnician language, in 1764, thanks to the bilingual Malta inscription . . . . *p.* 12

BASALT — Dark grey stone of volcanic origin, sometimes imported and used by Mesopotamian sculptors . . . . *e. g. fig.* 92

BASRA — City of modern Iraq, on the Shatt el-Arab (mouth of the Tigris and Euphrates) . . . . *p.* 15

BAU — Goddess, consort of Ningirsu, worshipped at Lagash. The name is sometimes read as Baba or Bawa (Sollberger). *p.* 136, 214, 240, 266, *fig.* 288, 328

BEE — Represented on Kassite cylinder seals, with an undetermined symbolic value. It appears nowhere else in Mesopotamian art. . . . *p.* 320, *fig.* 396*a*

BETHEL — Canaanite city, 11 miles north of Jerusalem, famous for a temple dedicated to El. Here Jacob had his vision of the heavenly ladder (Genesis, xxviii, 12), and Jeroboam, king of Israel, later erected an altar for the worship of the golden calf (I Kings, xii-xiii) . . . . *p.* 201, 238

BIANQUIS (André) — Member of the French archaeological expedition to Mari. Killed accidentally (April 3, 1936) at the end of the third season's excavations . . . . *p.* 259, *fig.* 36

BIBLE — Sacred book containing the Old Testament (in Hebrew) and the New Testament (in Greek). *p.* 12, 20

BILALAMA — King of Ashnunnak and law-giver. *p.* 305

BIRD-COMB — Decorative design on pottery of the Susa I style . . . . *p.* 62, *fig.* 80*a*, 80*e*

BIRD (Flying). . . . . *fig.* 120, 121

BIRD (Perched) — On boundary stones, emblem of the Kassite god Shuqamuna. . . . . . *p.* 319

BIRDS . . . . *fig.* 60*c*, 79, 96

BIRS NIMRUD (BORSIPPA) — Ancient site near Babylon, excavated by Koldewey in 1902. The god Nabu was worshipped there in the temple known as Ezida . . . . *p.* 32

BISMAYA (ADAB) — Site of the ancient dynastic city of Adab (the 9th after the Flood), SSE. of Nippur, excavated by E. J. Banks (1903-04) . . . *p.* 16, 180
Sculpture:
— Man's head . . . . *fig.* 217

BITCH SUCKLING PUPPIES . . . . . *fig.* 363

BITUMEN — Black hydrocarbon, found on the Middle Euphrates and Upper Tigris, much employed by the Mesopotamians in architecture, sculpture, implements, sumptuary arts, etc.

BOAT — Frequently represented in seal designs and also in clay, stone and metal models. Played an important part in religious ceremonies, when used by gods to navigate the canals (cylinder seals from Uruk) . . . . . . *p.* 74, 75, 80, *fig.* 91*a*, 91*b*, 306

BOAT-GOD . . . . *fig.* 198, 238

BORSIPPA, see BIRS NIMRUD

BOTTA (Paul-Emile) (1802-1870) — French consul at Mosul, discovered and excavated Khorsabad in 1843-44. . . . . *p.* 8, 12, 22, 28, *fig.* 14

BOUNDARY STONES, see KUDURRUS

BOXERS — On small figure plaques of the early 2nd millennium . . . . *p.* 293, *fig.* 359*d*

BRAIDWOOD (R. J.) — American archaeologist, specializing in protohistory. Has explored the Amuq plain (Antioch region) and northeastern Iraq (Jarmo) . . . . *p.* 25, 39

BRAZEN SEA — Large tank of bronze in the temple of Solomon at Jerusalem (I Kings, vii, 23-26). Perhaps a symbolic reminiscence of the *apsu**. . *p.* 332

BREASTED (James Henry) (1865-1935) — American Egyptologist, director of the Oriental Institute of Chicago, who did much to promote systematic exploration of the Ancient Near East. . . . . . . *p.* 22

BRECCIA — Conglomerate rock. 'Calcareous' breccia is a kind of marble . . . . *e. g. fig.* 148

BRICK (Baked) — Clay moulded into blocks, fired in kilns and used as building material.

BRICK (Moulded) — Used to form figures or decorations in relief. . . . . *fig.* 392

BRICK (Plano-convex) — A type of baked or unbaked brick flat on one side, curved on the other. Building material characteristic of the Early Dynastic or Pre-Sargonid period in Sumer. . . . . . . *p.* 97

BRICK (Unbaked) — Clay moulded into blocks and sun-dried, used as building material.

BROCADE STYLE — Name coined by Frankfort to describe certain form-distorting patterns of early 3rd-millennium seal designs . . . . . *e. g. fig.* 118

BRONZE — Alloy of copper and tin, much used from the early 3rd millennium on.

BRUEGEL THE ELDER (Pieter) (c. 1530-1569) — Flemish painter and engraver who painted several pictures representing the Tower of Babel, closely modelled on the Coliseum in Rome . . . . *fig.* 4

BUFFALO . . . . *e. g. fig.* 224

BULL — Very often represented in sculpture in the round (copper or bronze) from the Pre-Sargonid period on, and on the soundboxes of lyres. Many examples discovered at Ur (gold, silver, bronze) *fig.* 91*a*, 94-96, 108, 184*a*, 185, 186, 189*b*, 191, 292*b*

BULL-GOD — Represented on brick relief panels from the temple of Shushinak at Susa, 12th century B.C. Louvre . . . . *p.* 328, *fig.* 405

BULL (Human-headed) — Often represented in seals, reliefs, statuettes, apparently symbolizing a beneficent power under constant attack from an evil one (lion-headed eagle) . *p.* 10, 133, 140, 141, 150, 224, 290 *fig.* 25, 161*c*, 276*a*, 276*b*, 277

BULL (Human-headed) Muzzle of . . . . . *fig.* 170*b*

BULL-MAN — Composite figure of the Enkidu type. Represented in seal designs, stone and brick reliefs, and on small figure plaques. . . . . . . *p.* 140, 324

BULL-MUZZLE . . . . *fig.* 170*a*

BULL'S SKULL — Represented schematically on protohistorical pottery (Arpatchiya). Symbol of the storm god . . . . *e. g. fig.* 67*b*

BULL (Votive) . . . . *fig.* 100

BULLS (Winged) of Assurnasirpal II* . . . *fig.* 25

BURNEY PLAQUE — Terracotta plaque representing a naked, winged goddess with lions and owls . . . . *p.* 300, *fig.* 367*a*

BUR-SIN — Also read Amar-Sin, son of Dungi (Shulgi), third king of the Third Dynasty of Ur (2058-2050 B.C.) . . . . *p.* 203 — Hypogeum: discovered at Ur by Woolley in 1930-31. Built next to that of Dungi. . . . . *fig.* 249*e*

CADUCEUS — Beneficent emblem of Sumerian origin, often figuring in seal designs. The libation goblet of Gudea* (Louvre) shows a good example of it . . . . *p.* 237

CAILLOIS (Roger) — French writer born in 1913 *p.* 33

CAIN — Son of Adam, a husbandman, offered the 'fruit of the ground' as a sacrifice (Genesis, IV, 3) *p.* 71

CANAANITES — Large ethnic group of Semitic origin which had settled in the western part of the Near East by the early 3rd millennium. The area of their penetration and influence extends well beyond Palestine. . . . . *p.* 3

CANEPHORUS — Basket bearer. Name applied to a type of foundation figurine . . *fig.* 292*c*, 292*d*

CAPRIDAE. . . . . *e. g. fig.* 244

CARBON 14 — Method of dating based on the residual radioactivity of the isotope of carbon 14. Now extensively used in archaeological research . . . . *p.* 39

CARMEL — Small mountain range along the seacoast of Palestine, scarcely rising 1600 feet above the plain of Esdraelon. Famous for its associations with the Prophet Elijah (I Kings, XVIII) . . . . *p.* 46

CARPENTER — On a small figure plaque.
p. 293, *fig.* 359*e*

CELLA — The sacred precinct of the temple, the Holy of Holies, where the god resided and his statue stood, often surrounded by ex-votos *p.* 99, 114, 262, *fig.* 127*a*

CHAGAR BAZAR (SHUBAT ENLIL?) — Tell in the Upper Khabur region, excavated by Mallowan (1935-37) . . . . *p.* 23

CHALCOLITHIC AGE — Cultural phase characterized by the simultaneous use of metal (copper) and stone. One of the essential traits of the Halaf period.

CHALDEA — Name applied in the 19th century to Mesopotamia as a whole. It should be restricted to the area near the Persian Gulf and to the period of the first millennium B.C. . . . . *p.* 28

CHALDEANS — Name incorrectly used in many books to designate the Sumerians. Strictly speaking, it only applies to the tribes that settled Lower Mesopotamia in the 7th and 6th centuries B.C. . . . . . *p.* 10

CHALDEAN TEMPLE — Reconstruction of a ziggurat by Chipiez . . . . *fig.* 9

CHARIOT — Vehicle with solid wooden wheels represented from the early 3rd millennium on, in reliefs and mosaic panels (Ur, Mari) and small models made of copper (Tell Agrab) and clay (from all Mesopotamian sites) *p.* 133, 152, 153, *fig.* 181, 182 — War chariots: invented by the Sumerians, and developed and exploited tactically in the Assyrian period . . . . *p.* 136, 146, 149, *fig.* 175

CHERUBIM — Guardian animals of Paradise (Genesis, III, 24). May have taken the form of human-headed bulls, sphinxes or griffins (*cf.* Mari paintings, *fig.* 346)
p. 278

CHIERA (Edward) (1855-1933) — American Assyriologist, excavated Yorgan Tepe (Nuzi) from 1925 to 1928. . . . . *p.* 22

CHIPIEZ (Charles) (1835-1901) — French architect and draughtsman, collaborated with Georges Perrot in the publication of *Histoire de l'Art dans l'Antiquité* (*cf.* Bibliography) . . . . *p.* 7, 10 — Engravings by Chipiez . . . . *fig.* 7, 10 — Reconstruction by Chipiez . . . . . . *fig.* 9

CHOGA ZAMBIL — Elamite site in the Susa region, dominated by a five-storied ziggurat cleared by Ghirshman. . . . . *p.* 26, 322, 336 — Ziggurat: built by King Untash-Huban (12th century B.C.), excavated by Ghirshman . *fig.* 42, 43

CODE OF HAMMURABI*. . . . . *fig.* 373

COLUMNS OF SIT SHAMSHI*. . . . . *fig.* 408

COLOURS (Military) — Flag used first by the Sumerians and Akkadians, and later by the Neo-Sumerians and Assyrians. . . . . *p.* 176, *fig.* 213

CONE MOSAICS — Technique of wall decoration much employed in Lower Mesopotamia (at Uruk especially) in the Jemdet Nasr period (late 4th-early 3rd millennium) . . . . *fig.* 84*a*, 84*b*

CONTENAU (Georges) — French Orientalist born in 1877, honorary chief curator of the Louvre, excavated Tepe Giyan (1931-32) with Ghirshman. . . . *p.* 24

CRESCENT — Symbolic motif on Kassite seals and boundary stones, connected with Sin*
p. 319, 320, *e. g. fig.* 395*b*

CRETE — Aegean island called *Caftor* in the inscribed tablets found at Mari . . . . *p.* 281

CROS (Gaston) (?-1915) — French officer, excavated Telloh (1903-09) . . . . *p.* 16, 21

CROSS — Mesopotamian decorative motif, especially in protohistorical pottery and Kassite seal designs
p. 44, 320

CROSS (Greek) — Cross with four arms of equal length, figuring frequently on Susa pottery . . *p.* 62

CROSS (Maltese) — Decorative motif on protohistorical pottery, from the Samarra period on (5th millennium) . . . . *p.* 44, 50, 62, *fig.* 80*e*

CRYSTALLINE STONE . . . . *e. g. fig.* 97

CUNEIFORM WRITING — Name applied to the ancient Mesopotamian script, composed of wedge-shaped characters (Latin *cuneus*, a wedge). . . *p.* 94

CYCLOPS — On a small figure plaque from Khafaje. . . . . *p.* 291, *fig.* 358a

CYLINDER SEALS — Small cylindrical pieces of stone decorated in intaglio with religious or mythological scenes, so that when the seal is rolled over a soft clay tablet a raised impression is made. Many of them contain inscriptions.

DAGAN — Divinity worshipped at Mari and Terqa, upstream from the capital of Zimri-Lim
p. 259, 268, 286
— Bronze lions from the esplanade and entrance of the temple of Dagan (18th century B.C.). Louvre and Aleppo Museum . . . . *fig.* 322, 353

DATE PALM — Flourishes in the oases of Mesopotamia, but its fruit does not ripen north of Ana (Middle Euphrates) . . . . *p.* 278

DAVID — King of Israel, son-in-law of Saul, father of Solomon. . . . . *p.* 241

DEIR EL-MEDINEH — Small temple of the Ptolemaic period in Upper Egypt, where *ostraca* were found in excavations conducted by the Institut Français d'Archéologie. . . . . *p.* 150

DIACONICON — A room in Early Christian basilicas beside the central apse, reserved for the use of the deacons. . . . . *p.* 66

DIARBEKIR — The ancient Amida, now in Turkey on the right bank of the Upper Tigris . . . *p.* 174

DIEULAFOY Marcel (1844-1920) and Jeanne (1851-1916) — French excavators of Susa (1884-86). Brought back to the Louvre an extensive collection of Achaemenian works, including the Frieze of Archers and the so-called Achaemenian capital . . . . *p.* 16

DIORITE — An extremely hard, blue-black, eruptive rock, imported into Mesopotamia from the land of Magan (Arabia?). Several Gudea statues are carved in diorite. . . . . *e. g. fig.* 258

DISK (Rayed). . . . . . . *p.* 319, *e. g. fig.* 395a

DISTEMPER — A technique of painting in which the powdered colours, mixed with water, are applied to a dry surface with a brush dipped in hot glue *p.* 99

DIYALA — Tributary on the eastern side of the Tigris, which it joins about 12 miles SSE. of Baghdad . . . . *p.* 95

DIYALA REGION
p. 18, 22, 29, 98, 102, 110, 122, 153, 162, 166
Sculpture:
— Worshipper . . . . *fig.* 132
Figurines and plaques:
— Bitch suckling puppies . . . . *fig.* 363
— Harp-player . . . . *fig.* 359b
— Peasant . . . . *fig.* 360
— Woman . . . . *fig.* 140
Map: . . . . *fig.* 55

DOLERITE — Very hard, greenish blue, eruptive rock, imported into Mesopotamia and used in sculpture . . . . *e. g. fig.* 306

DOOR POST — Often represented in seal designs, with a loop or several pairs of rings attached to it . . . . *e. g. fig.* 200

DUDU — High priest of Ningirsu in the time of Entemena. Bituminous relief (Louvre) and statue (Baghdad Museum). Pre-Sargonid period. . . . *p.* 138
— Plaque of Dudu . . . . *fig.* 167a

DUMUZI — God of the Mesopotamian pantheon. His full name is Dumuzi-apsu . . . . . *p.* 65, 72

DUNGI (SHULGI) — One of the most famous kings of the Third Dynasty of Ur, a great builder, who reigned 48 years (2106-2059 B.C.). His name is now sometimes read as Shulgi . . *p.* 199, 203, 234, 250
Architecture:
— Hypogeum, discovered by Woolley at Ur in 1930-31, built next to that of Bur-Sin . . *fig.* 30, 249d, 249f
— Ziggurat built by Dungi . . . . *fig.* 247
Sculpture:
— Canephorus inscribed with Dungi's name. *fig.* 292c

DURA EUROPOS — City on the Middle Euphrates, founded by the Macedonians under Seleucos I Nicator (312-280 B.C.) and destroyed by the Persians in 256 A.D. . . . . *p.* 259

DUR KURIGALZU, see AQAR QUF.

DUR SHARRUKIN (fortress of Sargon), see KHORSABAD.

DUSSAUD (René) (1868-1958) — Eminent French Orientalist, for long Secretary of the Académie des Inscriptions et Belles-Lettres, curator of the Department of Oriental Antiquities at the Louvre, and an ardent promoter of French excavations in the Near East. . . . . *p.* 256

EA — Semitic name of the water god, called Enki* in Sumerian . . . . *p.* 188, 319

EAGLE — A frequent theme, treated both realistically and symbolically . . . . *fig.* 244, 308
— Lion-headed eagle, animal attribute of the god Ningirsu. . *p.* 131, 133, 137, 138, 158, *fig.* 161c, 187
— Spread eagle . . . . *fig.* 303, 304, 307

E-ANNA — Famous temple at Uruk, dedicated to the goddess Inanna. By extension the word also designates the whole temple complex. *p.* 65, 68, *fig.* 82

EANNATUM — King of Lagash, successor of Akurgal (c. 2700 B.C.). Among monuments left by this ruler is the Stele of the Vultures* (Louvre).
p. 135, 136, 172, *fig.* 164

EARLY DYNASTIC PERIOD — Name proposed by the Oriental Institute of Chicago and adopted by British and American archaeologists for the period between the end of the Jemdet Nasr period (c. 2800 B.C.) and the reign of Sargon of Akkad (began 2467 B.C.). Subdivided into three phases (I-II-III) by excavators. The term Pre-Sargonid* is used instead of Early Dynastic in this book.
p. 96

EBIH-IL — Steward of Mari who dedicated his statue in the temple of Ishtar. Louvre. . *p.* 118, *fig.* 147b

ECOLE BIBLIQUE ET ARCHEOLOGIQUE FRANÇAISE DE JERUSALEM — Conducted excavations at Neirab near Aleppo (1926-27). *p.* 22

EDDINGTON, Sir Arthur Stanley (1882-1944) — English astronomer and physicist . . . . . . *p.* 32

GLYPTICS — The art of engraving on precious stones.

GOATS . . . . *fig.* 110

GOAT'S HEAD — Bronze discovered at Shuruppak . . . . *p.* 155, *fig.* 184*b*

GOAT (Young) — Sacrificial animal often represented in statuettes, figurines and reliefs, held in both hands by a priest or worshipper
p. 264, 275, 328, *fig.* 294, 378, 382, 384

GOAT (Wild), see IBEX.

GOD (Two-faced) — Usmu, faithful minion of the god Enki-Ea, often represented in seal designs . *p.* 284

GOETZE (A.) — American Assyriologist, a leading authority on the civilization of ancient Anatolia . . . . *p.* 254

GOOSE — Generally accompanying the goddess Bau . . . . *fig.* 305

GUDEA — One of the most famous patesis of Lagash, lived in the Neo-Sumerian period (21st century B.C.). Portrayed in some thirty statues. The largest collection of them is in the Louvre
p. 8, 10, 15, 28, 31, 199, 204-207, 210, 211, 213-218, 220, 224, 226, 230, 234, 236, 237, 246, 250, 266, 290, 291, 318, *fig.* 6*a*, 49, 257, 260, 262, 266, 284
— 'Architect with a Plan' . . . . *fig.* 253
— Broad-shouldered Gudea . . . . . . *fig.* 255
— Gudea A . . . . *fig.* 256
— Gudea with a Flowing Vase . . . . . *fig.* 264
— Gudea with a Palm Branch . . . . . *fig.* 285
— Gudea as a Worshipper . . . . . *fig.* 263, 265
— Narrow-shouldered Gudea . . . . . *fig.* 254
— Small Seated Gudea . . . . *fig.* 251
— 'Turbaned Head': so called by Sarzec before it was identified as Gudea. Louvre . . . *fig.* 7, 8, 258

GUDEA (Basin of) — Adorned with lions' heads in high relief. Fragment in the Louvre . . . *p.* 236

GUDEA (Libation Goblet of) — Dedicated to Ningizzida, who is represented by her animal attributes. Louvre . . . . *p.* 236, *fig.* 289

GUDEA (Mace-head of) — Adorned with three lions' heads in high relief. Louvre . . . *p.* 236, *fig.* 291

GUDEA (Stele of) . . . . *fig.* 243, 284, 285, 288

GUDEA (Wife of) — Conjecturally identified in several steatite statuettes, including the so-called Woman with a Kerchief (Louvre) . . . . *p.* 220, *fig.* 272

GULA — Goddess of health, with a dog as her animal attribute . . . . *p.* 240, 296, 319

GUTI — Nomads who invaded Mesopotamia and put an end to the Akkadian dynasty (23rd century B.C.). They ruled the country for nearly a century
p. 197, 198, 246, 250, 313, 336

GYPSUM — Hydrous calcium sulfphate, a stone frequently used by sculptors of ex-votos *e. g. fig.* 147*a*

HADATU, see ARSLAN TASH.

HAGHIA TRIADA — Palace near Phaestos in Crete . . . . *p.* 278

HALAF PERIOD, see TELL HALAF.

HALL (H.R.) (1873-1930) — English Orientalist, excavated al 'Ubaid (1919), Eridu (1919), and began the exploration of Ur (1919) . . . . *p.* 20

HAMADAN — City of present-day Iran, identified with the ancient Ecbatana . . . . *p.* 331
Sculpture:
— Head of a dignitary . . . . *fig.* 406

HAMILTON (R.W.) — Assistant of R. Cambell Thompson in excavations at Nineveh (1930-31) and of Mallowan at Nimrud . . . . *p.* 22

HAMMURABI — The most famous king of the First Dynasty of Babylon, whose reign may be dated to 1792-1750 B.C. Established his hegemony over all Mesopotamia, conquering Larsa, Ashnunnak and Mari in turn. Several works are directly connected with him
p. 253, 254, 256, 259, 284, 291, 305, 306, 310, 313
— Figure in right profile on a relief in the British Museum (No. 22454), which H. R. Hall mistakenly calls the 'only known portrait' of Hammurabi (*Ars Asiatica*, XI, p. 34), forgetting the one on the Code stele . . . . *fig.* 374
— Head, discovered at Susa, very probably (but not certainly) representing Hammurabi. A replica in the Kansas City Museum appears to us to be a fake. Another now on the art market (1960) is equally doubtful . . . . *fig.* 375

HAMMURABI (Code of) — A black basalt boulder with 282 laws engraved beneath a scene showing Hammurabi before the god Shamash. Discovered at Susa by Morgan. Text translated by P. Scheil (1902). Louvre . . . *p.* 31, 179, 305, 314, *fig.* 373

HAMMURABI (Dynasty of) (First Dynasty of Babylon) — According to the chronology worked out by Sidney Smith and adopted here, it can be dated to 1894-1595 B.C. *Cf.* A. Parrot, *Archéologie mésopotamienne*, II, p. 332-445 . . . . *p.* 306

HARP-PLAYER — On a small figure plaque. *fig.* 359*b*

HASSUNA — Tell south of Mosul, excavated in 1943-44 by the Antiquities Department of Iraq. It revealed one of the earliest phases of Mesopotamian protohistory . . . . . *p.* 25, 41, 43, 44, 46, 52, 90
Architecture:
— Plan of the tell and of dwelling-houses *fig.* 59*a-b-c*
Pottery . . . . *fig.* 58, 63

HAUPTBURG — Name given by German archaeologists to a fortified complex lying outside the inner walls of Babylon . . . . *p.* 268

HAYNES (J.H.) — American archaeologist, first Peters' assistant, then in charge of excavations at Nippur (1893-1900) . . . . *p.* 15

HERO SUBDUING WILD ANIMALS, a theme of great antiquity in Mesopotamia (Gilgamesh), recurring on Luristan bronzes (early first millennium).

HERZFELD (Ernst) (1879-1948) — German Orientalist, took part in excavations at Assur, later in charge (with Sarre) of those at Samarra (1911-14) and Persepolis (1931-35) . . . . *p.* 17, 48

HIDDEKEL — The third river of the garden of Eden (Genesis, II, 14), undoubtedly the Tigris (in Assyrian *Idiglat*) . . . . *p.* 37

HIEL — A man of Bethel (I Kings, XVI, 34) who rebuilt Jericho and buried two of his sons in the foundations as sacrifices . . . . *p.* 238

JACOB — Hebrew patriarch, son of Isaac and Rebekah (Genesis, xxv) . . . . *p.* 201, 240

JARMO — Prehistoric settlement dated by Carbon 14 tests to about 5000 B.C. One of the oldest sites in Iraq, explored by Braidwood.
p. 25, 39, 40, 43, 48, 90

JASPER — A variety of quartz, coloured yellow, red or green, depending on its composition . . *e.g.fig.* 98*a*

JEBEL EL-ARAK (Knife from) — Egyptian work in the Louvre, valuable for the parallels it suggests with Mesopotamian art of the pre-dynastic period. The site is in Upper Egypt . . . . *p.* 80, *fig.* 99

JEDEIDEH — Arab name of a site in northern Syria excavated by the Oriental Institute of Chicago.
— Section showing the stratigraphy of the site under excavation . . . . *fig.* 28

JEMDET NASR — Site north-east of Kish excavated by the Langdon-Mackay-Watelin expedition (1925-28). . . . . *p.* 19, 20, 90, 93, 166

JEMDET NASR PERIOD — Phase of Mesopotamian protohistory (late 4th-early 3rd millennium), taking its name from the site north-east of Kish. *p.* 41, 63, 141

JERICHO — Canaanite city, besieged and destroyed by Joshua (Joshua, vi) . . . . *p.* 238

JERUSALEM — Royal capital and holy city. Originally a Canaanite settlement named Jebus, captured by David who made it the capital of his kingdom; here Solomon built the Temple. Ravaged by the Neo-Babylonians (586 B.C.) and restored under Ezra and Nehemiah, it went through many vicissitudes until the Roman conquest. Destroyed by Titus in 70 A.D. . . . . *p.* 332

JEZIREH, UPPER — Region in northern Syria, between the Tigris and Euphrates, watered by the Khabur. . . . . *p.* 25

JOKHA (UMMA) — Sumerian city, the great rival of Lagash. . . . . *p.* 135

JORDAN (Julius) (1878-1945) — German archaeologist, disciple of Koldewey, excavator of Warka (1912-31), then Director of Antiquities in Iraq . *p.* 16, 21

JUDGES — Magistrates who governed Israel from Joshua's death (13th century B.C.) till Saul was chosen king (11th century B.C.) . . . . *p.* 136

KALAKH, see NIMRUD.

KARAINDASH — Kassite king (15th century B.C.) who built a temple at Uruk decorated with brick reliefs (gods and goddesses with the flowing vase). *p.* 316, 328
Architecture :
— Temple of Karaindash (plan) . . . . . *fig.* 391*a*
Sculpture :
— Mural decoration of the Temple of Karaindash *fig.* 392

KASHAN — Modern Persian city, near Sialk* . *p.* 24

KASSITES — Invaders from the mountains north-east of Mesopotamia who put an end to the First Dynasty of Babylon (last king: Samsuditana, 1625-1595 B.C.) and founded a new dynasty (36 kings, reigning 576 years, from 1730 to 1155 B.C.).
p. 306, 313, 314, 316, 318, 319, 333, 336

KAUNAKES — Article of clothing worn by the Mesopotamians in the 3rd millennium B.C., represented as a robe or kilt composed of narrow strips. Its exact nature is still a matter of discussion. We take it to be made of strips of sheepskin, rendered schematically . . . . *fig.* 183*b*

KHABUR — Tributary on the east bank of the Euphrates, taking its rise in the Upper Jezireh, on the confines of the present Turkish frontier.
p. 3, 17, 23, 30, 48, 51, 95, 174

KHAFAJE (TUTUB?) — Site in the Diyala region, east of Baghdad, excavated by the Oriental Institute of Chicago, then by the Joint Expedition of the British Museum and the University Museum of Pennsylvania (*cf.* A. Parrot, *Archéologie mésopotamienne*, I, p. 377), from 1930 to 1938. Yielded very important works of Pre-Sargonid architecture and sculpture.
p. 22, 82, 86, 98, 102, 133, 139-141, 151, 166, 291
Architecture:
— Temple on a high platform (reconstruction) *fig.* 124
Sculpture:
— Arm-rest (in the form of a bull-muzzle). *fig.* 170*b*
— Man's head . . . . *fig.* 143*b*
— Vases decorated with reliefs, showing a tangled profusion of wild animals and birds of prey, with human figures trying to set some order in the mêlée. . . . . *fig.* 168*d*
— Woman's head . . . . *fig.* 139*c*
— Worshippers . . . . . *fig.* 130*a*, 130*b*, 180, 183*a*
Figure plaques:
— Banquet scene . . . . *fig.* 161*a*
— God killing a Cyclops . . . . *fig.* 358*a*
Cylinders seals:
— Abstract designs. . . . . *fig.* 118
— Animals . . . . *fig.* 111, 113, 119
— Gilgamesh* and Enkidu*. . . . . . *fig.* 169*b*
— Mythological scenes. . . . . . . *fig.* 112, 169*c*

KHANI — God of fertility, consort of Nidaba*. Large temple at Tell Harmal. . . . . *p.* 288

KHORSABAD (DUR SHARRUKIN) — Site 10 miles NNE. of Mosul, where in 1843 Botta discovered the palace of Sargon II of Assyria (721-705 B.C.)
p. 9, 12, 14, 16, 22, 28, 31, 32
Sculpture:
— Reliefs from the palace of Sargon* . . . *fig.* 50
— Works discovered by Botta . . . . *fig.* 5

KIDNUM — Mesopotamian city sometimes identified with Jemdet Nasr . . . . *p.* 63

KINGS (Books of the) — Two books of the Old Testament, relating the history of Israel from the death of David to the taking of Jerusalem by the Neo-Babylonians. The Vulgate includes the two books of Samuel under this name, thus giving four Books of Kings: I and II (Samuel), III and IV (Kings).
p. 46, 238

KISH, see AL 'OHEIMIR.

KNOSSOS — Town in Crete with a famous ancient palace (early 2nd millennium) . . . . . *p.* 278

KOLDEWEY (Robert Johann) (1855-1925) — German architect and archaeologist, began his career as an excavator in 1882 at Assos (an ancient city in Mysia, Asia Minor, opposite Lesbos) and went on to Mesopotamia, where he distinguished himself above all in the exploration of Babylon (1899-1917). . . . . *p.* 16, 21, 264, 268, *fig.* 16

KUDURRUS — Black boundary stones, decorated with reliefs, covered with inscriptions and deposited in temples, where they were supposed to ensure the permanence of the boundary. Kassite period.
p. 318-320, 336, *fig.* 387, 395*a-b-c-d*

KURDISTAN — Province in north-western Iran *p.* 174

KURLIL (or EKUR) — Name engraved on a basalt statue discovered at al 'Ubaid . . . . . . *fig.* 144

KUTIR-NAKHUNTE — Son of Shutruk-Nakhunte (12th century B.C.), Elamite king who put an end to the Kassite dynasty of Babylon. . . . . *p.* 328

KUYUNJIK (NINEVEH) — Tell north of the Khoser, on the left bank of the Tigris, opposite Mosul. One of the capitals of the Assyrian kingdom, famous for the palaces of Sennacherib and Assurbanipal. A whole phase of protohistory has also been revealed there.
p. 12, 14, 22, 26, 31, 48, 53, 170, 194
Sculpture:
— Bronze head, identified by Mallowan with Sargon of Akkad (Baghdad Museum). . . . *fig.* 206, 208
— Dying lioness. . . . . *fig.* 6*c*
— Feast in the Garden. . . . . *fig.* 20
— Flood tablet . . . . *fig.* 21

LABAN — Patriarch of the family of Abraham. Son of Nahor and father-in-law of Jacob (Genesis, XXIX). . . . . *p.* 240

LADY WITH A TIMBREL — Woman represented naked, holding a timbrel with both hands against her breast. On Neo-Sumerian figure plaques. . *p.* 291

LAGASH, see TELLOH.

LAMGI-MARI — King of Mari (Pre-Sargonid dynasty). Statue found in 1934 in the temple of Ishtar (Aleppo Museum). . . . *p.* 116, *fig.* 145

LAMP — Symbol of Nusku. Often represented on boundary stones . . . . . *p.* 319, *e. g. fig.* 395*b*

LANGDON (Stephen Herbert) (1876-1937) — English Assyriologist, in charge of the Joint Expedition to Kish and Jemdet Nasr (1923-33) . . . . . *p.* 20

LAPIS LAZULI — Azure blue stone composed of silicates, imported from Media, where there was a 'lapis mountain.'

LARSA, see SENKEREH.

LARSA PERIOD.
Sculpture:
— Head of Humbaba* . . . . *fig.* 370
— Winged goddess. . . . . *fig.* 376*c*
Figurine plaques:
— Burney* Plaque. . . . . *fig.* 367*a*
— Humbaba* . . . . *fig.* 369
— Itinerant showman exhibiting monkeys *fig.* 359*c*
— Naked woman . . . . *fig.* 365
— Nintu* . . . . *fig.* 368
— War scene . . . . *fig.* 358*c*

LAYARD (Sir Austen Henry) (1817-94) — English archaeologist and diplomatist, excavator of Nineveh, Nimrud, Assur, Babylon and Kish (1845-51)
p. 14, *fig.* 12
— Drawings by Layard . . . . *fig.* 25

LEES (G.M.) — English geologist who has advanced a new theory regarding the formation of the Mesopotamian delta . . . . *p.* 38

LIBATION — Religious rite often represented in reliefs and seal designs. The celebrant (king, priest or simple worshipper), naked or clad, pours water into a vase from which a plant emerges
p. 188, 228, 282, *fig.* 161*b*, 178, 281
— Libation vase. . . . . *fig.* 367*b*

LION — Very frequently represented, either under its natural aspect or in composite form (winged lion, centaur-lion, human-headed lion)
fig. 2, 95, 101, 168*c*, 225, 291
— attacking . . . . *fig.* 162, 362
— from Babylon* . . . . *fig.* 6*b*
— guardians: temple of Dagan* . . . *fig.* 322, 353
          temple of Tell Harmal* . *fig.* 354, 356
— passant . . . . *fig.* 1, 364
— roaring . . . . *fig.* 355, 356
— winged . . . . *fig.* 311, 386
— with foundation tablet . . . . *fig.* 220

LION-MUZZLES — Similar to the lions from Tell Harmal . . . . *p.* 286

LIONESS (Dying). . . . . *p.* 10, *fig.* 6*c*

LIONESS (Head of) — Monster with a human body and the head of a lioness (Brooklyn Museum) *fig.* 97

LIONESS FROM WARKA — Fine example of animal art, of uncertain date (Assyrian, if not Neo-Babylonian). Baghdad Museum. . . . *p.* 318, *fig.* 394

LIPIT-ISHTAR — Fifth king of the Isin dynasty (21st century B.C.), law-giver. . . . . . . *p.* 305

LOCUST — In Kassite seal designs and on a monument from Assur. . . . . *p.* 320

LOFTUS (Sir William Kennet) — English archaeologist, excavated Susa (1851), explored southern Babylonia (Nippur, Uruk, Ur, Eridu) and Larsa, and was sent to Nineveh and Nimrud by Rawlinson (1854). Found the relief of Assurbanipal and the 'Feast in the Garden' (British Museum) and a large collection of ivories (British Museum) . . . . *p.* 14

LUGALKISALSI — King of the Sumerian city of Uruk.
— Lugalkisalsi's Grandson . . . . . *fig.* 259, 261

LUGALZAGGISI — Sumerian king of the Third Dynasty of Uruk (c. 2500 B.C.), destroyed Lagash and perhaps Mari. Defeated by Sargon of Akkad
p. 169, 170, 194

LULUBI — Mountain tribe of Kurdistan, defeated by an army led by Naram-Sin, who commemorated the victory on a famous stele (Louvre). . . . *p.* 176

LYRES — Many examples found in the 'royal' tombs of Ur . . . . *p.* 144, 150, 162

MACE — Weapon often represented in the hands of gods. . . . . *e. g. fig.* 160 *a-b*

MACKAY (Ernest) (1880-1943) — American archaeologist, field director of the Joint Expedition to Kish and Jemdet Nasr (1923-25) . . . . *p.* 20

MADAULE (Jacques) — French writer born in 1898 . . . . *p.* 32

MALLOWAN (M.E.L.) — English archaeologist born in 1904, excavated Nineveh, Arpatchiya (1933), Chagar Bazar, Tell Brak (1935-39), Nimrud (from 1949 on) and Balawat (1956). A leading authority on Mesopotamian pottery and the Assyrian period
p. 22, 23, 25, 48

MALTA — A cippus (in the Louvre) from Malta with a bilingual inscription in Greek and Phoenician enabled Abbé Barthélemy to decipher the Phoenician language (1764). . . . . *p.* 12

MALTESE CROSS — Decorative theme on proto-historical pottery of the Samarra period (5th millennium B.C.) . . . . *p.* 44, 50, 62, *fig.* 80*e*

MANISHTUSU — Third king of the Akkadian dynasty, son of Sargon. Obelisk inscribed with his name (Louvre) . . . . *p.* 179
— Obelisk . . . . *fig.* 215
— Robe. . . . . *fig.* 214

MARASH (MARQASI) — Hittite city on the road from Anatolia into Syria. Among several works from Marash is a lion entirely covered with inscriptions in Hittite hieroglyphics . . . . *p.* 10

MARDUK — Son of Ea, god of Babylon, worshipped in the temple known as Esagila. . . . . . *p.* 319

MARDUK-APAL-IDDIN — Name of several kings: I (1187-1175 B.C.), Kassite dynasty; II (722-711 B.C.), 'J' dynasty. The boundary stone in the Berlin Museum belongs to the latter. . . . . . . *p.* 318

MARDUK-NADIN-AKHE — King of the Second Dynasty of Isin (1116-1101 B.C.). Boundary stone (British Museum) and sword (Louvre) inscribed with his name. . . . . *p.* 319
— Boundary stone of Marduk-nadin-akhe. *fig.* 395*c*

MARI, see TELL HARIRI.

MARRU — Hoe-shaped tool, presumably the symbol of the god Marduk . . . . *fig.* 80*b*

MARTU — Figure in the Mesopotamian iconography characterized by his headdress (a turbaned cap) and his weapon (a mace). Probably a variant of the god Adad . . . . *fig.* 381

MASPERO (Gaston) (1846-1916) — French Egyptologist, author of an *Histoire ancienne des Peuples de l'Orient* (*cf.* Bibliography) . . . . *p.* 7

MATTA (D.) — Lebanese member of the French archaeological expedition to Mari . . . . . *fig.* 36

MECQUENEM (Roland de) (1877-1958) — French mining engineer, joined the archaeological expedition to Susa where he succeeded J. de Morgan in 1912. Carried on explorations till 1945, when the work was taken over by Ghirshman. . . . . *p.* 24

MEDES — A confederation of tribes in the Iranian region, famous for their cavalry. Their political importance began with Cyaxares, about 625 B.C. *p.* 3

MELISHIPAK II — Kassite king (1202-1188 B.C.) whose name figures on several boundary stones (Louvre). . . . . *p.* 318
— Boundary stone of Melishipak II. . *fig.* 395 *a-b*

MEMPHIS — City in Lower Egypt, capital and residence of the Pharaohs at several different periods . . . . *p.* 33

MESANNIPADDA — King of the First Dynasty of Ur, whose name was found in 1919 on a foundation tablet of the temple of al 'Ubaid . . . . *p.* 95

MESILIM — King of Kish (Pre-Sargonid period), for a time ruler of Lagash. . . . . . . *p.* 131, 236
— Mace of Mesilim (Louvre) . . . . . *fig.* 160*a-b*

MESKALAMDUG — An important personage buried in the 'royal' cemetery of Ur (Tomb 755) with a treasure beside him: helmet, weapons, plate (gold, electrum, silver) and ornaments. . . . . . *p.* 160
— Helmet of Meskalamdug, of solid gold, discovered in the tomb of the 'good hero of the land.' A masterpiece of Sumerian goldsmiths' work (Baghdad Museum) . . . . *p.* 160, 170, *fig.* 189*c*

MESOPOTAMIA — The region between the Tigris and Euphrates. *p.* 1-3, 22, 24, 28, 32, 38-41, 46, 51, 53, 64, 80, 90, 95, 96, 153, 199, 259, 272, 284, 310, 313, 314, 333
— Maps of Mesopotamia . . . *fig.* 55, 56, 205, 419
— Mesopotamian sites . . . . . *fig.* 51, 417, 418

MESOPOTAMIANS — Generic name of the inhabitants of Mesopotamia
p. 98, 112, 140, 142, 155, 238, 324

MICHAL — Daughter of Saul and wife of David (I Samuel, XVIII) . . . . *p.* 241

MICHAUX STONE — Kassite boundary stone brought back to France in 1786 by the botanist André Michaux. Preserved in the Cabinet des Médailles, Bibliothèque Nationale, Paris . . . . *p.* 12, *fig.* 10, 11

MILGA — Name of a priest cited in the inscription on the statue of Puzur-Ishtar, governor of Mari (early 2nd millennium B.C.) . . . . *p.* 268

MITANNIANS — A people who settled between the Tigris and the Khabur, particularly powerful during the 2nd millennium, down to the 14th century B.C.. . . . . *p.* 3

MONKEY — On a small figure plaque . . . *fig.* 359*c*

MONSTER with a human body and the head of a lioness (Brooklyn Museum) . . . . . *p.* 78, *fig.* 97

MONSTERS with distended necks, in pre-dynastic seal designs. Many examples from Warka
p. 80, *fig.* 98*a-b*

MOORTGAT (Anton) — German Orientalist born in 1897 . . . . *p.* 25, 64, 160

MORGAN (Jacques de) (1857-1924) — French mining engineer, former Director General of Egyptian Antiquities, head of the French Delegation to Persia, began the exploration of Susa and the surrounding region in 1897. . . . . *p.* 16, 264

MOSAICS, see CONE MOSAICS.

MOSES ON MOUNT SINAI — Compared with Hammurabi on the mountain receiving the laws from Shamash . . . . *p.* 305

MOSUL — City in Iraq, on the right bank of the Tigris, opposite ancient Nineveh . . . . . . *p.* 12

MOTHER-GODDESS — Divinity represented in Mesopotamian art as early as the 5th millennium B.C. in clay figurines . *p.* 39, 48, 54, 90, *fig.* 64 ,65

MOUFLONS — Wild sheep with large curving horns . . . . *fig.* 110

MOULDS — Used from the late 3rd millennium on to produce stock figurines in large numbers *fig.* 361, 362

MUALLAFAT — Site of the earliest known settlement in Mesopotamia, in north-eastern Iraq. Discovered by the Braidwood Expedition . *p.* 25, 39, 40, 43, 90

MUDROS — Seaport on the Aegean island of Lemnos, where the armistice with Turkey was signed on October 30, 1918. . . . . *p.* 17

MUQAYYAR (or MUGEYER) (UR) — Present name ('mound of pitch') of the Sumerian city of Ur, referred to in Genesis (XI, 31) as 'Ur of the Chaldees' (*Ur Kasdim*). Capital of the First (early 3rd millennium) and Third Dynasties (22nd-19th century B.C.). Systematically excavated from 1922 to 1934 by the Joint Expedition of the British Museum and the University Museum of Pennsylvania, led by C. (later Sir) Leonard Woolley. The most sensational discovery made was that of the 'royal tombs' *p.* 4, 14, 20, 22, 26, 30, 76, 82, 93, 95, 96, 100, 102, 122, 140, 144, 153, 155, 159, 160, 166, 170, 182, 198-203, 226, 234, 238, 241, 250, 253, 264, 290, 305, 310, 316, 318

Architecture:
— Chapel of Pa-Sag . . . . *fig.* 249*b*
— Hypogeum of Bur-Sin* . . . . *fig.* 249*e*
— Hypogeum of Dungi* . . . . . . *fig.* 30, 249*d-f*
— Pater Noster Street . . . . *fig.* 249*c*
— Quiet Street . . . . *fig.* 249*a*
— Royal cemetery, explored by Woolley from 1927 to 1929. Some Orientalists explain the funerary rites, with their human sacrifices, as ceremonies connected with fertility cults. Date: first half of the 3rd millennium. . . . . *fig.* 29
— Royal tombs. . . . . *fig.* 31
— Tomb of Shubad* . . . . *fig.* 32
— Ziggurat (Third Dynasty) . . . . . *fig.* 247
— Ziggurat (Third Dynasty), reconstruction *fig.* 248

Sculpture:
— Bau* . . . . *fig.* 328
— Bull's head: soundbox of a harp . . . . *fig.* 191
                soundbox of a lyre . . . . *fig.* 189*b*
— Figurines . . . . *fig.* 73, 74, 76, 77
— Gaming board . . . . *fig.* 173*c*
— Goddess with flowing vase . . . . . *fig.* 301
— Helmet of Meskalamdug* . . . . . . *fig.* 189*c*
— Nannar* . . . . *fig.* 279, 282
— Ningal* . . . . *fig.* 278, 281
— Ram . . . . *fig.* 190
— Ram's head, in steatite, found in a dwelling house of the Isin-Larsa period (21st-18th century B.C.) *fig.* 357*a*
— Rein-ring . . . . *fig.* 188*a*
— Ritual bowl . . . . *fig.* 94
— Soundbox of a harp . . . . *fig.* 179
— Stele of Ur-Nammu* . . . . . . *fig.* 279-282

Metal-work:
— Goblet and bowl of Shubad* . . . . . *fig.* 189*a*

Mosaic:
— 'Standard of Ur,' a mosaic panel inlaid on both sides, one with scenes of war, the other with scenes of peace. Discovered in the 'royal' cemetery (Tomb 779). British Museum. . . *p.* 146-150, *fig.* 175-178

Glyptics and cylinder seals:
— Banquet scene . . . . *fig.* 197, 202
— Combat of animals and hero . . . . *fig.* 195
— Hero between two animals . . . . . *fig.* 193
— Mythological scenes . . . . *fig.* 239, 240, 242

MUSICIAN — On a small figure plaque
                          p. 293, *fig.* 359*a*

MUSICIANS WITH A DRUM . . . . . *fig.* 286

MUSIC-MAKING ANIMALS — Theme of Mesopotamian art, e.g. on a lyre from Ur (Tomb 789) and a relief from Tell Halaf . . . . *p.* 150

NABU — Son of Marduk, god of scribes and writing, worshipped at Borsippa in the temple known as Ezida . . . . *p.* 319

NAJI AL-ASIL — Former director general of Antiquities in Iraq, in charge of excavations at Eridu and in 1954 at Nebi Yunus (Nineveh) . . . . . *p.* 24

NANA — Daughter of Anu and wife of Nabu. A variant of Ishtar, goddess of love . . . . *p.* 318

NANI — High-ranking official of Mari, whose statue was found in the temple of Ninni-Zaza
                          p. 116, *fig.* 147*a*

NANNAR — Sumerian name of the moon god, worshipped chiefly at Ur
                p. 188, 226, 228, 316, *fig.* 279, 282

NAPIR-ASU — Wife of Untash-Huban. Bronze statue (13th century B.C.) in the Louvre
                p. 322, 336, *fig.* 398, 399

NARAM-SIN — King of the Akkadian dynasty (c. 2300 B.C.), grandson of Sargon. Palace at Tell Brak. His daughters were high priestesses at Mari and Ur. *p.* 174, 176, 179, 194, 234, 314, *fig.* 212, 216
— Stele of Naram-Sin, victory stele found at Susa by Morgan (Louvre) . . . . *fig.* 211-213

NARMER — Egyptian king of the pre-Thinite period (3300-3000 B.C.). It may have been Narmer, and not Menes, who united Egypt.
— Palette of Narmer . . . . *fig.* 98*b*

NEBUCHADNEZZAR I — King of the Second Dynasty of Isin (1146-1123 B.C.). Boundary stone with his name found at Abu Habba (British Museum)
                p. 268, 319, *fig.* 387, 395*d*

NEIRAB — Near Aleppo, excavated by the Ecole Biblique et Archéologique Française de Jérusalem (1926-27). Two Aramaean steles from this site were acquired by the Louvre at the end of the 19th century. Reliefs and inscriptions . . . . . . *p.* 22

NEOLITHIC PERIOD — A phase of prehistoric culture, characterized by agriculture and the domestication of animals, with no evidence of metalworking. A Neolithic phase without pottery is now also known . . . . *p.* 39

NEO-SUMERIANS — The Sumerians who regained political control of the country between the overthrow of the Guti (22nd century) and the fall of Ur (2016 B.C.). . . . . *p.* 198, 199, 234, 237, 238, 240, 246

NERGAL — God of the underworld, worshipped at Kutha . . . . *p.* 319, *fig.* 380

NERIBTUM — Ancient site sometimes identified with Ishchali* . . . . *p.* 22

NEW YEAR FESTIVAL, during which the rites of hierogamy* were celebrated. . . *p.* 72, 133, *fig.* 161*a*

NIDABA — Goddess of vegetation and writing, consort of Khani*. Large temple at Tell Harmal*. *p.* 288

NIHAVEND — Modern site, not far from Tepe Giyan, excavated in 1931-32. A type of painted pottery known by this name, with figurative and geometric designs, comes from this region . . . . . . *p.* 24

NILE — The great river, rising in East Africa, which waters Egypt. Sacred river of ancient Egypt *p.* 1, 8

NIMRUD (KALAKH) — One of the Assyrian capitals, south of Nineveh, excavated by Layard (1845-51) and Mallowan (since 1949) . . . . . . *p.* 14, 25

NINEVEH, see KUYUNJIK.

NINGAL — Goddess worshipped at Ur and Harran, consort of the moon god Nannar. Represented on the Stele of Ur-Nammu (University Museum, Philadelphia) . . . . . . *p.* 226, 228, *fig.* 278, 281

NINGIRSU — God of fertility, worshipped at Lagash in particular. His emblem is the lion-headed eagle . . . . . *p.* 136, 137, 214, 230, 319, *fig.* 165

NINGIZZIDA — Personal god of Gudea, patesi of Lagash. His most famous monument is the Berlin stele. . . . . . . *p.* 214, 230, 237, 319, *fig.* 284
— Dedication to Ningizzida . . . . . *fig.* 289, 290

NINHURSAG — Goddess of fertility (literally, 'lady of the mountain'), worshipped throughout Mesopotamia. Temple at Mari *p.* 99, 139, 319, 328, *fig.* 161*b*, 167*b*, 405

NINLIL — Goddess, consort of Enlil, god of Nippur . . . . *p.* 314

NINNI-ZAZA — Divinity hitherto unknown, whose temple was discovered at Mari in 1952 . . . *p.* 99
— Temple of Ninni-Zaza: inner court. . . *fig.* 127*b*
plan of the temple *fig.* 127*c*
reconstruction . . *fig.* 127*a*

NINSUN — Mother of Gilgamesh. Relief in the Louvre.
— Small plaque with a woman, dedicated to Ninsun. . . . . *fig.* 287

NINTU — Goddess of fecundity. Temple at Khafaje . . . . *p.* 102, *fig.* 368

NINURTA — War god . . . . . . *p.* 314, 319

NIPPUR — Sumerian city, residence of the god Enlil. Excavated from 1889 to 1900, and since 1948 by an American joint expedition
p. 15, 21, 25, 96, 130, 166, 169, 200, 238, 316
— Excavations in the scribal quarter . . . . *fig.* 39
Sculpture:
— Foundation figurine (canephorus). . *fig.* 292*d*
— Plaques, with offerings and libation before a divinity, presumably Enlil (Istanbul Museum)
fig. 158*c-d*

NISABA, see NIDABA.

NÖLDEKE (Arnold) — German archaeologist, disciple of Koldewey and excavator of Warka (1934-39)
p. 16, 21

NURAGHI — Stone constructions peculiar to Sardinia, datable to the Bronze Age . . . . . . *p.* 8

NUSKU — Fire god, symbolized by a lamp . *p.* 319

NUZI, see YORGAN TEPE.

OMEGA — A sign of this type figures on small plaques and in particular on boundary stones. Symbol of Ninhursag* or Nintu*, both goddesses of fecundity and fertility. . . . . *e. g. fig.* 368

ONAGERS — Wild asses of the Mesopotamian desert, domesticated and harnessed to chariots (represented in works from Ur, Mari and Khafaje)
p. 146, 152, 159, *fig.* 181, 188*a*

OPPENHEIM (Max Freiherr von) (1860-1946) — German archaeologist and traveller, excavated Tell Halaf (1911-1913-1929) . . . . *p.* 17, 29

ORIENTAL INSTITUTE OF CHICAGO — Has sponsored important expeditions to the Diyala region, Khorsabad and Nippur (*cf.* Breasted)
p. 22, 25, 29, 152

ORONTES — River in central Syria (now called Nahr el-Asi), empties into the Mediterranean near Suedia. . . . . *p.* 3

OSTRACA — Fragments of pottery used as writing tablets . . . . *p.* 150

OWL — Represented on the Burney Plaque, on either side of the winged goddess . . . . *p.* 300, *fig.* 367*a*

OX, Humped . . . . *fig.* 360

PALAEOLITHIC PERIOD — Phase of prehistoric culture, characterized by rough or chipped stone implements. Generally subdivided into three stages: Lower, Middle (Neanderthal man) and Upper (homo sapiens) . . . . *p.* 39

PALESTINE — The Holy Land of Biblical history, extending from Dan in the north (foothills of the Hermon) to Beersheba in the south (near the Egyptian frontier), bounded on the west by the Mediterranean, on the east by the Syrian desert. Successively inhabited by the Canaanites, the Hebrews, the Israelites and the Jews. The Greek name is derived from the Hebrew *Pelesheth*, 'land of the Philistines,' who settled there in the 12th century B.C. . . . . *p.* 3

PALM TREE — Widely cultivated in Mesopotamia. Famous palm groves at Basra, Hilleh (near Babylon) and Ana (on the Middle Euphrates). Ceases to grow beyond a point about 60 miles north of Abu Kemal. Very frequently represented in Mesopotamian art. . . . . *p.* 140, 328

PANTHER . . . . *fig.* 68

PARADISE — Called the Garden of Eden in Genesis (II), presumably located in Mesopotamia
p. 37, 90, 278

PAROS — Greek island in the Cyclades, famous for its quarries of white marble . . . . . . *p.* 8, 42

PATESI — Also read *ishak* or *ensi*. High dignitary performing religious and political functions, as the representative of the divinity. Acted as both king and priest . . . . *p.* 203, 204, 250

PAYEN (Jean) — Member of the French archaeological expedition to Mari, third season (1935-36) . *fig.* 36

PEARSON (F.) — Member of the archaeological expedition to Dura Europos. Specialist in the removal of wall paintings (synagogue and *mithraeum* of Dura). Performed the same operation for the Investiture painting at Mari (Court 106 of the palace) . *p.* 259

PEASANT — On a small figure plaque . . *fig.* 360

PENNSYLVANIA (University of) — Has sponsored important expeditions to Mesopotamia (Nippur, Ur, Fara, Nuzi, Tepe Gawra, Tell Billa) . *p.* 21, 22, 25

PERROT (Georges) (1832-1914) — French professor and archaeologist, author of a monumental *Histoire de l'Art dans l'Antiquité* (*cf.* Bibliography). . *p.* 7, 9

PERSIAN GULF — The shore of the Gulf now lies about 45 miles below Basra. . *p.* 30, 38, 52, 95, 169, 313

PERSIANS — A federation of agricultural and nomadic tribes, of which the Achaemenians formed one clan . . . . *p.* 3

PETERS (John P.) — American professor of Hebrew and excavator of Nippur (1889-90) . . . . . *p.* 15

PFEIFFER (Robert H.) (1892-1958) — In charge of excavations at Nuzi (1928-29) and curator of the Harvard Semitic Museum . . . . *p.* 22

PHAEDRUS — Latin fabulist (1st century B.C.-1st century A.D.) . . . . *p.* 150

PHOENICIANS — An ancient Semitic people of sea-farers and traders, inhabiting the Mediterranean seaboard between Latakia and Mount Carmel . *p.* 3

PICTOGRAPHIC WRITING — The earliest type of writing used in Mesopotamia (late 4th-early 3rd millennium), exemplified in texts from Uruk, Jemdet Nasr and Kish. Some good specimens in the Louvre. . . . . *p.* 93, 94, *fig.* 122

PILASTERS — Engaged piers projecting from the wall, used to break up the monotony of uniform wall surfaces and set up plays of light and shade
e. g. fig. 392

PIR HUSSEIN — In Kurdistan . . . . . *p.* 174
— Stele of Naram-Sin* . . . . *fig.* 211

PISON — One of the rivers in the Garden of Eden (Genesis, II, 11), sometimes identified with the Indus . . . . *p.* 37

PLACE (Victor) (1818-75) — French consul, excavator of Khorsabad (1852-54). The greater part of his finds were lost in an accident which sent them to the bottom of the Tigris. Two notable works, however, reached the Louvre: a human-headed bull and a large winged genius with a situla. *p.* 14, 16, 22

PLOUGH — Emblem of Ningirsu on a boundary stone from Susa. Often represented in seal designs. Decorative element on the enamelled brick panels of the palace of Khorsabad. . . . *p.* 319, *fig.* 232

PLUMED HEADDRESS (Man with a) — A curious bas-relief discovered at Lagash, showing a worshipper wearing two (ostrich?) plumes on his head. Early Pre-Sargonid period. Louvre. . *p.* 129, 130, *fig.* 158*a-b*

PODIUM — A low pedestal in Mesopotamian temples, where the divine statue stood.

POLOS — A high headdress, tapering off at the top and fastened at the bottom with a broad ribbon
fig. 153, 154

POTNIA THERON — On a vase with reliefs from Khafaje (British Museum). . . . . *p.* 139

PREHISTORY — Phase of civilization which, in Mesopotamia, ends about 5000 B.C. The first proto-historical period thereafter is that of Hassuna
p. 25, 39, 40

PRE-SARGONID PERIOD — Follows the Jemdet Nasr period and ends with Sargon of Akkad. Called the Early Dynastic Period by British and American archaeologists, and sometimes referred to in older books as the 'period of the early patesis.' Datable to 2800-2470 B.C. . . . *p.* 96, 98, 100, 141, 166, 256

PRE-SARGONIDS . . . . *p.* 96, 98, 142

PROTHESIS — A room in Early Christian basilicas beside the central apse, symmetrical with the dia-conicon* . . . . *p.* 66

PROTO-ELAMITES — Inhabitants of the Iranian plateau in the 4th millennium B.C. . . . . . *p.* 3

PROTOHISTORY — Phase of civilization beginning at the end of prehistoric times (c. 5000 B.C.) and ending when recorded history begins (early 3rd millennium B.C.) . . . *p.* 3, 17, 19-22, 25, 40, 65, 86

PUZUR-ISHTAR — Governor of Mari. Headless statue found by Koldewey at Babylon (Istanbul Museum); the head is now in the Berlin Museum
p. 268, *fig.* 334, 335

PYRAMIDS — Massive constructions with a polygonal base and plane triangular sides meeting in an apex. The stepped pyramid of Saqqara* recalls the architecture of the ziggurats. . . . . *p.* 200

QALAAT SHERGAT (ASSUR) — One of the capitals of the Assyrian kingdom, on the right bank of the Tigris, excavated by Andrae (1903-14)
p. 14, 16, 26, 98, 102, 180, 253
Architecture:
— Plan of the excavations. . . . . *fig.* 26
— Plan of the temple of Ishtar* . . . . . *fig.* 326*b*
Sculpture:
— Woman's head. . . . . *fig.* 218

RACHEL — Daughter of Laban, wife of Jacob, died in giving birth to Benjamin (Genesis, xxxv). *p.* 240

RAI — Site in the Susa region where some remarkable pottery has been found . . . . *p.* 51
— Potsherd with frieze of dancers . . . . *fig.* 69

RASSAM (Hormuzd) (1826-1910) — A Chaldean Christian who excavated most of the cities of Assyria and Babylonia for the British Museum. For an appreciation of his methods, see A. Parrot, *Archéologie mésopotamienne,* I, p. 52. . . . . *p.* 14

RAS SHAMRA (UGARIT) — One of the largest Phoenician cities of the 2nd millennium B.C., on the Mediterranean seaboard north of Latakia. Excavations, begun in 1929 by C. Shaeffer, entered their 20th season in 1959. . . . . *p.* 254

RAWLINSON (Sir Henry Creswicke) (1810-1895) — English archaeologist, regarded by English scholars as the 'father of Assyriology.' Played a very important part in the archaeological exploration of Assyria and Babylonia, which he supervised for many years (1843-55) . . . . *p.* 14

REEDS (Bundle of) — Tied together at the top, symbol of Inanna, goddess of Uruk . . . . *p.* 70

REINACH (Salomon) (1858-1932) — French writer, classical philologist and archaeologist . . . . *p.* 10

RIMUSH — King of the Akkadian dynasty and son of Sargon. . . . . *p.* 172
— Stele of Rimush. . . . . *fig.* 210

ROCKEFELLER (John D., Jr.) (1874-1960) — American industrialist and philanthropist, founder of the Oriental Institute of Chicago (1919) . . . . *p.* 22

ROSETTE — Symbolic theme in Kassite seal designs. . . . . *p.* 320

SACRED GROVE — Part of the Semitic high place. Appears in the so-called Tablet of Sit Shamshi *p.* 332

SACRIFICIAL OFFERING — Of an ibex, a young goat or a sheep. Very frequently represented on small figure plaques and in reliefs and statuettes *p.* 240, 242, 272, 276, 328, *fig.* 294, 297, 341, 378, 382, 384, 404*a-b*

ST. LOUIS, CITY ART MUSEUM — Acquired in 1952 a copper bull's head, of the same type as the one found in the 'royal tombs' of Ur . . . . . . *p.* 156
— Bull's head . . . . *fig.* 186

SAINT-SAVIN-SUR-GARTEMPE — Small town in the Vienne department of France, world-famous for the Romanesque paintings (12th century A.D.) in the church.
Painting:
— The Tower of Babel . . . . *fig.* 3

SAMARRA — City on the left bank of the Tigris, north of Baghdad, excavated in 1914 by Herzfeld. It revealed a phase of protohistorical culture. *p.* 17, 19 25, 41, 44, 46, 48, 90
Pottery. . . . . *fig.* 60-63

SAMSON — Hebrew judge, prototype of the Oriental Hercules. His exploits are related in Judges (XIII-XVI). Many traits in common with the Mesopotamian Gilgamesh . . . . *p.* 136

SAMUEL — Last of the judges in Israel. He abdicated in favour of Saul, who became the first king. . . . . *p.* 241

SAQQARA — City in Lower Egypt, famous for its necropolis and the stepped pyramid of the Pharaoh Zoser (IIIrd Dynasty) . . . . *p.* 200

SARDINIA, see NURAGHI.

SARGON OF AKKAD — Founder of the Akkadian dynasty. Dates proposed: 2470-2412 B.C. The famous head from Nineveh is a portrait of him *p.* 96, 162, 169-174, 179, 194, 199, *fig.* 206, 208
— Stele of Sargon . . . . *fig.* 207, 209

SARGON OF ASSYRIA (721-705 B.C.) — Conqueror of Samaria and builder of Khorsabad (Dur Sharrukin). The largest collection of his reliefs is in the Louvre. . . . . *p.* 118
— Reliefs from the palace of Sargon. . . . *fig.* 50

SARZEC (Ernest de) (1837-1901) — French vice-consul at Basra, excavated Telloh from 1877 to 1900 . . . . *p.* 15, 16, 21, 28, *fig.* 13

SAUL — First king of Israel. . . . . . . *p.* 241

SCHIST — Dark grey rock having a foliated structure and readily split into slabs or sheets.

SCHMIDT (Erich) — American archaeologist, born in 1897, excavated Fara (1931) and Persepolis and Surkh Dum (1938) . . . . *p.* 21

SCORPION — Animal attribute of the goddess Ishara, who presides over marriage *p.* 44, 319, *fig.* 60*d*, 305

SCORPION-MAN — Composite figure in Assyro-Babylonian mythology. Represented on the sound-box of a lyre from Ur (Tomb 789) and in statues from Tell Halaf . . . . *p.* 150

SEA-LAND DYNASTIES — Ruled the whole of Lower Mesopotamia from the 18th to the 11th century B.C.. . . . . *p.* 306, 313

SEGUIA — Irrigation furrow dug in their fields by the present-day fellahs. . . . . *p.* 62

SEMITES — Ethnic group originating in Arabia, divided into several branches established in every part of ancient western Asia *p.* 3, 29, 64, 95, 96, 162, 218, 246, 253, 272, 310, 332

SENKEREH (LARSA) — Prospected by Loftus (1853-54) and Andrae (1903), soundings made by A. Parrot (1933). The Larsa Dynasty (2023-1761 B.C.) was founded by Naplanum and ended with Rim-Sin, defeated by Hammurabi, king of Babylon. *Cf.* LARSA PERIOD *p.* 18, 21, 182, 194, 200, 253, 254, 264, 284, 291, 300, 310
Architecture:
— Ziggurat, built in the centre of a *temenos* (sacred area). Located but not yet excavated. . . *fig.* 57
Sculpture:
— Ibexes* back to back . . . . *fig.* 349
— Libation vase, discovered in 1933, decorated with a scene showing a naked winged goddess accompanied by various animals (Louvre). . . . . . . *fig.* 367*b*
— Worshipper, inscribed bronze, dedicated for the life of Hammurabi. Looted from the site. Louvre . . . . *fig.* 350
Figurine plaque:
— Naked woman . . . . *fig.* 358*b*
Cylinder seal:
— Nergal* . . . . *fig.* 380

SENNACHERIB — King of Assyria (705-681 B.C.), represented at the siege of Lachish (British Museum) . . . . *p.* 118

SEURAT (Georges) (1859-91) — French painter whose pointillist technique is foreshadowed in the protohistorical pottery of Mesopotamia . . . *p.* 51

SEVRES — Town in the suburbs of Paris, famous for its porcelain manufactory . . . . . . *p.* 60, 90

SEYRIG (Henri) — French archaeologist, born 1895, director of the Antiquities Service of the Haut Commissariat Français from 1929 to the Second World War, now director of the Institut Français d'Archéologie at Beirut. . . . . *p.* 256

SHADUPPUM, see TELL HARMAL.

SHAKKANAK — Name of a high Mesopotamian official, a kind of prince-governor. *p.* 259, 266, 268

SHAMASH — Sun god, worshipped at Larsa and Sippar in particular *p.* 99, 174, 188, 305, 319, *fig.* 2

SHANIDAR — Palaeolithic site in northern Iraq, not far from the Great Zab (tributary of the Tigris, left bank). . . . . *p.* 39

SHARKALISHARRI (Cylinder seal of) — A famous work dedicated by Ibnisharru for the life of Sharka-lisharri, king of Akkad. De Clercq Collection *p.* 186, *fig.* 223

SHARRUKENU — Meaning 'lawful king,' name taken by Sargon, founder of the Akkadian dynasty (after 2500 B.C.). . . . . *p.* 169

SHAUSHATAR — King of the Mitannians, contemporary with the Pharaoh Amenophis II (1447-1420 B.C.).
— Cylinder seal of Shaushatar . . . . . *fig.* 416

SHELL — Frequently used in the Pre-Sargonid period for inlaid work. . . . . *e. g. fig.* 171*a*

SHILHAK-IN-SHUSHINAK — Elamite ruler, a great builder, son of Shutruk-Nakhunte (12th century B.C.) . . . . *p.* 328, 332

SHINAR — Akkadian name of Babylonia. . . . *p.* 97

SHUBAD — 'Queen' buried in the cemetery of Ur (Tomb 800) with a treasure of *objets d'art* (270 pieces): vessels of gold, silver and stone, a harp, ornaments, etc. . . . . *p.* 160
— Goblet and bowl of Shubad. . . . . . *fig.* 189*a*
— Tomb of Shubad (plan) . . . . *fig.* 32

SHUBAT ENLIL, see CHAGAR BAZAR.

SHULGI, see DUNGI.

SHUQAMUNA — Kassite divinity, presiding over the fecundity of the flocks. . . . . *p.* 319

SHURUPPAK, see FARA.

SHUTRUK-NAKHUNTE — Elamite ruler, famous for his raids in Babylonia (12th century B.C.), from which he carried off many works as war trophies *p.* 313, 328

SIALK — Iranian site excavated by Ghirshman (1933-37). Some very important archaeological evidence was revealed by its early settlements and cemeteries. . . . . *p.* 24, 41, 51
— Samarra* pottery with dancers . . . . . *fig.* 62*c*
— Vase . . . . *fig.* 68

SIDON — Phoenician port, whose king Abdi-milkutti is represented on the stele of Asarhaddon (Assyrian king, 680-668 B.C., son of Sennacherib). The necropolis has yielded many sarcophagi, including the one named after Alexander (Istanbul Museum) . . . . *p.* 270
— Sarcophagus of Alexander* . . . . . . *fig.* 337

SIN — Semitic name of the moon god, worshipped at Ur and Harran in particular (*cf.* Nannar)
p. 188, 319

SINAI — Mountain on the Sinai peninsula where Moses received the Law (Exodus, XIX, 20) . . *p.* 305

SIPPAR, see ABU HABBA.

SIT SHAMSHI (so-called Tablet of)—Bronze model of a high place, inscribed with the name of Shilhak-in-Shushinak (12th century B.C.). Louvre
p. 332, *fig.* 408, 409
— Columns, compared with those of the temple of Jerusalem . . . . *p.* 332

SLIP — Liquid clay with which ancient pottery was sometimes coated . . . . *p.* 60

SLUGHIS — Greyhounds represented on Susa goblets (Style I) and on a mould from Mari.
p. 61, 295, *fig.* 79

SMITH (George) (1840-76) — Famous English Assyriologist who, at Nineveh in 1873, discovered the missing fragment of the cuneiform account of the Flood, which he had first identified on some Ninevite tablets in the British Museum in 1872 . . *p.* 15

SNAKE — Very frequently represented (in pottery, seal designs and reliefs) and regarded, paradoxically enough, as possessing a beneficent virtue *fig.*168*c*, 290

SNAKE (Horned) — A type of snake similar to the 'horned viper,' whose bite is fatal . . . . . *p.* 319

SNAKE-HEADED FIGURINES of the al 'Ubaid period, discovered at Ur . . . *p.* 55, *fig.* 74, 76, 77

SOLOMON — Son of David and king of Israel, who built the temple of Jerusalem (10th century B.C.)
p. 52

SPEISER (E.) — American archaeologist, excavated Tepe Gawra (1931-32 and 1936-37) and Tell Billa (1930-33). . . . . *p.* 22

SPIRAL PATTERN — A symbolic design frequent in Mesopotamian and Aegean iconography . *p.* 278

STAG . . . . *e. g. fig.* 162, 187

STANDARD OF UR — One of the most famous works discovered in the 'royal tombs' of Ur* (British Museum) . . . . *fig.* 175-178

STARR (Richard F.S.) — American archaeologist, excavated Yorgan Tepe (Nuzi) from 1929 to 1931 *p.* 22

STEATITE — A variety of medium-hard, greenish-blue stone in which the Mesopotamians carved many statuettes, figurines and cylinder seals . *e. g. fig.* 193

STELE — A commemorative slab or pillar of stone generally rounded off at the top, decorated with reliefs and often inscribed . . . . . . *e. g. fig.* 213

STRATIGRAPHIC TECHNIQUE — An excavating technique which consists in clearing a site stage by stage, working downwards through successive strata or levels . . . . *fig.* 27, 28

SUBARIANS — A people who settled in Upper Mesopotamia in very early times, probably before the arrival of the Sumerians (4th millennium B.C.) *p.* 29

SUBARTU — The northern part of Mesopotamia, roughly corresponding to the Assyrian region.
p. 170, 182

SUMER — A region of Lower Mesopotamia, south of Kish, largely confined to the area between Nippur and Eridu. The great majority of the inhabitants were Sumerians.
p. 21, 22, 68, 93, 95, 166, 170, 199, 238

SUMERIANS — A non-Semitic people who settled in Lower Mesopotamia in the middle of the 4th millennium B.C., probably during the Uruk period.
p. 3, 10, 12, 15, 29, 42, 63, 64, 66, 68, 82, 90, 93, 95, 96, 159, 162, 169, 170, 178, 197, 246, 250, 254, 272

SUMU-ILU — King of the Larsa dynasty and ruler of Lagash (20th century B.C.). . . . . . *p.* 182, 190
— Dog of Sumu-ilu, a votive statuette inscribed with Sumu-ilu's name, discovered at Telloh by Commandant Cros (Louvre) . . . . *fig.* 357*b*

SUN-GOD . . . . *fig.* 237

SUSA — A great metropolis in south-western Iran, systematically excavated since 1897, where some of the most precious works of Mesopotamian art have been found. . . . *p.* 10, 14, 16, 24, 26, 33, 41, 60, 62, 64, 90, 174, 238, 264, 290, 320, 328, 336
— Tell of Susa . . . . *fig.* 23
Sculpture:
— Boundary stone of Melishipak II* . . *fig.* 395*a-b*
— Bowls decorated with ibexes* . . . . *fig.* 357*c-d*
— Double vase . . . . *fig.* 168*a*
— Hammurabi* . . . . *fig.* 373, 375
— Innina* . . . . *fig.* 203
— Kneeling god . . . . *fig.* 293
— Manishtusu*: obelisk. . . . . *fig.* 215
                          robe. . . . . *fig.* 214
— Men's heads . . . . *fig.* 403, 407
— Napir-Asu* . . . . *fig.* 398, 399
— Naram-Sin: feet of a statue of . . . . . *fig.* 216
                     stele of . . . . *fig.* 212, 213

TEMPLE — House of God (*E* in Sumerian, *bit* in Akkadian).

TEMPTATION SEAL — Mesopotamian cylinder seal in the British Museum (No. 89326). . *p.* 37, *fig.* 53

TEPE GAWRA — Site north-east of Nineveh, explored from 1927 to 1938, where a well-preserved superposition of levels yielded evidence of each successive cultural phase from the Neolithic Age to the mid-2nd millennium B.C.. . . . . *p.* 2, 53, 54, 66, 316
Architecture:
— Gawra VIII temple (plan) . . . . . . *fig.* 391*b*
— Temple on Level XIII (plan). . . . . *fig.* 72*b*

TEPE GIYAN — Iranian tell excavated by Contenau and Ghirshman in 1931-32. It yielded a large quantity of pottery of the early Iranian period. *p.* 24, 41

TERAPHIM — Household idols of the Jews and other Semitic peoples (Genesis, XXXI, 19, 30). *p.* 240, 241

THOMPSON (R. Campbell) (1876-1941) — English Assyriologist, excavated Nineveh and (before 1914), Eridu (1918) and Nineveh (1927-32) . . *p.* 20, 22

THUNDERBOLT — Stylized representation in the form of a branch with jagged offshoots. . . *p.* 319

THUREAU-DANGIN (François) (1872-1944) — Famous French Assyriologist, excavated Arslan Tash (1928) and Tell Ahmar (1921-31) . . . . . *p.* 23

TIGRIS — One of the two great Mesopotamian rivers. . . . . . . *p.* 2, 8, 37, 51, 68, 80, 95, 96

TIGRIS, UPPER — From Jezireh-ibn-Omar to Assur, and the surrounding region.
                              p. 3, 22, 48, 53, 95, 162, 253

TIL BARSIP, see TELL AHMAR.

TISARI — King of Urkish on the Upper Khabur, builder of the temple of Pirigal ('the great lioness,' probably a warlike variant of Ishtar). . . . *p.* 182

TORTOISE — Represented on the Larsa* vase (Louvre) . . . . *fig.* 367*b*

TOWER OF BABEL (Genesis, XI, 1-9) — Identifiable with one of the ziggurats of Babylonia, perhaps with that of Babylon itself. . *p.* 32, 68, 97, *fig.* 3, 4

TOYNBEE (Arnold) — English historian, born in 1889, former Director of Studies at the Royal Institute of International Affairs (1925-55), professor at London University, and author of *A Study of History* in ten volumes . . . . *p.* 32, 33

TRANSCASPIAN REGION — Province east of the Caspian Sea. . . . . *p.* 64

TREE OF LIFE — In the Garden of Eden (Genesis, III, 22). A frequent theme or symbol in Mesopotamian reliefs and seal designs, represented either very realistically or very schematically (Assyrian reliefs) . . . . *p.* 162, 278, *fig.* 314

TURA-DAGAN — A governor of Mari in the early 2nd millennium B.C. . . . . *p.* 268

TURBANED HEAD — So called when first discovered, later identified as Gudea* (Louvre).
                              p. 10, 211, *fig.* 7, 8, 258

TURIN PAPYRI — Several important Egyptian papyrus scrolls preserved in the Turin Museum. . *p.* 150

TUTANKHAMEN — Egyptian pharaoh of the XVIIIth Dynasty whose tomb was discovered in the Valley of the Kings by Lord Carnavon and Howard Carter (1922-24) . . . . *p.* 20

TUTUB — Ancient site sometimes identified with Khafaje* . . . . *p.* 22

TYRE — Phoenician city south of Sidon, founded in the 3rd millennium B.C., seat of the cult of the god Melqart, and a famous seaport (Ezekiel, XXVII). Built on an island off the coast, it was linked to the mainland by Alexander the Great, who besieged the city in 332 B.C. . . . . *p.* 332

UGARIT, see RAS SHAMRA.

UGME — Son of Ur-Ningirsu and Patesi of Lagash. His hypogeum was discovered in 1932. . . . *p.* 203
— Hypogeum of Ugme . . . . *fig.* 250

UM EL-AGHAREB — Small site in the neighbourhood of Lagash. The Arab name means 'mother of scorpions.' Ancient name unidentified.
— Man's head . . . . *fig.* 143*a*

UMMA, see JOKHA.

UNIVERSITY MUSEUM OF PENNSYLVANIA, see PENNSYLVANIA.

UNTASH-HUBAN — Elamite king (13th century B.C.), builder of the ziggurat of Choga Zambil*
                              p. 322, 324
— Stele of Untash-Huban . . . . . . *fig.* 401, 402

UR, see MUQAYYAR.

URGAR — Patesi of Lagash, son-in-law of Ur-Bau (Gudea's predecessor as Patesi). Neo-Sumerian period.
— Human-headed bull inscribed with Urgar's name . . . . *fig.* 277

URKISH — Hurrian city situated in the Khabur triangle. A number of works have been looted from the site by clandestine excavators, e.g. some votive lions in bronze (Louvre and Metropolitan Museum) . *p.* 182
— Lion and foundation tablet . . . . . . *fig.* 220

UR-NAMMU — Founder of the Third Dynasty of Ur, author of a code of laws identified by Kramer. A great builder (2124-2107 B.C.).
                       p. 199, 226, 250, 305, *fig.* 281, 282

BIBLIOGRAPHY

I. HISTORIES OF ART

ANDRAE (Walter) and SCHAEFER (H.). — DIE KUNST DES ALTEN ORIENTS. DIE KUNST VORDERASIENS, in PROPYLÄEN KUNSTGESCHICHTE, II, pp. 133-168, Berlin, Propyläen Verlag, 1925.
Short presentation of the masterpieces of Mesopotamian art; excellent plates (pp. 467-580), brief descriptive notices, and basic bibliography.

CONTENAU (Georges). — L'ART DE L'ASIE OCCIDENTALE ANCIENNE, Paris and Brussels, G. van Oest, 1928.
Concise general survey (55 pages, 64 figures) of Oriental art, including Hittite art, from the origins to the third century A.D.

CONTENAU (Georges) and CHAPOT (V.). — L'ART ANTIQUE: ORIENT, GRÈCE, ROME, in L'HISTOIRE UNIVERSELLE DES ARTS, edited by Louis Réau, Paris, Armand Colin, 1930.
Studies the monuments by millennia and continually intermingles Egypt and Asia.

CONTENAU (Georges). — L'ANTIQUITÉ ORIENTALE, in L'HISTOIRE GÉNÉRALE DE L'ART, I, pp. 35-65, Paris, Flammarion, 1950.
Concise but substantial account; well-chosen, well-reproduced illustrations.

DELAPORTE (Louis). — L'ART DE L'ASIE ANTÉRIEURE in NOUVELLE HISTOIRE UNIVERSELLE DE L'ART, edited by Marcel Aubert, I, pp. 27-51, Paris, Firmin-Didot, 1932.
Brief account of a field greatly broadened and enriched since the date of publication.

DELAPORTE (Louis). — L'ART DE L'ASIE OCCIDENTALE AVANT LA CONQUÊTE D'ALEXANDRE, in L'ART DES ORIGINES A NOS JOURS, edited by Léon Deshairs, I, pp. 27-42, Paris, Larousse, 1932.
Sixteen pages (including illustrations) can obviously not give a complete picture of Mesopotamian art; yet well-chosen illustrations include some of the latest finds then available (notably from the excavations at Ur).

Encyclopédie Photographique de l'Art (parts 6-13), Paris, Editions Tel, 1935-36.
Excellent reproductions, from unpublished photographs by André Vigneau, of the most important and aesthetically interesting works in the Oriental collections of the Louvre; short descriptive captions.

FRANKFORT (Henri). — THE ART AND ARCHITECTURE OF THE ANCIENT ORIENT, in THE PELICAN HISTORY OF ART, Harmondsworth and Baltimore, Penguin Books, 1954.
One of the best and most recent histories of the art of the ancient Near East (279 pages, 192 plates), by an outstanding specialist on the region, who died prematurely in 1954.

HUYGHE (René). (editor). — L'ART ET L'HOMME, vol. I, Paris, Larousse, 1958.
General survey laid out along new lines, showing the interpenetration of different civilizations; early periods of Mesopotamia treated by Dr Contenau (pp. 65-70, 129-140). Contains a 'précis d'histoire de l'art,' written by Philippe Jean (pp. 164-168).

PERROT (Georges) and CHIPIEZ (Charles). — HISTOIRE DE L'ART DANS L'ANTIQUITÉ, vol. II: CHALDÉE ET ASSYRIE, Paris, Hachette, 1884.
The first comprehensive study of Oriental art, under the two general headings: Assyria (excavations of the Assyrian triangle) and 'Chaldea' (Sarzec's excavations at Telloh). Well-documented and abundantly illustrated with line engravings.

POPE (A. Upham). — A SURVEY OF PERSIAN ART FROM PREHISTORIC TIMES TO THE PRESENT, vol. IV, London and New York, Oxford University Press, 1938.
Magnificent survey of the most famous and most characteristic monuments of Iranian civilization: pottery, bronze vessels and enamelled panels from Susa, Luristan bronzes, reliefs from Persepolis, etc. Plates are commented on in a volume of text (vol. I).

REINACH (Salomon). — APOLLO: HISTOIRE GÉNÉRALE DES ARTS PLASTIQUES (6th ed.), Paris, Hachette, 1910. APOLLO, tr. from the French by Florence Symmonds. new ed., Heinemann, London, 1907.
Very few pages (pp. 23-30) are devoted to the art of 'Chaldea and Persia.'

TERRASSE (Charles). — HISTOIRE DE L'ART DEPUIS LES ORIGINES JUSQU'A NOS JOURS, vol. I: L'ART DE L'ASIE OCCIDENTALE, pp. 49-75, Paris, Henri Laurens, 1938.
Very succinct account (14 pages devoted to Mesopotamia, including illustrations); dates, however, need to be moved forward in time to bring them into line with the new chronology.

II. REPRODUCTIONS AND ILLUSTRATED SURVEYS

CONTENAU (Georges). — MUSÉE DU LOUVRE, DÉPARTEMENT DES ANTIQUITÉS ORIENTALES. LES ANTIQUITÉS ORIENTALES. I. Sumer, Babylonie, Elam. II. Monuments hittites, assyriens, phéniciens, perses, judaïques, cypriotes, araméens. Paris, Morancé, 1927-30.
Presentation of the outstanding works in the Department of Oriental Antiquities, with descriptive notices; excellent reproductions (108 collotype plates).

GRESSMANN (Hugo). — ALTORIENTALISCHE BILDER ZUM ALTEN TESTAMENT (2nd ed.), Berlin and Leipzig, Walter de Gruyter, 1927.
Valuable selection of works from the Ancient Near East (678 figures) chosen for their possible bearing on the Old Testament; excellent descriptive and bibliographical notices.

HALL (Harry Reginald). — BABYLONIAN AND ASSYRIAN SCULPTURE IN THE BRITISH MUSEUM, Paris and Brussels, G. van Oest, 1928.
Presentation of the finest examples of Mesopotamian sculpture in the British Museum, from the Jemdet Nasr period to Assyrian times.

MALRAUX (André). — LE MUSÉE IMAGINAIRE DE LA SCULPTURE MONDIALE, Paris, La Galerie de la Pléiade, Gallimard, 1952.
Mesopotamia is abundantly represented in this extraordinary panorama, in which the works of each period and place are seen in due perspective as part of an organic whole. Mesopotamian sculpture: figs. 6-30, 45-53, 94-102.

MALRAUX (André). — Vol. II. LE MUSÉE IMAGINAIRE DE LA SCULPTURE MONDIALE, DES BAS-RELIEFS AUX GROTTES SACRÉES, Paris, La Galerie de la Pléiade, Gallimard, 1954.
Many works from Mesopotamia (figs. 58-106 bis) take their place in this long sequence of bas-reliefs from many different periods and places.

PARROT (André). — MARI, Neuchâtel, Ides et Calendes 1953.
Photographs of the most attractive works (sculpture, painting, architecture, glyptics) discovered at Mari from 1933 to 1953 (132 collotype figures, 3 plans, 132 descriptive notices).

PRITCHARD (J.B.). — THE ANCIENT NEAR EAST IN PICTURES RELATING TO THE OLD TESTAMENT, Princeton, University Press, 1954.
Excellent reproductions of 769 works, with accurate descriptive notices and bibliography. Covers the entire Near East, including Egypt.

SPEISER (Werner). — VORDERASIATISCHE KUNST, Berlin, Safari, 1952.
Good general outline of Oriental art, from the earliest times to the Parthians.

ZERVOS (Christian). — L'ART DE LA MÉSOPOTAMIE DE LA FIN DU QUATRIÈME MILLÉNAIRE AU XVe SIÈCLE AVANT NOTRE ÈRE. ELAM, SUMER, AKKAD. Paris, Editions 'Cahiers d'Art,' 1935.
Photographic survey of the most important monuments of ancient Mesopotamia. Works from Susa are also included.

III. HISTORICAL WORKS

AYMARD (André) and AUBOYER (Jeannine). — L'ORIENT ET LA GRÈCE ANTIQUE, in HISTOIRE GÉNÉRALE DES CIVILISATIONS, edited by Maurice Crouzet, Vol. I, Paris, Presses Universitaires de France, 1953.
Part II (pp. 111-178), devoted to 'Mesopotamian Civilization,' contains an up-to-date chapter on 'les créations artistiques.' A few pages (191-206) on the Achaemenians. Well-chosen, well-reproduced illustrations.

Cambridge Ancient History. — I. EGYPT AND BABYLONIA, 1924. III. THE ASSYRIAN AND PERSIAN EMPIRES, 1925. IV. THE PERSIAN EMPIRE AND THE WEST, 1926. Cambridge, University Press.

DELAPORTE (Louis). — LES PEUPLES DE L'ORIENT MÉDITERRANÉEN. I. LE PROCHE-ORIENT ASIATIQUE, Paris, Collection 'Clio,' Presses Universitaires de France, 1938.
Excellent account of the history of the Near East from the earliest times to Alexander, with an extensive bibliography. Needs to be supplemented, however, with the knowledge acquired since the date of publication.

DHORME (Edouard) and CONTENAU (Georges). — LES PREMIÈRES CIVILISATIONS, first volume of the series 'Peuples et Civilisations,' Paris, Presses Universitaires de France, 1950.
Several chapters contributed by these two authors.

EDZARD (Dietz Otto). — DIE 'ZWEITE ZWISCHENZEIT' BABYLONIENS, Wiesbaden, Otto Harrassowitz, 1957.
Scrupulously accurate account of the Babylonian period from the accession of Ishbi-Irra of Isin to that of Rim-Sin of Larsa.

GHIRSHMAN (Roman). — L'IRAN, DES ORIGINES A L'ISLAM, Paris, Payot, 1951. IRAN: FROM THE EARLIEST TIMES TO THE ISLAMIC CONQUEST, Harmondsworth, Penguin Books, 1954.
The civilization, history and archaeology of Iran up to the Islamic conquest. A few reproductions of objects from the Sakkiz treasure (Ziwiyeh).

GOOSSENS (Godefroy). — ASIE OCCIDENTALE ANCIENNE, in HISTOIRE UNIVERSELLE I, Encyclopédie de la Pléiade, pp. 289-495, Paris, Gallimard, 1957.
One of the most recent syntheses of the history of Western Asia in ancient times, making full use of the latest archaeological discoveries.

KING (L.W.). — A HISTORY OF SUMER AND AKKAD, London, Chatto and Windus, 1910.

From the earliest times to the founding of the dynasty of Babylon. Still valuable as a record of the state of historical knowledge before the First World War, i.e. when the protohistory of these regions was still unknown.

KING (L.W.). — A HISTORY OF BABYLON FROM THE FOUNDATION OF THE MONARCHY TO THE PERSIAN CONQUEST, London, Chatto and Windus, 1915.

Historical study of the great capital with an account of archaeological explorations. Needs to be brought up to date.

MASPERO (Gaston). — HISTOIRE ANCIENNE DES PEUPLES DE L'ORIENT CLASSIQUE, 3 volumes, Paris, Hachette, 1895-1899.

Despite the vast increase in our knowledge, this remains a masterly study remarkable for its broad, synthetic grasp of the subject and the depth and penetration of the author's views. Will long remain a standard work.

MASPERO (Gaston). — THE DAWN OF CIVILISATION, EGYPT AND CHALDAEA, ed. by A.H. Sayce, tr. by M.L. McClure, 5th ed., London, Society for Promoting Christian Knowledge, 1910. New York and Toronto, The Macmillan Co., 1922.

MASPERO (Gaston). — THE STRUGGLE OF THE NATIONS, EGYPT, SYRIA AND ASSYRIA, ed. by A.H. Sayce, tr. by M.L. McClure, 2nd ed., London, Society for Promoting Christian Knowledge, 1910.

MASPERO (Gaston). — THE PASSING OF THE EMPIRES, 850 B.C. - 330 B.C., ed. by A.H. Sayce, tr. by M.L. McClure, 1st ed. (no later editions), London, Society for Promoting Christian Knowledge, 1900.

The three preceding works published as:

MASPERO (Gaston). — HISTORY OF EGYPT, SYRIA, BABYLONIA AND ASSYRIA, ed. by A.H. Sayce, tr. by M.L. McClure, London, The Grolier Society, Limited Edition, 1903.

MEYER (Eduard). — GESCHICHTE DES ALTERTUMS, 5 volumes, Stuttgart and Berlin, 1884-1902. HISTOIRE DE L'ANTIQUITÉ, vol. III: LA BABYLONIE ET LES SÉMITES JUSQU'A L'ÉPOQUE KASSITE, tr. by E. Combe, Paris, Geuthner, 1926.

Regarded at the time of publication as one of the best histories of antiquity. Now inevitably incomplete and out of date.

MOORTGAT (Anton) and SCHARFF (Alexander). — AEGYPTEN UND VORDERASIEN IM ALTERTUM (pp. 193-535), Munich, E. Bruckmann, 1950.

One of the most recent histories of the Ancient Near East, from the earliest times to Alexander, by specialists fully conversant with the latest archaeological discoveries.

OLMSTEAD (A.T.). — A HISTORY OF ASSYRIA, New York and London, Charles Scribner, 1923.

Begins with the archaic temples of Assur and ends with the fall of Nineveh.

SCHMÖKEL (Hartmut). — GESCHICHTE DES ALTEN VORDERASIENS. HANDBUCH DER ORIENTALISTIK, ed. by B. Spuler, Vol. 2, Leiden, Brill, 1957.

Excellent reappraisal of the history of the Ancient Near East, taking the latest discoveries into account.

SCHMÖKEL (Hartmut). — HAMMURABI VON BABYLON: DIE ERRICHTUNG EINES REICHS, Munich, R. Oldenburg, 1958.

The reign of King Hammurabi of Babylon, studied in the light of the latest discoveries, drawing in particular on the royal archives of Mari.

SMITH (Sidney). — EARLY HISTORY OF ASSYRIA TO 1000 B.C., London, Chatto and Windus, 1928.

Despite the title, this is more particularly a history of Babylon, written by one of the foremost authorities on the chronology of ancient history.

IV. ARCHAEOLOGY

AMANDRY (Pierre). — FRENCH BIBLIOGRAPHICAL DIGEST. ARCHAEOLOGY (1945-1955). II. THE NEAR EAST. New York, The Cultural Center of the French Embassy, 1957.

An accurate, detailed, fully documented bibliography of French archaeological publications.

ANDRAE (Walter). — DAS GOTTESHAUS UND DIE URFORMEN DES BAUENS IM ALTEN ORIENT, Berlin, Hans Schoetz, 1930.

An important study of sacred architecture and its distant antecedents in the form of reed constructions. A book that will be consulted for a long time to come.

ANDRAE (Walter). — DIE IONISCHE SÄULE. BAUFORM ODER SYMBOL? Berlin, Koldewey Gesellschaft, 1933.

The author's theory is that the Ionic column and capital may have originated in the cluster of reeds bound into a solid bundle.

ANDRAE (Walter). — DIE ARCHAISCHEN ISCHTARTEMPEL IN ASSUR, WISSENSCHAFTLICHE VERÖFFENTLICHUNGEN DER DEUTSCHEN ORIENT-GESELLSCHAFT, 39, Leipzig, J.C. Hinrichs, 1922.

Official publication of the temples of Ishtar found on the earliest levels (H-D). Reproduction of plans and numerous objects (pre-Sargonid worshipper statues).

ANDRAE (Walter). — DAS WIEDERERSTANDENE ASSUR, Leipzig, J.C. Hinrichs, 1938.

Remarkable synthesis of the results obtained by the archaeological exploration of the Assyrian capital. All the essential monuments are reproduced (86 plates).

ANDRAE (Walter). — VORDERASIEN, see OTTO (W.).

ASIL (Naji al-), see NAJI AL-ASIL.

BAQIR (Taha). — A HARVEST PLANNING CENTRE IN THE BABYLON OF 4000 YEARS AGO (TELL HARMAL), in ILLUSTRATED LONDON NEWS, August 3, 1946, pp. 116-117.
Report of the discovery at the gates of Baghdad of a second-millennium city, with a sanctuary guarded by terracotta lions. Many inscriptions brought to light.

BAQIR (Taha). — IRAQ GOVERNMENT EXCAVATIONS AT AQUAR QUF, in IRAQ SUPPLEMENTS, 1944, 1945, 1946.
Exploration of the Kassite capital Dur Kurigalzu (ziggurat, wall paintings, etc.).

BARRELET (Marie-Thérèse). — UNE PEINTURE DE LA COUR 106 DU PALAIS DE MARI, in STUDIA MARIANA, pp. 9-35, Leiden, E.J. Brill, 1950.
New interpretation of the painting known as 'The Investiture,' which was described by A. Parrot in Syria, XVIII (1937), pp. 335-346.

BARRELET (Marie-Thérèse). — NOTES SUR QUELQUES SCULPTURES MÉSOPOTAMIENNES DE L'ÉPOQUE D'AKKAD, in SYRIA, XXXVI (1959), pp. 20-37.
A reassessment of various pieces of sculpture, including the head from Nineveh identified with Naram-Sin.

BASMADSCHI (Faradsch). — LANDSCHAFTLICHE ELE-MENTE IN DER MESOPOTAMISCHEN KUNST DES IV. UND III. JAHRTAUSENDS, Basel, E. Birkhäuser, 1943.
On the representation of plants and landscape in ancient Mesopotamian glyptics.

BIROT (Pierre) and DRESCH (Jean). — LA MÉDI-TERRANÉE ET LE MOYEN-ORIENT, vol. II: LA MÉDITERRANÉE ORIENTALE ET LE MOYEN-ORIENT, Paris, Presses Universitaires de France, 1956.
Sound, up-to-date treatment of the subject from both the physical and human points of view.

BRAIDWOOD (R.J.), BRAIDWOOD (Linda), and others. — NEW CHALCOLITHIC MATERIAL OF SAMARRAN TYPE AND ITS IMPLICATIONS, in JOURNAL OF NEAR EASTERN STUDIES, III (1944), pp. 47-72.
Study of the so-called Samarra phase of culture, in the light of the discovery of Baghuz (cf. BUISSON, R. du Mesnil du).

BRAIDWOOD (R.J.). — THE WORLD'S FIRST FARMING VILLAGES, in ILLUSTRATED LONDON NEWS, April 28, 1956, pp. 410-411.
The most recent account of the mission to northern Iraq sponsored by the Oriental Institute of the University of Chicago.

BRITISH MUSEUM. — A SUMMARY GUIDE TO THE ANTIQUITIES OF WESTERN ASIA, London, British Museum, 1952.
Contains a few reproductions: Gudea with shaven head, Lion Hunt of Assurbanipal, ivories from Nimrud, bracelet from the Oxus treasure.

BUDGE (E.A. Wallis). — A GUIDE TO THE BABYLO-NIAN AND ASSYRIAN ANTIQUITIES (3rd edition), London, British Museum, 1922.

BUISSON (R. du Mesnil du). — BAGHOUZ, L'ANCIENNE CORSOTE, Leiden, E.J. Brill, 1948.
Important for the documentation it contains relating to the Samarra culture (cf. BRAIDWOOD, New Chalcolithic Material. . .).

BERAN. — DIE BABYLONISCHE GLYPTIK DER KASSITEN-ZEIT, in ARCHIV FÜR ORIENT-FORSCHUNG, XVIII (1958), pp. 255-278.
Methodical study of Kassite cylinder seals, classified in three groups.

BUSINK (T.A.). — DE BABYLONISCHE TEMPELTOREN, Leiden, E.J. Brill, 1949.
Well-informed, up-to-date monograph by one of the best qualified specialists on the subject, a professional architect.

CHILDE (V. Gordon). — NEW LIGHT ON THE MOST ANCIENT EAST (4th edition), London, Routledge and Kegan Paul, 1952. Reprinted with additions, 1954.
New, revised edition of a work first published as The Most Ancient East (1928), *then as* New Light on the Most Ancient East (1934).

CHRISTIAN (Viktor). — ALTERTUMSKUNDE DES ZWEI-STROMLANDES, 1 vol. of text, 1 vol. of 444 plates, Leipzig, Karl W. Hiersemann, 1940.
Exhaustive repertory of the documentation relating to Mesopotamian art and archaeology, from the earliest times to the end of the second millennium.

CONTENAU (Georges). — MANUEL D'ARCHÉOLOGIE ORIENTALE, DEPUIS LES ORIGINES JUSQU'A L'ÉPOQUE D'ALEXANDRE, 4 volumes of text (2378 pages), abundantly illustrated (1311 figures in the text), Paris, Picard, 1927, 1931, 1947.
Exhaustive recapitulation of the results obtained from many excavation sites in the Near East, up to a fairly recent date.

CONTENAU (Georges). — L'ÉPOPÉE DE GILGAMESH, POÈME BABYLONIEN, Paris, L'Artisan du Livre, 1939.
A French translation of the epic poem whose hero figures so prominently in the Mesopotamian iconography.

CONTENAU (Georges) and GHIRSHMAN (Roman). — FOUILLES DU TÉPÉ-GIYAN PRÈS DE NÉHA-VEND, 1931 ET 1932, Paris, Geuthner, 1935.
Publication of the excavations at Tepe Giyan, which revealed the early periods of Iranian civilization. The examples of pottery are among the most important found so far.

CONTENAU (Georges). — MONUMENTS MÉSOPOTA-MIENS NOUVELLEMENT ACQUIS OU PEU CONNUS. MUSÉE DU LOUVRE. Paris, Editions d'Art et d'Histoire, 1934.
Works ranging from the Jemdet Nasr period to Achaemenian times (stone, bronze, shell).

Corpus of Ancient Near Eastern Seals in North American Collections, edited by Edith Porada, 2 volumes, Washington, Bollingen Foundation, 1948.
Excellent publication on the Oriental glyptics in the Pierpont Morgan Collection, with 176 plates of the highest order illustrating 1157 items.

DELAPORTE (Louis). — CATALOGUE DES CYLINDRES ORIENTAUX ET DES CACHETS ASSYRO-BABYLONIENS, PERSES ET SYRO-CAPPADOCIENS DE LA BIBLIOTHÈQUE NATIONALE. INSTITUT DE FRANCE, FONDATION EUGÈNE PIOT. 1 vol. of text, 1 vol. of plates, Paris, Ernest Leroux, 1910.

Descriptive catalogue of 650 seals preserved in the Bibliothèque Nationale.

DELAPORTE (Louis). — CATALOGUE DES CYLINDRES ORIENTAUX. MUSÉE DU LOUVRE. I. Fouilles et Missions, 1920. II. Acquisitions, 1923, Paris, Hachette.

Exhaustive catalogue of the cylinder seals preserved in the Louvre.

DELORME (Jean). — CHRONOLOGIE DES CIVILISATIONS, Paris, Collection 'Clio,' Presses Universitaires de France, 1949.

Chronology of the world's great civilizations, based on the latest researches.

DELOUGAZ (P.). — THE TEMPLE OVAL AT KHAFAJAH (Oriental Institute Publications, LIII), Chicago, The University of Chicago Press, 1940.

Architectural study of an archaic temple discovered at Khafaje.

DELOUGAZ (P.) and LLOYD (Seton) with chapters by Henri FRANKFORT and Thorkild JACOBSEN. — PRE-SARGONID TEMPLES IN THE DIYALA REGION (OIP, LVIII), Chicago, The University of Chicago Press, 1942.

Architectural study of the Pre-Sargonid temples discovered at Khafaje (Sin, Nintu), Tell Asmar (Abu), and Tell Agrab (Shara).

DOSSIN (Georges). — L'INSCRIPTION DE FONDATION DE LAHDUN-LIM, ROI DE MARI, in SYRIA, XXXII (1955), pp. 1-28.

Inscription of historical and religious import (157 lines) found in several copies on foundation bricks buried in the substructure of the temple of Shamash at Mari. Discovered in 1953.

DUSSAUD (René). — EX-VOTO AU DIEU AMOURROU POUR LA VIE D'HAMMURABI, MUSÉE DU LOUVRE, in MONUMENTS ET MÉMOIRES DE LA FONDATION PIOT, XXXIII (1933), pp. 1-10.

Publication of the work often referred to as the 'Larsa bronze.'

FRANKFORT (Henri). — CYLINDER SEALS, A DOCUMENTARY ESSAY ON THE ART AND RELIGION OF THE ANCIENT NEAR EAST, London, Macmillan, 1939.

One of the most valuable compilations of Oriental glyptics, not only grouping the seals chronologically and geographically but also interpreting them. The best general study of the subject so far made.

FRANKFORT (Henri). — SCULPTURE OF THE THIRD MILLENNIUM B.C. FROM TELL ASMAR AND KHAFAJEH (Oriental Institute Publications, XLIV), Chicago, The University of Chicago Press, 1939.

An historical and stylistic introduction followed by a catalogue of the sculptures found at Tell Asmar (Square Temple) and Khafaje (Temple Oval, Temple of Sin), with 115 plates.

FRANKFORT (H.), LLOYD (Seton) and JACOBSEN (Thorkild) with a chapter by J. MARTINEZ. — THE GIMILSIN TEMPLE AND PALACE OF THE RULERS OF TELL ASMAR (Oriental Institute Publications, XLIII), Chicago, The University of Chicago Press, 1940.

Publication of several architectural discoveries, including the Audience Hall of Naram-Sin.

FRANKFORT (Henri). — MORE SCULPTURE FROM THE DIYALA REGION (OIP, LX), Chicago, The University of Chicago Press, 1943.

Stylistic study of Mesopotamian sculpture from the earliest times to Babylon. I. Catalogue of the sculptures, completing and in some cases correcting the catalogue given in OIP, XLIV.

FRANKFORT (Henri). — A NOTE ON THE LADY OF BIRTH, in JOURNAL OF NEAR EASTERN STUDIES, III (1944), pp. 198-200.

The omega sign interpreted as an amulet for pregnant women, auguring a happy delivery (cf. VAN BUREN, A Clay Relief.).

FRANKFORT (Henri). — THE BIRTH OF CIVILIZATION IN THE NEAR EAST, London, Williams and Norgate, and Bloomington, Indiana University Press, 1951.

Stress is laid on the similarities and connections that can be traced between Egypt and Mesopotamia.

FRANKFORT (Henri). — STRATIFIED CYLINDER SEALS FROM THE DIYALA REGION (Oriental Institute Publications, LXXII), Chicago, The University of Chicago Press, 1955.

The seals are arranged, not in chronological order, but according to the sites where they were found.

GADD (C.J.). — HISTORY AND MONUMENTS OF UR, London, Chatto and Windus, 1929.

General survey of the history of the great Sumerian capital, illustrated with works excavated there, including the 'royal' tombs.

GHIRSHMAN (Roman). — FOUILLES DE SIALK PRÈS DE KASHAN, 1933, 1934, 1937. Louvre, Département des Antiquités Orientales, Paris, Geuthner, 1938, 1939.

Painted pottery, with a sober elegance of design. Cultural parallels drawn between Iran and Mesopotamia, from the earliest times.

GROENEWEGEN-FRANKFORT (H.A.). — ARREST AND MOVEMENT: AN ESSAY ON SPACE AND TIME IN THE REPRESENTATIONAL ART OF THE ANCIENT NEAR EAST, London, Faber and Faber, 1951.

Analysis of styles, themes and composition in Mesopotamian art, pp. 145-181.

GOVERNMENT OF IRAQ. — Directorate General of Antiquities. A GUIDE TO THE IRAQ MUSEUM COLLECTIONS, Baghdad, Government Press, 1942.

Excellent guide with good reproductions of famous works (Warka vase, statuettes from Khafaje and Ashnunnak, woman's head from Warka, helmet of Meskalamdug from Ur, statue of Alla from Lagash, Assyrian reliefs from Khorsabad).

HALL (H.R.) and WOOLLEY (C.L.). — UR EXCAVATIONS. I: AL 'UBAID, London, The Oxford University Press, 1927.
Official report of the excavations at al 'Ubaid (1919-24).

HEINRICH (Ernst). — KLEINFUNDE AUS DEN ARCHAISCHEN TEMPELSCHICHTEN IN URUK, Leipzig, Otto Harrassowitz, 1936.
Publication of important finds made at Uruk on the Jemdet Nasr level.

HEINRICH (Ernst). — DIE STELLUNG DER URUKTEMPEL IN DER BAUGESCHICHTE, in ZEITSCHRIFT FÜR ASSYRIOLOGIE (1949), pp. 21-44.
Study of outstanding importance in which the Uruk sanctuaries are assigned their due place in the architectural tradition of Mesopotamia. Needs to be supplemented now with the discoveries made at Eridu.

HERZFELD (Ernst). — DIE AUSGRABUNGEN VON SAMARRA V: DIE VORGESCHICHTLICHEN TÖPFEREIEN, Berlin, Dietrich Reimer, 1930.
Documentation bearing on the so-called Samarra culture of protohistorical Mesopotamia.

HEUZEY (Léon). — LES ORIGINES ORIENTALES DE L'ART, Paris, Leroux, 1891-1915.
This 'recueil de mémoires archéologiques et de monuments figurés' contains a number of studies devoted to Mesopotamian works (Stele of the Vultures, the flowing vase, maceheads, statuette of Assurdan, etc.). Also contains a curious article on 'Oriental Antiquity' at the Paris World's Fair of 1889.

HEUZEY (Léon). — MUSÉE NATIONAL DU LOUVRE. CATALOGUE DES ANTIQUITÉS CHALDÉENNES, Paris, Librairies-Imprimeries Réunies, 1902.
Catalogue dealing entirely with Sumerian works from Lagash (Telloh) acquired for the Louvre by Ernest de Sarzec.

HEUZEY (Léon) and THUREAU-DANGIN (F.). — NOUVELLES FOUILLES DE TELLO PAR LE COMMANDANT GASTON CROS, Paris, Leroux, 1910-14.
The results of excavations conducted from 1903 to 1909.

HINKE (W.J.). — A NEW BOUNDARY STONE OF NEBUCHADREZZAR I FROM NIPPUR, Philadelphia, University of Pennsylvania, 1907.
Deals with the discovery of a kudurru. Useful contribution to the study of Kassite boundary stones.

KING (L.W.). — BABYLONIAN BOUNDARY-STONES AND MEMORIAL TABLETS, London, British Museum, 1912.
Exhaustive publication of the kudurrus in the British Museum.

KOLDEWEY (Robert). — DAS WIEDERERSTEHENDE BABYLON, Leipzig, J.C. Hinrichs, 1913, later edition, 1925. English edition: THE EXCAVATIONS AT BABYLON, London, Macmillan, 1914.
Synthesis of the results obtained in the excavations at Babylon. All the essential works are reproduced (255 figures in the text, several inset plates).

KRAMER (S.N.). — FROM THE TABLETS OF SUMER, Indian Hills, Colorado, The Falcon's Wing Press, 1956. Subsequent editions: HISTORY BEGINS AT SUMER, London, Thames and Hudson, and New York, Doubleday and Company, 1957.
A new study, with additions, of the literary documentation dealt with in the same author's Sumerian Mythology. Many iconographic parallels are proposed.

LANGDON (Stephen Herbert). — EXCAVATIONS AT KISH, I, 1923-24, Paris, Geuthner, 1924.
Though well-documented as regards the shell inlays found at Kish, this publication is rendered largely unserviceable by its neglect of stratigraphy.

LAYARD (Austen Henry). — DISCOVERIES IN THE RUINS OF NINEVEH AND BABYLON, London, John Murray, 1853, and New York, Harper and Brothers, 1856.
An account written in the style of the period but full of valuable information. Lavishly illustrated with outline drawings.

LEBRETON (L.). — THE EARLY PERIODS AT SUSA, in IRAQ, XIX (1957), pp. 79-123.
A careful study of the material from Susa, accurately classified in accordance with a new terminology (Susa A-D), with parallels drawn between Iran and Mesopotamia. Must now be regarded as the most reliable assessment of the finds made at Susa by Morgan and Mecquenem.

LEES (G.M.) and FALCON (N.R.). — THE GEOGRAPHICAL HISTORY OF THE MESOPOTAMIAN PLAINS, in THE GEOGRAPHICAL JOURNAL, vol. 118, I, March 1952. Cf. REVUE D'ASSYRIOLOGIE ET D'ARCHÉOLOGIE ORIENTALE, XLVIII (1954), pp. 28-29.
These two geographers maintain that the Persian Gulf had exactly the same coastline in ancient times that it has today.

LEGRAIN (L.). — UR EXCAVATIONS X, SEAL CYLINDERS, London and Philadelphia, Trustees of the British Museum and of the University Museum, University of Pennsylvania, 1951.
Descriptive catalogue of the seals found at Ur, dating from the Jemdet Nasr period to Seleucid and even Parthian times.

LENZEN (Heinrich). — DIE ENTWICKLUNG DER ZIKURRAT, VON IHREN ANFÄNGEN BIS ZUR ZEIT DER III. DYNASTIE VON UR, Leipzig, Otto Harrassowitz, 1941.
General study of Mesopotamian ziggurats, from the archaic periods to the Third Dynasty of Ur.

LENZEN (Heinz). — DIE SUMMER, Berlin, Gebr. Mann, 1948.
Brief presentation, archaeological and artistic, of some Sumerian masterpieces in the Berlin Museum (61 pages, 39 figures in the text).

LENZEN (H.J.). — DIE TEMPEL DER SCHICHT ARCHAISCH IV IN URUK, in ZEITSCHRIFT FÜR ASSYRIOLOGIE, N.F. XV (1949), pp. 1-20.
A study of capital importance, with plans, dealing in detail with the architecture of the great temples of the Jemdet Nasr period at Uruk.

LENZEN (H.J.). — ZUR DATIERUNG DER ANU-ZIKURRAT IN WARKA, in MITTEILUNGEN DER DEUTSCHEN ORIENTGESELLSCHAFT, LXXXIII (1951), pp. 1-32.
A careful study of the different architectural levels of the ziggurat of Anu at Uruk (Warka), in an attempt to specify and date them.

LLOYD (Seton). — THE OLDEST CITY: A PRE-SUMERIAN TEMPLE DISCOVERED AT PREHISTORIC ERIDU, in ILLUSTRATED LONDON NEWS, May 31, 1947, pp. 581-583.

On the superimposed temples of Enki at the foot of the ziggurat of the Ur III period.

LLOYD (Seton). — THE OLDEST CITY OF SUMERIA: ESTABLISHING THE ORIGINS OF ERIDU, in ILLUSTRATED LONDON NEWS, September 11, 1948, pp. 303-305.

On an impressive cemetery of the al 'Ubaid period, found intact, and superimposed archaic temples.

LLOYD (Seton) and SAFAR (Fuad). — TELL UQAIR. EXCAVATIONS BY THE IRAQ GOVERNMENT DIRECTORATE OF ANTIQUITIES IN 1940 AND 1941, in JOURNAL OF NEAR EASTERN STUDIES, II, 2 (1943), pp. 131-158, pls. III-XXXI.

Report on the excavations at Tell Uqair.

LLOYD (Seton) and SAFAR (Fuad). — TELL HASSUNA: EXCAVATIONS BY THE IRAQ GOVERNMENT DIRECTORATE GENERAL OF ANTIQUITIES IN 1943 AND 1944, in JOURNAL OF NEAR EASTERN STUDIES, IV, 4 (1945), pp. 255-289, pls. I-XXI.

Official report on the excavations which revealed a new cultural phase in the protohistory of Mesopotamia.

McCOWN (Donald E.). — THE COMPARATIVE STRATIGRAPHY OF EARLY IRAN (Studies in Ancient Oriental Civilization, XXIII), Chicago, University of Chicago Press, 1942.

A monograph of the highest value, with a system of equivalences between different sites.

MACKAY (E.). — A SUMERIAN PALACE AND THE 'A' CEMETERY AT KISH, MESOPOTAMIA, II, Dept. of Anthropology, Memoirs, Vol. I, Nos. 1, 2, Chicago, Field Museum of Natural History, 1929.

For all its lacunae, this work is indispensable for a knowledge of the early periods at Kish.

MACKAY (E.). — REPORT ON EXCAVATIONS AT JEMDET NASR, IRAQ, Dept. of Anthropology, Memoirs, Vol. I, No. 3, Chicago, Field Museum of Natural History, 1931.

Basic documentation on the so-called Jemdet Nasr period of protohistory, named after the site where it was first discovered.

MALLOWAN (M.E.L.) and ROSE (Cruikshank). — EXCAVATIONS AT TELL ARPACHIYAH, 1933, London, separate reprint from IRAQ, II, Part I, 1935.

Publication of exceptional interest for the wealth of its documentation. The Halaf period, in particular, here takes on a new lustre.

MALLOWAN (M.E.L.). — THE BRONZE HEAD OF THE AKKADIAN PERIOD FROM NINEVEH, in IRAQ, III (1936), pp. 104-110.

Though this bronze head was found on an Assyrian level (by R. Campbell Thompson and R.W. Hamilton in 1931), Mallowan makes out a case for identifying it with Sargon.

MALLOWAN (M.E.L.). — EXCAVATIONS AT BRAK AND CHAGAR BAZAR, in IRAQ, IX (1947).

The excavation zone dealt with here forms the link between the upper valleys of the Tigris and Euphrates.

MALLOWAN (M.E.L.). — TWENTY-FIVE YEARS OF MESOPOTAMIAN DISCOVERY (1932-56), London, The British School of Archaeology in Iraq, 1958.

A remarkable summing up of the results obtained on sites excavated by the British School of Archaeology, in Iraq (Arpachiyah, Nimrud) and Syria (Khabur and Balikh region).

MEISSNER (Bruno). — GRUNDZÜGE DER ALTBABYLONISCHEN PLASTIK, Leipzig, J.C. Hinrichs, 1914 (Part I of GRUNDZÜGE DER BABYLONISCH-ASSYRISCHEN PLASTIK, 1915).

Still a valuable work, though allowance must be made for the state of archaeological knowledge at the time.

MEISSNER (Bruno). — BABYLONIEN UND ASSYRIEN, I-II, Heidelberg, Carl Winter, 1920-25.

After a quarter of a century this remains a fundamental contribution to our knowledge of the Mesopotamian milieu under all its aspects. The picture it gives naturally needs to be filled out on the basis of discoveries made since 1925.

MEYER (G.R.). — STAATLICHES MUSEUM ZU BERLIN. DURCH VIER JAHRTAUSENDE ALTVORDERASIATISCHER KULTUR, Berlin, Vorderasiatisches Museum, 1956.

This catalogue includes some important works of Mesopotamian art from Babylon, Assur, Warka, Telloh and Mari.

MOORTGAT (Anton). — FRÜHE BILDKUNST IN SUMER, Leipzig, J.C. Hinrichs, 1935.

A very thorough study of Sumerian art of the late fourth and the early third millennium.

MOORTGAT (Anton). — VORDERASIATISCHE ROLLSIEGEL, Berlin, Gebr. Mann, 1940.

Publication of the collection of cylinder seals in the Berlin Museum. Catalogue of 783 works, fully described and extremely well reproduced (92 plates).

MOORTGAT (Anton). — DIE ENTSTEHUNG DER SUMERISCHEN HOCH KULTUR, in DER ALTE ORIENT, 43, Leipzig, J.C. Hinrichs, 1945.

A first-rate survey of Mesopotamian protohistory.

MOORTGAT (Anton). — GRUNDLAGEN UND ENTFALTUNG DER SUMERISCH-AKKADISCHEN KULTUR, in HISTORIA MUNDI, II, pp. 224-260, Berne, Francke, 1953.

Very succinct account of the period extending from Neolithic times to the Neo-Sumerians. Essential bibliography (p. 626). Very well informed.

MORGAN (Jacques de). — MÉMOIRES DE LA DÉLÉGATION DE PERSE (referred to as MDP), Paris, Vols. I-XIII, Leroux, 1900-12.

The series thereafter changed its name several times:
MÉMOIRES DE LA MISSION ARCHÉOLOGIQUE DE SUSIANE, Vol. XIV, 1913.
MISSION ARCHÉOLOGIQUE DE PERSE, Vol. XV, 1914.
MÉMOIRES DE LA MISSION ARCHÉOLOGIQUE DE PERSE. MISSION EN SUSIANE, Vols. XVI-XXVIII, 1921- 39.
MÉMOIRES DE LA MISSION ARCHÉOLOGIQUE EN IRAN. MISSION EN SUSIANE, Vol. XXIX on.

NAJI AL-ASIL. — ERIDU, in SUMER, III (1947), p. 3; EXCAVATIONS AT ERIDU, ibid., pp. 43-44; VI (1950), pp. 3-4.

An account of excavations in Iraq which have yielded a considerable amount of material, revealing, among other things, a great deal of archaic architecture.

NÖLDEKE (Arnold), HEINRICH (E.), SCHOTT (E.). — FÜNFTER VORLÄUFIGER BERICHT... (Uruk Vorläufiger Bericht, V), Berlin, 1934.

Lion Hunt Stele (pls. 12-13). Archaic glyptics (pls. 22-29).

NÖLDEKE (Arnold) and LENZEN (H.). — ELFTER VORLÄUFIGER BERICHT (Uruk Vorläufiger Bericht, XI), Berlin, 1940.

The frontispiece reproduces a woman's head in white marble of the Jemdet Nasr period.

NORTH (R). — STATUS OF THE WARKA EXPEDITION, in ORIENTALIA, XXVI (1957), pp. 185-256.

A summing up of sixteen seasons of excavation at Warka.

OPITZ (Dietrich). — DIE VOGELFÜSSIGE GÖTTIN AUF DEN LÖWEN, in ARCHIV FÜR ORIENT-FORSCHUNG, XI (1937), pp. 350-353.

A study of the famous Burney plaque, throwing doubt on its authenticity.

OPPENHEIM (Max Freiherr von). — TELL HALAF, I: DIE PRÄHISTORISCHEN FUNDE, by Hubert Schmidt, Berlin, Walter de Gruyter, 1943.

Official publication of the finds which revealed the so-called Halaf culture of Mesopotamian protohistory.

OSTEN (H.H. von der). — ANCIENT ORIENTAL SEALS IN THE COLLECTION OF MRS. E.T. NEWELL (Oriental Institute Publications, XXII), Chicago, University of Chicago Press, 1934.

One of the finest collections of Oriental glyptics, published with painstaking care (695 items on 41 plates). Includes several very clever fakes.

OSTEN (H.H. von der). — ANCIENT ORIENTAL SEALS IN THE COLLECTION OF MRS. AGNES BALDWIN BRETT (OIP, XXXVII), Chicago, University of Chicago Press, 1936.

Descriptive catalogue of 166 seals, with a study of the themes and motifs represented.

OTTO (W.). — HANDBUCH DER ARCHAEOLOGIE. VORDERASIEN by W. Andrae, Munich, C.H. Beck, 1939.

Handbook with an excellent survey of Mesopotamian archaeology (pp. 643-796), abundantly illustrated (pls. 113-182) and giving architecture the place it deserves.

PALLIS (S.A.). — CHRONOLOGY OF THE SHUBAD CULTURE, Copenhagen, Povl Branner-Norregade, 1941.

A study of the culture revealed by the 'royal tombs' of Ur. This culture corresponds to that of the First Dynasty of Ur.

PALLIS (S.A.). — THE ANTIQUITY OF IRAQ, Copenhagen, Einar Munksgaard, 1956.

Contains a wealth of documentary material on the excavations, history and civilization of Mesopotamia.

PARROT (André). — LES PEINTURES DU PALAIS DE MARI, in SYRIA, XVIII (1937), pp. 325-354.

General presentation of the wall paintings from various rooms and courts of the palace of Mari.

PARROT (André). — ARCHÉOLOGIE MÉSOPOTAMIENNE. I. LES ÉTAPES, Paris, Albin Michel, 1946.

General study of the progress of archaeological research in Mesopotamia.

PARROT (André). — ARCHÉOLOGIE MÉSOPOTAMIENNE. II. TECHNIQUE ET PROBLÈMES, Paris, Albin Michel, 1953.

On excavation technique and problems of Mesopotamian archaeology (protohistory, chronology).

PARROT (André). — TELLO. VINGT CAMPAGNES DE FOUILLES (1877-1933), Paris, Albin Michel, 1948.

A summing up of the excavations conducted at Lagash (Telloh), with reproductions of all important works from this site.

PARROT (André). — ZIGGURATS ET TOUR DE BABEL, Paris, Albin Michel, 1949.

Comprehensive study of the Mesopotamian ziggurats and the problems (literary, epigraphical, archaeological, architectural and religious) which they raise.

PARROT (André). — ACQUISITIONS ET INÉDITS DU MUSÉE DU LOUVRE. ANTIQUITÉS 'MÉSOPOTAMIENNES,' in SYRIA, XXXI (1954), pp. 1-13.

Publication of a new statue of Gudea (AO, 20164), a human-headed bull inscribed with Gudea's name (AO, 20152), terracotta lion-muzzles (AO, 19807-808), and a copper foundation lion (AO, 19937).

PARROT (André) and LAMBERT (Maurice). — GLYPTIQUE MÉSOPOTAMIENNE. Fouilles de Lagash (Tello) et de Larsa (Senkereh) (1931-33), Paris, Imprimerie Nationale, 1954.

Descriptive catalogue of 325 cylinder seals and stamps found in excavations at Lagash and Larsa. They range from the Jemdet Nasr period to Neo-Babylonian times.

PARROT (André). — MISSION ARCHÉOLOGIQUE DE MARI. I. LE TEMPLE D'ISHTAR, Paris, Geuthner, 1956.

Definitive publication of the Temple of Ishtar. Reproductions of several statues referred to in the present volume, among others Lamgi-Mari, Ebih-il the Steward and Idi-Narum; and of shell inlays, the Warrior with an Adze, etc.

PARROT (André). — MISSION ARCHÉOLOGIQUE DE MARI. II. LE PALAIS, Vol. I, ARCHITECTURE; Vol. II, PEINTURES MURALES; Vol. III, DOCUMENTS ET MONUMENTS (with the collaboration of Mme Barrelet and MM. Dossin, Ducos and Bouchud), Paris, Geuthner, 1958-59.

Definitive publication of the palace of the Zimri-Lim dynasty, with methodical studies of its architecture, wall paintings, statuary, furniture, implements, glyptics, etc.

PERKINS (Ann Louise). — THE COMPARATIVE STRATI-GRAPHY OF EARLY MESOPOTAMIA (Studies in Ancient Oriental Civilization, XXIII), Chicago, University of Chicago Press, 1949.

Highly important monograph, with a classification of the protohistorical pottery of Mesopotamia.

PEZARD (M.) and POTTIER (E.). — MUSÉE NATIONAL DU LOUVRE. CATALOGUE DES ANTIQUITÉS DE LA SUSIANE (2nd edition), Paris, Musées Nationaux, 1926.

Scrupulously accurate catalogue of works from Susiana, classified in chronological order under several main headings.

PIRENNE (Jacques). — CIVILISATIONS ANTIQUES, Paris, Albin Michel, 1951.

A panoramic survey of the ancient civilizations, with a fairly well-balanced treatment of Mesopotamia and the West (Aegean and Greek civilization).

PORADA (Edith). — THE COLLECTION OF THE PIER-PONT MORGAN LIBRARY, in CORPUS OF ANCIENT NEAR EASTERN SEALS IN NORTH AMERICAN COLLECTIONS, 1 vol. of text, 1 vol. of plates, Washington, Bollingen Foundation, 1948.

Remarkable publication of a very important collection of glyptics (1157 items, including some fakes), by one of the best specialists in the field.

POTTIER (Edmond). — ETUDE HISTORIQUE ET CHRO-NOLOGIQUE SUR LES VASES PEINTS DE L'ACRO-POLE DE SUSE, in MÉMOIRES DE LA DÉLÉGATION DE PERSE, XIII, pp. 27-103, Paris, Leroux 1912,

Remains the standard study of the so-called First and Second Styles of painted pottery from Susa.

SARZEC (Ernest de) and HEUZEY (Léon). — DÉCOUVERTES EN CHALDÉE, Paris, Leroux, 1884-1912.

'Description des fouilles de Tello' by Sarzec and 'Description des monuments' by Heuzey.

SCHARF (A.). — DIE FRÜHKULTUREN ÄGYPTENS UND MESOPOTAMIENS (Der Alte Orient, 41), Leipzig, J.C. Hinrichs, 1942.

Basic work for the comparative study of the early periods in Mesopotamia and Egypt. The author makes full use of the material from Susa and Warka.

SCHMÖKEL (Hartmut). — UR, ASSUR UND BABYLON. DREI JAHRTAUSENDE IM ZWEISTROMLAND, Stuttgart, Gustav Kilpper, 1955. French edition: LE MONDE D'UR, ASSUR ET BABYLONE, Paris, Buchet-Chastel, 1957.

Mesopotamian art from the earliest times to the Neo-Babylonians. Excellent reproductions (118 plates) of the most important works.

SPEISER (E.). — EXCAVATIONS AT TEPE GAWRA, I, Philadelphia, University of Pennsylvania Press, 1935.

Official publication of the discoveries made on the first eight levels. For the second volume, see TOBLER.

STARR (Richard F.S.). — NUZI. REPORT ON THE EXCAVATIONS AT YORGAN TEPE NEAR KIRKUK, IRAQ, 1927-31, 1 vol. of text, 1 vol. of plates, Cambridge, Mass., 1937-39.

Unusually well-illustrated report (142 plates and 44 plans) of the discoveries made at Nuzi.

THUREAU-DANGIN (F.). — STATUETTES DE TELLO, in MONUMENTS ET MÉMOIRES DE LA FONDATION PIOT, XXVII (1924), pp. 97-111, Paris.

Publication of three important statues: Gudea, in the Ny Carlsberg Glyptothek, Copenhagen; Ur-Ningirsu, the 'high priest of Nina'; and the Ur-Ningirsu in the Louvre (AO, 9504).

TOBLER (Arthur John). — EXCAVATIONS AT TEPE GAWRA, II, LEVELS IX-XX, Philadelphia, University of Pennsylvania Press, 1950.

Official publication of the discoveries made on the oldest levels of the site. For the first volume, see SPEISER.

UNGER (Eckhard). — SUMERISCHE UND AKKADISCHE KUNST, Breslau, F. Hirt, 1926.

The Sumerians were the founders, the Akkadians and Neo-Sumerians the promoters, and the Babylonians and Amorites the heirs, of archaic Mesopotamian art.

VAN BUREN (Elizabeth Douglas). — CLAY FIGURINES OF BABYLONIA AND ASSYRIA, YALE ORIENTAL SERIES, Researches Vol. 16, New Haven, Yale University Press, 1930.

Catalogue of the most characteristic Mesopotamian figurines, grouped according to types and themes. Includes 1334 items.

VAN BUREN (Elizabeth Douglas). — FOUNDATION FIGURINES AND OFFERINGS, Berlin, Hans Schoetz, 1931.

Monograph on the various types of foundation figurines found in the substructure of Mesopotamian edifices.

VAN BUREN (Elizabeth Douglas). — THE FLOWING VASE AND THE GOD WITH STREAMS, Berlin, Hans Schoetz, 1933.

Iconographical study of the frequently recurring theme of the god or man holding a flowing vase.

VAN BUREN (Elizabeth Douglas). — A CLAY RELIEF IN THE IRAQ MUSEUM, in ARCHIV FÜR ORIENT-FORSCHUNG, IX (1933-34), pp. 165-171.

Study of a figure in the Baghdad Museum identical with one in the Louvre. The author interprets the enigmatic omega sign found on certain boundary stones as a representation of the goddess Ninhursag (cf. FRANKFORT, A Note...).

VAN BUREN (Elizabeth Douglas). — A FURTHER NOTE ON THE TERRACOTTA RELIEF, in ARCHIV FÜR ORIENT-FORSCHUNG, XI (1937), pp. 354-357.

Deals with the Burney relief and the question of its authenticity.

VANDEN BERGHE (L.) and MUSSCHE (H.F.). — BIBLIOGRAPHIE ANALYTIQUE DE L'ASSY-RIOLOGIE ET DE L'ARCHÉOLOGIE DU PROCHE-ORIENT, Leiden, Brill, 1956.

Excellent bibliography classified by regions, with each region subdivided into several main headings.

VANDEN BERGHE (L.). — ARCHÉOLOGIE DE L'IRAN ANCIEN, Leiden, Brill, 1959.
A general survey of Iranian archaeology from the earliest times to the Sassanians. The early periods (at Susa, Giyan and Sialk) are treated at length.

WEBER (Otto). — ALTORIENTALISCHE SIEGELBILDER, in DER ALTE ORIENT, XVII-XVIII, Leipzig, J.C. Hinrichs, 1920.
A study of ancient Oriental glyptics, classified by themes and scenes.

WETZEL (Friedrich). — ASSUR UND BABYLON, Berlin, Gebr. Mann, 1949.
A small volume (70 pages) containing excellent reproductions of Assyrian, Kassite and Babylonian works in the Berlin Museum.

WILKINSON (Charles K.). — THE ART OF THE ANCIENT NEAR EAST, in THE METROPOLITAN MUSEUM OF ART BULLETIN, March 1949, pp. 186-198.
Reproductions of important Sumerian sculptures: heads of Gudea (?) and Ur-Ningirsu, and a worshipper statue from Ashnunnak; of three metal objects: the head of a bearded bull (Ur type), a foundation figurine (Shulgi type), and the head of an Elamite; and of Achaemenian reliefs.

WISEMAN (D.J.). — CYLINDER SEALS OF WESTERN ASIA, London, Batchworth Press, 1959.
A selection of 118 seals from the British Museum, many of them hitherto unpublished.

WOOLLEY (C.L.). — THE DEVELOPMENT OF SUMERIAN ART, London, Faber and Faber, 1935.
An historical introduction followed by studies of the successive cultural periods of ancient Mesopotamia: al 'Ubaid, Uruk, Jemdet Nasr, Early Dynastic (royal tombs of Ur, dated here 3500-3200 B.C., which may now be regarded as rather too early a date), Akkad, Ur III. Carefully illustrated (72 plates).

WOOLLEY (C.L.). — THE SUMERIANS, Oxford University Press, 1928.
General survey of Sumerian culture, largely based on the discoveries made at Ur and al 'Ubaid.

WOOLLEY (C.L.). — UR EXCAVATIONS, V: THE ZIGGURAT AND ITS SURROUNDINGS, London and Philadelphia, 1939.
Official publication of the ziggurat of Ur, from the first archaic construction to the Neo-Babylonian tower of Nabonidus. Numerous reconstructions.

WOOLLEY (Sir C.L.). — EXCAVATIONS AT UR, A RECORD OF TWELVE YEARS' WORK, 1st edition, London, Ernest Benn, and New York, Crowell, 1954.
Woolley's Ur of the Chaldees (1929; latest edition 1950) summed up the results of seven years' excavations. This new book is a well-illustrated résumé along the same lines, but for a full account of the Ur excavations the reader is referred to the official publications of the Joint Expedition of the British Museum and the Pennsylvania University Museum.

WOOLLEY (C.L.). — UR EXCAVATIONS, II: THE ROYAL CEMETERY, A REPORT ON THE PREDYNASTIC AND SARGONID GRAVES EXCAVATED BETWEEN 1927-31, London and Philadelphia, British Museum and Pennsylvania University Museum, 1934.
Official publication, lavishly illustrated (1 volume of 274 plates accompanying the volume of text), of one of the most sensational archaeological discoveries made in Mesopotamia.

WOOLLEY (Sir C.L.). — UR EXCAVATIONS, IV: THE EARLY PERIODS, London and Philadelphia, British Museum and Pennsylvania University Museum, 1956.
Publication of works extending from the al 'Ubaid period to the Third Dynasty of Ur.

LIST OF ILLUSTRATIONS

PREFACE

The Roman numerals refer to the corresponding pages of the Preface by André Malraux.

XII. *Sumero-Babylonian Art. Mari.* Worshipper with a Lamb. *2nd millennium B.C. Aleppo Museum. Stone, height 20 1/2 inches. (Schneider-Lengyel).*

XIV. *Saharan Art. Tassili. Rock Painting.* Four Tutelary Goddesses. *Egyptian Period (XVIIIth Dynasty). (Lhote Expedition Photo).*

XVa. *Iranian Art. Susa. Cylinder Seal.* Pastoral Scene, detail. *First half of the 3rd millennium B.C. Louvre, Paris. Height 1 1/4 inches. (Tel-Vigneau).*

XVb. *Magdalenian Art. Cueva de los Casares, Spain. Rock Drawing.* Fishing Scene, detail. *(Juan Cabré).*

XVIa. *Sumerian Art (?).* Goddess. *3rd millennium B.C. Baghdad Museum. Terracotta, height 6 1/2 inches. (Schneider-Lengyel).*

XVIb. *Sumerian Art (?).* Goddess of Fecundity. *3rd millennium B.C. Private Collection. Terracotta, height 4 1/4 inches. (Roger Parry).*

XVIIa. *Sumerian Art (?).* Idol. *Aleppo Museum. Terracotta, height 6 5/8 inches. (Schneider-Lengyel).*

XVIIb. *Sumerian Art (?).* Idol. *Baghdad Museum. Terracotta, height 5 7/8 inches. (Schneider-Lengyel).*

XVIII. *Mesopotamian Art (?).* Goddess of Fecundity, detail. *3rd millennium B.C. Private Collection. Terracotta, height 5 inches. (Roger Parry).*

XIX. *Mesopotamian Art (?).* Idol. *3rd millennium B.C. Aleppo Museum. Terracotta, height 5 7/8 inches. (Schneider-Lengyel).*

XX. *Mesopotamian Art (?).* Idol, detail. *3rd millennium B.C. Aleppo Museum. Terracotta, height 5 7/8 inches. (Schneider-Lengyel).*

XXI. *Mesopotamian Art (?).* Idol. *Damascus Museum. Terracotta, height 1 1/4 inches. (Schneider-Lengyel).*

XXIII. *Mesopotamian Art (?). Diyala Region. Tell Asmar.* Man holding a Cup, detail. *3rd millennium B.C. Oriental Institute, Chicago. Stone, height 19 1/8 inches. (Oriental Institute).*

XXIV. *Mesopotamian Art. Diyala Region. Tell Asmar.* The God Abu (?), detail. *First half 3rd millennium B.C. Baghdad Museum. Veined gypsum, hair and beard in bitumen, eyes made of shell inlaid with black stone and ringed with bitumen. Height 28 3/8 inches. (Oriental Institute, Chicago).*

XXV. *Mesopotamian Art. Diyala Region. Tell Asmar.* Goddess (?). *First half 3rd millennium B.C. Baghdad Museum. Veined gypsum, height 23 1/4 inches. (Schneider-Lengyel).*

XXVII. *Akkadian Art. Telloh (Lagash).* Woman's Head. *Second half 3rd millennium B.C. Louvre, Paris. Limestone, height 2 5/8 inches. (Tel-Vigneau).*

XXVIII. *Neo-Sumerian Art. Telloh (Lagash).* 'Turbaned Head.' *23rd century B.C. Louvre, Paris. Diorite, height 9 inches. (Tel-Vigneau).*

XXIX. *Akkadian Art. Nineveh.* Head of King Sargon (?). *Second half 3rd millennium B.C. Baghdad Museum. Bronze, height 11 3/4 inches. (Schneider-Lengyel).*

XXXa. *Mesopotamian Art.* Head of a Woman with a Kaunakes. *First half 3rd millennium B.C. Louvre, Paris. Limestone, height 8 5/8 inches. (Tel-Vigneau).*

XXXb. *Gothic Art. Chartres Cathedral, Royal Portal.* Woman's Head, detail of a column statue. *1145-1150 A.D. (Roger Parry).*

XXXIa. *Mesopotamian Art. Middle Euphrates. Mari.* Idi-Narum, the 'Miller,' detail. *First half 3rd millennium B.C. Aleppo Museum. Pink breccia, height 8 inches. (Schneider-Lengyel).*

XXXIb. *Gothic Art. Saint-Loup-de-Naud (Seine-et-Marne, France).* St Loup. *1170-1175 A.D. (Ina Bandy).*

XXXII. *Egyptian Art. Saqqara.* Seated Scribe. *Second half 3rd millennium B.C. Louvre, Paris. Painted limestone, height 20 7/8 inches. (Tel-Vigneau).*

XXXIII. *Neo-Sumerian Art. Telloh (Lagash).* Gudea Statue (Sarzec-Cros) known as the 'Small Seated Gudea.' *22nd century B.C. Louvre, Paris. Diorite, height 17 3/4 inches. (Tel-Vigneau).*

XXXIVa. *Neo-Sumerian Art. Telloh (Lagash).* Small Seated Gudea, detail: Clasped Hands. *22nd century B.C. Louvre, Paris. Diorite. (Tel-Vigneau).*

XXXIVb. *Mesopotamian Art. Telloh (?).* Statue of Lugalkisalsi's Grandson, detail: Clasped Hands. *Mid-3rd millennium B.C. Louvre, Paris. Limestone, over-all height 11 inches. (Tel-Vigneau).*

XXXVa. *Mesopotamian Art. Diyala Region. Khafaje.* Mythological Scene with Schematized Animals and Figures. *First half of the 3rd millennium B.C. Oriental Institute, Chicago. Shell, height 1 1/8 inches. (Oriental Institute).*

XXXVb. *Mesopotamian Art.* Seal impression, detail. Acolyte with Wheat. *Late 4th or early 3rd millennium B.C. Louvre, Paris. White limestone, height 2 1/2 inches. (Tel-Vigneau).*

XXXVc. *Akkadian Art. Susa.* Stele of Sargon, detail: Naked Captive. *Second half 3rd millennium B.C. Louvre, Paris. Diorite, height 18 1/8 inches. (Roger Parry).*

XXXVII. *Mesopotamian Art. Middle Euphrates. Mari.* Ur-Nina (or Ur-Nanshe), 'The Great Singer.' *First half 3rd millennium B.C. Damascus Museum. Gypsum, height 10 1/4 inches. (André Parrot). Shoulders and broken places retouched photographically.*

XXXVIIIa. *Akkadian Art. Assur.* Woman's Head. *Second half 3rd millennium B.C. Berlin Museum. Gypsum, height 2 3/4 inches. (Marburg).*

XXXVIIIb. *Neo-Sumerian Art. Telloh (Lagash).* Man's Head (Gudea ?). *22nd century B.C. Metropolitan Museum of Art, New York. (Metropolitan Museum).*

XXXIX. *Neo-Sumerian Art. Telloh (Lagash).* Woman's Head. *22nd century B.C. Berlin Museum. Steatite. (Marburg).*

XL. *Neo-Sumerian Art. Telloh (Lagash).* Man's Head (Gudea ?). *22nd century B.C. Metropolitan Museum of Art, New York. (Metropolitan Museum).*

XLIa. *Mesopotamian Art. Diyala Region. Tell Asmar.* Goddess (?), detail. *First half 3rd millennium B.C. Baghdad Museum. Veined gypsum, over-all height of statue 23 1/4 inches. (Schneider-Lengyel).*

XLIb. *Neo-Sumerian Art. Telloh (Lagash).* Woman's Head. *22nd century B.C. Berlin Museum. Steatite. (Marburg).*

XLIc. *Mesopotamian Art.* Head of a Woman with a Kaunakes. *First half 3rd millennium B.C. Louvre, Paris. Limestone, height 8 5/8 inches. (Tel-Vigneau).*

XLId. *Babylonian Art. Middle Euphrates. Mari.* Warrior with a Chin-piece. *18th century B.C. Aleppo Museum White stone, height 7 7/8 inches. (Schneider-Lengyel).*

XLIIa. *Modern Art. School of Paris.* Constantin Brancusi. Mademoiselle Pogany. *1913. Museum of Modern Art, New York. Bronze, height 17 3/8 inches.*

XLIIb. *Modern Art. School of Paris.* Constantin Brancusi. Mademoiselle Pogany. *1931. Brancusi Estate. Marble.*

XLIIIa. *Neo-Sumerian Art. Telloh (Lagash).* Gudea, detail. *22nd century B.C. British Museum, London. Over-all height, 28 3/4 inches. (British Museum).*

XLIIIb. *Modern Art. School of Paris.* Constantin Brancusi. Mademoiselle Pogany, detail. *1931. Brancusi Estate. Marble.*

XLIV. *Modern Art. Paris.* Auguste Rodin. Balzac, Nude Study. *Musée Rodin, Paris. Plaster. (Marc Foucault).*

XLV. *Modern Art. Paris.* Auguste Rodin. Balzac, Draped Study. *1891-1898. Musée Rodin, Paris. Plaster, height 9 ft 10 inches. (Roger Parry).*

XLVI. *Thai Art.* Walking Buddha. *After the 13th century A.D. Formerly Peytel Collection. Bronze, 6 5/8 inches. (Galerie de la Pléiade).*

XLVIIa. *Japanese Art.* Statue of Amida, detail. *11th century A.D. Byodo-in Temple, Kyoto. (Tatsuzo Sato).*

XLVIIb. *Mesopotamian Art. Middle Euphrates. Mari.* The Steward Ebih-il, detail. *First half 3rd millennium B.C. Louvre, Paris. Alabaster, over-all height 20 5/8 inches. (Tel-Vigneau).*

XLVIIc. *Elamite Art (?). Susa.* Worshipper, detail. *3rd millennium B.C. Louvre, Paris. Limestone, over-all height, 5 7/8 inches. (Tel-Vigneau).*

SUMER

1. *Iranian Art. Susa. Cylinder Seal.* Lion Passant. *Early 3rd millennium B.C. Louvre, Paris. Stone, height* 1 13/16 *inches. (Tel-Vigneau).*

2. *Mesopotamian Art. Akkadian Period.* The God Shamash scaling the Two-peaked Mountain, in a doorway guarded by lions. *Mid-3rd millennium B.C. British Museum, London. (British Museum).*

3. *Romanesque Art. Saint-Savin-sur-Gartempe, Vienne, France.* The Building of the Tower of Babel. *12th century. Fresco, Church of Saint-Savin. (Draeger).*

4. The Tower of Babel, *by Pieter Bruegel the Elder (c.* 1530-1569*). Boymans - Van Beuningen Museum, Rotterdam. (Giraudon).*
This painting was undoubtedly based on the architecture of the Coliseum in Rome.

5. *Khorsabad (Dur Sharrukin).* The First Discoveries of Botta, reproduced from his drawings. *7th century B.C. (Le Magasin Pittoresque,* 1844*).*

6a. *Sumerian Art. Telloh (Lagash).* Statue of Gudea. *22nd century B.C. Louvre, Paris. Diorite.*
PERROT and CHIPIEZ, *Histoire de l'Art dans l'Antiquité,* vol. II, pl. 6 *(engraved by J. Bourgoin).*

6b. *Neo-Babylonian Art* (?). *Babylon.* The Babylon Lion. *7th-6th centuries B.C. Babylon. Basalt.*
The date of this sculpture is a matter of controversy. Specialists hesitate between the Assyrian and Neo-Babylonian periods; one (Unger) has even assigned it to the 13th century A.D.!

6c. *Assyrian Art. Kuyunjik (Nineveh).* The Dying Lioness. *7th century B.C. British Museum, London. Alabaster.*
PERROT and CHIPIEZ, *Histoire de l'Art dans l'Antiquité,* vol. II, pl. 270 *(drawing by Saint-Elme Gautier).*

6d. *Assyrian Art. Nimrud (Kalakh).* Statue of Assurnasirpal. *9th century B.C. British Museum, London. Alabaster, height* 41 3/4 *inches.*
PERROT and CHIPIEZ, *Histoire de l'Art dans l'Antiquité,* vol. II, pl. 250.
G. MASPERO, *Histoire ancienne des Peuples de l'Orient classique,* vol. III, p. 567 *(drawing by Faucher-Gudin).*

7. *Sumerian Art. Telloh (Lagash).* 'Turbaned Head.' *22nd century B.C. Louvre. Diorite, height* 9 *inches.*
PERROT and CHIPIEZ, *Histoire de l'Art dans l'Antiquité,* vol. II, pl. 7 *(engraved by J. Bourgoin).*

8. *Sumerian Art. Telloh (Lagash).* 'Turbaned Head.' *22nd century B.C. Louvre. Diorite, height* 9 *inches. (Tel-Vigneau).*
So called from the way the hair is dressed. It was not known at the time of discovery that the work represented Gudea, *patesi of Lagash.*

9. *'Chaldean Temple.'* Reconstruction *by Charles Chipiez.*
PERROT and CHIPIEZ, *Histoire de l'Art dans l'Antiquité,* vol. II, pl. 4.

10. *Kassite Art. Babylonia.* Detail of the 'Michaux Stone.' *13th-12th centuries B.C. Cabinet des Médailles, Bibliothèque Nationale, Paris. Diorite.*
Brought back to France in 1786 by the botanist André Michaux and deposited by him in the Bibliothèque Nationale.
PERROT and CHIPIEZ, *Histoire de l'Art dans l'Antiquité,* vol. II, fig. 301 *(drawing by Saint-Elme Gautier).*

11. *Kassite Art. Babylonia.* The 'Michaux Stone.' *13th-12th centuries B.C. Cabinet des Médailles, Bibliothèque Nationale, Paris. Diorite, height* 17 3/4 *inches; circumference* 24 3/8 *inches. (Tel-Vigneau).*

12. Sir Austen Henry LAYARD (1817-94). Excavator of Nineveh, Kalakh and Assur. *Gersheim Collection. (Lock and Whitfield).*

13. Ernest DE SARZEC (1837-1901). Excavator of Telloh.

14. P.E. BOTTA (1802-70). Excavator of Khorsabad. *Painting by Champartin, Louvre. (Marc Foucault).*

15. Walter ANDRAE (1875-1956). Excavator of Assur.

16. Robert KOLDEWEY (1855-1925). Excavator of Babylon and Borsippa.

17. Henri FRANKFORT (1897-1954). Excavator of Tell Asmar, Khafaje, Tell Agrab, Ishchali and Khorsabad. *(Otto Fein).*

18. *Assyrian Art.* Presentation of the first collection of Assyrian antiquities at the Louvre, May 1, 1847.
These works were discovered by P.E. Botta in the course of his excavations at Khorsabad. They reached Paris in February 1847.

19. *Assyrian Art.* The main gallery of 'Chaldeo-Assyrian' antiquities at the Louvre in 1890. These works were excavated by Botta and Mace at Khorsabad.

20. *Assyrian Art. Kuyunjik (Nineveh).* The 'Feast in a Garden,' relief from Assurbanipal's Palace. *7th century B.C. British Museum. Gypseous alabaster, height* 20 7/8 *inches. (British Museum)*
Upon his return from an expedition to Elam, the king recounts his adventures to the queen.

21. *Kuyunjik (Nineveh).* 'Deluge' Tablet. *7th century B.C. British Museum. Clay. (British Museum).*
Discovered by George Smith in 1872 in the storerooms of the British Museum, among a heap of cuneiform tablets excavated at Nineveh. It gives the Babylonian version of the Flood described in the Book of Genesis (VI-VII).

22. The Ruins of Babylon, about 1850, before excavations began.
HŒFFER, *L'Assyrie et la Chaldée,* pl. X *(engraved by Lemaître).*

23. The tell of Susa before the excavations of Loftus and the Dieulafoys.
G. MASPERO, *Histoire ancienne des Peuples de l'Orient classique,* vol. II, p. 34 *(drawing by Faucher-Gudin).*

24. *Nimrud (Kalakh).* The Excavations conducted by Hormuzd Rassam.
G. MASPERO, *Histoire ancienne des Peuples de l'Orient classique*, vol. III, p. 49 *(drawing by Boudier from a photograph by Rassam).*

25. *Assyrian Art. Nimrud (Kalakh).* Winged Bulls of Assurnasirpal.
G. MASPERO, *Histoire ancienne des Peuples de l'Orient classique*, vol. III, p. 46 *(drawing by Faucher-Gudin from a sketch by Layard).*

26. Detail of an excavation plan of Assur.
C. PREUSSER, *Die Paläste in Assur*, pl. 1.

27. Stratigraphic cross-section of the excavations at Warka (Uruk).
Uruk Vorlaüfiger Bericht, 3, pl. 12.

28. *Jedeideh.* Stratigraphic cross-section of the excavations, showing characteristic objects discovered at each level. Syrian Expedition of the Oriental Institute of Chicago, 1937. *(Oriental Institute).*

29. *Ur.* Excavations in the 'Royal' Cemetery. *(Expedition Photo).*
The 'royal' cemetery was cleared from 1927 to 1929 by a Joint Expedition of the British Museum and the University of Pennsylvania, led by Sir Leonard Woolley.

30. *Sumerian Art. Ur.* Hypogeum of Shulgi, a king of the Third Dynasty of Ur. *21st century B.C. (Expedition Photo).*
Discovered during the excavations of 1930-31.

31. *Ur.* The 'Royal' Tombs. Reconstitution of a Sacrificial Procession of the first half of the third millennium.
C.L. WOOLLEY, *Ur Excavations*, II, pl. 30 *(drawing by A. Forestier).*

32. *Ur.* The 'Royal' Tombs. Plan of the tomb of 'Queen' Shubad showing the arrangement of the sacrificial victims (men, women and animals).
C.L. WOOLLEY, *Ur Excavations*, II, pl. 29.

33. *Mesopotamian Art. Diyala Region. Tell Asmar (Ashnunnak).* Statuettes from the *favissa* of the Temple of Abu. *First half of the 3rd millennium B.C. Baghdad Museum and Oriental Institute, Chicago. (Expedition Photo).*
This group of statuettes was found buried under the altar of Cella II in the Square Temple, dedicated to Abu, the god of fertility.

34. *Mari.* Clearing the Court of the Steward in the Palace of Mari. *Early 2nd millennium B.C.*
Excavations of the Musées Nationaux de France (1933-39), led by André Parrot. *(André Parrot).*

35. *Mari.* Clearing the head of the Goddess of the Flowing Vase, in Court 106 of the Palace. *Aleppo Museum. (André Parrot).*

36. Members of the French Expedition to Mari with the Goddess of the Flowing Vase (1936). From left to right: Jean Payen, Gustave Tellier, Paul François, André Parrot, André Bianquis and D. Matta. *(André Parrot).*

37. *Mesopotamian Art. Middle Euphrates.* Group of Statuettes discovered in the Temple of Ishtar at Mari in 1934. *First half of the 3rd millennium B.C. Aleppo Museum and Louvre, Paris.*
The large statue in the middle does not come from the Temple of Ishtar, but from another temple in the centre of the city. *(André Parrot).*

38. *Mari.* Clearing the Throne Room 65 of the Palace of Mari (1935). *(André Parrot).*

39. *Sumerian Art.* Excavations in the Scribal Quarter at Nippur, conducted by the University Museum of Pennsylvania in 1889-90. *(Reuben Goldberg).*

40. *Assyrian Art.* Mallowan's Excavations at Nimrud in 1949.
Illustrated London News, July 22, 1950, p. 149, fig. 6.

41. *Sumerian Art.* Interior of the White Temple at Warka (Uruk).
Excavations of 1930-32 conducted by the German expedition of the Notgemeinschaft der deutschen Wissenschaft, led at that time by J. Jordan.
H.J. LENZEN, *Die Entwicklung der Zikurrat*, pl. 22a.

42. *Elamite Art. Choga Zambil.* The Ziggurat. *12th century B.C. (Roman Ghirshman).*
Excavations sponsored by the Commission des Fouilles, Direction Générale des Affaires Culturelles et Techniques, Ministère des Affaires Etrangères, Paris, and led by Roman Ghirshman.

43. *Elamite Art. Choga Zambil.* The Ziggurat Stairway. *12th century B.C. (Roman Ghirshman).*

44. *Subarian-Mitannian Art. Tell Halaf.* Large Statue of the Goddess with Hanging Braids. *10th century B.C. Tell Halaf Museum, Berlin. Basalt, height 6 ft 3 1/2 inches. (Destroyed in an air raid in 1943).*
M.F. VON OPPENHEIM, *Tell Halaf*, III, pl. 1.

45. *Mesopotamian Art. Middle Euphrates.* Some of the Statuettes found in the Temple of Ishtar at Mari. *First half of the 3rd millennium B.C. Aleppo Museum and Louvre, Paris. (André Parrot).*

46. The Asiatic Room in the Louvre in 1911. *(Louvre).*
In the glass case in the middle of the room are Sumerian reliefs from Lagash (Telloh).

47. *Iranian Art.* The Susa Antiquities in the Dieulafoy Room of the Louvre in 1911. *(Louvre).*

48. *Iranian Art.* Miscellaneous objects from Susa exhibited in the Louvre in 1911. *(Louvre).*

49. *Sumerian Art.* Department of Oriental Antiquities at the Louvre. The Gudea Room, 1947 arrangement. *(Marc Foucault).*

50. *Assyrian Art. Khorsabad.* Reliefs from the Palace of Sargon of Assyria, drawn by Eugène Flandin. These reliefs no longer exist.
P.E. BOTTA, *Monument de Ninive*, vol. I, 1849, with drawings by Flandin.

51. Location and chronology of excavation sites in Mesopotamia.

52. *Iranian Art. Susa.* Vase of the Susa I Style. *Second half of the 4th millennium B.C. Louvre, Paris. Terracotta, height* 11 7/8 *inches. (Louvre).*

53. *Mesopotamian Art.* So-called Temptation Seal. *Mid-3rd millennium B.C. British Museum, London. (British Museum.)*

54. Mesopotamian landscape.

55. Map of Northern Mesopotamia, from the 'Assyrian Triangle' to the Diyala.

56. Map showing some of the sites of ancient Mesopotamia, from Tell Halaf to Eridu.

57. The site of Senkereh (Larsa) before excavation. The Ziggurat Mound (1933). *(André Parrot).*

58a. Hassuna Pottery: 'Painted Archaic.' *5th millennium B.C. Baghdad Museum. Terracotta.*

58b. Hassuna Pottery: 'Typical Painted.' *5th millennium B.C. Baghdad Museum. Terracotta.*

58c. Hassuna Pottery: 'Typical Engraved.' *5th millennium B.C. Baghdad Museum. Terracotta.*

58d. Hassuna Pottery: 'Engraved and Painted.' *5th millennium B.C. Baghdad Museum. Terracotta.*

59a. Excavation plan of the Hassuna Tell. Excavations sponsored by the Department of Antiquities of Iraq (1943-44) and led by Fuad Safar.

59b. *Mesopotamian Art. Hassuna.* Plan of Dwelling-houses on Level IV. *5th millennium B.C.*

59c. *Mesopotamian Art. Hassuna.* Reconstruction of a Dwelling-house on Level IV. *5th millennium B.C.*

60a. and b. *Mesopotamian Art.* Samarra Pottery decorated with Ibexes. *5th millennium B.C. Terracotta.*

60c. *Mesopotamian Art.* Samarra Pottery decorated with Birds and Fish. *5th millennium B.C. Terracotta.*

60d. *Mesopotamian Art.* Samarra Pottery. Women with Wind-blown Hair and Pattern of Scorpions. *5th millennium B.C. Terracotta.*

61a. *Mesopotamian Art.* Samarra Pottery showing the Transition from Figurative to Abstract. *5th millennium B.C. Terracotta.*
Schematic representation of four ibexes running round a pool.

61b. *Mesopotamian Art.* Samarra Pottery. *5th millennium B.C. Terracotta.*
More advanced schematization of the four ibexes.

61c. *Mesopotamian Art.* Samarra Pottery. *5th millennium B.C. Terracotta.*
Schematization gives way to abstraction.

62a. *Mesopotamian Art. Baghuz and Arpatchiya.* Samarra Pottery with the 'Garland' Design. *5th millennium B.C. Terracotta.*

62b. *Mesopotamian Art. Mussian.* Samarra Pottery with the 'Dancers' Design. *5th millennium B.C. Terracotta.*

62c. *Iranian Art. Sialk.* Samarra Pottery with the 'Dancers' Design. *5th millennium B.C. Terracotta.*

63. *Mesopotamian Art. Hassuna.* Samarra Pottery. Neck of a Hassuna Vase decorated with a Human Figure. *5th millennium B.C. Baghdad Museum. Terracotta. (Schneider-Lengyel).*

64. *Mesopotamian Art. Tell Halaf.* Seated Figurine of Mother Goddess. *5th-4th millennia B.C. Terracotta, height 3 1/8 inches.*
M.F. VON OPPENHEIM, *Tell Halaf*, I, pl. CV.

65. *Mesopotamian Art. Tell Brak.* Headless Figurine of Mother Goddess. *5th-4th millennia B.C. Aleppo Museum. Terracotta, height 2 inches. (Schneider-Lengyel).*

66. *Mesopotamian Art. Telloh (Lagash).* Headless Female Figurine. *Al 'Ubaid Style, 4th millennium B.C. Louvre, Paris. Terracotta, height 2 1/2 inches. (Roger Parry).*

67a. *Mesopotamian Art. Tell Halaf.* Painted Pottery decorated with Animals. *5th-4th millennia B.C. Terracotta.*

67b. *Mesopotamian Art. Arpatchiya.* Painted Pottery decorated with Bull Skulls. *5th-4th millennia B.C. Baghdad Museum and British Museum, London. Terracotta.*
The bull skull is considered to be the symbol of the storm god.

67c. *Mesopotamian Art. Arpatchiya.* Painted Pottery decorated with Geometric and Symbolic Designs (Double-headed Axe). *5th-4th millennia B.C. Baghdad Museum and British Museum, London. Terracotta.*
The double-headed axe is later represented in the hands of the storm god (Hadad, Teshub).

67d. *Mesopotamian Art. Tell Halaf.* Painted Pottery decorated with Human Figures. *5th-4th millennia B.C. Terracotta.*

68a. *Iranian Art. Sialk.* Painted Vase decorated with Panthers in a Woodland Setting, detail. *4th millennium B.C. Louvre, Paris. Terracotta. (Louvre).*

68b. *Iranian Art. Sialk.* Painted Vase decorated with Panthers in a Woodland Setting. *4th millennium B.C. Louvre, Paris. Terracotta, height 11 3/4 inches. (Louvre).*

69. *Iranian Art. Rai.* Painted Fragment of a Vase with a Frieze of Dancers. *4th millennium B.C. Louvre, Paris. Terracotta, height 3 1/8 inches. (Louvre).*

70. *Mesopotamian Art. Abu Shahrein (Eridu).* Plan of Temples on Levels XV to XVIII. *5th millennium B.C.*

71. *Mesopotamian Art. Telloh (Lagash).* Painted Fragments decorated with Ibexes. *Al 'Ubaid Period, 4th millennium B.C. Louvre, Paris. Terracotta, height 3 3/4 and 4 inches. (Louvre).*

72a. *Mesopotamian Art. Abu Shahrein (Eridu).* Plan of Temple VII. *4th millennium B.C.*

72b. *Mesopotamian Art. Tepe Gawra.* Plan of the Temple of Level XIII. *4th millennium B.C.*

73. *Mesopotamian Art. Ur.* Headless Figurine of a Woman holding a Child. *Al 'Ubaid Period, 4th millennium B.C. British Museum, London. Terracotta, height 5 1/4 inches. (British Museum).*

74. *Mesopotamian Art. Ur.* Snake-headed Female Figurine. *Al 'Ubaid Period, 4th millennium B.C. University Museum, Philadelphia. Terracotta, height 6 1/4 inches. (University Museum).*

75. *Mesopotamian Art. Abu Shahrein (Eridu).* Male Figurine. *Al 'Ubaid Period, 4th millennium B.C. Baghdad Museum. Terracotta, height 5 1/2 inches. (Baghdad Museum).*

76. *Mesopotamian Art. Ur.* Snake-headed Female Figurine, detail. *Al 'Ubaid Period, 4th millennium B.C. Baghdad Museum. Terracotta. (Iraq Museum).*

77. *Mesopotamian Art. Ur.* Figurine of a Snake-headed Woman holding a Child. *Al 'Ubaid Period, 4th millennium B.C. Baghdad Museum. Terracotta, height 5 1/2 inches. (Iraq Museum).*

78a. *Iranian Art. Susa.* Goblet in the Susa I Style. *4th millennium B.C. Louvre, Paris. Terracotta, height 10 3/8 inches. (Louvre).*

78b. *Iranian Art. Susa.* Goblet in the Susa I Style. *4th millennium B.C. Louvre, Paris. Terracotta, height 11 3/4 inches. (Louvre).*

79. *Iranian Art. Susa.* Goblet in the Susa I Style, decorated with Birds, Slughis and Ibexes. *4th millennium B.C. Louvre, Paris. Terracotta, height 11 1/4 inches. (Tel-Vigneau).*

80a. *Iranian Art. Susa.* Bowl in the Susa I Style decorated with 'Bird-combs.' *4th millennium B.C. Louvre, Paris. Terracotta, diameter 11 5/8 inches. (Louvre).*

80b. *Iranian Art. Susa.* Bowl in the Susa I Style, with a Man standing between Two 'Marus.' *4th millennium B.C. Louvre, Paris. Terracotta, diameter 7 7/8 inches. (Louvre).*

80c. *Iranian Art. Susa.* Bowl in the Susa I Style, with an Archer. *4th millennium B.C. Louvre, Paris. Terracotta, diameter 7 inches. (Louvre).*

80d. *Iranian Art. Susa.* Bowl in the Susa I Style, with a Swastika. *4th millennium B.C. Louvre, Paris. Terracotta, diameter 9 3/8 inches. (Louvre).*

80e. *Iranian Art. Susa.* Bowl in the Susa I Style, with Bird-combs and a Maltese Cross. *4th millennium B.C. Louvre, Paris. Terracotta, diameter 7 7/8 inches. (Louvre).*

81. *Warka (Uruk).* Plan of the Site.

82. *Warka (Uruk).* The Ziggurat and the E-Anna Sector.

83a. *Mesopotamian Art. Warka (Uruk).* Archaic Temples on Levels V and IV. *Second half of the 4th millennium B.C.*

83b. *Mesopotamian Art. Warka (Uruk).* Archaic Temples (C, D, and Red) on Level IVa. *Second half of the 4th millennium B.C.*

83c. *Mesopotamian Art. Warka (Uruk).* Detail Plan of Temple D on Level IVa. *Second half of the 4th millennium B.C.*

84a. *Mesopotamian Art. Warka (Uruk).* Cone Mosaics in an Archaic Temple. *Second half of the 4th millennium B.C. (British Museum).*

84b. *Mesopotamian Art. Warka (Uruk).* Mosaic Panels in an Archaic Temple. *Second half of the 4th millennium B.C. Uruk Vorlaüfiger Bericht, VII, 1935, pl. 17 A.*

85. *Mesopotamian Art. Warka (Uruk).* Plan of the White Temple of the Anu Ziggurat. *Second half of the 4th millennium B.C.*
So called because of the white coating of the walls.

86. *Mesopotamian Art. Warka (Uruk).* The White Temple and the Stairway leading to it. *Second half of the 4th millennium B.C. (Expedition Photo).*

87. *Mesopotamian Art. Warka (Uruk).* Vase with Religious Scenes. *4th-3rd millennia B.C. Baghdad Museum. Alabaster, height 41 3/8 inches. (Baghdad Museum).*
The decoration in superimposed registers is highly characteristic of Sumerian art.

88. *Mesopotamian Art. Warka (Uruk).* Vase with Religious Scenes, detail. *4th-3rd millennia B.C. Baghdad Museum. Alabaster. (Baghdad Museum).*

89. *Mesopotamian Art. Warka (Uruk).* The Three Registers of the Warka Vase. *4th-3rd millennia B.C. Baghdad Museum. Alabaster.*

90. *Mesopotamian Art. Warka (Uruk).* Detail of the Top Register of the Warka Vase. *4th-3rd millennia B.C. Baghdad Museum. (Schneider-Lengyel).*

91a. *Mesopotamian Art. Warka (Uruk).* Cylinder Seal. Sacred Boat. *Early 3rd millennium B.C. Berlin Museum. Lapis lazuli, height 1 11/16 inches. (Marburg).*
This was a canal boat used to transport objects connected with the cult of the gods. Recognizable here are models of a temple and an altar, the latter on the back of a bull.

91b. *Mesopotamian Art. Tell Billa.* Cylinder Seal. Boat and Ritual Scene. *Early 3rd millennium B.C. Baghdad Museum. Diorite, height 1 5/8 inches, diameter 1 7/16 inches. (Baghdad Museum).*

92. *Mesopotamian Art. Warka (Uruk).* The Lion-Hunt Stele. *Early 3rd millennium B.C. Baghdad Museum. Basalt, height 31 1/2 inches. (Schneider-Lengyel).*
The hunter represented on this stele has much in common with a figure that appears in several Egyptian works, dressed in the same costume (on the Jebel el-Arak knife and in a tomb painting from Hierakonpolis).

93. *Mesopotamian Art. Tell Agrab.* Ritual Vase with Animals in High Relief. *Early 3rd millennium B.C. Oriental Institute, Chicago. Height 5 7/8 inches. (Oriental Institute).*

94. *Mesopotamian Art. Ur.* Decorated Ritual Bowl: Bulls and Wheat. *Early 3rd millennium B.C. Baghdad Museum. Steatite, height 2 3/16 inches, diameter 5 3/8 inches. (Schneider-Lengyel).*

95. *Mesopotamian Art. Warka (Uruk).* Decorated Ritual Vase: Bulls and Lions in High Relief. *Early 3rd millennium B.C. Baghdad Museum. Limestone, height 11 7/8 inches, diameter 4 1/2 inches. (Schneider-Lengyel).*

96. *Mesopotamian Art. Uruk (?).* Decorated Ritual Vase: Gilgamesh, Bulls, Birds. *Early 3rd millennium B.C. British Museum, London. Grey limestone, height 5 inches. (British Museum).*

97. *Iranian Art. Unknown provenance.* Human-bodied, Lion-headed Monster. *Early 3rd millennium B.C. Brooklyn Museum. Crystalline limestone, height 3 1/2 inches. (Brooklyn Museum).*

98a. *Mesopotamian Art. Cylinder Seal.* Monsters with Intertwined Necks. *Early 3rd millennium B.C. Louvre, Paris. Green jasper, height 1 3/4 inches. (Tel-Vigneau).*

98b. *Egyptian Art. Kom el-Ahmar (Hierakonpolis).* Palette of Narmer: Monsters with Intertwined Necks. *First Dynasty, c. 3000 B.C. Cairo Museum. Schist, height 25 1/8 inches. (Tel-Vigneau).*

99. *Egyptian Art. Jebel el-Arak.* Knife Handle decorated with scenes inspired by Mesopotamian art. *Louvre, Paris. Ivory and flint. Length of blade 7 3/8 inches; length of handle 3 3/4 inches. (Tel-Vigneau).*

100. *Mesopotamian Art.* Votive Bull. *Early 3rd millennium B.C. British Museum, London. Grey limestone, length 8 1/2 inches. (British Museum).*

101. *Mesopotamian Art.* Ritual Vase decorated with Lions in High Relief. *Early 3rd millennium B.C. Louvre, Paris. Limestone, height 6 5/8 inches. (Louvre).*

102. *Iranian Art. Susa.* Ram. *Early 3rd millennium B.C. Louvre, Paris. Terracotta, height 2 1/2 inches. (Tel-Vigneau).*

103a. *Iranian Art. Susa.* Bird-shaped Perfume Jar. *Early 3rd millennium B.C. Louvre, Paris. Alabaster, height 1 7/8 inches. (Tel-Vigneau).*

103b. *Iranian Art. Susa.* Perfume Jar. *Early 3rd millennium B.C. Louvre, Paris. Limestone, height 4 1/2 inches. (Tel-Vigneau).*

103c. *Iranian Art. Susa.* Dog-headed Statuette. *Early 3rd millennium B.C. Louvre, Paris. Limestone, height 5 1/4 inches. (Tel-Vigneau).*

104. *Iranian Art. Susa.* Female Worshipper. *Early 3rd millennium B.C. Louvre, Paris. Alabaster, height 2 1/2 inches. (Tel-Vigneau).*

105. *Mesopotamian Art. Warka (Uruk).* Female Head. *Early 3rd millennium B.C. Baghdad Museum. Height 7 7/8 inches. (Schneider-Lengyel).*

106. *Mesopotamian Art. Cylinder Seal, detail.* Acolyte with Wheat. *Late 4th - early 3rd millennium B.C. Louvre, Paris. White limestone, height 2 7/16 inches. (Tel-Vigneau).*

107. *Iranian Art. Susa. Cylinder Seal, detail.* Pastoral Scene. *First half of the 3rd millennium B.C. Louvre, Paris. Shell, height 1 1/4 inches. (Tel-Vigneau).*

108. *Mesopotamian Art. Cylinder Seal.* Bulls Passant and Sheafs of Wheat. *Late 4th - early 3rd millennium B.C. Louvre, Paris. Stone, height 1 1/2 inches. (Tel-Vigneau).*

109. *Iranian Art. Susa. Cylinder Seal.* Three Rows of Animals Passant. *Early 3rd millennium B.C. Louvre, Paris. Limestone, height 2 1/2 inches. (Tel-Vigneau).*

110. *Iranian Art. Susa. Cylinder Seal.* Two Rows of Animals, Mouflons and Goats. *Early 3rd millennium B.C. Louvre, Paris. Limestone, height 1 15/16 inches. (Tel-Vigneau).*

111. *Mesopotamian Art. Diyala Region. Khafaje. Cylinder Seal.* Animals with Antlers. *Baghdad Museum. Steatite, height 2 inches. (Baghdad Museum).*

112. *Mesopotamian Art. Diyala Region. Khafaje. Cylinder Seal.* Mythological Scene. *Baghdad Museum. Limestone, height 1 5/8 inches, diameter 1 3/8 inches. (Baghdad Museum).*

113. *Mesopotamian Art. Diyala Region. Khafaje. Cylinder Seal.* Animals in the Sacred Precincts. *Baghdad Museum. Limestone, height 2 3/8 inches. (Baghdad Museum).*

114. *Mesopotamian Art. Cylinder Seal.* Horned Animals. *Pierpont Morgan Collection, New York. Marble, height 1 9/16 inches. (Morgan Library).*

115. *Mesopotamian Art. Cylinder Seal.* Women seated on Low Tables and Large Spider. *Late 4th - early 3rd millennium B.C. Louvre, Paris. Reddish limestone, height 1 inch. (Louvre).*

116. *Mesopotamian Art. Cylinder Seal.* 'Abstract' Pattern evoking Pyramidal Constructions.

117. *Iranian Art. Susa. Cylinder Seal.* Abstract Design. *Early 3rd millennium B.C. Louvre, Paris. Bituminous limestone, height 1 5/16 inches. (Tel-Vigneau).*

118. *Mesopotamian Art. Diyala Region. Khafaje. Cylinder Seal.* Abstract Design. *Oriental Institute, Chicago. Steatite, height 2 inches. (Oriental Institute).*
An example of the 'brocade' style of ornamentation (name proposed by Henri Frankfort).

119. *Mesopotamian Art. Diyala Region. Khafaje. Cylinder Seal.* Frieze of highly schematized Animals. *Oriental Institute, Chicago. Stone, height 2 3/16 inches. (Oriental Institute).*

120. *Mesopotamian Art. Warka (Uruk).* Bird in Flight. *Early 3rd millennium B.C. British Museum, London. (British Museum).*

121. *Mesopotamian Art. Warka (Uruk).* Bird in Flight. *Early 3rd millennium B.C. British Museum, London. (British Museum).*

122. Pictographic Script *(c. 3000 B.C.).*
In this early phase of picture writing, the Mesopotamian alphabet numbered nearly 900 signs, including a sign meaning *word* and another meaning *sound.* The sign for *arrow,* read TI, also meant *life.*

123. *Mesopotamian Art. Tell 'Uqair.* The Temple on a High Platform. *Early 3rd millennium B.C. (Expedition Photo).*
The temples on high platforms (Eridu, Uruk, Tell Brak, Tell 'Uqair, al 'Ubaid, Khafaje) preceded the ziggurats in the development of religious architecture.

124. *Mesopotamian Art. Khafaje.* Reconstruction of a Temple on a High Platform. *Early 3rd millennium B.C.*

125. *Mesopotamian Art. Kish.* Representation of a Ziggurat on the lower register of a Cylinder Seal. *Early 3rd millennium B.C. Oriental Institute, Chicago. Shell, height 1 1/8 inches. (Oriental Institute).*

126. *Iranian Art. Susa.* Representation of Two Ziggurats on a Vase from Susa. *Early 3rd millennium B.C. Teheran Museum. Terracotta, height 2 1/4 inches.*

127a. *Mesopotamian Art. Middle Euphrates. Mari.* Reconstruction of the Temple of Ninni-Zaza. *First half of the 3rd millennium B.C.*
Temple of the 'house' type, with inner court and cella. A sacred stone (baetylus) stood in the court.

127b. *Mesopotamian Art. Middle Euphrates. Mari.* Inner Court of the Temple of Ninni-Zaza, with Baetylus *in situ. First half of the 3rd millennium B.C.*

127c. *Mesopotamian Art. Middle Euphrates. Mari.* Plan of the Temples of Ishtarat and Ninni-Zaza. *First half of the 3rd millennium B.C.*

128a. *Mesopotamian Art. Kish.* Plan of the Palace. *First half of the 3rd millennium B.C.*

128b. *Mesopotamian Art. Kish.* Reconstruction of the Palace. *First half of the 3rd millennium B.C.*

129. *Mesopotamian Art. Diyala Region. Tell Asmar (Ashnunnak).* Statues from the *favissa* of the Temple of Abu. *First half of the 3rd millennium B.C. Baghdad Museum and Oriental Institute, Chicago. (Oriental Institute).*

130a. *Mesopotamian Art. Diyala Region. Khafaje.* Worshipper Statuette. *First half of the 3rd millennium B.C. University Museum, Philadelphia. Alabaster, height 14 1/2 inches. (University Museum).*

130b. *Mesopotamian Art. Diyala Region. Khafaje.* Worshipper Statuette. *First half of the 3rd millennium B.C. Baghdad Museum. Alabaster, height 11 3/4 inches. (Schneider Lengyel).*

130c. *Mesopotamian Art. Diyala Region. Tell Asmar (Ashnunnak).* Worshipper Statuette. *First half of the 3rd millennium B.C. Baghdad Museum. Gypsum, height 16 1/8 inches. (Schneider-Lengyel).*

130d. *Mesopotamian Art. Diyala Region. Tell Asmar (Ashnunnak).* Worshipper Statuette. *First half of the 3rd millennium B.C. Baghdad Museum. Limestone, height 11 3/8 inches. (Schneider-Lengyel).*

131. *Mesopotamian Art. Diyala Region. Tell Asmar (Ashnunnak).* Worshipper Statuette, detail. *First half of the 3rd millennium B.C. Baghdad Museum. Gypsum, height 11 3/8 inches. (Schneider-Lengyel).*

132. *Mesopotamian Art. Diyala Region.* Worshipper Statuette. *First half of the 3rd millennium B.C. Baghdad Museum. Limestone. (Schneider-Lengyel).*

133. *Mesopotamian Art. Diyala Region. Tell Agrab.* Worshipper Statuette. *First half of the 3rd millennium B.C. Baghdad Museum. Gypsum, height 11 inches. (Schneider-Lengyel).*

134a. *Mesopotamian Art. Diyala Region. Tell Asmar (Ashnunnak).* Detail of the Nose and Eyes of the God Abu (?). *First half of the 3rd millennium B.C. Baghdad Museum. Veined gypsum. (Schneider-Lengyel).*
The huge staring eyes are no doubt meant to convey the idea that the divinity sees everything and never loses sight of the faithful. But the identification of the statue with a god or prince remains problematic.

134b. *Mesopotamian Art. Diyala Region. Tell Asmar (Ashnunnak).* Detail of the Eyes of the Goddess (?). *First half of the 3rd millennium B.C. Baghdad Museum. Veined gypsum. (Schneider-Lengyel).*

135. *Mesopotamian Art. Diyala Region. Tell Asmar (Ashnunnak).* Goddess and the God Abu (?). *First half of the 3rd millennium B.C. Baghdad Museum. Veined gypsum, height of the god 28 1/4, height of the goddess 23 1/4 inches. Cf. fig. 134. (Schneider-Lengyel).*

136. *Mesopotamian Art. Diyala Region. Tell Asmar (Ashnunnak).* Head of the Goddess (?). *First half of the 3rd millennium B.C. Baghdad Museum. Veined gypsum. (Schneider-Lengyel).*

137. *Mesopotamian Art. Diyala Region. Tell Asmar (Ashnunnak).* Head of the God Abu (?). *First half of the 3rd millennium B.C. Baghdad Museum. Veined gypsum. (Schneider-Lengyel).*

138a. *Mesopotamian Art. Diyala Region. Tell Agrab.* Female Head. *First half of the 3rd millennium B.C. Baghdad Museum. Limestone, height 3 1/8 inches. (Schneider-Lengyel).*

138b. *Mesopotamian Art. Diyala Region. Tell Asmar (Ashnunnak).* Female Head. *First half of the 3rd millennium B.C. Louvre, Paris. Limestone, height 4 1/8 inches. (Louvre).*

139a. *Mesopotamian Art. Diyala Region. Khafaje.* Female Head. *First half of the 3rd millennium B.C. Baghdad Museum. Limestone, height 2 1/2 inches. (Iraq Museum).*

139b. *Mesopotamian Art. Diyala Region. Tell Agrab.* Female Head. *First half of the 3rd millennium B.C. Baghdad Museum. Limestone, height 4 3/4 inches. (Schneider-Lengyel).*

140. *Mesopotamian Art. Diyala Region.* Statuette of a Woman. *First half of the 3rd millennium B.C. Baghdad Museum. Limestone, height 14 1/2 inches. (Schneider-Lengyel).*

141. *Sumerian Art. Telloh (Lagash).* Head of a Woman. *First half of the 3rd millennium B.C. Louvre, Paris. Alabaster, height 3 1/8 inches. (Tel-Vigneau).*

142. *Mesopotamian Art.* Female Head and Bust. *First half of the 3rd millennium B.C. Louvre, Paris. Limestone, height 8 5/8 inches. (Tel-Vigneau).*

143a. *Sumerian Art. Um el-Aghareb.* Male Head. *First half of the 3rd millennium B.C. Louvre, Paris. Limestone, height 2 3/4 inches. (Louvre).*

143b. *Mesopotamian Art. Diyala Region. Khafaje.* Male Head. *First half of the 3rd millennium B.C. Oriental Institute, Chicago. Gypsum, height 2 inches. (Oriental Institute).*

144. *Sumerian Art. Al 'Ubaid.* Statue of Kurlil (or Ekur), 'Warrior Chief of Uruk.' *First half of the 3rd millennium B.C. British Museum, London. Basalt, height 14 3/4 inches. (British Museum).*

145. *Mesopotamian Art. Middle Euphrates. Mari.* Statue of King Lamgi-Mari. *First half of the 3rd millennium B.C. Aleppo Museum. White stone, height 10 5/8 inches. (Schneider-Lengyel).*
The inscription on this statue enabled us to identify Tell Hariri as the ancient city of Mari (January 23, 1934).

146. *Mesopotamian Art. Middle Euphrates. Mari.* Head of King Iku-Shamagan. *First half of the 3rd millennium B.C. Damascus Museum. Gypsum, height 36 1/4 inches. (Schneider-Lengyel).*

147a. *Mesopotamian Art. Middle Euphrates. Mari.* Statue of Nani. *First half of the 3rd millennium B.C. Damascus Museum. Gypsum, height 18 1/4 inches. (Schneider-Lengyel).*

147b. *Mesopotamian Art. Middle Euphrates. Mari.* The Steward Ebih-il. *First half of the 3rd millennium B.C. Louvre, Paris. Alabaster, height 20 5/8 inches. (Tel-Vigneau).*

148. *Mesopotamian Art. Middle Euphrates. Mari.* Idi-Narum, the 'Miller.' *First half of the 3rd millennium B.C. Aleppo Museum. Pink breccia, height 8 inches. (Schneider-Lengyel).*

149. *Mesopotamian Art. Middle Euphrates. Mari.* Head of a Male Worshipper ('The Bedouin'). *First half of the 3rd millennium B.C. Damascus Museum. Gypsum, height 17 3/8 inches. (Schneider-Lengyel).*

150. *Mesopotamian Art. Middle Euphrates. Mari.* 'Caricatural' Head of a Worshipper. *First half of the 3rd millennium B.C. Damascus Museum. Gypsum, height 5 inches. (André Parrot).*

151. *Sumerian Art. Ur.* Head of a Female Worshipper. *First half of the 3rd millennium B.C. British Museum, London. White marble, height 8 7/8 inches. (British Museum).*

152. *Mesopotamian Art. Middle Euphrates. Mari.* Female Worshipper (Queen?) with a Branch. *First half of the 3rd millennium B.C. Louvre, Paris. Gypsum, height 7 5/8 inches. (André Parrot).*

153. *Mesopotamian Art. Middle Euphrates. Mari.* Female Head with a 'Polos.' *First half of the 3rd millennium B.C. Damascus Museum. Gypsum, height of the statuette 9 3/4 inches. (Schneider-Lengyel).*

154. *Mesopotamian Art. Middle Euphrates. Mari.* Female Head with 'Polos' and Shawl. *First half of the 3rd millennium B.C. Damascus Museum. Gypsum, height of the statuette 14 1/4 inches. (Schneider-Lengyel).*

155a and b. *Mesopotamian Art. Middle Euphrates. Mari.* Ur-Nina (or Ur-Nanshe), 'The Great Singer.' *First half of the 3rd millennium B.C. Damascus Museum. Gypsum, height 10 1/4 inches. (Schneider-Lengyel).*

156. *Mesopotamian Art. Middle Euphrates. Mari.* Ur-Nina (or Ur-Nanshe), 'The Great Singer.' *First half of the 3rd millennium B.C. Damascus Museum. Gypsum, height 10 1/4 inches. (André Parrot).*

157. *Mesopotamian Art. Middle Euphrates. Mari.* 'The Embracing Couple.' *First half of the 3rd millennium B.C. Aleppo Museum. Gypsum, height 5 inches. (Schneider-Lengyel).*

158a and b. *Sumerian Art. Telloh (Lagash).* Bas-relief. Man with a Plumed Headdress. *Early 3rd millennium B.C. Louvre, Paris. Limestone, height 7 inches. (Tel-Vigneau).*

158c. *Sumerian Art. Nippur.* Votive Relief dedicated to Enlil. *First half of the 3rd millennium B.C. Archaeological Museum, Istanbul. Schist, height 7 1/2 inches. (Archaeological Museum).*

158d. *Sumerian Art. Nippur.* Votive Relief dedicated to Enlil. *First half of the 3rd millennium B.C. University Museum, Philadelphia. Limestone, height 1 5/8 inches. (University Museum).*

159a. *Sumerian Art. Telloh (Lagash).* Genealogical Bas-relief of Ur-Nina (or Ur-Nanshe). *First half of the 3rd millennium B.C. Louvre, Paris. Limestone, height 15 3/4 inches. (Tel-Vigneau).*
The reading of this name is still uncertain. Some Assyriologists now decipher it as Ur-Nina, while others still prefer Ur-Nanshe.

159b. *Sumerian Art. Telloh (Lagash).* Detail of the Genealogical Bas-relief: The King Ur-Nina (or Ur-Nanshe) carrying a Basket. *First half of the 3rd millennium B.C. Louvre, Paris. Limestone. (Tel-Vigneau).*

160a. *Sumerian Art. Telloh (Lagash).* Mace-head of Mesilim. *First half of the 3rd millennium B.C. Louvre, Paris. Limestone, height 7 1/2 inches. (Tel-Vigneau).*
Mesilim, king of Kish, also ruled over Lagash.

160b. *Sumerian Art. Telloh (Lagash).* Detail of the Mace-head of Mesilim. *First half of the 3rd millennium B.C. Louvre, Paris. Limestone. (Tel-Vigneau).*

161a. *Mesopotamian Art. Diyala Region. Khafaje.* Perforated Plaque. Banquet Scene. *First half of the 3rd millennium B.C. Baghdad Museum. Limestone, height 11 5/8 inches. (Schneider-Lengyel).*
Such reliefs as this presumably represent the celebration of the New Year.

161b. *Sumerian Art. Telloh (Lagash).* Perforated Plaque. Libation before the Goddess Ninhursag. *First half of the 3rd millennium B.C. Louvre, Paris. Limestone, height 6 3/4 inches, width 5 7/8 inches. (Tel-Vigneau).*

161c. *Sumerian Art. Al 'Ubaid.* Bas-relief. Lion-headed Eagle attacking a Human-headed Bull. *First half of the 3rd millennium B.C. University Museum, Philadelphia. Limestone, height 5 3/4 inches, width 5 1/2 inches. (University Museum).*

162. *Mesopotamian Art. Kish.* Bas-relief. Lion attacking a Stag. *First half of the 3rd millennium B.C. Baghdad Museum. Limestone, width 7 1/8 inches. (Baghdad Museum).*

163a. *Sumerian Art. Telloh (Lagash).* Detail of the Stele of the Vultures. *First half of the 3rd millennium B.C. Louvre, Paris. Limestone. (Tel-Vigneau).*

163b. *Sumerian Art. Telloh (Lagash).* Stele of the Vultures, mythological side. *First half of the 3rd millennium B.C. Louvre, Paris. Limestone, height 6 ft 2 inches. (Tel-Vigneau).*

163c. *Sumerian Art. Telloh (Lagash).* Stele of the Vultures, historical side. *First half of the 3rd millennium B.C. Louvre, Paris. Limestone, height 6 ft 2 inches. (Tel-Vigneau).*

164. *Sumerian Art. Telloh (Lagash).* Detail of the Stele of the Vultures: King Eannatum at the Head of his Troops. *First half of the 3rd millennium B.C. Louvre, Paris. Limestone. (Tel-Vigneau).*

165. *Sumerian Art. Telloh (Lagash).* Detail of the Stele of the Vultures: The God Ningirsu with his Mace. *First half of the 3rd millennium B.C. Louvre, Paris. (Tel-Vigneau).*

166. *Sumerian Art. Telloh (Lagash).* Detail of the Stele of the Vultures: The Prisoners in the Net. *First half of the 3rd millennium B.C. Louvre, Paris. (Tel-Vigneau).*

167a. *Sumerian Art. Telloh (Lagash).* Plaque of Dudu, Priest of Lagash. *First half of the 3rd millennium B.C. Louvre, Paris. Bituminous stone, height 9 7/8 inches. (Tel-Vigneau).*

167b. *Sumerian Art. Telloh (Lagash).* Fragment of a Vase with the Goddess Ninhursag. *First half of the 3rd millennium B.C. Berlin Museum. Basalt, height 9 7/8 inches. (Marburg).*

168a. *Iranian Art. Susa.* Double Vase with Architectural Ornamentation. *First half of the 3rd millennium B.C. Louvre, Paris. Steatite, height 7 1/4 inches. (Tel-Vigneau).*

168b. *Mesopotamian Art. Middle Euphrates. Mari.* Vase decorated with a Double Torsade. *First half of the 3rd millennium B.C. Aleppo Museum. Steatite, height 10 1/4 inches. (Schneider-Lengyel).*

168c. *Mesopotamian Art. Middle Euphrates. Mari.* Fragment of a Vase with a Lion fighting a Snake. *First half of the 3rd millennium B.C. Aleppo Museum. Steatite, height 4 3/4 inches. (Schneider-Lengyel).*

168d. *Mesopotamian Art. Diyala Region. Khafaje.* Vase decorated with a Welter of Animals. *First half of the 3rd millennium B.C. British Museum, London. Steatite, height 4 inches. (British Museum).*

169a. *Mesopotamian Art. Middle Euphrates. Mari.* Vase with Mythological Scenes. *First half of the 3rd millennium B.C. Damascus Museum. Steatite, height 7 7/8 inches. (Schneider-Lengyel).*

169b. *Mesopotamian Art. Cylinder Seal.* Gilgamesh and Enkidu subduing Wild Animals. *First half of the 3rd millennium B.C. Royal Dutch Cabinet of Medals, The Hague. Serpentine, height 1 3/4 inches. (Royal Dutch Cabinet of Medals).*

169c. *Mesopotamian Art. Diyala Region. Khafaje.* Mythological Scene with schematized Animals and Figures. *First half of the 3rd millennium B.C. Baghdad Museum. Shell, height 1 1/8 inches. (Baghdad Museum).*

170a. *Sumerian Art.* Arm-rest with the Muzzle of a Bull. *First half of the 3rd millennium B.C. Louvre, Paris. Gypsum, height 5 1/2 inches. (Louvre).*

170b. *Mesopotamian Art. Diyala Region. Khafaje.* Arm-rest with the Muzzle of a Human-headed Bull. *First half of the 3rd millennium B.C. University Museum, Philadelphia. Alabaster, height 2 3/4 inches. (University Museum).*

171a. *Mesopotamian Art. Middle Euphrates. Mari.* The 'Standard': Dignitaries. *First half of the 3rd millennium B.C. Louvre, Paris, and Aleppo Museum. Mother of pearl, height 4 1/4 inches. (Expedition Photo).*

171b. *Mesopotamian Art. Middle Euphrates. Mari.* Ritual Sacrifice of a Ram. *First half of the 3rd millennium B.C. Aleppo Museum. Ivory, height 2 3/4 inches, width 1 1/4 inches. (Schneider-Lengyel).*

171c. *Mesopotamian Art. Middle Euphrates. Mari.* Worshippers. *First half of the 3rd millennium B.C. Damascus Museum. Ivory, height 1 5/8 inches. (Schneider-Lengyel).*

172. *Mesopotamian Art. Middle Euphrates. Mari.* Seated Figure with a Goblet. *First half of the 3rd millennium B.C. Damascus Museum. Shell, height 2 7/8 inches. (André Parrot).*

173a. *Mesopotamian Art. Middle Euphrates. Mari.* Female Worshipper. *First half of the 3rd millennium B.C. Damascus Museum. Shell, height 1 1/4 inches. (Schneider-Lengyel).*

173b. *Mesopotamian Art. Middle Euphrates. Mari.* Porters. *First half of the 3rd millennium B.C. Damascus Museum. Shell, height 1 3/4 and 1 1/4 inches, width 1 3/8 and 1 inch. (André Parrot).*

173c. *Sumerian Art. Ur.* Inlaid Gaming Board. *First half of the 3rd millennium B.C. British Museum, London. Inlay of shell, bone, lapis lazuli, red paste and red limestone on wood, set with bitumen. Length 10 5/8 inches. (British Museum).*

174. *Mesopotamian Art. Middle Euphrates. Mari.* Kneeling Captive. *First half of the 3rd millennium B.C. Damascus Museum. Shell, height 2 3/4 inches. (André Parrot).*

175. *Sumerian Art. Ur.* Detail of the 'Standard': War Chariot. *First half of the 3rd millennium B.C. British Museum, London. Inlay of shell, lapis lazuli and red limestone. Length 18 1/2 inches, height 7 7/8 inches. (Draeger).*

176. *Sumerian Art. Ur.* The 'Standard': Panel representing War. *First half of the 3rd millennium B.C. British Museum, London. (Draeger).*

177. *Sumerian Art. Ur.* The 'Standard': Panel representing Peace. *First half of the 3rd millennium B.C. British Museum, London. (Draeger).*

178. *Sumerian Art. Ur.* The 'Standard.' Peace, detail: Libation Scene. *First half of the 3rd millennium B.C. British Museum, London. (Draeger).*

179. *Sumerian Art. Ur.* Inlaid Soundbox of a Harp from the 'Royal' Tombs. *First half of the 3rd millennium B.C. University Museum, Philadelphia. Mother of pearl, height c. 8 1/2 inches. (British Museum).*

180. *Mesopotamian Art. Diyala Region. Khafaje.* Worshipper on a Pedestal. *First half of the 3rd millennium B.C. Oriental Institute, Chicago. Copper, height 16 1/8 inches. (Oriental Institute).*

181. *Mesopotamian Art. Diyala Region. Tell Agrab.* Votive Chariot drawn by Four Animals. *First half of the 3rd millennium B.C. Baghdad Museum. Copper, height 2 3/4 inches. (Schneider-Lengyel).*

182. *Mesopotamian Art. Diyala Region. Tell Agrab.* Votive Chariot drawn by Four Animals. *First half of the 3rd millennium B.C. Baghdad Museum. Copper, height 2 3/4 inches. (Schneider-Lengyel).*

183a. *Mesopotamian Art. Diyala Region. Khafaje.* Worshipper Figurine on a Four-footed Stand. *First half of the 3rd millennium B.C. Baghdad Museum. Bronze, height 21 3/4 inches. (Baghdad Museum).*

183b. *Sumerian Art.* Worshipper Figurine with a Kaunakes Skirt. *First half of the 3rd millennium B.C. Louvre, Paris. Bronze, height 5 7/8 inches. (Louvre).*

183c. *Mesopotamian Art. Diyala Region. Tell Agrab.* Two Men wrestling with Vases on their Heads. *First half of the 3rd millennium B.C. Baghdad Museum. Copper, height 3 7/8 inches. (Schneider-Lengyel).*

184a. *Sumerian Art. Telloh (Lagash).* Bull's Head with Inlaid Eyes. *First half of the 3rd millennium B.C. Louvre, Paris. Bronze, height 7 1/2 inches. (Tel-Vigneau).*

184b. *Sumerian Art. Shuruppak.* Goat's Head with In- laid Eyes. *First half of the 3rd millennium B.C. University Museum, Philadelphia. Bronze, height 7 inches. (University Museum).*
The provenance of this work is given as Shuruppak by Hilprecht, *Explorations in Bible Lands*, p. XIX, whereas Frankfort, *The Art and Architecture of the Ancient Orient*, pl. 29B, gives Nippur.

185. *Sumerian Art. Al 'Ubaid.* Bull from the Temple Frieze. *First half of the 3rd millennium B.C. British Museum, London. Bronze plaque on wood, height 24 3/8 inches, width 24 3/8 inches. (British Museum)*
Another technique was also used at al 'Ubaid: copper plaques on bitumen.

186. *Sumerian Art.* Bull's Head. *First half of the 3rd mil- lennium B.C. City Art Museum, St. Louis, Mo. Copper, height 9 inches. (City Art Museum).*

187. *Sumerian Art. Al 'Ubaid.* Lion-headed Eagle bet- ween Two Stags. *First half of the 3rd millennium B.C. British Museum, London. Bronze, height 3 ft 6 1/8 inches, width 7 ft 9 1/2 inches. (British Museum).*

188a. *Sumerian Art. Ur.* Rein Ring with an Onager. *First half of the 3rd millennium B.C. British Museum, London. Electrum and silver, height 5 1/4 inches, length 4 inches. (British Museum).*

188b. *Sumerian Art. Telloh (Lagash).* Silver Vase of Entemena, Patesi of Lagash. *First half of the 3rd millen- nium B.C. Louvre, Paris. Silver and bronze, height 13 3/4 inches. (Louvre).*
The *patesi* (also read *ishak*) was a ruler invested with both temporal and religious powers. His office was that of priest-king.

189a. *Sumerian Art. Ur.* Goblet and Bowl of 'Queen' Shubad. *First half of the 3rd millennium B.C. University Museum, Philadelphia. Gold. Height of goblet 5 7/8 inches. Height of bowl 1 5/8 inches; width of bowl 3 1/4 inches. (University Museum).*

189b. *Sumerian Art. Ur.* Bull's Head from the Sound- box of a Lyre. *First half of the 3rd millennium B.C. Uni- versity Museum, Philadelphia. Gold and lapis lazuli, width 9 7/8 inches. (University Museum).*

189c. *Sumerian Art. Ur.* Helmet of Meskalamdug. *First half of the 3rd millennium B.C. Baghdad Museum. Gold, height 9 inches, width 10 1/4 inches. (Schneider- Lengyel).*

190. *Sumerian Art. Ur.* Ram resting against a Flower- ing Shrub. *First half of the 3rd millennium B.C. British Museum, London. Gold, lapis lazuli, shell, silver, etc. Height 19 3/4 inches. (Draeger).*

191. *Sumerian Art. Ur.* Bull's Head from the Sound- box of a Harp. *First half of the 3rd millennium B.C. Baghdad Museum. Gold, height 11 5/8 inches. (Schneider- Lengyel).*

192. *Sumerian Art.* Cylinder Seal. Combat of Animals. *Pierpont Morgan Collection, New York. Marble, height 1 5/8 inches. (Morgan Library).*

193. *Sumerian Art. Ur.* Cylinder Seal. Hero fighting Two Animals. *British Museum, London. Steatite, height 1 3/8 inches. (British Museum).*

194. *Iranian Art. Susa.* Cylinder Seal. Hero fighting Four Animals. *Louvre, Paris. Black limestone, height 1 inch. (Tel-Vigneau).*

195. *Sumerian Art. Ur.* Cylinder Seal. Animals fight- ing and Hero. *British Museum, London. Shell, height 1 1/2 inches. (British Museum).*

196. *Sumerian Art.* Cylinder Seal. Animals fighting and Hero. *Pierpont Morgan Collection, New York. Shell, height 7/8 of an inch. (Morgan Library).*

197. *Sumerian Art. Ur.* Cylinder Seal. Banquet Scene in a Boat. *University Museum, Philadelphia. Steatite, height 1 3/8 inches. (University Museum).*

198. *Mesopotamian Art. Mari.* Cylinder Seal. The Boat-God. *Louvre, Paris. Shell, height 1 3/8 inches. (Tel-Vigneau).*

199. *Tell Asmar.* Cylinder Seal. Animal with Antlers. *Baghdad Museum. Haematite, height 1 3/8 inches. (Bagh- dad Museum).*

200. *Tell Agrab.* Cylinder Seal. Temple and Mask of a God (?). *Baghdad Museum. Limestone, height 2 inches. (Baghdad Museum).*

201. *Mesopotamian Art.* Cylinder Seal. Men and Various Animals. *Pierpont Morgan Collection, New York. Onyx, height 1 1/2 inches. (Morgan Library).*

202. *Sumerian Art. Ur.* Cylinder Seal. Banquet Scenes. *University Museum, Philadelphia. Lapis lazuli, height 1 1/2 inches. (University Museum).*

203. *Iranian Art. Susa.* The Goddess Innina. *Second half of the 3rd millennium B.C. Louvre, Paris. Limestone, height 33 1/2 inches. (Tel-Vigneau).*

204. *Akkadian Art.* Cylinder Seal. Mythological Scene: Gods in Combat. *Second half of the 3rd millennium B.C. Mrs William M. Moore Collection. Lapis lazuli, height 1 1/8 inches. (Courtesy Mrs William M. Moore).*

205. Map of Mesopotamia. 'The Four Quarters of the World.'

206. *Akkadian Art. Nineveh.* Head of King Sargon (?). *Second half of the 3rd millennium B.C. Baghdad Museum. Bronze, height 11 3/4 inches. (Schneider-Lengyel).*

207. *Akkadian Art. Susa.* Detail of the Stele of Sargon: Captives. *Second half of the 3rd millennium B.C. Louvre, Paris. Diorite, height of stele 18 inches. (Roger Parry).*

208. *Akkadian Art. Nineveh.* Head of King Sargon (?). *Second half of the 3rd millennium B.C. Baghdad Museum. Bronze, height 11 3/4 inches. (Schneider-Lengyel).*

209. *Akkadian Art. Susa.* Detail of the Stele of Sargon. *Second half of the 3rd millennium B.C. Louvre, Paris. Diorite, height of stele 18 inches. (Louvre).*

210. *Akkadian Art. Telloh (Lagash).* Stele of Rimush. *Second half of the 3rd millennium B.C. Louvre, Paris. Limestone, height 13 3/8 inches. (Louvre).*

211. *Akkadian Art. Pir Hussein.* Stele of Naram-Sin. *Second half of the 3rd millennium B.C. Archaeological Museum, Istanbul. Basalt, height* 21 5/8 *inches.* (*Archaeological Museum*).

212. *Akkadian Art. Susa.* Detail of the Stele of Naram-Sin: The King trampling Enemy Soldiers. *Second half of the 3rd millennium. Louvre, Paris. Pink sandstone.* (*Tel-Vigneau*).
This stele came originally from Babylonia, but was carried off to Susa by Shutruk-Nakhunte in the 12th century B.C.

213. *Akkadian Art. Susa.* Stele of Naram-Sin. *Second half of the 3rd millennium B.C. Louvre, Paris. Pink sandstone, height* 6 *ft* 6 3/4 *inches, width* 3 *ft* 5 1/4 *inches.* (*Tel-Vigneau*).

214. *Akkadian Art. Susa.* Robe of Manishtusu. *Second half of the 3rd millennium B.C. Louvre, Paris. Diorite, height* 37 *inches.* (*Tel-Vigneau*).

215. *Akkadian Art. Susa.* Obelisk of Manishtusu. *Second half of the 3rd millennium B.C. Louvre, Paris. Diorite, height* 4 *ft* 7 1/8 *inches.* (*Louvre*).

216. *Akkadian Art. Susa.* Feet of a Statue of Naram-Sin. *Second half of the 3rd millennium B.C. Louvre, Paris. Diorite, height* 18 1/2 *inches.* (*Louvre*).

217. *Akkadian Art. Bismaya (Adab).* Man's Head. *Second half of the 3rd millennium B.C. Oriental Institute, Chicago. Gypsum, height* 3 1/2 *inches.* (*Oriental Institute*).

218. *Akkadian Art. Assur.* Woman's Head. *Second half of the 3rd millennium B.C. Berlin Museum. Gypsum, height* 2 3/4 *inches.* (*Marburg*).

219. *Akkadian Art.* Head of a Bearded Man. *Second half of the 3rd millennium B.C. Louvre, Paris. Limestone, height* 3 1/4 *inches.* (*Tel-Vigneau*).

220. *Hurrian Art.* Lion and Foundation Tablet dedicated by Tisari, King of Urkish. *Mid-3rd millennium B.C. Louvre, Paris. Bronze and stone. Height of figurine* 4 3/4 *inches, width* 3 3/8 *inches. Tablet* 4 3/4 *by* 3 3/8 *inches.* (*Louvre*).

221. *Akkadian Art. Telloh (Lagash).* Head of a Woman. *Second half of the 3rd millennium B.C. Louvre, Paris. Limestone, height* 2 5/8 *inches.* (*Tel-Vigneau*).

222. *Akkadian Art. Telloh (Lagash).* Head of a Divinity. *Second half of the 3rd millennium B.C. Louvre, Paris. Terracotta, height* 4 *inches.* (*Tel-Vigneau*).

223. *Akkadian Art.* Cylinder Seal of Sharkalisharri. *Second half of the 3rd millennium B.C. De Clercq Collection, Paris. Brown jasper, height* 1 5/8 *inches.* (*De Clercq*).

224. *Akkadian Art. Mari.* Cylinder Seal, detail. Gilgamesh grappling with a Buffalo. *Second half of the 3rd millennium B.C. Damascus Museum. Stone, height* 1 3/8 *inches.* (*Damascus Museum*).

225. *Akkadian Art.* Cylinder Seal, detail. Gilgamesh grappling with a Lion. *Second half of the 3rd millennium B.C. British Museum, London. Agate, height* 1 7/16 *inches.* (*British Museum*).

226. *Akkadian Art.* Cylinder Seal. Myth of Etana. *Second half of the 3rd millennium B.C. Berlin Museum. Serpentine, height* 1 3/4 *inches.* (*Marburg*).

227. *Akkadian Art.* Cylinder Seal. Procession of Gods. *Second half of the 3rd millennium B.C. Pierpont Morgan Collection, New York. Shell, height* 1 5/16 *inches.* (*Morgan Library*).

228. *Akkadian Art. Mari.* Cylinder Seal. The God Anu and Other Deities. *Second half of the 3rd millennium B.C. Damascus Museum. White stone, height* 2 1/2 *inches.* (*Schneider-Lengyel*).

229. *Akkadian Art.* Fragment of a Vase with a Captive. *Second half of the 3rd millennium B.C. Louvre, Paris. Steatite, height* 2 1/4 *inches.* (*Tel-Vigneau*).

230. *Akkadian Art.* Vase with a Captive, detail. *Second half of the 3rd millennium B.C. Louvre, Paris. Steatite, height* 2 1/4 *inches.* (*Tel-Vigneau*).

231. *Akkadian Art.* Cylinder Seal. Watering a Garden. *Louvre, Paris. Shell, height* 1 1/4 *inches.* (*Tel-Vigneau*).

232. *Akkadian Art. Diyala Region. Tell Asmar.* Cylinder Seal. God with a Plough. *Oriental Institute, Chicago. Stone, height* 7/8 *of an inch.* (*Oriental Institute*).

233. *Akkadian Art.* Cylinder Seal. Mythological Scene. *Second half of the 3rd millennium B.C. Pierpont Morgan Collection, New York. Serpentine, height* 1 1/2 *inches.* (*Morgan Library*).

234. *Akkadian Art.* Cylinder Seal. Mythological Scene connected with Agriculture. *Second half of the 3rd millennium B.C. Pierpont Morgan Collection, New York. Black serpentine, height* 1 3/8 *inches.* (*Morgan Library*).

235. *Akkadian Art.* Cylinder Seal. Mythological Scene. *Second half of the 3rd millennium B.C. Louvre, Paris. Steatite, height* 1 3/8 *inches.* (*Louvre*).

236. *Akkadian Art. Diyala Region. Tell Asmar.* Cylinder Seal. Mythological Scene. *Second half of the 3rd millennium B.C. Baghdad Museum. Shell, height* 1 3/8 *inches.* (*Baghdad Museum*).

237. *Akkadian Art.* Cylinder Seal of Adda. Mythological Scene: Liberation of the Sun-God. *Second half of the 3rd millennium B.C. British Museum, London.* (*British Museum*).

238. *Akkadian Art. Diyala Region. Tell Asmar.* Cylinder Seal. Mythological Scene: The Boat-God. *Second half of the 3rd millennium B.C. Oriental Institute, Chicago. Shell, height* 1 1/2 *inches.* (*Oriental Institute*).

239. *Akkadian Art. Ur.* Cylinder Seal. Mythological Scene. *Second half of the 3rd millennium B.C. Shell, height* 1 3/8 *inches.*

240. *Akkadian Art. Ur.* Cylinder Seal. Mythological Scene: The God Enki (Ea) in his Water House. *Second half of the 3rd millennium B.C. Baghdad Museum. Stone, height* 1 3/8 *inches.* (*Baghdad Museum*).

241. *Akkadian Art. Telloh (Lagash).* Cylinder Seal. Mythological Scene: Combat of Animals and Heroes. *Second half of the 3rd millennium B.C. Louvre, Paris. Marble, height* 2 1/8 *inches.* (*Louvre*).

242. *Akkadian Art. Ur.* Cylinder Seal. Mythological Scene: Gilgamesh and Enkidu fighting Wild Animals. *Second half of the 3rd millennium B.C. Steatite, height* 1 1/2 *inches.*

243. *Neo-Sumerian Art. Telloh (Lagash).* Bas-relief adorned with Flowing Vases. *23rd century B.C. Louvre, Paris. Limestone, height 5 7/8 inches. (Marc Foucault).* Belonged to a stele of Gudea.

244. *Neo-Sumerian Art. Telloh (Lagash).* Cylinder Seal. Eagle and Capridae. *22nd century B.C. Baghdad Museum. Limestone, height 1 5/16 inches. (Baghdad Museum).*

245. French Excavations at Lagash (Telloh), 1930-31 season. *(André Parrot).*

246. *Mesopotamian Art.* Matrix inscribed with the Name of Ur-Ningirsu, Patesi of Lagash. *Baghdad Museum. (Baghdad Museum).* Bricks stamped with this were used to build the hypogeum of Ur-Ningirsu.

247. *Neo-Sumerian Art. Ur.* The Third-Dynasty Ziggurat. *22nd-21st centuries B.C.* Built by the kings Ur-Nammu and Shulgi (Dungi). *(André Parrot).*

248. *Neo-Sumerian Art. Ur.* Reconstruction of the Third-Dynasty Ziggurat. *22nd-21st centuries B.C.*

249a. *Neo-Sumerian Art. Ur.* 'Quiet Street.' *19th century B.C.* In a residential quarter. *(British Museum).*

249b. *Neo-Sumerian Art. Ur.* Chapel of Pa-Sag. *20th century B.C.* In a residential quarter. *(British Museum).*

249c. *Neo-Sumerian Art. Ur.* 'Paternoster Street.' *20th century B.C.* In a residential quarter. *(British Museum).*

249d. *Neo-Sumerian Art. Ur.* Hypogeum of Shulgi (Dungi), stairs. *22nd-21st centuries B.C. (British Museum).*

249e. *Neo-Sumerian Art. Ur.* Hypogeum of Bur-Sin, stairs leading to the tombs. *21st century B.C. (British Museum).*

249f. *Neo-Sumerian Art. Ur.* Hypogeum of Shulgi (Dungi). *22nd-21st centuries B.C. (British Museum.)*

250. *Neo-Sumerian Art. Telloh (Lagash).* Hypogeum of the Patesis Ur-Ningirsu and Ugme. *22nd century B.C. (André Parrot).*

251. *Neo-Sumerian Art. Telloh (Lagash).* Gudea Statue known as the 'Small Seated Gudea.' *22nd century B.C. Louvre, Paris. Diorite, height 17 3/4 inches. (Tel-Vigneau).* The head was found by Sarzec and the body by Cros a few years later.

252. *Sumerian Art.* Seated Figure. *Mid-3rd millennium B.C. Ny Carlsberg Glyptothek, Copenhagen. (Ny Carlsberg Glyptothek).* This statue is inserted here as a basis of comparison in order to show the evolution of this style. It is similar in type to the statue of Kurlil (No. 144).

253. *Neo-Sumerian Art. Telloh (Lagash).* Gudea, the Architect with a Plan. *22nd century B.C. Louvre, Paris. Diorite, height 36 5/8 inches. (Roger Parry).*

254. *Neo-Sumerian Art. Telloh (Lagash).* Gudea 'with Narrow Shoulders.' *22nd century B.C. Louvre, Paris. Diorite, height 55 1/8 inches. (Tel-Vigneau).*

255. *Neo-Sumerian Art. Telloh (Lagash).* Gudea 'with Broad Shoulders.' *22nd century B.C. Louvre, Paris. Diorite, height 55 1/8 inches. (Tel-Vigneau).*

256. *Neo-Sumerian Art. Telloh (Lagash).* Gudea 'A'. *22nd century B.C. Louvre, Paris. Diorite, height 48 3/4 inches. (Marc Foucault).*

257. *Neo-Sumerian Art. Telloh (Lagash).* Unnamed Head (Gudea?). *22nd century B.C. Louvre, Paris. Limestone, height 3 1/2 inches. (Louvre).*

258. *Neo-Sumerian Art. Telloh (Lagash).* Turbaned Head (Gudea). *22nd century B.C. Louvre, Paris. Diorite, height 9 inches. (Tel-Vigneau).* Discovered by Sarzec. So called from the way the hair is dressed. It was not known at the time of discovery that the work represented Gudea.

259. *Mesopotamian Art. Telloh (?).* Statue of Lugalkisalsi's Grandson, detail: Clasped Hands. *Mid-3rd millennium B.C. Louvre, Paris. Limestone. (Tel-Vigneau).*

260. *Neo-Sumerian Art. Telloh (Lagash).* Statue of Gudea, detail: Clasped Hands. *21st century B.C. Louvre, Paris. Diorite. (Tel-Vigneau).* These two details form an interesting comparison: they show that worshippers clasped their hands in different ways at different periods.

261. *Mesopotamian Art. Telloh (?).* Lugalkisalsi's Grandson. *Mid-3rd millennium B.C. Louvre, Paris. Limestone, height 11 inches. (Tel-Vigneau).*

262. *Neo-Sumerian Art. Telloh (Lagash).* Gudea. *22nd century B.C. British Museum, London. Height, 28 3/4 inches. (British Museum).* Although uninscribed, this statue can safely be identified with Gudea.

263 a and b. *Neo-Sumerian Art. Telloh (Lagash).* Gudea worshipping. *22nd century B.C. Ny Carlsberg Glyptothek, Copenhagen. Steatite, height 32 5/8 inches. (Ny Carlsberg Glyptothek).*

264. *Neo-Sumerian Art. Telloh (Lagash).* Gudea with Flowing Vase. *22nd century B.C. Private Collection. Dolerite, height 24 3/4 inches.*

265. *Neo-Sumerian Art. Telloh (Lagash).* Gudea worshipping. Uninscribed Statue. *22nd century B.C. Louvre, Paris. Dolerite, height 41 3/8 inches. (Marc Foucault).*

266. *Neo-Sumerian Art. Telloh (Lagash).* Head of Gudea (?). *22nd century B.C. Metropolitan Museum of Art, New York. (Metropolitan Museum).*

267. *Neo-Sumerian Art. Telloh (Lagash).* Ur-Ningirsu with a Beard. *21st century B.C. Berlin Museum. Dolerite, height 7 7/8 inches. (Marburg).*

268. *Neo-Sumerian Art. Telloh (Lagash).* Headless Statue of Ur-Ningirsu. *21st century B.C. Louvre, Paris. Alabaster, height 18 1/8 inches. (Tel-Vigneau).* The head of this statue is in the Metropolitan Museum, New York, which acquired it from the Brummer estate.

269. *Neo-Sumerian Art. Telloh (Lagash).* Headless Statue of Ur-Ningirsu, detail: Base with Tributaries. *21st century B.C. Louvre, Paris. Alabaster. (Tel-Vigneau).*

270. *Neo-Sumerian Art. Telloh (Lagash).* Head of a Young Man (Ur-Ningirsu?). *21st century B.C. Louvre, Paris. Diorite, height 6 1/4 inches. (Franceschi).*

271. *Neo-Sumerian Art. Telloh (Lagash)*. Head of a Man. *22nd-21st centuries B.C. Louvre, Paris. Diorite, height 2 1/4 inches. (Tel-Vigneau)*.

272. *Neo-Sumerian Art. Telloh (Lagash)*. Woman with a Kerchief (Gudea's Wife?). *22nd century B.C. Louvre, Paris. Steatite, height 6 3/4 inches. (Tel-Vigneau)*.

273. *Neo-Sumerian Art. Telloh (Lagash)*. Woman holding an Aryballos. *22nd-21st centuries B.C. Louvre, Paris. Alabaster, height 7 1/2 inches. (Tel-Vigneau)*.

274. *Neo-Sumerian Art. Telloh (?)*. Female Worshipper. *22nd-21st centuries B.C. Berlin Museum. (Marburg)*.

275. *Neo-Sumerian Art. Telloh (Lagash)*. Head of a Woman. *22nd century B.C. Berlin Museum. Steatite. (Marburg)*.
Head of the same type as that of the Woman with a Kerchief (No. 272).

276a. *Neo-Sumerian Art. Telloh (Lagash)*. Human-headed Bull. *22nd century B.C. Louvre, Paris. Steatite, height 4 inches. (Tel-Vigneau)*.
Bulls of this type, all of them found at Telloh, should be assigned to the time of Gudea. Cf. *Syria*, XXXI (1954), p. 5.

276b. *Neo-Sumerian Art. Telloh (Lagash)*. Human-headed Bull. *22nd century B.C. Louvre, Paris. Steatite, height 4 3/4 inches. (Tel-Vigneau)*.

277. *Neo-Sumerian Art. Telloh (Lagash)*. Human-headed Bull inscribed with the Name of the Patesi Urgar. *22nd century B.C. Baghdad Museum. Steatite, length 5 5/8 inches. (André Parrot)*.
Urgar, son-in-law of Ur-Bau.

278. *Neo-Sumerian Art. Ur*. Woman's Head, sometimes identified with the Goddess Ningal. *22nd-21st centuries B.C. University Museum, Philadelphia. Marble, height 2 3/4 inches. (British Museum)*.

279. *Neo-Sumerian Art. Ur*. Detail of the Stele of Ur-Nammu: The God Nannar. *22nd century B.C. University Museum, Philadelphia. Stone. (British Museum)*.

280. *Neo-Sumerian Art. Ur*. Stele of Ur-Nammu. *22nd century B.C. University Museum, Philadelphia. Stone, height 9 ft 11 1/2 inches. (British Museum)*.

281. *Neo-Sumerian Art. Ur*. Detail of the Stele of Ur-Nammu: The King making a Libation before Ningal. *22nd century B.C. University Museum, Philadelphia. (British Museum)*.

282. *Neo-Sumerian Art. Ur*. Detail of the Stele of Ur-Nammu: The King worshipping Nannar (above) and carrying a Mason's Tools (below). *22nd century B.C. University Museum, Philadelphia. (British Museum)*.

283. *Neo-Sumerian Art. Telloh (Lagash)*. Cylinder Seal. Scene of Presentation. *22nd-21st centuries B.C. Baghdad Museum. Diorite, height 1 1/4 inches. (Schneider-Lengyel)*.

284. *Neo-Sumerian Art. Telloh (Lagash)*. Stele of Gudea. The Patesi 'presented' by Ningizzida. *22nd century B.C. Berlin Museum. Limestone, height 13 3/8 inches. (Marburg)*.

285. *Neo-Sumerian Art. Telloh (Lagash)*. Stele of Gudea. The Patesi carrying a Palm Branch. *22nd century B.C. Louvre, Paris. Limestone, height 9 1/2 inches. (Tel-Vigneau)*.

286. *Neo-Sumerian Art. Telloh (Lagash)*. Detail of a Vase: Musicians with a Drum. *22nd century B.C. Louvre, Paris. Blackish stone, height 4 3/4 inches. (Giraudon)*.

287. *Neo-Sumerian Art*. Small Plaque. Woman and Dedication to Ninsun. *22nd-21st centuries B.C. Louvre, Paris. Steatite, height 5 1/2 inches. (Tel-Vigneau)*.

288. *Neo-Sumerian Art. Telloh (Lagash)*. Fragment of the Stele of Gudea: The Goddess Bau. *22nd century B.C. Louvre, Paris. Limestone, height 7 1/2 inches. (Tel-Vigneau)*.

289. *Neo-Sumerian Art. Telloh (Lagash)*. Gudea's Libation Goblet, with Dedication to Ningizzida. *22nd century B.C. Louvre, Paris. Steatite, height 9 inches. (Tel-Vigneau)*.

290. *Neo-Sumerian Art. Telloh (Lagash)*. Cover of a Lamp adorned with Snakes, with a Dedication to Ningizzada. *22nd century B.C. Louvre, Paris. Steatite, length 4 3/8 inches. (Tel-Vigneau)*.

291. *Neo-Sumerian Art. Telloh (Lagash)*. Gudea's Mace-head adorned with Lion-muzzles. *22nd century B.C. Louvre, Paris. Veined breccia, height 3 1/2 inches, width 5 1/2 inches. (Louvre)*.

292a. *Neo-Sumerian Art. Telloh (Lagash)*. Foundation Figurine. Kneeling God driving in a Stake. *22nd century B.C. Louvre, Paris. Bronze, height 7 7/8 inches. (Tel-Vigneau)*.

292b. *Neo-Sumerian Art. Telloh (Lagash)*. Foundation Figurine. Reclining Bull. *22nd century B.C. Louvre, Paris. Bronze, height 10 1/4 inches. (Tel-Vigneau)*.

292c. *Neo-Sumerian Art. Susa*. Foundation Figurine. Basket Carrier inscribed with the Name of Shulgi (Dungi). *21st century B.C. Louvre, Paris. Bronze, height 9 7/8 inches. (Tel-Vigneau)*.
Though found at Susa, this figurine came originally from Ur, i.e. from the Sumerian region.

292d. *Neo-Sumerian Art. Nippur*. Foundation Figurine. Basket Carrier with a Dedication to Ur-Nammu. *22nd century B.C. Bronze, height 12 3/4 inches. (Illustrated London News)*.

293. *Iranian Art. Susa*. Bas-relief. Kneeling God driving in a Stake. *Second half of the 3rd millennium B.C. Louvre, Paris. Limestone, height 22 1/2 inches. (Louvre)*.
This scene was directly inspired by the foundation figurine illustrated here (No. 292a).

294. *Neo-Sumerian Art. Telloh (Lagash)*. Small Figure-plaque. Man carrying a Goat. *22nd-21st centuries B.C. Louvre, Paris. Terracotta, height 4 1/8 inches. (Louvre)*.

295. *Neo-Sumerian Art. Telloh (Lagash)*. Small Figure-plaque. Woman suckling a Child. *22nd-21st centuries B.C. Louvre, Paris. Terracotta, height 4 1/8 inches. (Louvre)*.

296. *Neo-Sumerian Art. Telloh (Lagash)*. Small Figure-plaque. Husband and Wife. *22nd-21st centuries B.C. Louvre, Paris. Terracotta, height 4 1/4 inches. (Louvre)*.

297. *Neo-Sumerian Art. Telloh (Lagash)*. Figurine. Offering Bearer. *22nd-21st centuries B.C. Louvre, Paris. Terracotta, height 3 inches. (Tel-Vigneau)*.

298. *Neo-Sumerian Art. Telloh (Lagash).* Lion-headed Demon. *22nd-21st centuries B.C. Louvre, Paris. Terracotta, height 5 1/8 inches. (Tel-Vigneau).*

299. *Neo-Sumerian Art. Telloh (Lagash).* Figurine. Bearded Warrior with an Adze. *21st century B.C. Baghdad Museum. Terracotta, height 7 1/2 inches. (Schneider-Lengyel).*

300. *Neo-Sumerian Art. Tell Asmar.* Female Figurine, perforated (for cones). *21st century B.C. Louvre, Paris. Terracotta, height 5 1/4 inches. (Roger Parry).*

301. *Neo-Sumerian Art. Ur.* Figurine. Goddess with a Flowing Vase. *21st-20th centuries B.C. Terracotta, height 29 1/2 inches. (British Museum).*

302. *Neo-Sumerian Art.* Head of a Divine Figurine. *22nd-21st centuries B.C. Louvre, Paris. Terracotta, height 2 inches. (Roger Parry).*

303. *Neo-Sumerian Art. Cylinder Seal.* Spread Eagle between Two Seated Figures. *22nd-21st centuries B.C. Louvre, Paris. Marble, height 1 1/8 inches. (Marc Foucault).*

304. *Neo-Sumerian Art. Cylinder Seal.* Spread Eagles between Reclining Animals. *22nd-21st centuries B.C. Louvre, Paris. Shell, height 1 5/8 inches. (Marc Foucault).*

305. *Neo-Sumerian Art. Telloh (Lagash). Cylinder Seal.* Scorpions and Geese. *22nd-21st centuries B.C. Louvre, Paris. Diorite, height 1 1/4 inches. (Marc Foucault).*

306. *Neo-Sumerian Art. Telloh (Lagash). Cylinder Seal.* Sacred Boat. *22nd-21st centuries B.C. Louvre, Paris. Dolerite, height 15/16 of an inch. (Marc Foucault).*

307. *Neo-Sumerian Art. Telloh (Lagash). Cylinder Seal.* Spread Eagle, Garland, and Pyramidal Structures. *22nd-21st centuries B.C. Louvre, Paris. Stone, height 7/8 of an inch. (Marc Foucault).*

308. *Neo-Sumerian Art. Telloh (Lagash). Cylinder Seal.* Eagle between Two Animals. *22nd-21st centuries B.C. Louvre, Paris. Stone, height 1 1/8 inches. (Marc Foucault).*

309. *Neo-Sumerian Art. Telloh (Lagash). Cylinder Seal.* Presentation Scene, with Inscription. *22nd-21st centuries B.C. Louvre, Paris. Marble, height 1 5/8 inches. (Marc Foucault).*

310. *Neo-Sumerian Art. Telloh (Lagash). Cylinder Seal.* Combat against Wild Animals. *22nd-21st centuries B.C. Louvre, Paris. Diorite, height 15/16 of an inch. (Marc Foucault).*

311. *Neo-Sumerian Art. Telloh (Lagash). Cylinder Seal.* Gilgamesh and Enkidu subduing a Winged Lion. *22nd-21st centuries B.C. Louvre, Paris. Serpentine, height 1 inch. (Marc Foucault).*

312. *Neo-Sumerian Art. Telloh (Lagash). Cylinder Seal.* Presentation Scene. *22nd-21st centuries B.C. Louvre, Paris. Schist, height 1 1/8 inches. (Marc Foucault).*

313. *Neo-Sumerian Art. Telloh (Lagash). Cylinder Seal.* Presentation Scene. *22nd-21st centuries B.C. Louvre, Paris. Serpentine, height 1 1/4 inches. (Marc Foucault).*

314. *Neo-Sumerian Art. Cylinder Seal.* Worshippers on either side of the Sacred Tree. *22nd-21st centuries B.C. Louvre, Paris. Serpentine, height 7/16 of an inch. (Marc Foucault.)*

315. *Babylonian Art. Susa.* Scene of Warfare. *Early 2nd millennium B.C. Louvre, Paris. Basalt, height 1 5/8 inches. (Tel-Vigneau).*

316. *Babylonian Art. Cylinder Seal.* Scene of Worship. *Early 2nd millennium B.C. Pierpont Morgan Collection, New York. Haematite, height 15/16 of an inch. (Morgan Library).*

317. *Babylonian Art. Middle Euphrates. Mari.* Palace of Zimri-Lim. *18th century B.C. (André Parrot).*

318. *Tell Hariri (Mari).* The Mounds of Tell Hariri before Excavation. Photograph taken in 1933. *(André Parrot).*

319. *Mari.* Aerial View of the Site: Temple of Ishtar and Palace. *(Aviation française du Levant).*

320. *Mari.* Clearing the Palace. *Early 2nd millennium B.C. (A. Bianquis).*

321. *Mari.* Axonometric Projection. Reconstruction of the Palace, from the plan of R. Duru.

322. *Mari.* Clearing a Bronze Lion guarding the Door of the Temple of Dagan. *(André Parrot).*

323. *Mari.* Clearing the Statue of the 'Governor' Ishtup-ilum. *(André Bianquis).*

324. *Mari.* Clearing a Male Head on the Step of a Stairway. *(R. Cans).*

325. *Mari.* Aerial View of the Palace from directly overhead. *(Aviation française du Levant).*

326a. *Mesopotamian Art. Ishchali.* Plan of the Temple of Ishtar-Kititum. *Early 2nd millennium B.C. (Drawing by Claude Abeille).*

326b. *Mesopotamian Art. Assur.* Plan of one of the Temples of Ishtar. *(Drawing by Claude Abeille).*

326c. *Mesopotamian Art. Telloh (Lagash).* Plan of a House. *Early 2nd millennium B.C.*

327. *Mesopotamian Art. Ishchali.* Reconstruction by Harold D. HILL of the Temple of Ishtar-Kititum. *Early 2nd millennium B.C. (Oriental Institute of Chicago).*

328. *Mesopotamian Art. Ur.* Statue of the Goddess Bau. *Early 2nd millennium B.C. Baghdad Museum. Diorite, height 11 3/8 inches. (Iraq Museum).*

329. *Babylonian Art. Susa.* Small Headless Statue of a Worshipper. *Early 2nd millennium B.C. Louvre, Paris. Diorite, height 24 3/8 inches. (Archives photographiques.)* This statue came originally from Ashnunnak. Like many other Babylonian works, it was carried off to Elam as a trophy of war by Shutruk-Nakhunte in the 12th century B.C. Morgan found many such works at Susa (cf. No. 212).

330. *Babylonian Art. Middle Euphrates. Mari.* Small Headless Statue of Idi-ilum, Governor of Mari. *Early 2nd millennium B.C. Louvre, Paris. Steatite, height 16 1/8 inches. (Roger Parry).*

331. *Babylonian Art. Middle Euphrates. Mari.* Statue of Ishtup-ilum, Governor of Mari. *Early 2nd millennium B.C. Aleppo Museum. Black stone, height 5 ft. (Schneider-Lengyel).*

332. *Babylonian Art. Middle Euphrates. Mari.* Statue of Ishtup-ilum, back view. *Early 2nd millennium B.C. Aleppo Museum. Black stone, height 5 ft. (Audrain-Arthaud).*

333. *Babylonian Art. Middle Euphrates. Mari.* Statue of Ishtup-ilum, detail of the head. *Early 2nd millennium B.C. Aleppo Museum. (Schneider-Lengyel).*

334. *Babylonian Art. Middle Euphrates. Mari.* Statue of Puzur-Ishtar, Governor of Mari. *Early 2nd millennium B.C. Berlin Museum and Archaeological Museum, Istanbul. Diorite, height 5 ft 9 inches. Photo Marburg (head) and Istanbul Museum (body).*
Head in the Berlin Museum (purchased on the art market), body in the Istanbul Museum (excavated by Koldewey).

335. *Babylonian Art. Middle Euphrates. Mari.* Head of Puzur-Ishtar. *Early 2nd millennium B.C. Berlin Museum. Diorite. (Marburg).*

336. *Babylonian Art. Middle Euphrates. Mari.* Warrior with a Chin-piece. *18th century B.C. Aleppo Museum. White stone, height 7 7/8 inches. (Schneider-Lengyel).*

337. *Hellenistic Art. Sidon.* So-called Sarcophagus of Alexander. *Hellenistic Period. Istanbul Museum. Marble, length 10 ft 5 inches, width 5 ft 5 3/4 inches, height 4 ft 1 5/8 inches. (Alinari).*

338. *Babylonian Art. Middle Euphrates. Mari.* Warrior with a Chin-piece. *18th century B.C. Aleppo Museum. White stone, height 7 7/8 inches. (Schneider-Lengyel).*

339. *Babylonian Art. Middle Euphrates. Mari.* Goddess with Flowing Vase. *18th century B.C. Aleppo Museum. White stone, height 4 ft 10 5/8 inches. (Schneider-Lengyel).*

340. *Babylonian Art. Middle Euphrates. Mari.* Goddess with Flowing Vase, detail of the head. *18th century B.C. Aleppo Museum. (Schneider-Lengyel).*

341. *Babylonian Art. Middle Euphrates. Mari.* Offering Bearer. *Early 2nd millennium B.C. Aleppo Museum. Gypsum, height 9 inches. (Schneider-Lengyel).*

342. *Babylonian Art. Middle Euphrates. Mari.* Wall Painting. Warrior with a Chin-piece riddled with Arrows. *18th century B.C. Painted on a surface coated with mud. (Roger Parry).*
This painting, like all the others decorating the palace of Mari, should not be described as a fresco. It was probably executed with pigments mixed with egg or glue.

343. *Babylonian Art. Middle Euphrates. Mari.* Wall Painting. A Fisherman. *18th century B.C. (Roger Parry).*

344. *Babylonian Art. Middle Euphrates. Mari.* Wall Painting. Scene of Sacrifice. *18th century B.C. Louvre, Paris. Painted on plaster, length 53 1/8 inches, height 31 1/2 inches. (Draeger).*

345. *Babylonian Art. Middle Euphrates. Mari.* Wall Painting. Scene of Sacrifice. *18th century B.C. Aleppo Museum. Length 19 5/8 inches, height 17 3/4 inches. (Schneider-Lengyel).*

346. *Babylonian Art. Middle Euphrates. Mari.* Wall Painting. Investiture of the King of Mari. *18th century B.C. Louvre, Paris. Length 8 ft 2 1/2 inches, height 5 ft 9 inches. (Draeger).*

347. *Babylonian Art. Middle Euphrates. Mari.* Wall Painting. Detail of the Investiture Scene: Blue Bird. *18th century B.C. Louvre, Paris. (Draeger).*

348a. *Babylonian Art. Middle Euphrates. Mari.* Wall Painting. Sacrificial Scene: Offering of Water and Fire. *18th century B.C. Length 11 ft, height c. 10 ft. (Photo Draeger, from the copy by P. Hamelin).*

348b. *Babylonian Art. Middle Euphrates. Mari.* Wall Painting. Sacrificial Scene: Offering of Water and Fire, detail. *18th century B.C. (Draeger).*

349. *Babylonian Art. Larsa.* Three Ibexes back to back. *19th-18th centuries B.C. Louvre, Paris. Bronze and gold, height 8 7/8 inches. (Tel-Vigneau).*

350. *Babylonian Art. Larsa.* Kneeling Worshipper, dedicated for the life of Hammurabi, King of Babylon. *18th century B.C. Louvre, Paris. Bronze and gold, height 7 5/8 inches. (Tel-Vigneau).*

351. *Babylonian Art. Diyala Region.* Ishchali (?). Four-faced God, with one foot on a ram. *19th century B.C. Oriental Institute, Chicago. Bronze, height 6 5/8 inches. (Oriental Institute).*

352. *Babylonian Art. Diyala Region.* Ishchali (?). Four-faced Goddess, seated. *19th century B.C. Oriental Institute, Chicago. Bronze, height 6 3/4 inches. (Oriental Institute).*

353. *Babylonian Art. Middle Euphrates. Mari.* Lion guarding the Temple of Dagan. *19th-18th centuries B.C. Louvre, Paris. Bronze and stone, length 27 1/2 inches. (Roger Parry).*

354. *Babylonian Art. Tell Harmal.* Lion guarding the Temple. *Early 2nd millennium B.C. Baghdad Museum. Terracotta, life-size. (Iraq Museum).*

355. *Babylonian Art.* Head of a Roaring Lion. *Early 2nd millennium B.C. Louvre, Paris. Terracotta, height 23 1/4 inches. (Roger Parry).*

356. *Babylonian Art. Tell Harmal.* Head of a Roaring Lion. *Early 2nd millennium B.C. Baghdad Museum. Terracotta. (Schneider-Lengyel).*

357a. *Babylonian Art. Ur.* Ram's Head. *Early 2nd millennium B.C. British Museum, London. Steatite, height 2 3/4 inches. (British Museum).*

357b. *Babylonian Art. Larsa Period.* Telloh (Lagash). Votive Dog of Sumu-ilu. *Early 2nd millennium B.C. Louvre, Paris. Steatite, height 3 1/4 inches. (Tel-Vigneau).*

357c. *Iranian Art. Susa.* Bowl, with stems decorated with ibexes. *Early 2nd millennium B.C. Louvre, Paris. Bitumen, height 6 3/4 inches. (Tel-Vigneau).*

357d. *Iranian Art. Susa.* Bowl adorned with an Ibex. *Early 2nd millennium B.C. Louvre, Paris. Bitumen, length 9 1/4 inches. (Tel-Vigneau).*

358a. *Babylonian Art. Larsa Period.* Khafaje. Small Figure-plaque. God killing a Cyclops. *Early 2nd millennium B.C. Oriental Institute, Chicago. Terracotta, height 4 1/4 inches. (Oriental Institute).*

358b. *Babylonian Art. Larsa Period. Larsa.* Small Figure-plaque. Nude Woman with clasped hands. *Early 2nd millennium B.C. Louvre, Paris. Terracotta, height 4 1/2 inches. (Roger Parry).*

358c. *Babylonian Art. Larsa Period.* Small Figure plaque. Warrior God marching over a Fortress. *Early 2nd millennium B.C. Louvre, Paris. Terracotta. (Louvre).*

359a. *Babylonian Art. Larsa Period. Ashnunnak.* Small Figure-plaque. Musician. *Early 2nd millennium B.C. Louvre, Paris. Terracotta, height 4 1/4 inches. (Louvre).*

359b. *Babylonian Art. Larsa Period. Diyala Region.* Small Figure-plaque. Harpist. *Early 2nd millennium B.C. Oriental Institute, Chicago. Terracotta, height 4 3/4 inches. (Oriental Institute).*

359c. *Babylonian Art. Larsa Period.* Small Figure-plaque. Itinerant Showman exhibiting Monkeys. *Early 2nd millennium B.C. Louvre, Paris. Terracotta, height 4 1/4 inches. (Louvre).*

359d. *Babylonian Art. Larsa Period. Ashnunnak.* Small Figure-plaque. Boxers. *Early 2nd millennium B.C. Louvre, Paris. Terracotta, height 4 1/8 inches. (Louvre).*

359e. *Babylonian Art. Larsa Period. Warka (Uruk).* Small Figure-plaque. Carpenter at Work. *Early 2nd millennium B.C. Louvre, Paris. Terracotta, height 3 1/8 inches. (Louvre).*

360. *Babylonian Art. Larsa Period. Diyala Region.* Small Figure-plaque. Peasant riding a Humped Ox. *Early 2nd millennium B.C. Oriental Institute, Chicago. Terracotta, height 2 3/4 inches. (Oriental Institute).*

361. *Babylonian Art. Middle Euphrates. Mari.* Mould. Stag Hunt. *18th century B.C. Aleppo Museum. Terracotta, length 9 1/4 inches, width 7 1/2 inches. (André Bianquis).*

362. *Babylonian Art. Middle Euphrates. Mari.* Mould. Lion attacking Oxen. *18th century B.C. Louvre, Paris. Terracotta, length 8 7/8 inches, width 7 3/4 inches. (André Bianquis).*

363. *Babylonian Art. Larsa Period. Diyala Region.* Small Figure-plaque. Bitch suckling Puppies. *Early 2nd millennium B.C. Oriental Institute, Chicago. Terracotta, height 3 7/8 inches.*

364. *Babylonian Art. Larsa Period. Mari.* Small Figure-plaque. Lion Passant, detail. *19th century B.C. Louvre, Paris. Terracotta, height 3 5/8 inches, width 5 inches. (Roger Parry).*

365. *Babylonian Art. Larsa Period.* Small Figure-plaque. Nude Woman with her Hands clasped on her Breast. *Early 2nd millennium B.C. Louvre, Paris. Terracotta, height 4 3/4 inches. (Roger Parry).*

366. *Babylonian Art. Larsa Period. Ashnunnak.* Small Figure-plaque. Nude Woman with her Hands clasped on her Breast. *Early 2nd millennium B.C. Louvre, Paris. Terracotta, height 5 1/8 inches. (Roger Parry).*

367a. *Babylonian Art. Larsa Period.* Nude Winged Goddess ('Burney Plaque'). *Early 2nd millennium B.C. Norman Colville Collection. Terracotta, height 19 5/8 inches. (The Warburg Institute).*

367b. *Babylonian Art. Larsa Period. Larsa.* Nude Winged Goddess adorning a Libation Vase. *Early 2nd millennium B.C. Louvre, Paris. Terracotta, height 10 5/8 inches. (Tel-Vigneau).*

367c. *Babylonian Art. Larsa Period.* Nude Winged Goddess standing on Two Ibexes. *Early 2nd millennium B.C. Louvre, Paris. Terracotta, height 7 7/8 inches. (Louvre).*

368. *Babylonian Art. Larsa Period.* Small Figure-plaque. The Goddess Nintu between Two Acolytes. *Early 2nd millennium B.C. Baghdad Museum. Terracotta, height 4 inches. (Schneider-Lengyel).*

369. *Babylonian Art. Larsa Period.* Small Figure-plaque. Humbaba. *Early 2nd millennium B.C. British Museum, London. Terracotta. (British Museum).*
Humbaba, guardian of the cedar forest, figures in the epic of Gilgamesh.

370. *Babylonian Art. Larsa Period.* Grimacing Mask of the Giant Humbaba. *Early 2nd millennium B.C. British Museum, London. Terracotta, height 2 3/4 inches. (British Museum).*

371. *Babylonian Art. Middle Euphrates. Mari.* Goddess smelling a Flower. *18th century B.C. Louvre, Paris. Stone, height 5 1/4 inches. (Tel-Vigneau).*

372. *Babylonian Art. Middle Euphrates. Mari.* Cylinder Seal dedicated for the life of Idi-ilum, Governor of Mari. Scene of Presentation. *Early 2nd millennium B.C. Aleppo Museum. Stone, height 1 1/16 inches. (Schneider-Lengyel).*

373. *Babylonian Art. Susa.* Stele with the Code of Hammurabi. *18th century B.C. Louvre, Paris. Basalt, height 7 ft 4 1/2 inches. (Tel-Vigneau).*

374. *Babylonian Art.* Bas-relief with a representation of Hammurabi, in right profile. *18th century B.C. British Museum, London. Limestone, height of the figure 5 ft. (British Museum).*

375. *Babylonian Art. Susa.* Head of Hammurabi (?), King of Babylon. *18th century B.C. Louvre, Paris. Steatite, height 5 7/8 inches. (Tel-Vigneau).*

376. *Babylonian Art.* Cylinder Seal. Scene of Worship. *Early 2nd millennium B.C. Pierpont Morgan Collection, New York. Haematite, height 1 1/8 inches. (Morgan Library).*

377. *Babylonian Art.* Cylinder Seal. Mythological Scene. *Early 2nd millennium B.C. Pierpont Morgan Collection, New York. Haematite, height 7/8 of an inch. (Morgan Library).*

378. *Babylonian Art.* Cylinder Seal. Offering of a Young Goat. *Early 2nd millennium B.C. Pierpont Morgan Collection, New York. Haematite, height 1 inch. (Morgan Library).*

379. *Babylonian Art.* Cylinder Seal. Nude Goddess. *Early 2nd millennium B.C. Louvre, Paris. Haematite, height 1 3/16 inches. (Tel-Vigneau).*

380. *Babylonian Art. Larsa Period. Larsa.* Cylinder Seal. The God Nergal trampling an Enemy. *Early 2nd millennium B.C. Baghdad Museum. Steatite, height 1 5/8 inches. (Baghdad Museum).*

381. *Babylonian Art. Cylinder Seal.* Goddess before 'Martu.' *Early 2nd millennium B.C. Pierpont Morgan Collection, New York. Black jasper, height* 1 3/16 *inches. (Morgan Library).*

382. *Babylonian Art. Cylinder Seal.* Offering of a Young Goat. *Early 2nd millennium. B.C. Museum of Fine Arts, Boston. (Museum of Fine Arts).*

383. *Iranian Art. Susa. Cylinder Seal.* Divinities and Scene of Execution. *Early 2nd millennium B.C. Louvre, Paris. Haematite, height* 1 *inch. (Louvre).*

384. *Babylonian Art. Diyala Region. Ashnunnak. Cylinder Seal.* Religious Scene, Offering of a Young Goat, and Ishtar Militant. *Early 2nd millennium B.C. Oriental Institute, Chicago. Brown stone, height* 1 3/16 *inches. (Oriental Institute).*

385. *Babylonian Art. Cylinder Seal.* Scene of Worship. *Early 2nd millennium B.C. Pierpont Morgan Collection, New York. Rock crystal, height* 1 *inch. (Morgan Library).*

386. *Babylonian Art. Diyala Region. Ishchali. Cylinder Seal.* Scene of Worship and Gilgamesh fighting the Winged Lion. *Early 2nd millennium B.C. Baghdad Museum. Grey stone, height* 7/8 *of an inch. (Baghdad Museum).*

387. *Kassite Art. Abu Habba.* Boundary Stone of Nebuchadnezzar I. *12th century B.C. British Museum, London. Limestone (?), height* 25 3/8 *inches.*
In the purest Kassite style, this *kudurru* was carved at the behest of Nebuchadnezzar I (1146-1123 B.C.), a king of the Second Dynasty of Isin.

388. *Kassite Art. Cylinder Seal.* Mythological Scene. *Louvre, Paris. Chalcedony, height* 1 7/16 *inches. (Tel-Vigneau).*

389. *Kassite Art. Aqar Quf (Dur Kurigalzu).* Wall Painting. Procession. *14th century B.C. (Iraq Museum).*

390. *Kassite Art. Aqar Quf (Dur Kurigalzu).* Ziggurat. *14th-13th centuries B.C. Baked bricks. (Iraq Museum).*

391a. *Kassite Art. Uruk (Warka).* Plan of the Temple of Karaindash. *15th century B.C.*

391b. *Mesopotamian Art. Tepe Gawra.* Plan of Temple Gawra VIII. *Late 4th millennium B.C.*
The plan of this early temple is given here as a basis of comparison.

392. *Kassite Art. Uruk (Warka).* Mural Decoration of the Temple of Karaindash. Gods and Goddesses with Flowing Vase. *15th century B.C. Berlin Museum. Baked bricks, height* 6 *ft* 10 3/4 *inches. (Marburg).*

393. *Kassite Art. Aqar Quf (Dur Kurigalzu).* Lioness. *14th century B.C. Baghdad Museum. Terracotta, height* 2 *inches. (Iraq Museum).*

394. *Kassite Art. Uruk (Warka).* Lioness. *Kassite Period (?). Baghdad Museum. Unbaked clay, length* 29 1/2 *inches, height* 19 5/8 *inches. (Uruk Vorläufiger Bericht, III, pl. 24).*
There is some doubt as to the date of this figurine, as it did not come to light *in situ*. It seems to us to be in the Kassite style, and we have accordingly grouped it with other Kassite works. Some authorities, however, assign it to the Neo-Babylonian Period.

395a. *Kassite Art. Susa.* Boundary Stone of Melishipak. *12th century B.C. Louvre, Paris. Diorite, height* 35 3/8 *inches. (Tel-Vigneau).*
This work, like many others, was found by Morgan at Susa, where it had been brought as war booty by the Elamite king Shutruk-Nakhunte in the 12th century B.C.

395b. *Kassite Art. Susa.* Boundary Stone of Melishipak. *12th century B.C. Louvre, Paris. Black limestone, height* 26 3/4 *inches. (Tel-Vigneau).*

395c. *Kassite Art.* Boundary Stone of Marduk-nadin-akhe. *12th century B.C. British Museum, London. Black limestone, height* 20 3/4 *inches. (British Museum).*

395d. *Kassite Art.* Boundary Stone of Nebuchadnezzar, king of the Second Dynasty of Isin. *12th century B.C. British Museum, London. Limestone, height* 25 3/8 *inches, width* 8 1/4 *inches. (British Museum).*

396a. *Kassite Art. Cylinder Seal.* Scene of Worship and Animals confronted. *13th-12th centuries B.C. Berlin Museum. Height* 1 9/16 *inches, diameter* 5/8 *of an inch. (Marburg).*

396b. *Kassite Art. Cylinder Seal.* Animals confronted. *Berlin Museum. Height* 2 7/8 *inches, diameter* 11/16 *of an inch. (Marburg).*

397. *Elamite Art. Susa.* Stele showing a King standing before a God. *Louvre, Paris. Basalt, height* 26 3/8 *inches. (Tel-Vigneau).*

398. *Elamite Art. Susa.* Statue of Queen Napir-Asu, Wife of Untash-Huban. *C.* 1250 *B.C. Louvre, Paris. Bronze, height* 4 *ft* 2 3/4 *inches. (Tel-Vigneau).*
The name of Untash-Huban was formerly read Untash-Gal.

399. *Elamite Art. Susa.* Detail of the Statue of Queen Napir-Asu. *Louvre, Paris. Bronze. (Tel-Vigneau).*

400. *Elamite Art. Susa.* Procession of Warriors. *Late 2nd millennium B.C. Louvre, Paris. Bronze, height* 14 1/2 *inches. (Tel-Vigneau).*

401. *Elamite Art. Susa.* Detail of the Stele of Untash-Huban. *C.* 1250 *B.C. Louvre, Paris. Stone, over-all height* 8 *ft* 7 *inches. (Tel-Vigneau).*

402. *Elamite Art. Susa.* Detail of the Stele of Untash-Huban. *C.* 1250 *B.C. Louvre, Paris. Stone. (Tel-Vigneau).*

403. *Elamite Art. Susa.* Head of a Man. *Mid-2nd millennium B.C. Louvre, Paris. Terracotta, height* 4 1/4 *inches. (Tel-Vigneau).*

404a. *Elamite Art. Susa.* Offering Bearer. *Mid-2nd millennium B.C. Louvre, Paris. Electrum, height of the statuette* 2 1/2 *inches, height of the base* 5/8 *of an inch. (Tel-Vigneau).*

404b. *Elamite Art. Susa.* Offering Bearer. *Mid-2nd millennium B.C. Louvre, Paris. Silver, height of the statuette* 2 3/8 *inches, height of the base* 5/8 *of an inch. (Tel-Vigneau).*

404c. *Elamite Art. Susa.* Worshipper. *Second half of the 2nd millennium B.C. Louvre, Paris. Bronze, height* 4 3/4 *inches. (Tel-Vigneau).*

405. *Elamite Art. Susa.* Mural Decoration of Moulded Bricks. Bull-God and the Goddess Ninhursag. *Second half of the 2nd millennium B.C. Louvre, Paris. Baked bricks, height 54 inches. (Tel-Vigneau).*

406. *Elamite Art. Hamadan.* Head of an Elamite Dignitary. *Second half of the 2nd millennium B.C. Metropolitan Museum of Art, New York. Bronze, height 13 1/2 inches. (Courtesy Metropolitan Museum of Art, Rogers Fund, 1948).*

407. *Elamite Art. Susa.* Head of a Bearded Man. *Early 1st millennium B.C. (?). Louvre, Paris. Terracotta, height 9 3/8 inches. (Tel-Vigneau).*

408. *Elamite Art. Susa.* So-called Tablet of Sit Shamshi. *12th century B.C. Louvre, Paris. Bronze, length 23 5/8 inches, width 15 3/4 inches. (Tel-Vigneau).*
Dated thanks to an inscription by Shilhak-in-Shushinak. This ex voto is the model of an Elamite 'high place,' showing all the characteristic features of the Semitic cult.

409. *Elamite Art. Susa.* So-called Tablet of Sit Shamshi, detail: Two Worshippers. *12th century B.C. Louvre, Paris. Bronze. (Tel-Vigneau).*

410. *Kassite Art. Cylinder Seal.* Scene of Worship. *Second half of the 2nd millennium B.C. Louvre, Paris. Chalcedony, height 1 1/4 inches, diameter 9/16 of an inch. (Roger Parry).*

411. *Kassite Art. Cylinder Seal.* Scene of Worship. *First half of the 2nd millennium B.C. Pierpont Morgan Collection, New York. Red jasper, height 1 1/4 inches, diameter 11/16 of an inch. (Morgan Library).*

412. *Kassite Art. Cylinder Seal.* Scene of Worship. *Second half of the 2nd millennium B.C. Louvre, Paris. Steatite, height 1 1/4 inches, diameter 9/16 of an inch. (Louvre).*

413. *Cylinder Seal.* Divinity. *Louvre, Paris. Chalcedony, height 1 3/8 inches. (Roger Parry).*

414. *Cylinder Seal.* Scene of Worship and Symbolic Themes. *Louvre, Paris. White jasper flecked with brown, height 1 5/8 inches. (Roger Parry).*

415. *Kassite Art. Cylinder Seal.* Seated Divinity and Frieze of Animals. *Second half of the 2nd millennium B.C. Collection of Mrs Agnes Baldwin Brett. Yellow chalcedony, height 1 9/16 inches. (Courtesy Mrs Agnes Baldwin Brett).*

416. *Mitannian Art. Nuzi.* Cylinder Seal of Shaushatar, King of Mitanni. *First half of the 2nd millennium B.C. Harvard Semitic Museum, Cambridge. (Harvard Semitic Museum).*

417. *Maps.* Mesopotamian Sites. 4th to 2nd millennium B.C. Zones of Influence.

418. *Map.* Mesopotamian Sites.

419. General Map of the Ancient Near East.

Drawings by Claude ABEILLE

from original documents or reproductions in André PARROT, *Archéologie mésopotamienne*, I and II.

Maps drawn by Henri JACQUINET,

Marius CAGNION and Roger GRAINDORGE.

MAPS

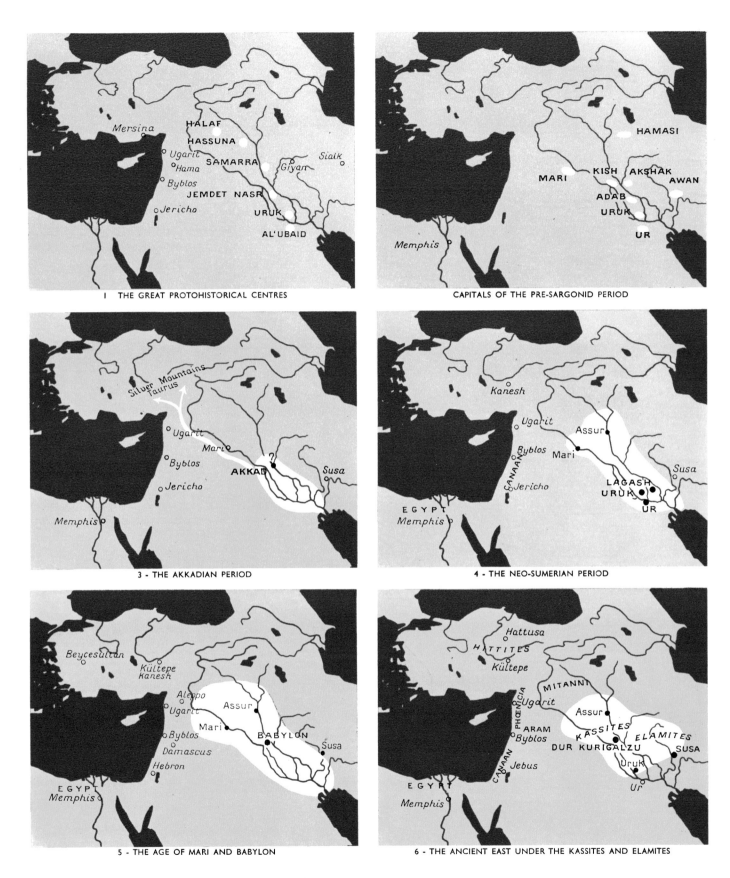

1   THE GREAT PROTOHISTORICAL CENTRES

CAPITALS OF THE PRE-SARGONID PERIOD

3 - THE AKKADIAN PERIOD

4 - THE NEO-SUMERIAN PERIOD

5 - THE AGE OF MARI AND BABYLON

6 - THE ANCIENT EAST UNDER THE KASSITES AND ELAMITES

417 - MESOPOTAMIAN SITES FROM THE FOURTH TO THE SECOND MILLENNIUM B.C. - ZONES OF INFLUENCE

418 - MESOPOTAMIAN SITES →

ALPHABETICAL TABLES OF THE SITES

Opposite: Modern Names - Ancient Names
Below: Ancient Names - Modern Names
Reference Maps : A. Mesopotamian Sites
                 B. The Ancient Near East
                 * Map of the Discoveries

Some modern names designate sites whose ancient names have not yet been identified.

Ancient Names	Modern Names	A	B
Adab	Bismaya	d 7	
Agade	Deir (?)	c 6	
Aleppo	Aleppo		D 2
Amida	Diarbekir		E 2
Arbela	Erbil	c 2	F 2
Ashnunnak	Tell Asmar	c 5	F 3
Assur	Qalaat Shergat	b 3	E 3
Babylon	Babil	c 6	F 3
Barsip (Til)*	Tell Ahmar		
Borsippa	Birs Nimrud	c 6	
Byblos	Jebail		C 3
Carchemish	Jerablus		D 2
Damascus	Esh Sham		D 3
Dur Kurigalzu	Aqar Quf	c 5	F 3
Dur Sharrukin	Khorsabad	b 2	E 2
Dur Untashi	Choga Zambil	g 6	
Ecbatana	Hamadan	g 4	G 3
Eridu	Abu Shahrein	e 8	F 4
Guzana	Tell Halaf		E 2
Hadatu*	Arslan Tash		
Hattusa	Boghazkeuy		C 2
Isin	Ishan Bahriyat	d 7	
Jericho	Er Riha		C 4
Jerusalem	Jerusalem or El Quds		C 4
Kalakh	Nimrud	b 2	
Kanesh	Kultepe		C 2
Kish	al 'Oheimir	c 6	
Lagash	Telloh	e 7	F 4
Larsa	Senkereh	d 7	F 4
Mari	Tell Hariri		E 3
Megiddo	Tell Mutesellim		C 3
Nerab*	Neirab		
Nineveh	Kuyunjik	b 2	E 2
Nippur	Niffer	d 6	
Nuzi	Yorgan Tepe	c 3	
Palmyra	Tadmor		D 3
Qadesh	Tell Nebi Mend		D 3
Qatna	Mishrifeh		D 3
Sidon	Saida		C 3
Sippar	Abu Habba	c 5	
Susa	Shushan	g 6	G 3
Terqa	Asharah		
Troy	Hissarlik		A 2
Tyre	Sur		C 3
Ugarit	Ras Shamra		C 3
Umma	Jokha	d 7	
Ur	Muqayyar	e 8	F 4
Uruk	Warka	d 7	F 4

BLACK SEA

Troy

Ankara

Hattusa
(Boghazkeuy)

HITTITES

A n a t o l i a

Halys (Kizil Irmak)

Kanesh (Kultepe)

Taurus

Amanus

Carchemish

Aleppo

CYPRUS

Ugarit
(Ras Shamra)

MEDITERRANEAN SEA

Qatna (Mishrifeh)

Lebanon

Qadesh

Orontes

Byblos

Baalbek

Sidon

Tyre

Litani

PHOENICIA

Megiddo

PALESTINE

Jericho

Jerusalem

DEAD
SEA

Sais   Tanis

DELTA

Memphis

FAYUM

MIDDLE
EGYPT

Nile

El Amarna

UPPER
EGYPT

Thebes

A r a b i a n   D e s e r t

Sinai

RED SEA

A r a b i a n   De

A r m e n i

Lake
Van

K u r d

Amida
(Diarbekir)

H U R R I A N S

Chagar Bazar

Halaf   Tell Brak

Khorsabad

Nineveh

Mosul

ASSYRI

Hassuna

Assur

Khabur

Mari
(Tell Hariri)

Tadmor

Palmyra

S y r i a n

Damascus

D e s e r t

Euphrates

Tigris

Great

Little

Dur Kuriga
(Aqar Qu

Bab

Km   300
Miles   200

Modern Names	Ancient Names	A	B
Abu Habba	Sippar	c 5	
Abu Shahrein	Eridu	e 8	F 4
Agrab (Tell)		d 5	
Ahmar (Tell)*	Til Barsip		
Akshak		c 6	
Aleppo	Aleppo		D 2
Ankara	Ancyra		C 2
Aqar Quf	Dur Kurigalzu	c 5	F 3
Arpatchiya		b 2	
Arslan Tash*	Hadatu		
Asmar (Tell)	Ashnunnak	c 5	F 3
Baalbek	Heliopolis		D 3
Babil	Babylon	c 6	F 3
Baghdad		c 5	F 3
Balawat	Imgur Bel	b 2	
Basra		f 8	F 4
Bavian		b 2	
Billa (Tell)		b 2	
Birs Nimrud	Borsippa	c 6	
Bismaya	Adab	d 7	
Boghazkeuy	Hattusa		C 2
Brak (Tell)			E 2
Chagar Bazar	Shubat Enlil (?)		E 2
Chemchemal		c 3	
Choga Zambil	Dur Untashi	g 6	
Deir	Agade (?)	c 6	
Diarbekir	Amida		E 2
Dizful		g 6	
Djowi		g 6	
Erbil	Arbela	c 2	F 2
Er Riha	Jericho		C 4
Esh Sham	Damascus		D 3
Fara	Shuruppak	d 7	
Fecherijeh*	Washshukani (?)		
Gawra (Tepe)		b 2	
Giyan (Tepe)		g 5	G 3
Halaf (Tell)	Guzana		E 2
Hamadan	Ecbatana	g 4	G 3
Hariri (Tell)	Mari		E 3
Harmal (Tell)*	Shadupum		
Hassuna		b 3	E 3
Hissarlik	Troy		A 2
Hit		a 5	
Ishchali	Dur Rimush (?)	c 5	
Ishchali	Neribtum (?)	c 5	

Modern Names	Ancient Names	A	B
Ishchali	Shatlash (?)	c 5	
Ishan Bahriyat	Isin	d 7	
Jarmo		c 3	F 3
Jebail	Byblos		C 3
Jemdet Nasr		c 6	F 3
Jerablus	Carchemish		D 2
Jerusalem or El Quds	Jerusalem		C 4
Jezireh		a 1	
Jokha	Umma	d 7	
Khafaje	Tutub (?)	c 5	
Khorsabad	Dur Sharrukin	b 2	E 2
Kirkuk		c 3	
Kultepe	Kanesh		
Kuyunjik	Nineveh	b 2	C 2
Lahm (Tell El)		e 8	F 4
Malatya		b 2	
Mishrifeh	Qatna		D 3
Mosul		b 2	E 2
Muallafat		b 2	
Muqayyar	Ur	e 8	F 4
Mutesellim (Tell)	Meggido		C 3
Nebi Mend (Tell)	Qadesh		D 3
Neirab*	Nerab		
Niffer	Nippur	d 6	
Nimrud	Kalakh	b 2	
'Oheimir (al)	Kish	c 6	
Qalaat Shergat	Assur	b 3	E 3
Ras Shamra	Ugarit		C 3
Saida	Sidon		C 3
Samarra	Samarra	b 4	
Senkereh	Larsa	d 7	F 4
Shanidar		c 2	F 2
Shemshara*			
Shushan	Susa	g 6	G 3
Suleimaniya		d 3	
Sur	Tyre		C 3
Tadmor	Palmyra		D 3
Telloh	Lagash	e 7	F 4
Tepe Mussian		f 6	F 3
Tepe Sialk			G 3
'Ubaid (al)		d 8	F 4
'Uqair (Tell)		c 6	
Warka	Uruk	d 7	F 4
Yorgan Tepe	Nuzi	c 3	
Zarzi		d 3	

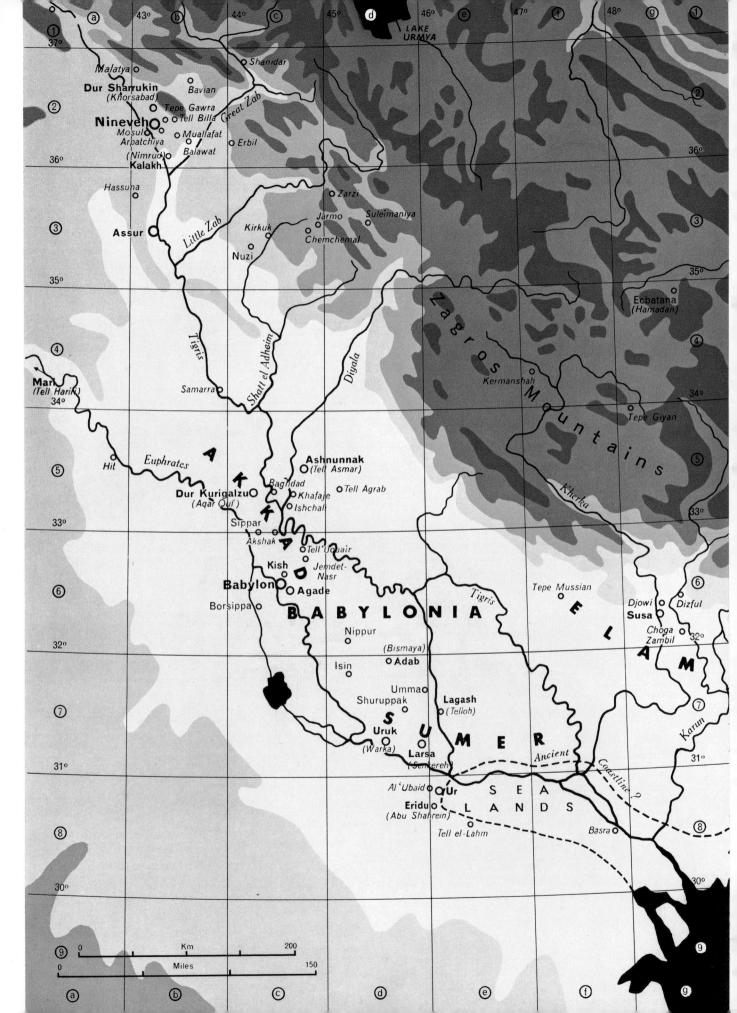

THIS, THE FIRST VOLUME OF THE SERIES 'THE ARTS OF MANKIND',
EDITED BY ANDRÉ MALRAUX AND GEORGES SALLES, HAS BEEN
PRODUCED UNDER THE SUPERVISION OF ALBERT BEURET, EDITOR-
IN-CHARGE OF THE SERIES. SET IN BASKERVILLE TYPE, THE BOOK
WAS DESIGNED BY ROGER PARRY. THE TEXT AND PLATES IN BLACK
AND WHITE WERE PRINTED BY L'IMPRIMERIE GEORGES LANG,
PARIS; PLATES IN SEPIA, METALLIC INKS AND COLOUR BY L'IMPRI-
MERIE DRAEGER, MONTROUGE. DESIGNED BY MASSIN, THE BINDING
WAS EXECUTED BY BABOUOT, GENTILLY.